Exploraciones

Vol. 1

Second Edition

Mary Ann Blitt | Margarita Casas

Australia • Brazil • Japan • Korea • Mexico • Singapore • Spain • United Kingdom • United States

Exploraciones: Student Edition, Second Edition

Exploraciones: Student Edition, Second Edition
Blitt | Casas

© 2016 Cengage Learning. All rights reserved.

For product information and technology assistance, contact us at
Cengage Learning Customer & Sales Support, 1-800-354-9706

For permission to use material from this text or product, submit all requests online at **cengage.com/permissions**
Further permissions questions can be emailed to
permissionrequest@cengage.com

This book contains select works from existing Cengage Learning resources and was produced by Cengage Learning Custom Solutions for collegiate use. As such, those adopting and/or contributing to this work are responsible for editorial content accuracy, continuity and completeness.

Compilation © 2016 Cengage Learning

ISBN: 9781337039406

WCN: 01-100-101

Cengage Learning
20 Channel Center Street
Boston, MA 02210
USA

Cengage Learning is a leading provider of customized learning solutions with office locations around the globe, including Singapore, the United Kingdom, Australia, Mexico, Brazil, and Japan. Locate your local office at:
www.international.cengage.com/region.

Cengage Learning products are represented in Canada by Nelson Education, Ltd.

For your lifelong learning solutions, visit **www.cengage.com/custom.**

Visit our corporate website at **www.cengage.com.**

The Department of Modern Languages

Why Study Spanish? *Perhaps because...*

- It is spoken by 500 million people in the world
- It is the official language in 21 countries
- It is the 3rd most spoken language after Chinese and English
- It is the 2nd most used language in international education, and an official language of the UN and its organizations
- It is the 2nd language most used in Facebook and Twitter
- 29 million of US residents over 5 yrs. of age speak Spanish at home
- Hispanic population has had an increase of 60% in the US in the last decade
- Latin American countries are experiencing strong economic growth and are important commercial partners
- Latin American culture continues to contribute greatly to world's art and literature
- Spanish is a Romance language, and as such it can be instrumental when travelling to France, Italy, and Brazil
- More than 20 million people study Spanish in the world
- It is a beautiful Romance language

Why Study Spanish at COC?

- Language immersion classes
- Supportive and fun classroom environment
- Communicative approach include small group activities every day
- Full integration of the 5Cs (Communication, Connection, Culture, Communities, Comparisons) and the 3Ps (Perspectives, Practices, Products)
- All language classes have an accompany online lab to support learning
- All language instructors have Masters Degrees or equivalents, native/near-native fluency and years of professional teaching experience
- Most instructors have lived and/or travelled extensively in Spanish-speaking countries
- Access to State of the Art Tutorial Lab Center (TLC) includes free tutoring
- Classrooms have audio/media equipment and designed as smart classroom

ML Webpage
Http://www.canyons.edu/departments/modernlanguages

The Department of Modern Languages

Spanish 101- Elementary Spanish I-

Student Learning Outcomes

At the end of the course the student will be able to:

- ❖ Demonstrate competence by communicating through reading, writing, speaking, and listening in Spanish at the <u>novice mid level</u>.

- ❖ Analyze the relationship between perspectives, practices and products of the Spanish culture at the <u>novice mid level</u>.

NOVICE MID LEVEL DESCRIPTORS

At the end of this course, each student **will** demonstrate proficiency in the four skills at the Novice Mid Level according to the ACTFL (American Council on the Teaching of Foreign Languages) guidelines:

Speaking Guidelines

Speakers at the Novice-Mid level communicate minimally and with difficulty by using a number of isolated words and memorized phrases limited by the particular context in which the language has been learned. When responding to direct questions, they may utter only two or three words at a time or an occasional stock answer. They pause frequently as they search for simple vocabulary or attempt to recycle their own and their interlocutor's words. Because of hesitations, lack of vocabulary, inaccuracy, or failure to respond appropriately. Novice-mid speakers maybe understood with great difficulty even by sympathetic interlocutors accustomed to dealing with non-natives. When called on to handle topics by performing functions associated with the intermediate level, they frequently resort to repetition, words from their native language, or silence.

Writing Guidelines

Writers at the Novice Mid level are able to copy or transcribe familiar words or phrases, and reproduce from memory a modest number of isolated words and phrases in context. They can supply limited information on simple forms and documents, and other basic biographical information, such as names, numbers, and nationality. Novice-Mid writers exhibit a high degree of accuracy when writing on well-practiced, familiar topics using limited formulaic language. With less familiar topics, there is a marked decrease in accuracy. Errors in spelling or in the representation of symbols may be frequent. There is little evidence of functional writing skills. At this level, the writing may be difficult to understand even by those accustomed to reading the texts of non-natives.

Listening Guidelines

Able to recognize the symbols of an alphabetic and/or syllabic writing system and/or a limited number of characters in a system that uses characters. The reader can identify an increasing number of highly contextualized words and/or phrases including cognates and borrowed words, where appropriate. Material understood rarely exceeds a single phrase at a time, and rereading may be required.

Reading Guidelines

Able to understand some short, learned utterances, particularly where context strongly supports understanding and speech is clearly audible. Comprehends some words and phrases from simple questions, statements, high-frequency commands and courtesy formulae about topics that refer to basic personal information or the immediate physical setting. The listener requires long pauses for assimilation and periodically requests repetition and/or a slower rate of speech.

ORAL EVALUATION

Points: 25

Name: _____

Course : _____ Grade: _____ /

Fluency:
1 Speech halting and fragmentary; long, unnatural pauses, or utterances left unfinished.
2 Speech very slow and uneven except for short or routine sentences.
3 Speech frequently hesitant and jerky; sentences may be left uncompleted.
4 Some definite stumbling, but manages to rephrase or continue.
5 Speech generally natural and continuous; only slight stumbling or unnatural pauses.

Vocabulary: (Breadth and precision of usage)
1 Lacks basic words; inadequate; inaccurate usage.
2 Often lacks needed words; frequent inaccurate usage.
3 Sometimes lacks needed words; some inaccurate usage.
4 Occasionally lacks basic words; generally accurate usage.
5 Rich and extensive vocabulary; very accurate usage.

Structure: (Grammar and sentence organization)
1 Very few utterances structurally correct.
2 Some utterances rendered correctly, but major structural problems remain.
3 Many correct utterances, but with definite structural problems.
4 Most utterances rendered correctly, with some minor structural errors.
5 Utterances almost always correct.

Comprehensibility:
1 Almost entirely/entirely incomprehensible to native speaker of Spanish.
2 Mostly incomprehensible; occasional phrases comprehensible.
3 Many errors, about half incomprehensible.
4 Some errors, but mostly comprehensible.
5 Almost entirely/entirely comprehensible to native speaker of Spanish; only an occasional word not comprehensible.

Listening Comprehension:
1 Student comprehends nothing/little of what instructor says.
2 Student comprehends some of what instructor says.
3 Student comprehends a lot of what instructor says.
4 Student comprehends most of what instructor says.
5 Student comprehends all of what instructor says.

Semana 1

1. ¿Cómo te llamas? Me llamo...

2. ¿Te gustan las enchiladas? Me gustan...

3. ¿Dónde vives? Vivo...

4. ¿Qué días es tu clase de español? Mi clase es...

5. ¿Hay muchos o pocos estudiantes en tu clase? Hay...

6. ¿Qué clases estudias en COC? Yo estudio...

7. ¿Trabajas por la noche?

8. ¿Te gusta el café? Me gusta...

1. ¿Cuál es tu dirección? Mi dirección es...

2. ¿Cuál es tu dirección electrónica? Mi email es...

3. ¿Tienes un Ipad? Sí/No. Tengo...

4. ¿Te gusta mandar textos? Me gusta...

5. ¿Eres inglés o estadounidense?

6. ¿Te gusta Shakira y Enrique Iglesias? Me gusta...

7. ¿Hablas español? Sí/No. Hablo español.

8. ¿Eres de California? Sí/No. Soy de ...

Nuevo vocabulario

_____

_____

_____

Semana 2

1. ¿Dónde vives?

2. ¿Cuál es tu apellido?

3. ¿Te gusta el golf o el fútbol?

4. ¿Quién es Antonio Banderas?

5. ¿De dónde es Penélope Cruz?

6. ¿Cómo se llama el presidente de Estados Unidos?

7. ¿Dónde está Colombia?

8. ¿Cómo se llama el Rey de España?

1. ¿Qué es una guitarra?

2. ¿Hay muchos estudiantes de España en tu clase?

3. ¿Cuál es tu programa de televisión favorito?

4. ¿Te gusta Outback?

5. ¿Cuántos años tienes?

6. ¿Dónde trabajas?

7. ¿Eres una persona alegre?

8. ¿Eres de Nueva York?

Nuevo vocabulario

_____

_____

_____

Semana 3

1. ¿Cómo te llamas? Me llamo...

2. ¿Qué clases estudias? Estudio...

3. ¿Dónde vives? Vivo en...

4. ¿Dónde estudias? Estudio en...

5. ¿Te gusta el tenis? Me gusta...

6. ¿Eres estadounidense? Soy...

7. ¿Eres de California? Soy de...

8. ¿Sos una persona romántica? Soy...

1. ¿Te gustan las enchiladas? Me gustan...

2. ¿Quién es tu actor favorito? Mi actor favorito es ...

3. ¿Eres una persona conflictiva? Soy...

4. ¿Tomas café en Starbucks or Peet's Coffee? Tomo...

5. ¿Cuál es el apellido de tu mamá? El apellido de mi mamá es ...

6. ¿Qué color no te gusta? No me gusta...

7. ¿Qué hora es? Son las...

8. ¿Hay una cafetería en tu college? Hay...

Nuevo vocabulario

_____

_____

_____

Semana 4

1. ¿Cuál es tu película favorita? Mi película favorita es…

2. ¿Cuál es tu música favorita?

3. ¿Cuál es tu playa favorita?

4. ¿Cuál es tu restaurante favorito?

5. ¿Cuál es tu comida favorita?

6. ¿Cuál es tu pasatiempo favorito?

7. ¿Cuál es tu libro favorito?

8. ¿Cuál es tu ciudad favorita?

1. ¿Cuál es tu videojuego favorito?

2. ¿Cuál es tu deporte favorito?

3. ¿Cuál es tu número de móvil?

4. ¿Cuál es tu clase favorita este semestre?

5. ¿Cuál es tu programa de televisión favorito?

6. ¿Cuál es tu museo favorito?

7. ¿Cuál es tu gimnasio favorito? Mi gimnasio favorito es…

8. ¿Cuál es tu ciudad favorita?

Nuevo vocabulario

_____

_____

_____

Semana 5

1. ¿Cuántas personas hay en tu familia?

2. ¿Te gusta la playa de Malibú?

3. ¿Deseas comprar un ipad?

4. ¿Tienes hermanos?

5. ¿Eres soltero o casado?

6. ¿Eres una persona conflictiva?

7. ¿Qué fruta no te gusta?

8. ¿Te interesa el arte?

1. ¿Qué quieres hacer este verano?

2. ¿Tienes una familia grande?

3. ¿Cómo es tu familia?

4. ¿Te gusta la ciudad donde vives?

5. ¿De dónde es tu familia?

6. ¿Te gusta tu auto?

7. ¿Te llevas bien con tus primos?

8. ¿Hablas portugués o alemán?

Nuevo vocabulario

_____

_____

_____

Semana 6

1. ¿Cuántas clases tomas este semestre?

2. ¿Es tu apellido italiano?

3. ¿Tienes una bicicleta?

4. ¿Qué idioma se habla en tu casa?

5. ¿Cómo se dice "librería" en inglés?

6. ¿Qué deseas hacer hoy?

7. ¿Trabajas los lunes?

8. ¿Visitas Costa Rica?

1. ¿Te gusta el chile?

2. ¿Qué vas a estudiar el próximo semestre?

3. ¿Qué haces para divertirte?

4. ¿Tienes muchos exámenes en tus clases?

5. ¿Sabes quién es Plácido Domingo?

6. ¿Te gusta cantar en el baño?

7. ¿Vives cerca o lejos de COC?

8. ¿Qué animales te gustan?

Nuevo vocabulario

_____

_____

_____

Semana 7

1. ¿Tienes novia/o?

2. ¿Te gusta la comida china?

3. ¿Eres rubio/a?

4. ¿Te gustan las montañas o prefieres la ciudad?

5. ¿Eres arrogante o humilde?

6. ¿Eres tímido/a en público?

7. ¿Vives con tus padres?

8. ¿Cuántos hermanos tienes?

9. Te gusta la comida mexicana?

10. ¿Eres una persona obsesiva?

11. ¿Qué haces para divertirte?

12. ¿Cuántos Jeans tienes?

13. ¿Qué deporte practicas?

14. ¿Vives en una casa o departamento?

15. ¿Tienes tu propio cuarto o compartes?

16. ¿Qué tipo de música escuchas?

Nuevo vocabulario

_____

_____

_____

Semana 8

1. ¿Qué programa de televisión quieres ver hoy ?

2. ¿Qué lugar en Estados Unidos te gusta mucho?

3. ¿Tomas café todo el día?

4. ¿Qué vas a hacer mañana?

5. ¿Vas al cine con frecuencia?

6. ¿Qué haces por las tardes los domingos?

7. ¿Haces yoga o karate?

8. ¿Viste/miraste una comedia?

9. ¿Quién su escritor favorito?

10. ¿Qué quieres hacer en las vacaciones?

11. ¿Cuándo vas a la biblioteca?

12. ¿Vas al psiquiatra regularmente?

13. ¿Andas en bicicleta o motocicleta?

14. ¿Te gusta leer novelas?

15. ¿Cómo te diviertes?

16. ¿Tienes planes de viaje?

Nuevo vocabulario

_____

_____

_____

Semana 9

1. ¿Tienes muchos amigos y amigas?

2. ¿Tienes un gato?

3. ¿Qué hacen tus padres? ¿A qué se dedican? (what do they do?)

4. ¿Eres un buen amigo? ¿Por qué?

5. ¿Vives con tus padres?

6. ¿Tienes buena relación con tus primos?

7. ¿Qué admiras de tus abuelos? ¿Los visitas?

8. ¿Piensas comprar una motocicleta en el futuro?

1. ¿Qué tradiciones o costumbres tiene tu familia?

2. ¿Te enojas mucho? ¿Por qué?

3. ¿Celebras tu cumpleaños? ¿Cómo?

4. ¿Qué hacen para el día de Acción de Gracias?

5. ¿Con quién te llevas muy bien?

6. ¿Hay mucho drama en tu familia?

7. Proporciona (give) tres adjetivos para describir a tu familia.

8. ¿A qué playa vas con frecuencia?

Nuevo vocabulario

_____

_____

_____

Semana 10

1. ¿A qué hora te levantas?

2. ¿Qué quieres ser o hacer profesionalmente en el futuro cercano?

3. ¿Dónde te gustaría trabajar?

4. ¿Deseas estudiar en una Universidad privada?

5. ¿Necesitas una beca (scholarship)?

6. ¿Tienes que tomar un examen de admisión?

7. ¿En que trabajas?

8. ¿Sos diligente?

1. ¿Cuál es tu horario de clases?

2. ¿Bebes gaseosas (sodas)?

3. ¿Mandas text durante la clase? ¿A quién?

4. ¿Asistes a conciertos de música Rock?

5. ¿Prefieres las montañas o la playa?

6. ¿Qué tipo de computador prefieres?

7. ¿Qué tienes ganas de hacer hoy?

8. ¿Te consideras una persona generosa?

Nuevo vocabulario

_____

_____

_____

Semana 11

1. ¿Vienes a clases los viernes? Vengo...

2. ¿Pones música en la noche antes de dormir? Pongo...

3. ¿Quieres ir a la biblioteca? Quiero...

4. ¿Sales a fiestas? Salgo...

5. ¿Qué tipo de persona sos? Soy

6. ¿Sabes quién es Marc Anthony? Sé ...

7. ¿Tienes ganas de un café? Tengo ganas de...

8. ¿Mandas emails?

1. ¿Conoces a Fernando Botero?

2. ¿Traes tu libro a clase?

3. ¿Vas a conciertos de Rock?

4. ¿Qué te gusta hacer los fines de semana?

5. ¿Oyes bien?

6. ¿Duermes poco durante la semana?

7. ¿Trabajas en un hospital?

8. ¿Buscas empleo?

Nuevo vocabulario

_____

_____

_____

Semana 12

1. ¿Qué sabes de Perú?

2. ¿Eres una persona ordenada?

3. Describe un día típico en tu vida.

4. ¿Qué acabas de comprar recientemente?

5. ¿Desayunas siempre?

6. ¿Cuál es tu comida favorita?

7. ¿Sales mucho a fiestas?

8. ¿Qué te gusta hacer el domingo?

1. Describe a tu mejor amigo/amiga.

2. ¿Eres una persona mandona?

3. ¿Lees mucho? ¿Qué cosas?

4. ¿Eres miedoso/miedosa?

5. ¿Qué opinas de la gente mentirosa?

6. ¿Qué no puedes comer?

7. ¿Bebes gaseosas y bebidas con azúcar?

8. ¿Qué va a hacer tu familia/amigos en la Navidad?

Nuevo vocabulario

_____

_____

_____

Semana 13

Escribe las preguntas relevantes a este capítulo y practícalas.

1.

2.

3.

4.

5.

6.

7.

8.

9.

10.

11.

12.

13.

14.

15.

Semana 14

1. ¿A qué restaurante te gusta frecuentar?

2. ¿Cuál es tu comida favorita?

3. ¿Qué sabes cocinar bien?

4. ¿Te gusta tener invitados en tu casa?

5. ¿Cuál es el menu para el día de Acción de Gracias?

6. ¿Qué comen los Estados Unidenses en La Navidad?

7. ¿Cuáles son los vegetales qué más te gustan?

8. ¿Comes pavo?

1. ¿Qué comida prefieres: el almuerzo o la cena?

2. ¿Tomas siestas?

3. ¿Comparte algo interesante de esta semana?

4. ¿Te vas a comprar ropa nueva el fin de semana?

5. ¿Tienes que pagar muchas cuentas?

6. ¿En el restaurante, pagas con tarjeta de crédito?

7. ¿Manejas rápido?

8. ¿Dejas propina en el restaurante?

Nuevo vocabulario

_____

_____

_____

Semana 15

1. ¿Fuiste a un restaurante elegante? Fui...

2. ¿Qué hiciste para el cuatro de julio?

3. ¿Visitaste un país en América del Sur?

4. ¿Qué comiste anoche para la cena?

5. ¿Cómo celebraste tu cumpleaños el año pasado?

6. ¿Trabajaste ayer?

7. ¿Recibiste un regalo especial el año pasado?

8. ¿Te compraste un ipad recientemente?

1. ¿Fuiste de vacaciones el verano pasado?

2. ¿Qué clases tomaste el semetre pasado?

3. ¿Qué película miraste últimamente?

4. ¿Qué hiciste la semana pasada?

5. ¿Fuiste al médico el otro día?

6. ¿Qué hizo tu familia para "Thanksgiving" el año pasado?

7. ¿Fuiste de vacaciones recientemente?

8. ¿Te compraste algo lindo últimamente?

Nuevo vocabulario

_____

_____

_____

Semana 16

Escribe 15 preguntas relacionadas a los capítulos estudiados.

1.

2.

3.

4.

5.

6.

7.

8.

9.

10.

11.

12.

13.

14.

15.

The Department of Modern Languages

Spanish Associate in Arts Degree

Program Requirements: Units Required: **18 Units**

SPAN-150 Beginning Conversational Spanish   3.0

SPAN-201 Intermediate Spanish I   4.0

SPAN-202 Intermediate Spanish 11   4.0

SPAN-240 Introduction to Latin American Literature   3.0

Plus four units from the following:

SPAN-102 Elementary Spanish II   4.0

SPAN·212 Spanish for Heritage Speakers II   4.0

Advisor
claudia.acosta@canyons.edu

Visit our Webpage
Http://www.canyons.edu/departments/modernlanguages

The Department of Modern Languages

Spanish Associate in Arts Degree for Transfer AA-T
Intended for students who plan to complete a Bachelors of Spanish at CSU

SPAN- 101 Elementary Spanish I   4.0

SPAN- 102 Elementary Spanish II   4.0

Plus eight units from the following:

SPAN- 201 Intermediate Spanish I   4.0
or
SPAN- 211 Heritage Speakers I   4.0

SPAN- 202 Intermediate Spanish II   4.0
or
SPAN- 212 Heritage Speakers II   4.0

Plus 3 units from the following:

SPAN 150- Beginning Conversational Spanish   3.0

SPAN-240 Introduction to Latin American Literature   3.0

If substitution of a course is needed due to testing out of required courses, students may choose from the followings: French 101 or 102; Italian 101; Spanish 150 or 240 or other approved by the Spanish advisor.

Total units required   19.0

Advisor
claudia.acosta@canyons.edu

Visit our Webpage
Http://www.canyons.edu/departments/modernlanguages

The Department of Modern Languages

New Honors Course!

Spanish 101H
Elementary Spanish I Honors

ML Webpage
Http://www.canyons.edu/departments/modernlanguages

The College of the Canyons
Department of Modern Languages
has a Facebook page!

Like our page today to get the latest information, including:

- **International Film Festival**

- **Modern Languages Film Series**

- **Study Abroad Programs**

- **International Poetry Reading**

- **Cultural Events on campus and in the community**

. . . and much more!

Sigma Delta Mu

National Honor Society in Spanish
Iota Chapter of California at COC

This society had its foundation in Sigma Delta Pi
The largest foreign language honor society. It recognizes excellence in Spanish.

The purposes of the society are:

- To honor those who seek and attain excellence in the study of the Spanish language and in the study of the literature and the culture of Spanish-speaking peoples;

- To honor those who strive to make the Hispanic contribution to modern culture better known to the English-speaking peoples;

- To encourage students to acquire a greater interest in, and a deeper understanding of Hispanic culture; and

- To foster friendly relations and mutual respect between the nations of Hispanic speech and those of English speech.

Membership Requirements:

- One course in Spanish with at least a letter B, and

- A min. cumulative GPA of 3.0

Cost:

- $30.00 (includes certificate, pin and candle provided during the installation ceremony)

COLLEGE OF THE CANYONS

canyons.edu/departments/modernlanguages

For more information, contact Dr. Claudia Acosta by email claudia.acosta@canyons.edu or phone at 661.362.3530

Sigma Delta Mu, Iota of California Chapter
The National Spanish Honor Society

Life-Time Membership Application

Name: _____ Student ID: _____

Address: _____
Street   City   Zip

Telephone: (home):_____ (cell):_____(work):_____

Email: _____

Major: _____ Cum. GPA _____

Number of college credits completed: _____ Expected Graduation: _____

Spanish Language college courses completed: _____

There is a one-time membership fee of $30.00 due at the time of application. Please indicate below the form of payment you are intending to use:

☐   Cash
☐   Money Order (Payable to Sigma Delta Mu): _____
☐   Other _____

Amount paid by the student: $ _____ Verified by: _____

_____   _____
Applicant   Date

Received by: _____ Faculty Advisor: _____

COLLEGE OF THE CANYONS

Return to Dr. Claudia Acosta at
the Department of Modern Languages

DEDICATORIA

To my parents and closest friends, I am forever grateful
for your unconditional love and support

To the Spanish faculty at MCC, thank you for all of your
encouragement

Para los estudiantes de español, que aprendan a apreciar
el idioma y sus culturas
(Mary Ann)

A mi queridísima familia: A Gordon, a mis padres, a mis
hermanos Luis, Alfonso y Fer, a Paty y a mis sobrinos.
Gracias por su apoyo y cariño incondicional.

To all my professors and friends at the Foreign Language
Department of Colorado State University.

To all our Spanish students!
(Margarita)

Scope and Sequence

Chapter	Objectives	Vocabulary

CAPÍTULO 1
Hola ¿qué tal?

At the end of the chapter, you will be able to:

- Greet and say goodbye to people in formal and informal situations
- Describe your classroom, your friends, and other people
- Use numbers up to 101, exchange telephone numbers
- Spell names

Exploraciones léxicas 1
Greetings, introductions, and goodbyes 4

Classroom 4

Alphabet 5

Numbers 0-101 9, 12

Exploraciones léxicas 2
Descriptive adjectives 18

CAPÍTULO 2
¿Cómo es tu vida?

At the end of the chapter, you will be able to:

- Describe your family and tell their age
- Talk about your classes
- Discuss your routine
- Express ownership

Exploraciones léxicas 1
Family members and pets 40

Exploraciones léxicas 2
Academic subjects 54

CAPÍTULO 3
¿Qué tiempo hace hoy?

At the end of the chapter, you will be able to:

- Talk about the weather and seasons
- Discuss clothing
- Express likes and dislikes
- Communicate dates and time
- Tell what you and others are going to do in the near future

Exploraciones léxicas 1
Seasons 78

Weather 78

Clothing 78

Colors 78

Exploraciones léxicas 2
Days of the week 92

Months 92

Time 92

Grammar	Reading/Listening	Culture
Exploraciones gramaticales 1 Stem-changing verbs 1: **(o→ue)** 118 **Exploraciones gramaticales 2** The verb **estar** with prepositions 121 **Exploraciones gramaticales 3** Question formation 132 **Exploraciones gramaticales 4** Stem-changing verbs 2: **(e→ie; e→i)** 135	**En vivo** Turismo local en Ecuador 125 Casas en venta 141 **Lectura** Algunas ciudades únicas en Latinoamérica 126 Soluciones a la vivienda 138 ▶ **Exploraciones profesionales** La arquitectura 142 **Exploraciones literarias** "Ida de otoño" de Juan Ramón Jiménez 148 "Canción de invierno" de Juan Ramón Jiménez 149	**Conexiones culturales** Ciudades fuera de lo común 116 Casas únicas 130
Exploraciones gramaticales 1 **Estar** with adjectives and present progressive 156 **Exploraciones gramaticales 2** **Ser** and **estar** 159 **Exploraciones gramaticales 3** Verbs with changes in the first person 170 **Exploraciones gramaticales 4** **Saber** and **conocer** 173	**En vivo** Entrevista a un actor 163 Solicitudes de trabajo 179 **Lectura** ¿Quiénes son más felices? 164 Trabajos poco comunes 176 ▶ **Exploraciones profesionales** El trabajo social 180	**Conexiones culturales** Las emociones y el bienestar 154 Las profesiones y la economía 168
Exploraciones gramaticales 1 Reflexive verbs 192 **Exploraciones gramaticales 2** Adverbs of time and frequency 195 **Exploraciones gramaticales 3** The preterite 206 **Exploraciones gramaticales 4** Stem-changing verbs in the preterite 209	**En vivo** Cómo mantenernos sanos 199 Un reportaje biográfico 215 **Lectura** La siesta 200 Deportistas famosos 212 ▶ **Exploraciones profesionales** La educación física 216 **Exploraciones literarias** "Cántico" de Donato Ndongo 222	**Conexiones culturales** La vida diaria 190 Los deportes en España y Latinoamérica 204

Scope and Sequence

Chapter	Objectives	Vocabulary

CAPÍTULO 7

¿Qué te gusta comer?

At the end of the chapter, you will be able to:

- Talk about food
- Order food in a restaurant
- Use numbers above 100

Exploraciones léxicas 1
Fruit, vegetables, and condiments 226

Exploraciones léxicas 2
Meals and utensils 240

Exploraciones léxicas 3
Numbers above 100

Learning Strategy

Study frequently

When learning a foreign language it is important to study every day. Aside from any written homework you may have, plan to spend some time each day learning the current vocabulary and verbs. For most students, it is more effective to study for 15–20 minutes three times a day than to spend a full hour on the subject. It might also be a lot easier for you to find time to study if you break it into smaller periods of time.

In this chapter you will learn how to:
- Greet and say goodbye to people in formal and informal situations
- Describe your classroom, your friends, and other people
- Use numbers up to 100 and exchange telephone numbers
- Spell names

© Image Source Plus/Alamy

Este es el salón de clases de Mariana. ¿Qué hay en la clase?

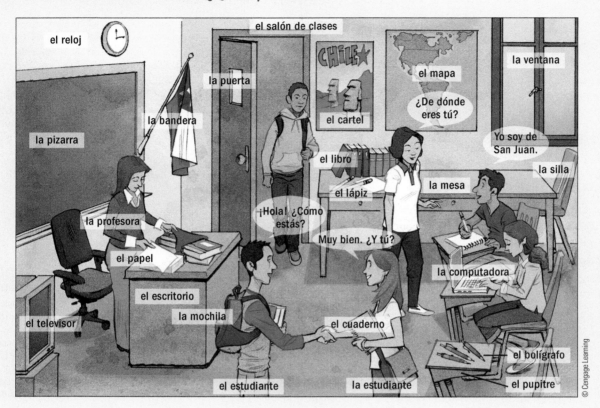

Saludos formales

Buenos días.
Buenas tardes.
Buenas noches.
¿Cómo está (usted)?

Respuestas

Buenos días.
Buenas tardes.
Buenas noches.
Bien, gracias. /
Mal. / Regular,
gracias.
¿Y usted?

Saludos informales

¡Hola!
¿Cómo estás
(tú)?
¿Qué tal?
¿Qué hay de
nuevo?
¿Qué pasa?

Respuestas

¡Hola!
Bien, gracias. /
Mal. / Regular,
gracias. ¿Y tú?
Nada.

Nada.

Despedidas

Adiós.	Goodbye.
Chao.	Goodbye.
	(informal)
Hasta luego.	See you later.
Hasta pronto.	See you soon.
Hasta mañana.	See you tomorrow.
¡Nos vemos!	See you later!
¡Que tengas un	Have a nice day!
buen día!	(informal)

Presentaciones

¿Cómo te	What is your name?
llamas?	(informal)
Me llamo...	My name is . . .
Le presento	I'd like to introduce
a...	you to . . . (formal)
Te presento	I'd like to introduce
a...	you to . . . (informal)

Encantado(a).	Nice to meet you.
Mucho gusto.	Nice to meet you.
¿Cómo se	How do you
escribe...?	spell . . . ?

Palabras interrogativas

¿Dónde?	Where?
¿Cuándo?	When?
¿Cuántos(as)?	How many?
¿Qué?	What?
¿Quién?	Who?
¿Por qué?	Why?

INVESTIGUEMOS EL VOCABULARIO

Vocabulary often varies from one Spanish-speaking country to another. For example, here are three different terms for the word for *pen*:

    el bolígrafo (Spain)   **la pluma** (Mexico)   **el lapicero** (Peru)

Another word that has variations is *computer:*

    la computadora (Latin America)   **el ordenador** (Spain)

A practicar

1.1 **Escucha y responde** Listen to the following list of common classroom items.
🔊 If the item is in your classroom, give a thumbs-up; if it is not, give a thumbs-down.
1-2

1.2 **En la mochila** Indicate which of these items could go into a student's backpack:
la pizarra, el cuaderno, el papel, la silla, el bolígrafo, el escritorio, la puerta, los lápices

1.3 **Un poco de lógica** Match each question or statement with a logical response.

1. ¿Cómo te llamas?
2. ¿De dónde eres?
3. ¿Cómo estás?
4. ¿Qué hay de nuevo?
5. Te presento a Jairo.

a. Soy de California.
b. Me llamo Marcos.
c. Nada.
d. Mucho gusto.
e. Bien, gracias. ¿Y tú?

INVESTIGUEMOS EL VOCABULARIO
When making introductions, male speakers use the form **encantado**. Female speakers use the form **encantada**.

1.4 **Mucho gusto** Read the dialogue aloud with a partner. Then, read it again, substituting all the parts in italics with your own information or greetings/farewells.

Estudiante 1: *¡Hola!*
Estudiante 2: *¡Hola!*
Estudiante 1: Me llamo *Rafael.* ¿Y tú? ¿Cómo te llamas?
Estudiante 2: Me llamo *Carlos.*

Estudiante 1: *Mucho gusto, Carlos.* ¿De dónde eres?
Estudiante 2: Soy de *México.* ¿Y tú?
Estudiante 1: Yo soy de *Argentina.*
Estudiante 2: *¡Qué bien!*
Estudiante 1: *Bueno... ¡adiós!*
Estudiante 2: *¡Chao!*

INVESTIGUEMOS EL VOCABULARIO
According to the Real Academia, **ch, ll,** and **rr** are not independent letters, so they are not listed as part of the Spanish alphabet. Additional changes made to the alphabet are the names of the letters **v, w,** and **y.** However, it is likely to hear the former letter names used as well.

🔊 # El alfabeto
1-3

Letra	Nombre de la letra	Letra	Nombre de la letra	Letra	Nombre de la letra	Letra	Nombre de la letra
A	a	H	hache	Ñ	eñe	U	u
B	be	I	i	O	o	V	uve
C	ce	J	jota	P	pe	W	doble uve
D	de	K	ka	Q	cu	X	equis
E	e	L	ele	R	ere	Y	ye
F	efe	M	eme	S	ese	Z	zeta
G	ge	N	ene	T	te		

1.5 **Correo electrónico** You and your partner are in charge of your school's Club Internacional. You have information for half of the new members on this page and your partner has the other half in Appendix B. Ask each other questions to complete the tables. You will need the following words: **arroba** (@) and **punto** (dot).

Modelo Estudiante 1: *¿Cuál es el correo electrónico de Pilar?*
Estudiante 2: *pilybonita@uden.es → p-i-l-y-b-o-n-i-t-a, arroba, u-d-e-n, punto, e-s*

Nombre	Correo electrónico
1. Marina	
2. Gabriel	gabmuñoz@inter.cl
3. Alejandro	
4. Valeria	valelapeña@clarotodo.pr

Conexiones...
a la geografía

Look at the map and write the names of all Spanish-speaking countries that you can locate. Then indicate in what region each country is located: North America (**América del Norte**), Central America (**América Central**), South America (**América del Sur**), the Caribbean (**el Caribe**), Europe (**Europa**), or Africa (**África**). When you finish your list, match each of the countries with its capital city from the box below. **¡OJO!** One of the countries has two capital cities.

© Cengage Learning

Asunción	**La Paz**	**San Juan**
Bogotá	**Lima**	**San Salvador**
Buenos Aires	**Madrid**	**Santiago**
Caracas	**Malabo**	**Santo Domingo**
Ciudad de Guatemala	**Managua**	**Sucre**
Ciudad de México	**Montevideo**	**Tegucigalpa**
Ciudad de Panamá	**Quito**	
La Habana	**San José**	

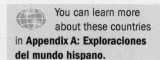
You can learn more about these countries in **Appendix A: Exploraciones del mundo hispano.**

Comparaciones

How different is the Spanish used in Spain from the Spanish spoken in Latin American countries? It is important to understand that it is the same language and both will be understood in every country where Spanish is spoken. However, there are regional differences in vocabulary as well as accents, just as there are between the English spoken in England and the English used in the United States. Come up with a list of five or six regional vocabulary variations in English and compare your list with a partner's. Do your words fit into specific categories (food, clothing, etc.)? What factors do you think influence differences in vocabulary within the same language? Write five words that you would expect to vary in Spanish-speaking countries. For some variations, check **Investiguemos el vocabulario** on page 4.

© Maridav/Shutterstock

Cultura

Cultural practices and products of Spanish-speaking countries vary from country to country. Putting aside preconceived ideas will help you gain a better understanding of these cultures. Work in groups of three or four to determine if the statements below are true or false. Then, search the Internet to correct the false statements.

1. All Latin Americans speak Spanish.
2. Flamenco is a popular dance throughout South America.
3. The majority of the population in Spanish-speaking countries is Catholic.
4. **Tortillas** are a typical dish in Spain.
5. Some indigenous people in Mexico and Guatemala still wear traditional clothing.
6. Chiles are a cooking staple in Paraguay, Uruguay, and Argentina.
7. Soccer is the most popular sport in South America.
8. In many Spanish-speaking countries, children can attend school in the morning or the afternoon.
9. Bullfighting is a popular sport in Cuba.
10. In most Spanish-speaking countries, the main meal is between 5:00 and 7:00 P.M.

Many people assume that the same foods are eaten in all of Latin America and Spain. Choose a country from the **Exploraciones del mundo hispano** section in **Appendix A** and research some of the typical dishes from that country. Share an image and the name of a dish you'd like to try and list the ingredients needed.

Comunidad

If there are any international students or ESL students in your school that are native Spanish speakers, introduce yourself to one of them and find out where he or she is from. You may want to become conversation partners.

INVESTIGUEMOS LA MÚSICA
Find the song "Latino" by Adolescent's Orquesta on the Internet and listen to it. What Latin American countries are named?

Exploraciones gramaticales

Throughout the program, you will be given examples of grammatical structures in Spanish and asked to discover the patterns of use based on those examples. This process not only helps you to remember how to use particular structures but will also help you to develop important skills such as inference and pattern recognition, which will make you a better language learner.

A analizar ▶

Professor Tobar is in his classroom making sure he has everything ready for the first day of classes. Watch the video and note whether there is one or more than one of everything you see. Read the passage and underline the vocabulary words. Then answer the questions.

© Cengage Learning

> Este es el salón de clases. Hay muchos estudiantes en la clase. Hay una pizarra. No hay carteles, pero hay un mapa. Hay muchas sillas. También hay un escritorio, hay lápices y bolígrafos en el escritorio... ¡no hay una computadora!

1. Which words that you underlined refer to more than one item (are plural)? How do you know?
2. Find the word above that is similar to **lápiz**. What differences do you notice?

A comprobar

Gender and number of nouns

1. A noun (**sustantivo**) is a person, place, or thing. In order to make a noun plural:

   - add an **-s** to words ending in a vowel — libro → libros — silla → sillas
   - add an **-es** to words ending in a consonant — profesor → profesores — papel → papeles
   - change a final **-z** to **-c** and add an **-es** — lápiz → lápices

2. You will notice that some nouns lose an accent mark or gain an accent mark when they become plural. You will learn more about accent marks in **Capítulo 2.**

   - televisión → televisiones
   - salón → salones
   - examen → exámenes

3. In Spanish, nouns have a gender. In other words, they are either masculine or feminine.

   The endings of nouns not referring to people often indicate a word's gender.

   Masculine nouns:
   - often end in **-o,** such as **el libro** and **el cuaderno**
   - can refer to a man, such as **el profesor** and **el estudiante**

   Feminine nouns:
   - often end in **-a,** such as **la silla** and **la pizarra**
   - can refer to a woman, such as **la profesora** and **la estudiante**

   There are some exceptions such as:

Masculine	Feminine
el día	la mano
el mapa	la foto
el problema	la moto

4. Here are the numbers from 0 to 20.

Los números

0	cero	7	siete	14	catorce
1	uno	8	ocho	15	quince
2	dos	9	nueve	16	dieciséis
3	tres	10	diez	17	diecisiete
4	cuatro	11	once	18	dieciocho
5	cinco	12	doce	19	diecinueve
6	seis	13	trece	20	veinte

A practicar

1.6 **De singular a plural** Change the following vocabulary words from singular to plural.

Modelo cuaderno → *cuadernos*

1. mochila
2. lápiz
3. papel
4. pupitre
5. reloj
6. bandera
7. libro
8. cartel
9. televisor
10. examen

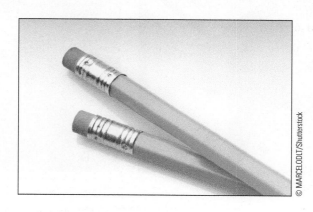

© MARCELODLT/Shutterstock

1.7 **Género** Using the rules that you have learned, decide whether the following words are masculine (**M**) or feminine (**F**).

	M	F
1. saludo	_____	_____
2. actriz	_____	_____
3. cafetería	_____	_____
4. rosa	_____	_____
5. doctor	_____	_____
6. teatro	_____	_____
7. día	_____	_____
8. supervisora	_____	_____
9. mapa	_____	_____
10. autor	_____	_____

1.8 **En la clase** Listen to Carolina describe how many of the following items are in her classroom. As you listen, write the number next to each item. Then tell how many of each of the items there are in your classroom.

1-4

Modelo You will hear: *Hay once escritorios.*
You will write: ___11___ escritorios

1. _____ estudiantes
2. _____ pizarras
3. _____ sillas
4. _____ ventanas
5. _____ mapas
6. _____ computadoras

1.9 **Los útiles** Look at the pictures below and identify the plural classroom items you have learned, telling how many there are. Then work with a partner and take turns identifying the school supplies you each have. ¡OJO! Pay attention to singular and plural forms of the vocabulary words.

© tobkatrina/Shutterstock

© hxdbzxy/Shutterstock

1.10 **La clase de matemáticas** Work with a partner and take turns saying the following mathematical equations in Spanish and giving their solutions. You will need the following words: **más (+), menos (–),** and **son (=).**

Modelo $6 + 10 =$
Seis más diez son dieciséis.

1. $4 + 5 =$
2. $16 - 6 =$
3. $20 - 2 =$
4. $7 + 9 =$
5. $3 + 12 =$
6. $11 - 4 =$
7. $13 + 1 =$
8. $14 + 5 =$

A analizar

Profesor Tobar is in his classroom. Watch the video again. Then read the paragraph below and answer the questions that follow.

> Este es el salón de clases. Hay muchos estudiantes en la clase. Hay una pizarra. No hay carteles, pero hay un mapa. Hay muchas sillas. También hay un escritorio, hay lápices y bolígrafos en el escritorio... ¡no hay una computadora! ¡¿Donde está la computadora?! Necesito hablar con el director.

© Cengage Learning

1. Write the word that comes before each of the following nouns. Do these words change according to the nouns that follow? Explain.

   _____ salón de clase   _____ escritorio

   _____ pizarra   _____ computadora

   _____ mapa   _____ director

2. What do you think **hay** means?

A comprobar

Definite and indefinite articles and **hay**

1. The definite article *the* is used with a specific noun or a noun that has previously been mentioned. In Spanish, the definite article indicates whether a noun is masculine or feminine as well as whether it is singular or plural. It can be expressed in four different ways.

   Artículos definidos

	masculino	femenino
singular	el	la
plural	los	las

   ¿De dónde es **el** profesor?
   *Where is **the** professor from?*

2. The indefinite articles *a/an* or *some* are used when referring to a noun that is not specific or that has not previously been mentioned. They also indicate gender (masculine/feminine) and number (singular/plural), and can be expressed in four different ways in Spanish.

   Artículos indefinidos

	masculino	femenino
singular	un	una
plural	unos	unas

   ¿Hay **una** ventana en el salón de clases?
   *Is there **a** window in the classroom?*

3. **Hay** means *there is* or *there are*. It is used with the indefinite article to talk about singular nouns and to indicate *some* with plural nouns. The indefinite article is often omitted after **hay** in plural expressions.

   Hay un escritorio.   No hay lápices.
   There is a desk.   *There are no pencils.*

   Hay (unas) ventanas.   No hay una pizarra.
   There are (some) windows. *There isn't a board.*

4. When using **hay** with numbers, do not use an article. You already know numbers 0–20; numbers 21 through 101 are below.

No hay tres libros.
There aren't three books.

Hay cinco libros.
There are five books.

21	veintiuno	28	veintiocho	60	sesenta
22	veintidós	29	veintinueve	70	setenta
23	veintitrés	30	treinta	80	ochenta
24	veinticuatro	31	treinta y uno	90	noventa
25	veinticinco	40	cuarenta	100	cien
26	veintiséis	50	cincuenta	101	ciento uno
27	veintisiete				

Numbers below 30 are only one word, whereas numbers above 30 take the word **y** *(and)*, for example, **treinta y uno.** With the numbers 21, 31, etc., **uno** changes to **un** when followed by a masculine noun: **Hay treinta y un libros** and **una** when followed by a feminine noun: **Hay treinta y una sillas.** Note that **veintiún** has an accent over the letter **u.**

A practicar

1.11 **¿Lógico o no?** Read the statements and decide if they are logical or not.

1. Hay un cuaderno en la mochila.
2. No hay una puerta en la clase.
3. Hay una estudiante en la clase.
4. Hay cinco libros en el escritorio.
5. Hay unos papeles en la mesa.
6. Hay una pizarra en la silla.

1.12 **Los artículos** Read the paragraph and decide if you need the definite article or the indefinite article. Circle the correct answer.

David es estudiante en (**1.** una / la) universidad de los Estados Unidos. En su salón de clases hay (**2.** unos / los) carteles y (**3.** una / la) ventana. (**4.** Una / La) ventana es muy grande. En (**5.** una / la) mochila de David hay (**6.** unos / los) libros. También hay (**7.** un / el) cuaderno para (**8.** una / la) clase de español de David.

David es estudiante.

1.13 **¿Cuántos hay?** Look at the picture below and take turns answering the following questions.

1. ¿Cuántos mapas hay?
2. ¿Cuántas sillas hay?
3. ¿Cuántos libros hay?

4. ¿Cuántos lápices hay?
5. ¿Cuántas banderas hay?
6. ¿Qué más hay? (*What else is there?*)

1.14 **¿Qué hay?** With a partner, take turns asking and answering the questions about the items in your classroom. If you have them in your classroom, tell how many there are. Remember, if there is only one item, you must use **un** or **una.**

Modelo ¿Hay mesas?
       Estudiante 1: *¿Hay mesas?*
       Estudiante 2: *Sí, hay una mesa. / Sí, hay dos mesas. / No, no hay mesas.*

1. ¿Hay relojes?
2. ¿Hay pizarras?
3. ¿Hay banderas?
4. ¿Hay mapas?

5. ¿Hay ventanas?
6. ¿Hay carteles?
7. ¿Hay computadoras?
8. ¿Hay sillas?

1.15 **El número, por favor** Look at the directory for a university in Nicaragua. Tell what numbers you would need to call to reach the following areas.

1. la oficina de admisión
2. las diferentes facultades (*departments*)
3. para participar en actividades

Contáctenos

Oficina de admisión 2214 7300

Facultades
Ciencia y Tecnología 2297 7210
Psicología 2249 3765
Sociología 2278 4403
Humanidades y Filosofía 2251 2030
Arquitectura 2259 8215

Deportes y cultura
Fútbol 2264 3911
Karate 2255 1290
Volibol 2213 8616
Ballet folclórico 2233 0961
Grupo de teatro 2292 4718

© Cengage Learning

1.16 **En la librería** It is the end of the year, and employees are taking inventory at the bookstore. Tell how many items they have using the verb **hay**.

1. 50 cuadernos
2. 85 diccionarios
3. 100 bolígrafos
4. 78 lápices
5. 21 computadoras
6. 94 paquetes de papel
7. 31 libros de español
8. 62 mapas
9. 49 calculadoras
10. 51 mochilas

© Monkey Business Images/Shutterstock

Entrando en materia

Where do you buy your school supplies?

Comprando artículos escolares

◀)) Maricarmen will start school next week, and she is looking for supplies at good
1-5 prices. Listen to two commercials where she can buy what she needs: the first one for Papelería El Gigante and the second one for La Bodega.

Vocabulario útil			
los artículos escolares	*school supplies*	**gratis**	*for free*
la copiadora	*copier*	**la impresora**	*printer*
el descuento	*discount*		

Comprensión

Listen to the commercials again and indicate where Maricarmen would get a better price for the following articles.

Maricarmen needs . . .	She should buy at . . .	
1. cuadernos	Papelería El Gigante	La Bodega
2. lápices	Papelería El Gigante	La Bodega
3. papel	Papelería El Gigante	La Bodega
4. una computadora	Papelería El Gigante	La Bodega
5. bolígrafos	Papelería El Gigante	La Bodega
6. una mochila	Papelería El Gigante	La Bodega

Más allá

What supplies do you use for your classes? Using the vocabulary in this chapter, make a list in Spanish and use Share It! to post a written or recorded list to share with the class.

© Nattika/Shutterstock

Lectura

Antes de leer

Look at the advertisement for a school. Using the cognates to help you, answer the questions.

LINGUA**MAX**

Establecido en 1980, **Linguamax** ofrece clases de inglés y francés para adolescentes y adultos.

- Profesores nativos con mucha experiencia
- Clases con un máximo de 5 estudiantes
- Precios razonables

Los cursos comienzan el 1° de junio

Para más información llame al 951-23-45-67 o visite **Linguamax** en la Avenida Bolívar, 203

¡Cursos de lenguas con garantía de calidad!

Obtenga un descuento del 10% al mencionar este anuncio.

---

1. When was the school established?
2. What classes are offered at the school?
3. Who can take classes?
4. What are three benefits of taking classes at this school?
5. When do classes begin?
6. How can you get more information?
7. How can you receive a discount?

Now look at the reading on the next page. The red, bold words are cognates. What do they mean?

© Keith Dannemiller / Alamy

A leer

La escuela es para todos

En los **países** latinoamericanos y en España, **la educación** es un **derecho** de los niños. En unos países la escuela **primaria** y la **secundaria** son **obligatorias**. En otros países la **preparatoria** es obligatoria. Para satisfacer la **demanda**, muchas escuelas tienen dos **turnos**: unos niños **asisten** a la escuela por la mañana, y otros por la tarde.

> la educación es un derecho de los niños

Por lo **general**, los libros de texto son **gratuitos**, pero las familias **deben comprar** otros **útiles** escolares. También en muchos **casos** las **familias** necesitan comprar **uniformes** para los niños porque es **común** usarlos.

countries/right

3 year pre-university course
shifts/attend

free
must buy
supplies

Una escuela en Cuba

© AFP/Getty Images

Comprensión

Decide whether the following statements are true (**cierto**) or false (**falso**).

1. En Latinoamérica la escuela primaria es obligatoria.
2. Todos (*All*) los niños están en la escuela por la mañana.
3. Es necesario comprar (*to buy*) los libros para la escuela.
4. Muchos niños usan uniformes.

Después de leer

Even though school is free, there are many expenses associated with it, such as purchasing uniforms, lab coats, fees for special equipment, etc. What expenses are associated with K–12 in the United States? Can you think of other hidden expenses?

Las descripciones de la personalidad

bueno(a) / malo(a)
cruel / cariñoso(a)
generoso(a) / egoísta
idealista / realista
inteligente / tonto(a)
interesante / aburrido(a)
optimista / pesimista
liberal / conservador(a)
paciente / impaciente
serio(a) / cómico(a)
tímido(a) / sociable

Más adjetivos

agresivo(a)	aggressive
atlético(a)	athletic
antipático(a)	unfriendly
amable	kind
corto(a)	short (length)
difícil	difficult
fácil	easy
famoso(a)	famous
gordo(a)	fat

guapo(a)	good-looking
honesto(a)	honest
largo(a)	long
nuevo(a)	new
perezoso(a)	lazy
pobre	poor
rico(a)	rich
simpático(a)	nice
trabajador(a)	hardworking

Palabras adicionales

muy	very
pero	but
un poco	a little
también	also
y	and

INVESTIGUEMOS EL VOCABULARIO

The word **gordo** is often used in Spanish endearingly, such as between spouses, and parents often call their children **gordito** or **gordita**. People often describe themselves using the diminutive as well: **Soy (un poco) gordito.** Another word commonly used instead of **delgado** is **flaco.**

A practicar

 Escucha y responde Look at the picture and listen to the different adjectives. Write the letter **D** on one piece of paper and the letter **S** on another. If the adjective you hear describes Don Quijote, hold up the **D**. If it describes Sancho Panza, hold up the **S**.

© Cengage Learning

1.18 Identificaciones Look around the classroom and identify someone that fits the following descriptions.

1. pelirrojo
2. alto
3. joven
4. guapo
5. moreno
6. rubio
7. bajo
8. delgado

1.19 Sinónimos Identify a word from the vocabulary list that has a similar meaning.

1. afectuoso
2. introvertido
3. sincero
4. tolerante
5. complicado
6. atractivo
7. simple
8. positivo

1.20 La personalidad y las profesiones Make a list of the ideal personality traits for the following jobs.

Modelo profesor
paciente, interesante, inteligente

1. policía
2. estudiante
3. actor
4. espía *(spy)*
5. político
6. doctor

1.21 Veinte preguntas Follow the steps below to play "twenty questions."

Paso 1 In groups of three, write a list of names of famous men who are familiar to everybody in the group.

Paso 2 One person in the group chooses a name from the list but doesn't say which name it is. The other two members of the group guess the name by asking yes/no questions.

Modelo ¿Es (Is he) *joven?*   ¿Es *rubio?*   ¿Es *alto?*

1.22 La fila Work with a partner to figure out the names of the people in the stands. One of you will look at this page, and the other will look at the picture in Appendix B. Take turns giving the name of a person and a description, so your partner will know who it is.

© Cengage Learning

Cultura

Francisco de Goya was a Spanish painter who made a living for many years painting portraits of the Spanish royal family. Goya painted *La familia de Carlos IV,* shown below, in 1800.

Pick three different people in the painting and describe them in Spanish using vocabulary from the chapter. You might speculate what their personalities are like.

La familia de Carlos IV, por Francisco de Goya

Research a different portrait painter from a Spanish-speaking country. Find a painting you like and upload the image to Share It! along with a description in Spanish of one of the people in the painting.

Comparaciones

There is great cultural diversity among Spanish-speaking countries. One thing all Hispanic countries have in common is that Spanish is spoken by the majority of the population, although it is not always an official language, and in most cases, it is not the only language. Why do you think there are "official" languages, and what impact do they have on communities? Look at the information below. How can you explain the variety of languages in these countries? What do you think is the difference between a "national" language and an "official" language?

SPAIN

Official language:	Spanish
Official regional languages:	Galician, Basque (Euskara), Catalan, Valenciano
Other languages spoken:	14

MEXICO

National language:	Spanish
Other languages spoken:	298 (nahuatl is the only one spoken by over one million speakers)

GUATEMALA

Official language:	Spanish
Other languages spoken:	55

BOLIVIA

Official languages:	Spanish, Quechua, Aymara
Other languages spoken:	45

UNITED STATES

National languages:	English (official in some states)
Regional languages:	Hawaiian, Spanish (in New Mexico)
Other languages spoken:	178

Sources: *The Ethnologue Report, Almanaque Mundial 2010*

INVESTIGUEMOS EL MUNDO HISPANO

You can learn more about these countries and their Spanish-speaking populations in Appendix A: **Exploraciones del mundo hispano**.

Conexiones... a la geografía

The people in the photos are all from Latin America. In Spanish, tell what country each person is from and describe him or her. If possible, locate the countries using Google Earth. Why do you think there is such great ethnic diversity in Latin America?

Rigoberta Menchú, Guatemala, activista política

Paulina Rubio, México, cantante

Evo Morales, Bolivia, presidente

David Ortiz, República Dominicana, beisbolista

Keiko Fujimori, Perú, política

Lionel "Leo" Messi, Argentina, futbolista

Comunidad

Interview a Spanish speaker from your school or community. Introduce yourself and ask him/her to describe the diversity in his/her home country: You may want to start by asking: **¿Cómo es la gente *(people)* en tu país?**

A analizar

Rosa is going to introduce herself and her friend Santiago. After watching the video, read the following paragraph, paying attention to the words in bold.

> Yo **soy** Rosa y **soy** de El Salvador. Mi mejor amigo **es** de España y se llama Santiago. Yo **soy** muy sociable, pero Santiago no; él **es** un poco tímido, pero nosotros **somos** muy buenos amigos… ¿Y tú? ¿Cómo **eres** tú?

1. In the paragraph, who does **yo** refer to? Who does **él** refer to? Does **nosotros** refer to one person or more than one person?

2. The verb **ser** *(to be)* is used throughout the paragraph. Its forms are in bold. Write the appropriate form that is used with each of the following pronouns.

   yo _____   él _____

   tú _____   nosotros _____

3. Look at the following conversations, paying attention to the use of **tú** and **usted**. Both mean *you* in English. What do you think the difference is?

Buenos días, señor Martínez. ¿Cómo está usted?

Bien, gracias. ¿Y tú?

¡Hola! ¿Cómo estás?

Bien. ¿Y tú?

A comprobar

Subject pronouns and the verb ser

singular		plural	
yo	*I*	**nosotros/nosotras**	*we*
tú	*you (familiar)*	**vosotros/vosotras**	*you (familiar in Spain)*
usted	*you (formal)*	**ustedes**	*you*
él	*he*	**ellos**	*they (group of males or a mixed group)*
ella	*she*	**ellas**	*they (group of females)*

1. When addressing one person, Spanish speakers use either **tú** or **usted** (sometimes abbreviated **Ud.**). **Tú** is informal. It is used with family, friends, classmates, and children. It denotes familiarity. **Usted** is formal. It is used with people in a position of authority, older people, strangers, and people in a professional setting. It denotes respect and more distance.

2. When referring to groups of females, use **nosotras** and **ellas,** and when referring to groups of males, use **nosotros** and **ellos.** When the groups are mixed, use the masculine forms **nosotros** and **ellos,** as they have a generic meaning that implies the presence of both genders.

3. In Spain, **vosotros** and **vosotras** are used to address a group of people and denote familiarity, and follow the same rules as **nosotros** and **nosotras** with regard to gender; **ustedes** is used to address a group of people and denotes respect. In Latin America, **ustedes** (sometimes abbreviated **Uds.**) is used to address any group of people, regardless of the relationship.

4. The verb **ser** means *to be.* Just as there are different forms of the verb *to be* in English (*I am*, *you are*, etc.), there are also different forms of the verb **ser** in Spanish. Changing a verb into its different forms to indicate who is doing the activity is called *conjugating.*

> **INVESTIGUEMOS LA GRAMÁTICA**
> In Spanish **ser** and **estar** both mean *to be*. You will learn more about **estar** in **Capítulo 4.**

ser

yo	**soy**	*I am*	**nosotros/nosotras**	**somos**	*we are*
tú	**eres**	*you are*	**vosotros/vosotras**	**sois**	*you (all) are*
usted	**es**	*you are*	**ustedes**	**son**	*you all are*
él/ella	**es**	*he/she is*	**ellos/ellas**	**son**	*they are*

5. Use **ser**
   - to describe what someone is like.
     Él **es** alto, pero ellos **son** bajos.
     *He **is** tall, but they **are** short.*
   - to identify someone or something
     Yo **soy** Manolo.   *I **am** Manolo.*
   - to ask or say where someone is from.
     ¿De dónde **eres** tú?   Yo **soy** de Lima, Perú.
     Where are you from?   *I **am** from Lima, Peru.*

A practicar

1.23 **¿Tú o usted?** Which pronoun would you use **to address** each of the following people?

Modelo un niño → *tú*

1. un policía
2. un profesor
3. mamá
4. un amigo
5. el presidente
6. un estudiante en la clase de español

1.24 Sustituciones Which pronoun would you use **to talk about** the following people?

Modelo Rebeca → *ella*

1. Felipe
2. Silvia y Alicia
3. tu amigo y Ricardo
4. Regina

5. la señora Marcos
6. Javier y yo
7. Lola, Ana, Sara y Luis
8. Miguelito

1.25 Parejas Match the subject with the remainder of the sentence.

1. Yo
2. Rafael y Carlos
3. La profesora
4. Tú
5. Maite y yo

a. es joven.
b. somos trabajadores.
c. soy optimista.
d. eres inteligente.
e. son guapos.

1.26 El verbo ser Complete the paragraph with the necessary form of the verb **ser**.

¡Hola! Yo (**1**) _____ Antonio y (**2**) _____ de Santiago, Chile. Mis amigos (**3**) _____ Laura y Víctor. Nosotros (**4**) _____ estudiantes en la Universidad de Santiago. Laura (**5**) _____ estudiante de biología y Víctor y yo (**6**) _____ estudiantes de ciencias políticas. Y tú, ¿también (**7**) _____ estudiante?

1.27 ¿De dónde son? In groups of three, look at the map and complete the following sentences telling where the different people are from. Then, find out from the other members of your group where they are from. Be sure to use the correct forms of the verb **ser.**

Modelo Carolina...
Carolina es de Chile.

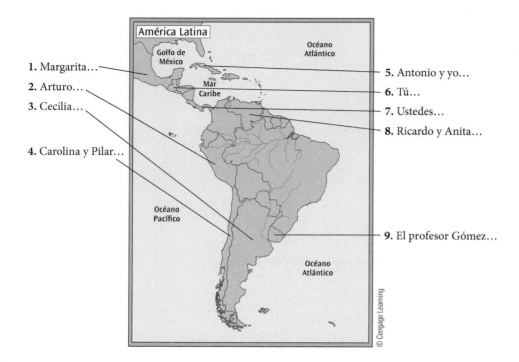

1. Margarita...
2. Arturo...
3. Cecilia...
4. Carolina y Pilar...

5. Antonio y yo...
6. Tú...
7. Ustedes...
8. Ricardo y Anita...
9. El profesor Gómez...

América Latina

Golfo de México
Océano Atlántico
Mar Caribe
Océano Pacífico
Océano Atlántico

© Cengage Learning

A analizar ▶

Rosa is going to introduce herself and her friend Santiago. Watch the video. Then read the paragraph that follows and underline the adjectives.

Yo soy Rosa y soy de El Salvador. Mi mejor amigo es de España y se llama Santiago. Yo soy muy sociable, pero Santiago no; él es un poco tímido, pero nosotros somos muy buenos amigos. Santiago es inteligente, muy simpático e idealista. Yo también soy inteligente y simpática pero no soy idealista. Soy realista, muy trabajadora y también soy liberal. Además, Santiago es alto, rubio y atlético, y yo soy baja y morena. Santiago y yo somos muy diferentes, pero lo importante es que somos buenos amigos.

Note the forms already filled in the chart and use the adjectives you underlined as well as what you learned about **encantado** and **encantada** in the box on page 5, to complete the chart.

masculine singular	masculine plural	feminine singular	feminine plural
bajo			
	inteligentes		
		idealista	
liberal			
			trabajadoras

A comprobar

Adjective agreement

Adjectives describe a person, place, or thing. In Spanish, adjectives must agree with the person or the object they describe both in gender (masculine/feminine) and in number (singular/plural).

Singular masculine adjectives		singular	plural
ending in **-o**	masculine	simpático	simpáticos
	feminine	simpática	simpáticas
ending in **-a**	masculine	idealista	idealistas
	feminine	idealista	idealistas
ending in **-e**	masculine	sociable	sociables
	feminine	sociable	sociables
ending in a consonant*	masculine	ideal	ideales
	feminine	ideal	ideales
*exception: ending in **-or**	masculine	trabajador	trabajadores
	feminine	trabajadora	trabajadoras

Mi amigo es simpático, sociable e idealista.
Mi amiga también es simpática, sociable e idealista.
Mis amigos son simpáticos, sociables e idealistas.

INVESTIGUEMOS LA PRONUNCIACIÓN

For pronunciation purposes, **y** (and) becomes **e** when followed by a word beginning with the letter(s) **i** or **hi.**

A practicar

1.28 **¿Quién es?** Listen to the six descriptive statements and decide which person is being described. In some cases, the description may apply to both. Place a check mark in the appropriate blanks. **¡OJO!** Pay attention to the adjective endings!

1. _____ Jennifer López   _____ Pitbull
2. _____ Lorena Ochoa   _____ Rafael Nadal
3. _____ Sofía Vergara   _____ George López
4. _____ Isabel Allende   _____ Gabriel García Márquez
5. _____ Christina Aguilera   _____ Gael García Bernal
6. _____ Penélope Cruz   _____ Mario López

1.29 **La atracción de los opuestos** Complete each sentence with an adjective that has the opposite meaning of the underlined word. **¡OJO!** Be sure the adjectives agree with the subject they are describing.

1. Susana es <u>generosa</u> y su esposo *(spouse)* es _____.
2. Fernando es <u>tímido</u> y su esposa es _____.
3. Mis amigas son <u>delgadas</u> y sus esposos son _____.
4. Marcos es <u>trabajador</u> y su esposa es _____.
5. Mis amigos son <u>cómicos</u> y sus esposas son _____.
6. Mi amigo es _____ y su esposa es _____.
   (Choose adjectives not used in the sentences above.)

1.30 **En el café** Work with a partner and take turns giving true/false statements about the people in the drawing. You should correct any false statements. **¡OJO!** Be sure the adjectives agree with the subject they are describing.

Modelo   Estudiante 1: *Vicente es calvo.*
         Estudiante 2: *Falso, él es rubio.*

1.31 **Los ideales** Complete the following statements expressing your own opinion regarding the ideal characteristics of each subject. Then compare your list with a partner's and come to an agreement on two characteristics for each.

1. La profesora ideal es… No es…
2. El estudiante ideal es… No es…
3. Los amigos ideales son… No son…
4. La madre *(mother)* ideal es… No es…
5. Los políticos ideales son… No son…
6. Las mascotas *(pet)* ideales son… No son…

1.32 **El horóscopo** Find your astrological sign below and read the descriptions. Choose two characteristics that describe you. You may use those listed for your sign or choose others that are more accurate. Then, talk to three classmates and find out their signs and the characteristics that describe them.

Modelo   Estudiante 1: *¿Cuál es tu signo?*
Estudiante 2: *Yo soy Aries.*
Estudiante 1: *¿Cómo eres tú?*
Estudiante 2: *Yo soy extrovertido y muy emocional.*

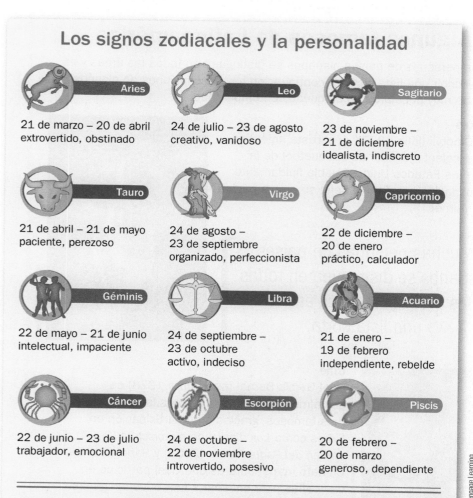

Los signos zodiacales y la personalidad

Aries
21 de marzo – 20 de abril
extrovertido, obstinado

Leo
24 de julio – 23 de agosto
creativo, vanidoso

Sagitario
23 de noviembre –
21 de diciembre
idealista, indiscreto

Tauro
21 de abril – 21 de mayo
paciente, perezoso

Virgo
24 de agosto –
23 de septiembre
organizado, perfeccionista

Capricornio
22 de diciembre –
20 de enero
práctico, calculador

Géminis
22 de mayo – 21 de junio
intelectual, impaciente

Libra
24 de septiembre –
23 de octubre
activo, indeciso

Acuario
21 de enero –
19 de febrero
independiente, rebelde

Cáncer
22 de junio – 23 de julio
trabajador, emocional

Escorpión
24 de octubre –
22 de noviembre
introvertido, posesivo

Piscis
20 de febrero –
20 de marzo
generoso, dependiente

© Cengage Learning

Lectura

Reading Strategy: Cognates

Read the first time through without using a dictionary. Underline any cognates that you see, as they will help you to understand the reading. Remember not to get hung up on understanding everything, but rather read for the general meaning.

Antes de leer

Write a list of names of famous contemporary U.S. citizens in the fields of pop culture, politics, movies, and sports. Why are they famous? Compare lists with a classmate. Together, try to come up with names of famous contemporary citizens of Spanish-speaking countries. What are their professions?

A leer

Algunos famosos de Latinoamérica

Muchas personas de países hispanos se distinguen en todas las áreas y es difícil escribir una lista corta. A continuación hay descripciones de algunas personas muy populares en el mundo contemporáneo.

Deportes

Manu Ginóbili (julio 1977), deportista argentino, es un excelente jugador de básquetbol de la NBA de los Estados Unidos. Habla fluidamente español, inglés e italiano y tiene su propia página en el Internet.

© Bob Pearson/epa/Corbis

[Muchas personas de países hispanos se distinguen en todas las áreas y es difícil escribir una lista corta.]

© Alastair Grant/AP Images

teach reading

Cine

Gael García Bernal (noviembre 1978) es actualmente uno de los actores latinoamericanos más famosos, gracias a su participación en filmes como *Los diarios de motocicleta* (2004), *El crimen del Padre Amaro* (2002) y *Babel* (2006). Un dato interesante es que Gael participó en campañas para **enseñar a leer** a los indígenas huicholes en el norte de México.

Música

Olga Tañón (abril 1967) es una cantante y actriz de Puerto Rico. Es famosa en Latinoamérica por su música rítmica, y ahora planea **grabar** música en inglés. Tañón participó en la controversial versión en español del himno estadounidense en 2006.

to record

Política

Michelle Bachelet (septiembre 1951) es presidente de Chile, doctora pediatra y también la primera mujer presidente de este país (2006–2010; 2014–2018). Es muy popular entre los chilenos y es la **segunda vez** que es elegida presidente. *Forbes* la considera una de las mujeres más influyentes del mundo. Bachelet se distingue por su trabajo para conseguir la **igualdad** entre hombres y mujeres.

second time

equality

Comprensión

To which of the people mentioned in the reading does the statement refer?

1. Es famosa por su música.
2. Estudió medicina.
3. Es un actor popular.
4. Es atlético.
5. Es puertorriqueña.
6. Juega al básquetbol.

Después de leer

What other famous people do you know from Spanish-speaking countries? Work with a partner to come up with a list of names, then choose one of the people on your list and write a short description of him/her. Read your description to the class and have them guess whom you are describing.

INVESTIGUEMOS LA MÚSICA

Find the Mocedades song "Eres tú" on the Internet and listen to it. Write down as many cognates as you can as well as words you recognize. What do you think the theme of the song is?

Redacción

Write a paragraph in which you describe yourself and your best friend.

Paso 1 Create a Venn diagram such as the one below. In the middle section where the circles overlap, write any adjectives that are common to both yourself and your best friend. Write any adjectives that are unique to yourself in the circle on the left and adjectives that are unique to your best friend in the circle on the right.

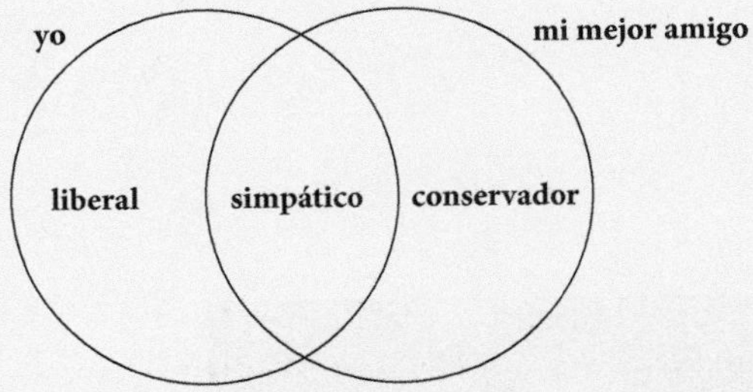

Estrategia

Be sure to brainstorm in Spanish rather than English to make the writing of the paragraph easier.

yo   mi mejor amigo

liberal   simpático   conservador

Paso 2 Write a sentence in which you introduce your reader to yourself and to your best friend.

Paso 3 Using the information you generated in **Paso 1**, continue your paragraph with two or three sentences in which you describe the qualities that you and your friend have in common and another two or three sentences where you describe the qualities that are unique to you and unique to your best friend.

Paso 4 Write a conclusion sentence that wraps up the paragraph.

Paso 5 Edit your paragraph:

1. Do the adjectives agree with the person they describe?
2. Check your spelling, including accent marks.
3. Are there any sentences that could be joined with either **y** or **pero**?
4. Can you vary some of the sentences by using expressions like **también** and **los/las dos** (both of us)?

En vivo

Entrando en materia

Look at the following sketches of people. Write down two or three adjectives that describe each person.

A   B   C   D   E   F

En busca de talento

A television network is looking for talent to participate in a new sitcom. The show requires several Hispanic characters, and they have a very specific idea of what they should look like. The descriptions that follow have been distributed to agents in the hopes of finding an exact match. Match the headshots to the descriptions.

NUEVO PROGRAMA BUSCA TALENTOS

Buscamos nuevos talentos para actuar en una comedia original. Es indispensable hablar español e inglés.

Leyre Morales Blanco
Edad: 5 años
Estatura: 1.10 **mts.**
Descripción: Delgada, morena, **pelo** largo. Leyre es tímida y seria, pero aventurera.

Rocío Leyva Zamora
Edad: 30 años
Estatura: 1.55 mts.
Descripción: Delgada, con pelo corto. Rocío es bonita, extrovertida y amable.

Aymar Ibañez Sodi
Edad: 12 años
Estatura: 1.50 mts.
Descripción: Alto para su edad, pelo negro y corto. Aymar es atlético, independiente y muy sociable. Es alérgico a los animales.

Florián González Calva
Edad: 75 años
Estatura: 1.60 mts.
Descripción: Bajo, calvo y un poco gordito. Carácter tímido y serio.

meters
hair

Comprensión

Which headshot corresponds to which description?

Más allá

 Think of a person you know well and describe that person to your partner, who will draw a portrait according to your description. Be sure to include the person's name and key identifiers such as height, hair color, etc. Switch roles so that you each have a turn to describe and draw.

> Now use the drawing you have just created to post a brief corresponding description to Share It! Don't forget to use correct adjective forms!

Más despacio, por favor.

© Cengage Learning

Vocabulario

Sustantivos

el acento	*accent*
la grabación	*recording*
el guión	*script*
el/la hablante nativo(a)	*native speaker*
la lengua meta	*target language*

Adjetivos

bilingüe	*bilingual*
neutro(a)	*neutral*

Verbos

ensayar	*to practice*
grabar	*to record*
hablar	*to speak*

Frases útiles

¡Grabando!	*Recording!*
¡Probando!	*Testing!*
Más despacio, por favor.	*Slowly, please.*
Repite la última oración.	*Repeat the last sentence.*

DATOS IMPORTANTES

Educación: Título universitario en comunicación; Los hablantes nativos de la lengua meta tienen preferencia; Es necesario producir un acento neutro en inglés y español

Salario: Promedio: $45.000/año – $33–50/hora

Dónde se trabaja: Empresas de publicidad, canales de televisión, editoriales, estudios de grabación

---

Vocabulario nuevo Choose the most logical answer.

1. Yo hablo (*I speak*) español pero mi _____ es muy fuerte.
   a. grabación
   b. acento
   c. lengua

2. Cuando hablo otro idioma, no hablo (*I don't speak*) rápido, hablo _____.
   a. bilingüe
   b. neutro
   c. despacio

3. Jorge habla italiano y español. Él es _____.
   a. acento
   b. meta
   c. bilingüe

Elisa Solís, voz en off

Elisa Solís, a voiceover professional, is going to work at a recording studio. Felipe Hernández is the studio technician. In the video, you will watch a segment of Elisa's recording session and observe Felipe's instructions.

Antes de ver

Bilingual voiceover professionals deliver messages and announcements and narrate videos, documentaries, and commercials. Voiceover narrators are heard but never seen. They must be professionally trained and speak the target language, such as Spanish, perfectly. What type of instruction do you think a voiceover professional receives at the recording studio? How long do you think it takes to record a one-minute commercial? Do you believe that voiceover professionals should be native speakers of English or of the target language? Why?

Comprensión

Decide whether the following statements are true (**cierto**) or false (**falso**).

1. El técnico se llama José.

2. Elisa no habla inglés.

3. Elisa es de Cuba.

4. El video es sobre (*about*) un festival.

5. Elisa quiere (*wants*) ensayar.

Después de ver

With a partner, play the roles of a voiceover professional and a recording studio technician. Write a short recording script using the vocabulary and expressions on page 32. The technician should give instructions and correct the voiceover professional when needed. Include both English and Spanish in the script. Determine who is the target audience and what is the message. Be creative!

1.33 **¿Qué hay?** A student is in her room studying. Mention five items that are in the room, and then mention one thing that is not.

Modelo *Hay unos libros.*

© Sofos Design/Shutterstock

1.34 **Los famosos** Tell where the following famous people are from. Search online for information on anyone you don't know.

1. Enrique y Julio Iglesias
2. Ricky Martin
3. Salma Hayek
4. Daisy Fuentes y Gloria Estefan
5. Carlos Mencia
6. Shakira y Juanes

1.35 **Mi amiga Mónica** Complete the paragraph with the appropriate forms of the verb **ser** and the adjectives, as indicated by the words in parentheses.

¡Buenos días! Yo (**1.** ser) _____ Jacobo y ella (**2.** ser) _____ Mónica. Nosotros (**3.** ser) _____ estudiantes en la Universidad Central de Venezuela. Mónica (**4.** ser) _____ estudiante de literatura, y es muy (**5.** inteligente) _____ y (**6.** trabajador) _____. Las clases (**7.** ser) _____ muy (**8.** difícil) _____, pero los profesores son (**9.** bueno) _____ y (**10.** simpático) _____.

1.36 **Entrevista** Talk to three different classmates to gather the following information about them.

1. What are their first and last names and how are they spelled?
2. Where they are from?
3. What they are like? (two descriptions each)

1.37 **Diferencias** Working with a partner, one of you will look at the picture on this page, and the other will look at the picture in Appendix B. Take turns describing the pictures using the expression **hay,** numbers, and the classroom vocabulary. Find the eight differences.

Modelo Estudiante 1: *En A hay una computadora.*
Estudiante 2: *Sí. En B, hay una silla.*
Estudiante 1: *No, en A no hay una silla.*

© Cengage Learning

1.38 **Somos similares** Work with a partner to identify the personality traits that you have in common.

Paso 1 Make a list of 7–8 adjectives that describe your personality. **¡OJO!** Pay attention to the adjective endings.

Paso 2 Take turns describing your personalities using the adjectives on your lists. Be sure to use complete sentences. When you determine a trait that you both have in common, circle it on your lists.

Paso 3 Report to the class on how you are similar by sharing the characteristics that you have in common.

🔊 Vocabulario 1

Saludos

bien	*fine*	mal	*bad*
Buenas noches.	*Good night.*	nada	*nothing*
Buenas tardes.	*Good afternoon.*	¿Qué hay de nuevo?	*What's new?*
Buenos días.	*Good morning.*	¿Qué pasa?	*What's going on?*
¿Cómo estás (tú)?	*How are you? (informal)*	¿Qué tal?	*How's it going?*
¿Cómo está (usted)?	*How are you? (formal)*	regular	*so-so*
gracias	*thank you*	¿Y tú?	*And you? (informal)*
hola	*hello*	¿Y usted?	*And you? (formal)*

Presentaciones

Encantado(a).	*Nice to meet you.*	Te presento a...	*I'd like to introduce you to . . . (informal)*
Me llamo...	*My name is . . .*		
Mucho gusto.	*Nice to meet you.*		
Le presento a...	*I'd like to introduce you to . . . (formal)*		

Despedidas

Adiós.	*Goodbye.*	Hasta pronto.	*See you soon.*
Chao.	*Bye.*	Nos vemos.	*See you later.*
Hasta luego.	*See you later.*	¡Que tengas un buen día!	*Have a nice day!*
Hasta mañana.	*See you tomorrow.*		

El salón de clases

la bandera	*flag*	la mochila	*backpack*
el bolígrafo	*pen*	el papel	*paper*
el cartel	*poster*	la pizarra	*chalkboard*
la computadora	*computer*	el (la) profesor(a)	*professor*
el cuaderno	*notebook*	la puerta	*door*
el diccionario	*dictionary*	el pupitre	*student desk*
el escritorio	*teacher's desk*	el reloj	*clock*
el (la) estudiante	*student*	el salón de clases	*classroom*
el lápiz	*pencil*	la silla	*chair*
el libro	*book*	el televisor	*television set*
el mapa	*map*	la ventana	*window*
la mesa	*table*		

Palabras interrogativas

¿Dónde?	*Where?*	¿Qué?	*What?*
¿Cuándo?	*When?*	¿Quién?	*Who?*
¿Cuántos(as)?	*How many?*	¿Por qué?	*Why?*

Los números   *See pages 9, 12*

Palabras adicionales

¿De dónde eres tú?	*Where are you from?*	Yo soy de...	*I am from . . .*
hay	*there is/there are*		

◀)) Vocabulario 2

Adjetivos para describir la personalidad

aburrido(a)	*boring*	interesante	*interesting*
agresivo(a)	*aggressive*	liberal	*liberal*
amable	*kind*	malo(a)	*bad*
antipático(a)	*unfriendly*	optimista	*optimist*
atlético(a)	*athletic*	paciente	*patient*
bueno(a)	*good*	perezoso(a)	*lazy*
cariñoso(a)	*loving*	pesimista	*pessimist*
cómico(a)	*funny*	pobre	*poor*
conservador(a)	*conservative*	realista	*realist*
cruel	*cruel*	rico(a)	*rich*
egoísta	*selfish*	serio(a)	*serious*
famoso(a)	*famous*	simpático(a)	*nice*
generoso(a)	*generous*	sociable	*sociable*
honesto(a)	*honest*	tímido(a)	*timid, shy*
idealista	*idealist*	tonto(a)	*dumb*
impaciente	*impatient*	trabajador(a)	*hardworking*
inteligente	*intelligent*		

Adjetivos para describir el aspecto físico

alto(a)	*tall*	guapo(a)	*good-looking*
bajo(a)	*short*	joven	*young*
bonito(a)	*pretty*	moreno(a)	*dark-skinned/ dark-haired*
calvo(a)	*bald*		
delgado(a)	*thin*	pelirrojo(a)	*red-haired*
feo(a)	*ugly*	pequeño(a)	*small*
gordo(a)	*fat*	rubio(a)	*blond(e)*
grande	*big*	viejo(a)	*old*

Otros adjetivos

corto(a)	*short (length)*	fácil	*easy*
difícil	*difficult*	largo(a)	*long*

Verbos

ser	*to be*

Palabras adicionales

el hombre	*man*	pero	*but*
la mujer	*woman*	un poco	*a little*
muy	*very*	también	*also*
el (la) niño(a)	*child*	y	*and*

Diccionario personal

_____

_____

Learning Strategy

Listen to and repeat vocabulary

When studying vocabulary, take time to listen to and repeat the pronunciation of the words. It will help your pronunciation, which in turn will help you learn to spell the words properly. You may click on the vocabulary in the eBook to hear it pronounced or you may want to download the audio files onto your MP3 player or cell phone, so they will be more accessible.

In this chapter you will learn how to:

- Describe your family and talk about ages
- Discuss your classes
- Discuss your routine
- Express ownership

© Ariel Skelley/Corbis

Esta es la familia de Hernán. ¿Cuántas personas hay en la familia?

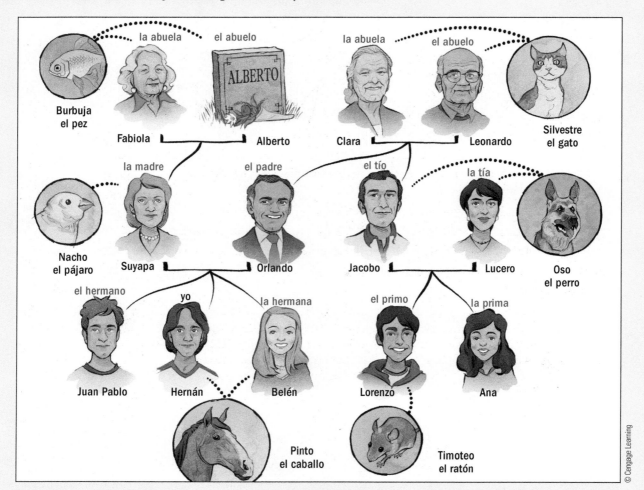

la abuela — el abuelo — la abuela — el abuelo

Burbuja el pez — Fabiola — ALBERTO — Alberto — Clara — Leonardo — Silvestre el gato

la madre — el padre — el tío — la tía

Nacho el pájaro — Suyapa — Orlando — Jacobo — Lucero — Oso el perro

el hermano — yo — la hermana — el primo — la prima

Juan Pablo — Hernán — Belén — Lorenzo — Ana

Pinto el caballo — Timoteo el ratón

© Cengage Learning

La familia

los parientes	relatives
esposo(a)	spouse
hijo(a)	son / daughter
nieto(a)	grandson / granddaughter
sobrino(a)	nephew / niece
hermanastro(a)	stepbrother / stepsister
madrastra	stepmother
padrastro	stepfather
medio(a) hermano(a)	half brother / half sister
suegro(a)	father-in-law / mother-in-law

Palabras adicionales

(mejor) amigo(a)	(best) friend
¿Cómo se llama...?	What is the name of . . . ?
la mascota	pet
novio(a)	boyfriend / girlfriend

INVESTIGUEMOS EL VOCABULARIO

Remember that most of the words in the vocabulary can be used to refer to a female by changing the final **o** to an **a**. When talking about a mixed group, the masculine plural form is used:

hijos   sons and daughters

hermanos   brothers and sisters

padres   parents

La mascota is used for both male and female pets.

A practicar

2.1 **Escucha y responde** Listen to the following statements about Hernán's family. Based on the drawing, give a thumbs up if the statement is true or a thumbs down if it is false.

🔊 1-10

2.2 **¿Cómo se llama...?** Give the names of the following people using the information provided in the drawing on p. 40.

1. la madre de Suyapa
2. el padre de Lorenzo
3. los padres de Orlando y Jacobo
4. la hermana de Juan Pablo
5. los tíos de Lorenzo
6. la mascota de Hernán

2.3 **¿Quién es?** Complete the following sentences about Hernán's family with the appropriate vocabulary word.

1. Suyapa es la _____ de Lorenzo.
2. Fabiola es la _____ de Suyapa.
3. Hernán es el _____ de Orlando.
4. Belén es la _____ de Lorenzo.
5. Jacobo y Orlando son _____.
6. Hernán es el _____ de Jacobo.
7. Clara es la _____ de Leonardo.
8. Fabiola es la _____ de Juan Pablo.

2.4 **En busca de...** Circulate throughout the classroom and find students to whom the following statements apply. Find a different student for each statement. **¡OJO!** Remember that the masculine word is used in a generic sense. For example **¿Tienes hermanos?** is asking if you have any siblings, which could include sisters as well as brothers.

Modelo Tiene gatos. *(Has cats.)*
    Estudiante 1: *¿Tienes gatos?* (Do you have cats?)
    Estudiante 2: *No, no tengo gatos. / Sí, tengo un gato.*
    (No, I don't have cats. / Yes, I have a cat.)

1. Tiene hijos.
2. Tiene hermanos.
3. Tiene primos.
4. Tiene caballos.
5. Tiene abuelos.
6. Tiene mascotas.
7. Tiene tíos.
8. Tiene sobrinos.

2.5 **Una familia** You and your partner each have half of the information about the Sofía Navarro family. One of you will look at the drawing on this page, the other one will look at the drawing in Appendix B. Take turns asking the names of the different people.

Modelo
Estudiante 1: *¿Cómo se llama la madre de Sofía?*
Estudiante 2: *Se llama Gloria.*

Gloria
Sofía
Emma
Pablo
Belén

© Cengage Learning

INVESTIGUEMOS LA CULTURA

In most countries where Spanish is spoken, families use two last names. Typically the first last name comes from the father's side, and the second last name comes from the mother's side. These are not middle names.

INVESTIGUEMOS LA MÚSICA

Pimpinela is an Argentine brother-sister duo whose songs are often conversations between a man and a woman. Find their song "Señorita" online and write down any family vocabulary words you hear in the song. Then, look up the words of the song online and check your understanding. To find lyrics, just type the word **letra** after the title of the song.

Cultura

What determines whether a group is considered a family? The painting entitled *La familia presidencial* (1965) was created by Colombian artist Fernando Botero. With this painting, the artist consolidated his now famous signature style of inflated, round figures. Look at the painting. Do you think that they are blood relatives, or are they related in a different way? Can you think of any other groups of people who are considered to be like families?

 Discover some other famous Colombians and identify their professions in **Exploraciones del mundo hispano.**

 Carmen Lomas Garza has painted numerous works depicting Hispanic families in the U.S. Find a painting you like. Why do you like it? Post the painting and your opinion on Share It!

familia presidencial, Fernando Botero

Comunidad

Find a native speaker of Spanish in your university or community who is willing to be interviewed and ask the following questions: **¿Tu familia es grande o pequeña? ¿Cuántas personas hay en tu familia? ¿Quiénes son? ¿Cuántos primos hay en tu familia extendida?**

 Post your findings to Share It! and read the information posted by your classmates.

Comparaciones

What are some of the important events that bring families together in the United States? In Spain and Latin America, numerous events allow families to get together. Some are religious celebrations such as Christmas (**Navidad**) and Holy Week (**Semana Santa**); others are non-religious occasions such as Mother's Day, Father's Day, Children's Day, and any family birthday or anniversary. The **quinceañera** celebration or **los quince años,** which marks a girl's 15th birthday, is a particularly important celebration.

Fiesta de quince años

While many of these days are also observed in the U.S., there are some important differences. For example, in Mexico, El Salvador, and Guatemala, Mother's Day is always on May 10, so it could fall on any day of the week. Paraguay and Nicaragua also have set dates in May, and Costa Rica in August. Many companies organize activities to honor mothers, and often allow employees to leave early so they can take their mothers out to eat. If the date falls on a weekend, many people will have a larger celebration with food and music.

The date to mark Children's Day also varies. For example, it is celebrated on June 1 in Ecuador and Nicaragua, April 12 in Bolivia, August 16 in Paraguay, and December 25 in Guinea Ecuatorial. It is usually celebrated with big parties at schools, city parades for children, and other types of entertainment. Many organizations will give away toys or other items for children on this day. This photo and the one on the previous page are of family events in Latin America. How are these photos similar to ones you might take during your own family events? How are they different?

Conexiones... a la sociología

In Spanish-speaking countries the family is very important and people tend to dedicate a lot of time to their family members. It is not uncommon for children to live with their parents until they marry. How can this impact other areas of society (for example, housing, jobs, eating habits, etc.)? Does it have any impact on the life of college students? What do you think are some advantages and disadvantages of living with your family until getting married?

Es común vivir con la familia hasta casarse.

A analizar

Rosa talks to Paula about her family. After watching the video, read part of their conversation, and note the words in bold. Then answer the questions below.

Paula:	¿Es esta una foto de **tu** familia, Rosa?
Rosa:	Sí. Esa foto es del Día de la Madre. Aquí está **mi** hermano Miguel y aquí está **mi** hermana Susana con **su** esposo Jaime. Este es **su** hijo Tomás. Y ellos son **mis** padres...
Paula:	¡¿Y este gato en la mesa?!
Rosa:	Es Bibi, **nuestra** gata. Es cómica y muy cariñosa... ¡pero muy mala con **nuestro** pobre perro!

The words in bold are used to show possession.

1. What are the two ways of expressing *my* in Spanish in the conversation above? What is the difference between the two forms? Why do you think they are different?

2. What are the two forms of **nuestro** in the conversation? What is the difference between the two forms? Why do you think they are different?

3. In the conversation the word **su** has two different meanings. Find the two uses of **su** above. How are they different?

A comprobar

Possessive adjectives

mi(s)	*my*	**mi** hermano, **mis** hermanos
tu(s)	*your*	**tu** primo, **tus** primos
su(s)	*his, her, its, your*	**su** mascota, **sus** mascotas
nuestro(s), nuestra(s)	*our*	**nuestro** primo, **nuestros** primos, **nuestra** prima, **nuestras** primas
vuestro(s), vuestra(s)	*your*	**vuestro** tío, **vuestros** tíos, **vuestra** tía, **vuestras** tías
su(s)	*their, your*	**su** abuelo, **sus** abuelos

INVESTIGUEMOS LA GRAMÁTICA

When using possessive adjectives in Spanish, keep in mind that the subject pronouns **tú, usted, vosotros,** and **ustedes** all mean *you*. Each of the possessive adjectives that indicate *your* corresponds to a different subject pronoun.

tú → tu(s)
usted → su(s)
vosotros/vosotras → vuestro(s)/vuestra(s)
ustedes → su(s)

1. Similar to other adjectives, possessive adjectives agree in number (singular / plural) with the noun they modify (that is, the object that is owned or possessed).

    Mi familia es muy grande.
    My family is very large.

    Sus padres hablan italiano.
    His parents speak italian.

2. **Nuestro** and **vuestro** agree in gender (masculine / feminine) as well as in number.

    Nuestra gata se llama Lili.
    Our cat is named Lili.

    ¿Cómo se llaman **vuestras hijas**?
    What are your daughters' names?

3. In Spanish, the *'s* does not exist. Instead, if you want to be more specific about who possesses or owns something, it is necessary to use **de** *(of)*. Notice that in this structure the item owned comes before the person who owns it.

Es la casa **de mi hermano.**
*It is **my brother's** house.*

Es **su** casa.
*It is **his** house.*

Ellas son las hijas **de Patricia.**
*They are **Patricia's** daughters.*

Ellas son **sus** hijas.
*They are **her** daughters.*

4. Just as there are contractions in English (can't, don't), there are also contractions in Spanish. However, these contractions are not optional. When using **de** in front of the masculine article **el,** it forms the contraction **del** (**de** + **el** = **del**).

Macarena es la esposa **del** profesor.
Macarena is the professor's wife.

De does not contract with the other articles.

Max es el perro **de la** familia Pérez.
Max is the Pérez family's dog.

A practicar

2.6 **Mi familia** Indicate whether each of the sentences requires **mi** or **mis.**

1. (Mi/Mis) madre es bonita.
2. (Mi/Mis) padre es alto.
3. (Mi/Mis) hermanas son cómicas.

4. (Mi/Mis) perro es pequeño.
5. (Mi/Mis) abuelos son simpáticos.
6. (Mi/Mis) amigos son inteligentes.

2.7 **Su familia** Complete the following paragraph with the correct form of **su** or **sus.**

Alberto, David y Óscar son hermanos y tienen un apartamento en Lima. (**1.**) _____ apartamento es pequeño, pero confortable. Alberto y David comparten *(share)* un cuarto *(bedroom)* y hay muchos carteles en (**2.**) _____ cuarto. (**3.**) _____ hermano, Óscar, tiene un cuarto pequeño. Él tiene dos gatos y un perro. (**4.**) _____ mascotas molestan *(bother)* mucho a (**5.**) _____ hermanos porque (**6.**) _____ perro siempre está en el sofá y (**7.**) _____ gatos siempre están en la mesa.

El perro siempre está en el sofá.

© Bryan Firestone/Shutterstock

2.8 **¿Qué tienen?** With a partner, take turns completing the sentences to tell what your friends and family have. You may complete the sentences with a person (**un hermano, un novio,** etc.), a pet (**un perro, un gato,** etc.), or an object (**una casa, un auto, una clase,** etc.). Then describe the person, pet, or object using a possessive pronoun and an adjective, as in the model.

Modelo La profesora tiene...
La profesora tiene un gato. Su gato es bonito.

1. Yo tengo...
2. Mi amigo tiene...
3. Mi familia tiene...
4. Mis amigos tienen..

2.9 **Andrés y Ana** Andrés and Ana are siblings, and they have left their things in the living room. Tell whether the items belong to Andrés or Ana.

Modelo los CDs *Los CDs son de Andrés.*

1. la pizza
2. los bolígrafos
3. el diccionario

4. la mochila
5. el cuaderno
6. los libros

7. los papeles
8. el cartel
9. la soda

2.10 **¿De quién es?** Andrés' mother is cleaning the living room where her children have left their things. She is unsure about what belongs to him and what belongs to his sister, Ana. With a partner, take turns playing Andrés and his mother. Look at the picture in Activity 2.9 to decide how Andrés answers her questions. Be sure to use the correct possessive adjective in the proper form.

Modelo Estudiante 1 (madre): *¿De quién (Whose) es el cuaderno?*
Estudiante 2 (Andrés): *Es su cuaderno.*
Estudiante 2 (madre): *¿De quién son los papeles?*
Estudiante 1 (Andrés): *Son mis papeles.*

1. ¿De quién es la mochila?
2. ¿De quién son los libros?
3. ¿De quién es el diccionario?
4. ¿De quién es el cartel?

5. ¿De quién son los bolígrafos?
6. ¿De quién es la soda?
7. ¿De quién es la pizza?
8. ¿De quién son los CDs?

2.11 **¿Cómo son?** Describe the following items that your family owns and ask your partner about the items his/her family owns.

Modelo el televisor
Estudiante 1: *Nuestro televisor es nuevo. ¿Cómo es su televisor?*
Estudiante 2: *Nuestro televisor es pequeño.*

1. la casa/el apartamento
2. el auto/los autos

3. la mascota
4. la computadora

5. los primos
6. la familia

Exploraciones **gramaticales**

A analizar ▶

Rosa talks about her family with Paula. After watching the video, read part of their conversation, paying attention to the endings of the words in bold. Then answer the questions.

Paula: ¿Dónde **trabajan** ellos?

Rosa: Mi madre **trabaja** en la universidad. Ella es profesora de historia. Y mi padre **trabaja** en una compañía internacional y viaja a los Estados Unidos con frecuencia.

Paula: ¡Qué interesante! ¿Tú **trabajas** también?

Rosa: No, yo no **trabajo**.

1. What does the word **trabajar** mean?

2. You have learned that the verb **ser** has different forms depending upon the subject. The verb **trabajar** also has different forms. Looking at the forms of the verb **trabajar** in the conversation, complete the following chart.

yo _____   nosotros(as) trabajamos

tú _____   vosotros(as) trabajáis

él, ella, usted _____   ellos, ellas, ustedes _____

A comprobar

Regular -ar verbs

1. An infinitive is a verb in its simplest form. It conveys the idea of an action, but does not indicate who is doing the action. The following are verbs in their infinitive form. You will notice that their English translations are all *to _____*.

ayudar	*to help*	**estudiar**	*to study*	**necesitar**	*to need*
bailar	*to dance*	**hablar (por**	*to talk (on*	**practicar**	*to practice; to*
buscar	*to look for*	**teléfono)**	*the phone)*	**(deportes)**	*play (sports)*
caminar	*to walk*	**limpiar**	*to clean*	**preguntar**	*to ask*
cantar	*to sing*	**llamar**	*to call*	**regresar**	*to return*
cocinar	*to cook*	**llegar (a)**	*to arrive (at)*	**(a casa)**	*(home)*
comprar	*to buy*	**mandar (un**	*to send (a*	**tomar**	*to take; to drink*
desear	*to want,*	**mensaje)**	*message)*	**(café)**	*(coffee)*
	to desire	**manejar**	*to drive*	**trabajar**	*to work*
enseñar	*to teach*	**mirar (la tele)**	*to look, to*	**usar**	*to use*
escuchar	*to listen*		*watch (TV)*	**viajar (a)**	*to travel (to)*
esquiar	*to ski*	**nadar**	*to swim*		

© Cengage Learning

2. Although it also means *to drink*, the verb **tomar** is used in many of the same ways that the verb *to take* is used in English.

tomar un examen *to take a test* **tomar una siesta** *to take a nap*
tomar fotos *to take photos* **tomar un taxi** *to take a taxi*
tomar notas *to take notes* **tomar vacaciones** *to take a vacation*

3. You learned that the verb **ser** must be conjugated in agreement with the subject. In other words, different forms of the verb indicate who the subject is. The verbs in the list on page 47 all end in **-ar** and are all conjugated in the same way. To form a present tense verb, the **-ar** is dropped from the infinitive and an ending is added that reflects the subject (the person doing the action).

llegar

yo	**-o**	llego	nosotros(as)	**-amos**	llegamos
tú	**-as**	llegas	vosotros(as)	**-áis**	llegáis
él, ella, usted	**-a**	llega	ellos, ellas, ustedes	**-an**	llegan

4. When using two verbs together that are dependent upon each other, the second verb remains in the infinitive.

> Él **necesita viajar** mucho.
> He **needs to travel** a lot.
>
> Ellas **desean estudiar** inglés.
> They **want to study** English.

However, notice that both verbs are conjugated in the following sentences because they are not dependent on each other.

> Yo **estudio** en la universidad y **trabajo** en un restaurante.
> I **study** in the university and **work** in a restaurant.
>
> Édgar **nada, esquía** y **practica** el tenis.
> Édgar **swims, skis,** and **plays** tennis.

5. When creating a negative statement, place the word **no** in front of the verb.

> Ella **no** baila bien.
> She **doesn't** dance well.
>
> No, yo **no** trabajo.
> No, I **don't** work.

6. In order to create a simple yes/no question, it is not necessary to use helping words. Simply place the subject after the verb and change the intonation, raising your voice at the end.

> ¿Estudias tú mucho?
> **Do** you study a lot?
>
> ¿Habla usted español?
> **Do** you speak Spanish?

> **INVESTIGUEMOS LA GRAMÁTICA**
>
> When the recipient of the action (direct object) is a person or a pet, an **a** is used in front of the object. This is known as the **a personal.** It is not translated into English. You will learn more about this concept in **Capítulo 5.**
>
> Los estudiantes buscan **a** la profesora.
> Los niños llaman **a** los perros.

A practicar

2.12 **Mi familia y yo** Decide which of the two phrases best completes the sentences. **¡OJO!** You must decide which verb ending agrees with the subject.

1. Mi padre...
   a. miro la tele mucho **b.** miran la tele mucho

2. Mis padres...
   a. manejamos un auto viejo **b.** manejan un auto viejo

3. Mi esposo...
   a. baila bien **b.** bailo bien

4. Mi hermana y yo...
   a. tomamos mucho café **b.** toman mucho café

5. ¿Tú...?
   a. estudia mucho **b.** estudias mucho

2.13 **La familia de Gabriela** Complete the paragraph with the appropriate form of the verb in parentheses.

Yo (**1.**) _____ (ser) Gabriela. Mi esposo se llama Nicolás y él (**2.**) _____ (trabajar) en un hospital. Él (**3.**) _____ (pasar – *to spend*) mucho tiempo en el trabajo. Nuestros dos hijos Dora y Ernesto (**4.**) _____ (estudiar) en la universidad. Mi esposo necesita (**5.**) _____ (trabajar) mucho, pero nosotros siempre (*always*) (**6.**) _____ (tomar) vacaciones en julio. La familia (**7.**) _____ (viajar) a Bariloche, Argentina, y nosotros (**8.**) _____ (esquiar). Yo no (**9.**) _____ (esquiar) muy bien, pero es muy divertido.

2.14 **El fin de semana** Working in pairs, find out if your partner does the following activities on the weekend.

Modelo hablar por teléfono
Estudiante 1: *¿Hablas por teléfono?*
Estudiante 2: *Sí, hablo por teléfono. / No, no hablo por teléfono.*

1. trabajar
2. estudiar español
3. limpiar la casa
4. tomar una siesta
5. practicar deportes

6. bailar en un club
7. mirar la tele
8. cantar en un coro (*choir*)
9. cocinar para (*for*) amigos
10. caminar con (*with*) el perro

2.15 **En los Estados Unidos** The following statements describe what some Spanish speakers in different countries often do. Using the **nosotros** form, state what we generally do in the United States.

Modelo Los colombianos practican fútbol.
Nosotros practicamos fútbol americano.

1. Los argentinos hablan español.
2. Los chilenos estudian inglés.
3. Los españoles viajan a Francia de vacaciones.
4. Los mexicanos escuchan música en inglés y español.
5. Los cubanos bailan salsa.
6. Los paraguayos esquían en Argentina.

Los cubanos bailan salsa.

Aleksandar Todorovic/Shutterstock

2.16 **Un día ocupado** Fedra and Bruno are very busy. Look at the drawings and describe what they do on a typical day.

Modelo *Fedra y Bruno toman un café.*

1.

2.

3.

4.

5.

6.

© Cengage Learning

2.17 **¡Yo también!** Place a check mark next to four of the following activities that you do. Then, find four different classmates, each of whom also does one of those activities. When you are finished, report to the class something that you and another classmate both do using the **nosotros** form.

_____ buscar un trabajo

_____ viajar con frecuencia *(frequently)*

_____ mirar la tele mucho

_____ trabajar en un restaurante

_____ cantar bien

_____ cocinar

_____ mandar muchos mensajes

_____ llamar a un amigo con frecuencia

_____ escuchar la radio

_____ usar la computadora

_____ nadar

_____ comprar muchos regalos *(gifts)*

_____ esquiar

_____ ¿?

2.18 **¿Quién?** Interview your partner to find out if he/she or someone he/she knows does the following activities. **¡OJO!** When asking the question you will need to use the **él/ella** form of the verb. When answering, be sure that the verb agrees with the subject.

Modelo viajar mucho
    Estudiante 1: *¿Quién viaja mucho?*
    Estudiante 2: *Mis padres viajan mucho. / Mi mejor amigo y yo viajamos mucho.*

1. manejar un auto nuevo

2. trabajar en un restaurante

3. practicar tenis

4. enseñar

5. estudiar biología

6. escuchar música clásica

7. cocinar bien

8. mandar muchos textos

Entrando en materia

¿Celebras tú el Día de la Madre ¿y el Día del Niño?

Celebrando a la familia

🔊 You are going to hear a fragment of a radio show. Listen carefully, then answer the
1-11 questions below.

Vocabulario útil

fecha fija	*fixed date*	**razón**	*reason*
mayo	*May*	**tercer domingo**	*third Sunday*
junio	*June*		

Comprensión

After listening to the radio announcers, read the statements below and decide if each one is
true (**cierto**) or false (**falso**).

1. Hoy es 30 de mayo.
2. El 30 de mayo es el Día del Padre en Nicaragua.
3. En Nicaragua no celebran el Día de la Suegra.
4. En Argentina el Día de la Suegra es el 17 de octubre.
5. En Perú, Colombia y Ecuador no celebran el Día del Padre.

Más allá

Look for another date that is celebrated in a Spanish-speaking country. What is the
celebration? Where does it take place? When? Here are a few keywords to help with your
search: **Independencia, Acción de Gracias, Día Nacional.**

Record your findings and post a brief summary to Share It!

El día de la Madre es importante en muchos países.

© mnoa357/Shutterstock

Lectura

Reading Strategy: Predicting

Read through the comprehension questions before reading the article. This will help give you a better idea as to what to expect.

Antes de leer

What does the modern American family look like? What do you think the modern Latin American family looks like?

A leer

La familia típica latinoamericana

Es difícil hablar de una familia típica latinoamericana, especialmente porque Latinoamérica es una región muy grande que comprende muchos países diferentes. Sin embargo, en todas las sociedades las familias **cambian** para adaptarse a los tiempos modernos. La familia típica latinoamericana urbana tiene pocos hijos, y el hombre y la mujer trabajan. Las familias extendidas son muy importantes, pero en la mayoría de las casas no **viven** muchos familiares. Por ejemplo, en Chile viven un **promedio** de 3.5 personas por casa; en México, viven 3.9 y en Colombia viven 4.2. En Colombia y en México en el 74% de las casas viven solamente los padres y los hijos o una pareja sin hijos. Solo en el 24% de las casas viven otros miembros de la familia **como** abuelos, nietos u otros familiares. **Es decir**, para muchos latinoamericanos es muy importante ayudar a los miembros de la familia, solo en una de cuatro casas vive un miembro de la familia extendida. Ahora también hay muchas familias donde los hijos viven con solo uno de sus padres, o **ninguno**. También hay muchas casas donde dos adultos cohabitan (viven **juntos** pero no están **casados**). En Colombia el 39% cohabitan, en México el 21% y en Chile el 12%.

change
live
average
such as
In other words
neither
together
married

[las familias extendidas son muy importantes]

© Andy Dean Photography/Shutterstock

Otro cambio importante en toda la región es el del **papel** de la mujer. La mayoría de las familias **está encabezada por** hombres, pero el número de familias encabezadas por mujeres **está aumentando** rápidamente.

En varios países latinoamericanos el divorcio es **cada vez más frecuente**. En Chile el divorcio es legal desde 2004 y ahora hay más divorcios que **casamientos**. En 2013 Chile fue el 3er país con más divorcios en el mundo con una tasa de 170% de divorcios. En México la tasa de divorcios es 16%, y en Colombia 24%.

Otra estadística interesante que habla de la importancia de la familia es la frecuencia con que las familias comen juntas. En toda Latinoamérica comer juntos es importante. En Argentina el 86% de las familias come junta, en contraste con Perú, donde solo el 69% come junta. En Estados Unidos el número es aproximadamente el 65%.

role
is headed by

is increasing

increasingly more frequent

marriages

© Monkey Business Images/Shutterstock

Sources: Sistema Nacional para el Desarrollo Integral de la Familia; Instituto Nacional de Estadística y Geografía; Instituto Nacional de Estadísticas; RevistaCredencial.com

Comprensión

Decide whether the following statements are true (**cierto**) or false (**falso**). Correct any false statements.

1. Las mujeres latinoamericanas no trabajan.
2. La familia extendida es muy importante en Latinoamérica.
3. Ahora hay más *(more)* familias encabezadas por mujeres.
4. En la mayoría de las casas viven tres generaciones (los abuelos, los padres y los hijos).
5. En Chile pocos matrimonios terminan *(end)* en divorcio.
6. En Colombia muchos adultos prefieren vivir juntos sin *(without)* estar casados.

Después de leer

 1. In groups of three or four, discuss the following questions in English.
   • Did any information surprise you? Why?
   • How does this information about Latin American families compare with U.S. families in general?

2. In the same groups, discuss the following questions in Spanish.
   • ¿Es importante la familia para ti?
   • ¿Qué personas consideras tú como parte de tu familia?
   • ¿Qué actividades haces *(do you do)* con tu familia?

Exploraciones léxicas

¿Cómo es tu universidad?

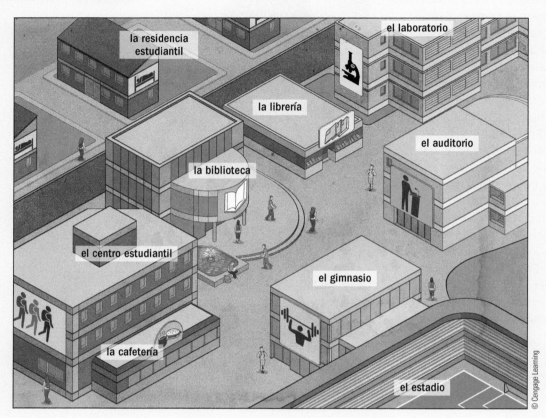

la residencia
estudiantil

el laboratorio

la librería

la biblioteca

el auditorio

el centro estudiantil

el gimnasio

la cafetería

el estadio

© Cengage Learning

Las materias académicas	*Academic subjects*	**las ciencias sociales**	*social studies*
el álgebra	*algebra*	**la física**	*physics*
el arte	*art*	**la economía**	*economy*
el cálculo	*calculus*	**la geografía**	*geography*
la criminología	*criminology*	**la historia**	*history*
la educación física	*physical education*	**la psicología**	*psychology*
la expresión oral	*speech*	**la química**	*chemistry*
la filosofía	*philosophy*		
la geografía	*geography*	**Las lenguas**	*Languages*
la informática	*computer science*	**el alemán**	*German*
la ingeniería	*engineering*	**el español**	*Spanish*
la literatura	*literature*	**el francés**	*French*
las matemáticas	*mathematics*	**el inglés**	*English*
la música	*music*	**el italiano**	*Italian*
los negocios	*business*		
el periodismo	*journalism*	**Palabras adicionales**	
la redacción	*writing, composition*	**el/la compañero(a)**	*classmate*
el teatro	*theater*	** de clase**	
		la nota	*grade*
Las ciencias naturales	*Natural science*	**el semestre**	*semester*
la biología	*biology*	**la tarea**	*homework*
las ciencias políticas	*political science*	**el trimestre**	*quarter*

Estrategia

Listen to and repeat vocabulary

When studying vocabulary, take time to listen to and repeat the pronunciation of the words included on the audio recordings. It will help your pronunciation, which in turn will help you learn to spell the words properly. You may want to download the audio files onto your MP3 player or cell phone so they will be more accessible.

A practicar

2.19 **Escucha y responde** Listen to the statements about activities that can be done at the university. Raise your right hand if the activity typically occurs in the classroom; raise your left hand if it typically occurs in another part of the campus, such as the cafeteria, gym, or stadium.

🔊 1–12

2.20 **Relaciones** Match each course from the first column with a related topic from the second column.

1. _____ periodismo
2. _____ ciencias políticas
3. _____ química
4. _____ alemán
5. _____ veterinaria
6. _____ informática

a. los animales
b. la computadora
c. los eventos internacionales
d. los elementos
e. los verbos
f. los presidentes

2.21 **En la universidad** Look at the list and determine where on campus students would do each activity.

1. tomar una siesta
2. escuchar un concierto
3. comprar libros
4. mirar un partido (*match*) de fútbol
5. tomar café con unos amigos
6. estudiar en silencio
7. usar un microscopio
8. practicar deportes

2.22 **Opiniones** With a classmate, take turns completing the sentences with a word from the vocabulary list and finishing the sentences logically.

1. Me gusta (*I like*) la clase de _____ porque (*because*) es...
2. No me gusta mucho la clase de _____ porque es...
3. El profesor/La profesora de la clase de _____ es...
4. Los exámenes en la clase de _____ son...
5. El libro para la clase de _____ es...
6. La tarea de la clase de _____ es...

> **INVESTIGUEMOS LA GRAMÁTICA**
> In order to talk about a specific class or a specific instructor, you can use the expressions **La clase de...** or **El profesor de...**
> **El profesor de historia es inteligente.**
> *The history instructor is intelligent.*

2.23 **La graduación** In order to graduate, each student must take one class in each of the following categories: natural science, social science, math, humanities (**las humanidades**), and language. You and your partner must check the transcripts of four students to determine which courses they have taken, and which ones they need. One of you will look at the information on this page and the other will look at Appendix B.

Modelo Estudiante 1: *¿Tiene (has) Raúl Ruiz Costa una clase de ciencias naturales?*
Estudiante 2: *Sí, Raúl tiene una clase de biología.*

Ramón Ayala Pérez	Andrea Gómez Ramos	Diana Salazar Casas	Hugo Vargas Díaz
	ingeniería		**biología**
	física		**geometría**
	alemán		**economía**
	cálculo		**negocios**

Conexiones culturales

La educación

Cultura

One of the largest universities in the world is the **Universidad Nacional Autónoma de México (UNAM).** The university is so large that the applicants have to take their admission exam in a sports stadium. UNAM is considered one of the best universities in the world and is free for Mexican citizens.

The Central University City Campus of UNAM is one of three universities in the world that was designated as a World Heritage site by UNESCO in 2007. It was designed by over 60 architects, engineers, and artists, and is an exceptional display of twentieth-century modernism. The campus has numerous impressive works of art, and is known especially for its murals and mosaics.

Is there art at your school or university? Where? What do you think of it? How many students attend your university?

Sources: Times Higher Education; UNESCO; www.topuniversities.com

Do an online search to explore a historic university in Spain or Latin America. Find out when it was built and what makes it special. Post an image of it on Share It! and share what you learned. Here are some keywords to help with your search: **universidad, histórica, primera, fundada, establecida.**

Comunidad

Find an international student from a Spanish-speaking country and ask him or her for additional information about their school system. Ask which subjects they study, the price of textbooks, and the number of hours they spend at school every day. The following are some possible questions for your interview:

¿De dónde eres?
¿Qué clases tienes?
¿Es similar la universidad en _____(country)_____?
¿Cuántas horas están en la escuela los estudiantes de primaria/secundaria/preparatoria?

¿Qué clases tienes?

Comparaciones

While in the United States students are required by law to attend school until they are 16, in Chile students are legally required to attend school only until they complete **nivel básico** at age 14. After that, students can choose the type of **liceo** they want to attend. Those who continue to **educación superior** can attend an **instituto profesional** and learn a trade, or attend university. Recently, however, several reforms have been introduced and are being implemented. These reforms call for a redistribution of the number of years spent in **nivel básico** and **enseñanza media**, and seek to update the system, improve the quality of education, and provide better access to education for everyone. How does the education system of the United States compare to the Chilean system? Complete the table with the U.S. equivalents.

Edad	Chile	Estados Unidos
2–6 años	preescolar (kinder)*	_____
6–14 años	nivel básico (8 años)*	_____
14–18 años	enseñanza media (liceo) (4 años)**	_____
18+	educación superior (instituto profesional/universidad) (2–4 años)	
	diplomados	_____
	maestría	_____
	doctorado	_____

* Compulsory
** Education can become specialized at this point. Students can choose between Humanities and Sciences, technical programs, or the Arts.

For more information on Chile, refer to Appendix A: **Exploraciones del mundo hispano.**

Conexiones... a la educación

In Spanish-speaking countries, elementary and secondary students commonly wear uniforms to school. What are the advantages and disadvantages of using them? Did you ever wear a uniform to school? Are uniforms popular in the United States? Why?

Niñas cubanas en sus uniformes

Exploraciones gramaticales

A analizar ▶

Paula and Santiago are talking about their classes. After watching the video, read Paula's comments, paying particular attention to the forms of the verb **tener** in bold. Then answer the questions below.

Tengo dos clases de psicología este semestre y son muy difíciles. **Tengo** que estudiar mucho. Nosotros **tenemos** mucha tarea y hay varios estudiantes que **tienen** miedo de recibir una mala nota. ¿**Tienes** tú una clase difícil este semestre?

1. What does the verb **tener** mean?
2. Using the examples in the paragraph, complete the chart with the forms of the verb **tener.**

   yo _____   nosotros, nosotras _____

   tú _____   vosotros, vosotras **tenéis**

   él, ella, usted _____   ellos, ellas, ustedes _____

3. Using context clues to help you, what does the expression **tener miedo** mean?

   a. to have to   **b.** to need   **c.** to be afraid

A comprobar

The verb **tener**

tener (to have)			
yo	**tengo**	nosotros(as)	**tenemos**
tú	**tienes**	vosotros(as)	**tenéis**
él, ella, usted	**tiene**	ellos, ellas, ustedes	**tienen**

*Notice that the original vowel **e** changes to **ie** in some of the forms. This is what is known as a stem-changing verb. You will learn more about stem-changing verbs in **Capítulo 3**.

1. There are a number of expressions in which the verb **tener** is used where *to be* would be used in English. The following are noun expressions with the verb **tener:**

tener… años	*to be . . . years old*
tener (mucho) calor	*to be (very) hot*
tener (mucho) cuidado	*to be (very) careful*
tener (mucho) éxito	*to be (very) successful*

tener (mucho) frío	*to be (very) cold*
tener ganas de + infinitive	*to feel like doing something*
tener (mucha) hambre	*to be (very) hungry*
tener (mucho) miedo	*to be (very) afraid*
tener (mucha) prisa	*to be in a (big) hurry*
tener que + infinitive	*to have to do something*
tener (mucha) razón	*to be right*
tener (mucha) sed	*to be (very) thirsty*
tener (mucho) sueño	*to be (very) sleepy*
tener (mucha) suerte	*to be (very) lucky*

2. Unlike adjectives, noun expressions do not change in gender and number.

   Mis hermanos tienen frío.
   My brothers are cold.

   Mi hermana tiene sueño.
   My sister is sleepy.

A practicar

2.24 **¿Qué tienen?** Match the sentences to the appropriate picture.

a.

b.

c.

d.

e.

f.

1. _____ Tenemos hambre.
2. _____ Tienen miedo.
3. _____ Tengo 5 años.

4. _____ Tiene sed.
5. _____ ¿Tienes sueño?
6. _____ Tiene prisa.

2.25 **¿Tienes ganas?** Read the the list of activities that Carla will do this week and decide whether each one is something she feels like doing (**tiene ganas de**) or has to do (**tiene que**).

1. estudiar para el examen de español hasta *(until)* las tres de la mañana
2. hablar con unos amigos en el centro estudiantil
3. trabajar por 18 horas
4. comprar los libros para sus clases en la librería
5. viajar a España
6. limpiar la casa
7. bailar en el club
8. mirar la tele con un amigo

2.26 **¿Cuántos años tienes?** Complete the paragraph with the correct forms of the verb **tener.**

Yo soy estudiante en la Universidad de Salamanca y (**1.**) _____ 20 años. Mis amigos Sara y Fernando (**2.**) _____ 19 años. Sara y yo (**3.**) _____ nuestros cumpleaños *(birthday)* en noviembre. Fernando (**4.**) _____ su cumpleaños en diciembre. ¿Y tú? ¿Cuántos años (**5.**) _____?

INVESTIGUEMOS LA MÚSICA

Find the song "Tengo tu love" by Puerto Rican singer and songwriter El Sie7e online and listen to it. What does he say that he has? What are some of the things he mentions that others have?

2.27 **¿Cuántos años tiene?** Ask your partner how old the following people are. If you are not sure, guess and use the expression **probablemente.**

Modelo   tu profesor de inglés
    Estudiante 1: *¿Cuántos años tiene tu profesor de inglés?*
    Estudiante 2: *Mi profesor (probablemente) tiene 35 años.*

1. tú

2. tu mejor amigo

3. tu profesor de la clase de español

4. el presidente de los Estados Unidos

5. tu actor favorito (¿Cómo se llama?)

6. tu actriz favorita (¿Cómo se llama?)

2.28 **¿Qué tienen?** Describe the scenes using expressions with **tener.**

Modelo   Ronaldo
    Ronaldo tiene razón.

1. Lola y yo

2. Marcia

3. yo

4. Isabel y Mar

5. tú

6. Rosario

© Cengage Learning

2.29 **Entrevista** Interview a classmate using the questions below.

En la casa

1. ¿Tienes mucho sueño en la noche?

2. ¿Tienes ganas de invitar a amigos a tu casa?

3. ¿Quién *(Who)* tiene que cocinar?

En la universidad

4. ¿En qué clase tienes éxito en los exámenes?

5. ¿Tienes miedo de un profesor? ¿Cómo se llama?

6. ¿Para qué clases tienes que estudiar mucho?

A analizar ▶

Paula and Santiago are talking about their classes. Watch the video again. Then read part of the conversation between Paula and Santiago and identify the adjectives. Then, answer the questions below.

Paula: Tengo dos clases de psicología este semestre y son muy difíciles. Tengo que estudiar mucho. Nosotros tenemos mucha tarea y hay varios estudiantes que tienen miedo de recibir una mala nota. ¿Tienes tú una clase difícil este semestre?

Santiago: Para mí, historia es una clase interesante pero muy difícil. ¡Tenemos exámenes muy largos! Afortunadamente tengo un buen profesor con mucha experiencia. Además es un hombre simpático e inteligente.

1. List all the adjectives you identified.

_____ _____ _____ _____

_____ _____ _____

_____ _____ _____ _____

2. Where are the adjectives placed in relation to the noun they describe? What are the exceptions?

A comprobar

Adjective placement

1. In Spanish, adjectives are generally placed *after* the nouns they describe.

> El cálculo es una clase **difícil**.
> *Calculus is a **difficult** class.*

> La señora Muñoz es una profesora **interesante**.
> *Mrs. Muñoz is an **interesting** professor.*

2. However, adjectives such as **mucho** *(a lot)*, **poco** *(few)*, and **varios** *(several)* that indicate quantity or amount are placed in front of the object.

> **Muchos** estudiantes estudian francés.
> ***Many** students study French.*

> Tengo **varios** libros para esta clase.
> *I have **several** books for this class.*

> Hay **pocos** estudiantes en clase hoy.
> *There are **few** students in class today.*

3. **Bueno** and **malo** are likewise generally placed in front of the noun they describe. They drop the **o** when used in front of a masculine singular noun.

> Él es un **buen** estudiante.
> *He is a **good** student.*

> Ellos son **buenos** estudiantes.
> *They are **good** students.*

> Es una **mala** clase.
> *It's a **bad** class.*

> Son **malas** clases.
> *They are **bad** classes.*

4. When using more than one adjective to describe an object, use commas between adjectives and **y** *(and)* before the last adjective.

> Tengo un cuaderno pequeño **y** rojo.
> *I have a small, red notebook.*

> El profesor es un hombre honesto, serio **e** inteligente.
> *The professor is an honest, serious, **and** intelligent man.*

A practicar

2.30 **Mi clase de español** Listen to the statements about your Spanish class and decide whether they are true (**cierto**) or false (**falso**).

1–13   Modelo *(you hear)* La clase de español tiene estudiantes simpáticos.
Cierto

2.31 **¿Cómo son?** Complete the sentences with a logical adjective from the list on the right.

Modelo   Eva Longoria es una actriz... talentosa.
Eva Longoria es una actriz talentosa.

1. Victor Cruz es un hombre...   **a.** largo.

2. Santana es un grupo...   **b.** atlético.

3. Sofía Vergara es una mujer...   **c.** guapa.

4. "Bésame mucho" es una canción *(song)*...   **d.** musical.

5. *Don Quijote de la Mancha* es un libro...   **e.** argentina.

6. Buenos Aires es una ciudad...   **f.** mexicana.

7. Puerto Rico es una isla...   **g.** altos.

8. Manu Ginobili y Rudy Fernández son basquetbolistas...   **h.** pequeña.

2.32 **Mis clases** With a classmate, complete each of the following sentences with the name of a class and an appropriate adjective.

Modelo   En la clase de _____ hay un profesor _____.
En la clase de historia hay un profesor inteligente.

1. El profesor de _____ es un hombre _____.

2. La profesora de _____ es una mujer _____.

3. En la clase de _____ tenemos un libro _____.

4. En la clase de _____ hay unos estudiantes _____.

5. En la clase de _____ tenemos exámenes _____.

6. _____ es una clase _____.

7. En la clase de _____ tenemos tarea _____.

8. En la clase de _____ hay un estudiante _____.

> **¿TE ACUERDAS?**
>
> Remember that adjectives must agree in both number (singular and plural) and gender (masculine and feminine) with the object they describe.

2.33 **En busca de...** Circulate throughout the classroom and find eight different students to whom one of the following statements applies. Be ready to report to the class; so remember to ask for the names of your classmates if you don't know them.

Modelo   Tiene un lápiz nuevo
Estudiante 1: *¿Tienes un lápiz nuevo?*
Estudiante 2: *Sí tengo un lápiz nuevo.*

1. Tiene una clase difícil.

2. Tiene mucha tarea este semestre.

3. Tiene un profesor rubio.

4. Tiene una computadora nueva.

5. Tiene pocos libros en la mochila hoy *(today)*.

6. Siempre *(Always)* tiene notas excelentes.

7. Tiene un muy buen profesor este semestre.

8. Tiene un compañero de clase muy inteligente.

© wavebreakmedia/Shutterstock

2.34 **¿Cierto o falso?** Complete the statement below to form four true / false statements that describe the people and objects in the classroom. Then read your statements to your partner, who will tell you whether they are true (**cierto**) or false (**falso**). ¡OJO! Pay attention to the position of the adjective.

En la clase hay...

Modelo Estudiante 1: *En la clase hay un estudiante calvo.*
          Estudiante 2: *Falso.*

2.35 **Hablemos de las clases** Interview a classmate with the following questions.

1. ¿Tienes muchas clases hoy? ¿Qué clases tienes?
2. ¿Tienes un profesor muy simpático este semestre? ¿Cómo se llama?
3. ¿Tienes una clase con pocos estudiantes? ¿Cuántos estudiantes hay?
4. ¿Tienes una clase favorita? ¿Qué clase es?
5. ¿En qué clase tienes exámenes muy largos?
6. ¿En qué clase tienes tarea difícil?

2.36 **¿Tienes...?** Use different adjectives to talk about the following items with a partner. Possible adjectives: **inteligente, simpático, viejo, nuevo, grande, pequeño, difícil, fácil, interesante, aburrido, largo, corto.**

Modelo una computadora
          Estudiante 1: *¿Tienes una computadora?*
          Estudiante 2: *Sí, tengo una computadora nueva.*
          Estudiante 1: *Yo tengo una computadora vieja. / Yo también*
                       tengo una computadora nueva.

1. una casa / un apartamento
2. un auto
3. clases
4. profesores
5. una familia
6. un amigo

Lectura

Antes de leer 👥

1. The title of this article is **"Otros sistemas universitarios."** Use your knowledge of cognates to deduce what it means, and then mention three ideas that you would expect to find in a text with this title.

2. Work with a partner to ask and answer the following questions.
   a. ¿Cuántas clases tienes este semestre?
   b. ¿Qué clases tomas?

A leer

Otros sistemas universitarios

world   Las universidades en diferentes partes del **mundo** usan diversos sistemas de educación. En muchas universidades de España y Latinoamérica los estudiantes no necesitan obtener un cierto número de créditos para graduarse.

Instead of   **En vez de** usar créditos tienen un "plan de estudios", que es una lista de las clases que los estudiantes

each   tienen que tomar **cada** semestre. A veces las universidades combinan el plan de estudios con el sistema de créditos, especialmente para ayudar a los estudiantes internacionales.

La Universidad de la Habana en Cuba

[en muchas universidades no hay clases de educación general]

En muchas universidades no hay clases de educación general. Un estudiante de literatura tiene diferentes clases de literatura y otras materias relacionadas, pero no necesita estudiar matemáticas ni ciencias si no son parte de su plan de estudios. En consecuencia, cuando un estudiante inicia **la licenciatura,**

tiene que especializarse inmediatamente en su área y toma casi todas sus clases en una sola **facultad.** Cuando un estudiante **termina** la licenciatura, puede usar el título de licenciado. En muchas partes del mundo, la educación universitaria es un **derecho** y es prácticamente **gratuita.** Sin embargo, un estudiante **puede** asistir a una universidad privada si lo prefiere y si tiene suficiente dinero.

bachelor's degree

department / finishes

right / free
can

Comprensión

Decide whether the statements are true (**cierto**) or false (**falso**). Correct the false statements.

1. En muchas universidades hispanas no existen los créditos.
2. La lista de clases que los estudiantes necesitan tomar se llama "el plan de estudios".
3. Los estudiantes en Latinoamérica y España necesitan tomar clases de educación general.
4. Normalmente los estudiantes tienen clases en diferentes facultades.
5. Las universidades privadas son gratuitas.

Después de leer

Look for a university in a Spanish-speaking country. Then find your major in the index and answer the following questions.

1. ¿Cuántos años de estudios son necesarios para completar la carrera?
2. ¿Qué cursos necesitan tomar?

La Universidad de Guanajuato en México

Redacción

Write an email to a new friend and tell him or her about your family and your classes.

Paso 1 Jot down a list of the members of your family.

Paso 2 Choose two family members and beside each one, write down his or her age and two adjectives that describe the person. Be sure to use different adjectives for each person so your paragraph will not be repetitive.

Paso 3 Jot down a list of the classes you are taking.

Paso 4 Choose one of the classes in the list and write an adjective to describe it (**fácil, difícil, aburrido, interesante,** etc). Then jot down a series of phrases about it including the following: how many students are in the class and what they are like, and who the teacher is and what he or she is like.

Paso 5 Start your email with **Hola** or **¿Qué tal?** *(How's it going?)* and introduce yourself. Tell him/her something about yourself, such as where you are from, your age, or what you are like.

Paso 6 Tell him/her whether you have a large or small family. Then tell who each of the members of your family are and give details about two of them using the ideas you generated in **Paso 2.**

Paso 7 Begin a second paragraph telling your friend that you are a student and where you are studying.

Paso 8 Tell your friend what classes you have this semester. Then introduce the class you brainstormed ideas for in **Paso 4,** giving your opinion of the class.

Paso 9 Using the information you generated in **Paso 4,** describe the class.

Paso 10 Finish the letter with **Hasta pronto** or **Tu amigo(a).**

Paso 11 Edit your letter:

1. Are there any sentences that are irrelevant to the topic? If so, get rid of them.
2. Are there any spelling errors?
3. Do adjectives agree with the person or object they describe?
4. Do verbs agree with the person doing the action?
5. Are there any sentences you can join using **y** or **pero**?

Entrando en materia

How many classes does a full-time student in the United States usually take?

Un plan de estudios

Look at the plan of study for a technical program from a school in Colombia.

Programas técnicos: Auxiliar de oficina

Plan de estudios

Semestre 1: Recepción de Información (336 horas, 7 créditos)
1. Desarrollo de habilidades comunicativas.
2. Utilización de los equipos de oficina.
3. Digitación de textos.
4. Manipulación y aplicación de herramientas informáticas I.
5. Formación Humana: Conciencia e identidad del ser integral.

Semestre 2: Procesamiento y disposición de la información (336 horas, 7 créditos)
1. Aplicación de técnicas de archivo.
2. Aplicación de las técnicas de correspondencia comercial.
3. Manipulación y aplicación de herramientas informáticas II.
4. Manejo de bases de datos en Access.
5. Construcción de valores para la vida, el liderazgo y la autonomía.

Semestre 3: Manejo de la información (288 horas, 6 créditos)
1. Aplicación de técnicas comerciales de oficina.
2. Servicio al cliente.
3. Etiqueta y protocolo empresarial.
4. El emprendedor y la empresa.

Semestre 4: Formación y práctica laboral (672 horas, 14 créditos)
1. Proyecto empresarial.
2. Práctica laboral.

Intensidad horaria semanal:
Estudia entre 14 y 16 horas semanales de **clase presencial.**

contact hours

Comprensión

1. ¿Qué programa es?
2. ¿Cuántas clases hay en el primer *(first)* semestre? ¿y en el tercer *(third)* semestre?
3. ¿Cuántas horas de clases hay por semana?

 **Más allá**

Choose another major or technical program and list classes you think would be appropriate for the first two semesters of study. Post your major and list of classes to Share It! and find out what your classmates have chosen.

Asistente de oficina ▶

© Yuri Arcurs/Shutterstock

Vocabulario

Sustantivos

buena presencia	*good appearance*
la cita	*appointment*
el formulario	*form*
la oficina	*office*
la reunión	*meeting*

Verbos

contestar el teléfono	*to answer the phone*
inscribir	*to register*
interpretar	*to interpret*
preparar informes	*to prepare reports*

Frases útiles

¿En qué puedo servirle?
How can I help you?

Un momento, por favor.
One moment, please.

Está ocupado. ¿Desea hacer una cita?
He is busy right now. Would you like to make an appointment?

¿Cuál es su número de teléfono?
What is your phone number?

Más despacio, por favor.
Slower, please.

Disculpe.
Excuse me. / I'm sorry.

Necesita hablar con...
You need to speak to . . .

¿Con quién quiere hablar?
Whom do you want to speak to?

Tiene que ver a...
You have to see . . .

DATOS IMPORTANTES

Educación: Escuela secundaria con entrenamiento especial en tecnología o *community college;* algunos puestos *(some positions)* requieren una licenciatura *(bachelor's degree)*

Salario: Entre $23 000 y $36 000

Dónde se trabaja: Variedad de organizaciones; aproximadamente 90% de los asistentes trabajan en la industria de servicio, como *(like)* la educación, el gobierno *(government)*, la salud *(health)* y ventas *(retail)*

Vocabulario nuevo Match the comments or questions from the first column with a logical response from the second column.

1. ¿En qué puedo servirle?
2. ¿Con quién quiere hablar?
3. ¿Cuál es su número de teléfono?
4. Tengo que ver al señor Gómez.
5. Disculpe...

a. Está ocupado.
b. Tengo una cita con el señor Pérez.
c. Necesito hablar con la Sra. Ávila.
d. Un momento, por favor.
e. Es el 555-333-2222.

▶ María Bravo, secretaria ejecutiva

María Bravo es secretaria ejecutiva y trabaja en una escuela privada. Allí hay muchos estudiantes de otros países *(countries)*. Ella necesita comunicarse en inglés y en español continuamente. María se encarga de *(is in charge of)* los trabajos administrativos de la escuela y ayuda a los padres y estudiantes que necesitan información. En el video, María habla con el padre de un estudiante que no habla inglés.

Antes de ver

Administrative assistants and executive secretaries are the connections between a company and their clients. What questions do you think a parent would ask a secretary at a private school? How important do you think it is to have bilingual administrative personnel in a school? Why?

Comprensión

Answer the following questions according to the video.

1. ¿Qué tiene que hacer *(to do)* el Sr. Molina?

2. ¿De dónde son el Sr. Molina y su familia?

3. ¿Cuántos años tiene el hijo del Sr. Molina?

4. Según la Sra. Bravo, ¿a qué grado entra el hijo del Sr. Molina?

5. ¿Cuántos maestros *(teachers)* bilingües hay?

Después de ver

👥 With a partner, play the roles of the parent of a Latin American student who has just arrived in the United States and the secretary of a school. Greet and introduce yourself to the secretary. The secretary should ask how he/she can help you. Explain what you need.

Begin your answer with this phrase.

Quiero inscribir a...   *I want to register . . .*

2.37 **La Universidad de Puerto Rico** Complete the paragraph with the appropriate form of the verb or the possessive in parentheses.

(1.) _____ (mi) hermana Victoria y yo (2.) _____ (estudiar) en la Universidad de Puerto Rico. (3.) _____ (nuestro) clases son difíciles y nosotras (4.) _____ (tener) mucha tarea. Los profesores son muy amables y (5.) _____ (ayudar) mucho. Yo (6.) _____ (tener) tres clases: cálculo, biología e inglés. La clase de inglés es muy interesante, y yo (7.) _____ (hablar) bien. Victoria (8.) _____ (tener) cuatro clases. Ella (9.) _____ (tomar) historia, filosofía, literatura y francés. (10.) _____ (su) clases favoritas son las de historia y de literatura.

2.38 **Así es mi familia** Add the adjectives in parentheses to the sentences. Be sure to put them in the proper place and in the proper form (masculine, feminine, singular, plural).

1. Tengo una familia. (interesante)
2. Tengo dos hermanas. (pequeño)
3. No tenemos mascotas. (mucho)
4. Tenemos un perro. (cariñoso)
5. Tenemos una gata. (perezoso)
6. Tengo parientes en la ciudad (city) donde vivo. (varios)

2.39 **¿Cómo son?** Using the descriptive adjectives in parentheses and the possessive adjectives (**mi, tu, su,** etc.), tell what the family members and pets of the people below are like. **¡OJO!** Be sure to use the correct form of the possessive and descriptive adjectives.

Modelo Natalia tiene perros. (agresivo)   *Sus perros son agresivos.*
        Mi hermano tiene una esposa. (rubio)   *Su esposa es rubia.*

1. Geraldo tiene una hermana. (simpático)
2. Mis abuelos tienen gatos. (cariñoso)
3. Nosotros tenemos un caballo. (viejo)
4. Tú tienes primos. (cómico)
5. Yo tengo una sobrina. (bonito)
6. Rufina tiene hijos. (grande)

Mi caballo es bonito.

Exploraciones de repaso: comunicación

2.40 **En familia** In groups of three, each student chooses a different photo to describe to the rest of the group. Imagine the following about the people in the photo: their names, what their relationship is, how old they are, what they are like, and what they are doing.

© Photos To Go

© Photos To Go

© Photos To Go

2.41 **Datos personales** Working with a partner, look at the chart below while your partner looks at the chart in Appendix B. Take turns asking questions to fill in the missing information.

Modelo   *¿Cuántos años tiene Diego?*   *Diego tiene veinte años.*
         ¿Qué parientes hay en la familia de Diego?   *Diego tiene dos hermanos.*
         ¿Qué clase tiene Diego?   *Diego tiene informática.*

Nombre	Edad	Familia	Clase
Diego	20	dos	informática
Alonso	18		química
Magdalena	22	padrastro	
Cristina			historia
Pablo		dos hijos	arte
Gabriel		una hermana	
Rufina	41		

2.42 **Buscando un amigo** You are looking to find some new friends to do things with.

Paso 1 Circle 5 or 6 activities below that you like to do.

bailar en un club   escuchar un concierto   nadar
caminar en el parque   esquiar   practicar deportes
cantar karaoke   hablar por teléfono   tomar café
cocinar   manejar una motocicleta   tomar fotos
comprar ropa *(clothing)*   mirar la tele   viajar

Paso 2 Interview your partner to find out whether he/she does the activities that you have circled.

Paso 3 Decide whether you and your partner are compatible and would be good friends. Share your decision with the class.

🔊 Vocabulario 1
1-14

La familia

el (la) abuelo(a)	*grandfather / grandmother*
el (la) amigo(a)	*friend*
el (la) esposo(a)	*spouse*
el (la) hermanastro(a)	*stepbrother / stepsister*
el (la) hermano(a)	*brother / sister*
el (la) hijo(a)	*son / daughter*
la madrastra	*stepmother*
la madre (mamá)	*mother*
el (la) medio(a) hermano(a)	*half brother / half sister*

el (la) nieto(a)	*grandson / granddaughter*
el (la) novio(a)	*boyfriend / girlfriend*
el padrastro	*stepfather*
el padre (papá)	*father*
la pareja	*couple; partner*
el pariente	*relative*
el (la) primo(a)	*cousin*
el (la) sobrino(a)	*nephew / niece*
el (la) suegro(a)	*father-in-law / mother-in-law*
el (la) tío(a)	*uncle / aunt*

Las mascotas

el caballo	*horse*
el (la) gato(a)	*cat*
el pájaro	*bird*

el (la) perro(a)	*dog*
el pez	*fish*
el ratón	*mouse*

Los verbos

ayudar	*to help*
bailar	*to dance*
buscar	*to look for*
caminar	*to walk*
cantar	*to sing*
cocinar	*to cook*
comprar	*to buy*
desear	*to wish*
enseñar	*to teach*
escuchar	*to listen*
esquiar	*to ski*
estudiar	*to study*
hablar (por teléfono)	*to talk (on the phone)*
limpiar	*to clean*
llamar	*to call*
llegar	*to arrive*

mandar (un mensaje)	*to send (a message)*
manejar	*to drive*
mirar (la tele)	*to look, to watch (TV)*
nadar	*to swim*
necesitar	*to need*
practicar (deportes)	*to practice; to play (sports)*
preguntar	*to ask*
regresar (a casa)	*to return (home)*
tomar (café)	*to take; to drink (coffee)*
trabajar	*to work*
usar	*to use*
viajar	*to travel*

Diccionario personal

_____

_____

_____

_____

🔊 Vocabulario 2

Las materias académicas

el alemán	*German*		la historia	*history*
el álgebra	*algebra*		la informática	*computer science*
el arte	*art*		la ingeniería	*engineering*
la biología	*biology*		el inglés	*English*
el cálculo	*calculus*		el italiano	*Italian*
las ciencias naturales	*natural science*		las lenguas	*languages*
las ciencias políticas	*political science*		la literatura	*literature*
las ciencias sociales	*social science*		las matemáticas	*mathematics*
la criminología	*criminology*		la música	*music*
la economía	*economy*		los negocios	*business*
la educación física	*physical education*		el periodismo	*journalism*
la expresión oral	*speech*		la psicología	*psychology*
la filosofía	*philosophy*		la química	*chemistry*
la física	*physics*		la redacción	*writing, composition*
el francés	*French*		el teatro	*theater*
la geografía	*geography*		la veterinaria	*veterinary medicine*
la geometría	*geometry*			

Los lugares en la universidad

el auditorio	*auditorium*		el gimnasio	*gymnasium*
la biblioteca	*library*		el laboratorio	*laboratory*
la cafetería	*cafeteria*		la librería	*bookstore*
el centro estudiantil	*student center*		la residencia estudiantil	*residence hall*
el estadio	*stadium*			

Expresiones con *tener*

tener... años	*to be . . . years old*		tener (mucho) miedo	*to be (very) afraid*
tener (mucho) calor	*to be (very) hot*		tener (mucha) prisa	*to be in a (big) hurry*
tener (mucho) cuidado	*to be (very) careful*		tener que + infinitive	*to have to do something*
tener (mucho) éxito	*to be (very) successful*		tener (mucha) razón	*to be right*
tener (mucho) frío	*to be (very) cold*		tener (mucha) sed	*to be (very) thirsty*
tener ganas de + infinitive	*to feel like doing something*		tener (mucho) sueño	*to be (very) sleepy*
tener (mucha) hambre	*to be (very) hungry*		tener (mucha) suerte	*to be (very) lucky*

Palabras adicionales

el (la) compañero(a) de clase	*classmate*		poco	*few*
el examen	*exam*		el semestre	*semester*
mucho	*a lot*		el trimestre	*quarter*
la nota	*grade*		varios	*several*

Exploraciones literarias

© Felipe Rodríguez/age fotostock

Gustavo Adolfo Bécquer

Biografía

Gustavo Adolfo Bécquer (1836–1870) was a Spanish writer associated with the post-romanticism movement. Some of his recurrent topics are the night, love, human fragility, and death. His best known book, *Rimas y leyendas*, is a collection of poems and tales that has become essential reading for anyone studying Spanish literature.

Antes de leer

1. In your opinion, what is poetry?
2. Have you ever written a poem?
3. Based on the title, what do you think this poem is going to be about?

¿Qué es poesía?

you say while you pierce

¿Qué es poesía?, **dices mientras clavas**
En mi pupila tu pupila azul.
¡Qué es poesía! ¿Y tú me lo preguntas?
Poesía eres tú.

© OlgaLis/Shutterstock

Source: Gustavo Adolfo Bécquer, "Rima XXI," *Rimas*.

Después de leer

A. Comprensión

1. To whom is the poetic voice talking?
2. In your opinion, what is meant by the last line, "Poesía eres tú"?

B. Conversemos

Why do people write poetry?

Investiguemos la literatura: La voz poética

The poetic voice is the person that speaks in the poem. It would be incorrect to say that the poet is actually speaking. He or she usually takes on the persona of someone in a particular situation. As you read through a poem, it is important to ask yourself who is speaking.

Gloria Fuertes
Biografía
Gloria Fuertes (1917–1998) was a Spanish writer born in Madrid. She wrote her first poem at the age of 14 and published her first poems in 1935. She continued writing during the Spanish Civil War (1936–1939) while working as an accountant and a secretary. The civil war had a profound effect on her as she struggled to understand how modern civilizations could go to war over things of little importance and with no concern for the children destroyed by it. As a result, a large percentage of her works were written for children.

Antes de leer

1. What do you know about Somalia?
2. What would you expect a poet to write about children in Somalia?

Niños de Somalia

eat

Yo **como**
Tú comes
Él come
Nosotros comemos
Vosotros coméis
¡Ellos no!

Source: Authorized by Luz María Jimenez, heiress of Gloria Fuertes.

Después de leer

A. Comprensión

1. According to the poem, who eats? Who does not?
2. What do you think is the message of the poem?

B. Conversemos

1. Both Becquer's and Fuertes' poems are simple, but they are very different in style. Which poem do you prefer? Why?
2. Do you enjoy reading poetry? Why?

Investiguemos la literatura: Interpretación

It is important to realize that there are often multiple interpretations of a literary piece. Each reader brings his or her own experiences to the reading, and these experiences influence his or her interpretation. So don't be afraid to express your ideas. Look for ways to support them with a part or parts of the text.

Learning Strategy

Understand before moving on

Learning a foreign language is like learning math: you will continue to use what you have already learned and will build upon that knowledge. Therefore, if you find you don't understand something, make an appointment to see your instructor or a tutor right away in order to get some extra help. For help with grammar topics, you can also watch the tutorials in iLrn.

In this chapter you will learn how to:
- Talk about the weather and seasons
- Discuss clothing
- Express likes and dislikes
- Communicate dates and times
- Tell what you and others are going to do in the near future

¿Qué tiempo hace hoy?

Christopher Pillitz/Getty Images

¿Qué estación es? ¿Qué ropa llevas?

El tiempo

Hace (muy) buen tiempo.	*The weather is (very) nice.*
Hace (muy) mal tiempo.	*The weather is (very) bad.*
Hace (mucho) calor.	*It's (very) hot.*
Hace fresco.	*It is cool.*
Hace (mucho) frío.	*It's (very) cold.*
Hace sol.	*It's sunny.*
Hace (mucho) viento.	*It's (very) windy.*
Está nublado.	*It is cloudy.*
Está despejado.	*It is clear.*
Llueve.	*It's raining. / It rains.*
Nieva.	*It's snowing. / It snows.*

La ropa

la bolsa	*handbag*

los calcetines	*socks*
la corbata	*tie*
el impermeable	*raincoat*
los lentes	*glasses*
los pantalones	*pants*
la pijama	*pajamas*
el traje	*suit*
el vestido	*dress*

Verbos

llevar	*to wear; to carry; to take*
llevar puesto(a)	*to be wearing*
tomar el sol	*to sunbathe*

Palabras adicionales

cómodo(a)	*comfortable*

Los colores

amarillo(a)	*yellow*
anaranjado(a)	*orange*
azul	*blue*
blanco(a)	*white*
café	*brown*
gris	*gray*
morado(a)	*purple*
negro(a)	*black*
rojo(a)	*red*
rosado(a)	*pink*
verde	*green*

INVESTIGUEMOS EL VOCABULARIO

Many Latin Americans use the word **el clima** to refer to the weather. Additionally, it is possible to say either **llevar** or **llevar puesto(a)** to say what you wear.

The following are lexical variations for clothing items:

handbag	**el bolso** (Spain), **la cartera**	*tennis shoes*	**las zapatillas de deportes** (Spain), **los campeones** (Paraguay)
jacket	**la chamarra** (Mexico)		
glasses	**las gafas** (Spain), **los anteojos**	*jeans*	**los pantalones de mezclilla** (Mexico), **los**
socks	**las medias** (Central and South America)		**mahones** (Puerto Rico), **los vaqueros** (Spain)
skirt	**la pollera** (Panama and South America)		

A practicar

3.1 **Escucha y responde** You are going to hear a list of different articles of clothing. If you wear the clothing when it is hot, give a thumbs up. If not, give a thumbs down.

1-16

3.2 **¿Qué tiempo hace?** Which season do you associate with each of the weather conditions?

1. Hace viento.
2. Nieva.
3. Hace mucho calor.

4. Está despejado.
5. Hace fresco.
6. Llueve.

7. Hace mucho sol.
8. Hace mucho frío.

3.3 **Identificaciones** Find a classmate who is wearing one of the articles of clothing in the list. For number 10, choose another item of clothing. Then, report to the class who is wearing what.

1. unos calcetines blancos
2. una chaqueta
3. un suéter
4. unas botas
5. una camiseta

6. una falda
7. unos pantalones negros
8. un vestido
9. unos tenis
10. ¿?

> **INVESTIGUEMOS LA GRAMÁTICA**
>
> Notice that the indefinite article is used when talking about what you are wearing, not the definite article. Articles can be omitted altogether if the clothing item is plural.
> **Llevo pantalones y una camisa.**

> **INVESTIGUEMOS LA MÚSICA**
>
> El Grupo Niche is a Colombian salsa band. Listen to their song "Gotas de lluvia" and write down any vocabulary words you hear.

3.4 **De vacaciones** With a partner, take turns asking about the weather in the following destinations, and the clothing that you need.

Modelo   Cancún / julio
Estudiante 1: *¿Qué tiempo hace en Cancún en julio?*
Estudiante 2: *Hace mucho calor y está despejado.*
Estudiante 1: *¿Qué ropa necesitas?*
Estudiante 2: *Necesito pantalones cortos, sandalias y un traje de baño.*

1. Buenos Aires / diciembre
2. Anchorage / abril
3. Miami / agosto

4. Londres / junio
5. La Habana / septiembre
6. Chicago / marzo

3.5 **Los regalos** A friend sent a care package for the rest of your friends but forgot to label who everything was for, so you and a classmate need to clarify. One of you will look at the drawing on this page, and the other at the drawing in Appendix B.

Modelo   Estudiante 1: *¿Para quién* (For whom) *son los calcetines rojos?*
Estudiante 2: *Los calcetines rojos son para Emilia.*

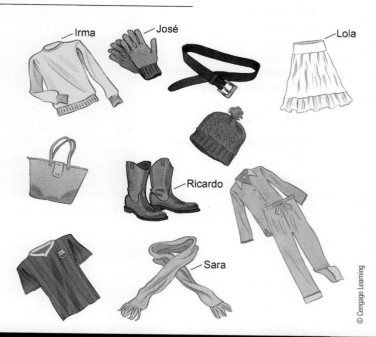

Conexiones culturales
El clima y la ropa

Cultura

Write a list in Spanish of colors and other things you associate with spring. Then read aloud the first verse of "De colores," a popular song in many Spanish-speaking countries. Afterward, answer the questions that follow.

De colores, de colores se visten los **campos**[1] en la primavera

De colores, de colores son los pajaritos que vienen de afuera

De colores, de colores es el **arco iris**[2] que vemos **lucir.**[3]

Y por eso los grandes amores de muchos colores me gustan a mí.[4]

Y por eso los grandes amores de muchos colores me gustan a mí.

Write your own one-stanza poem about colors and post to Share It!

[1]fields   [2]rainbow   [3]to shine   [4]I like

1. In your opinion, which of the following words best describe the song? Why?

   triste *(sad)*   alegre *(happy)*   nostálgica   rítmica   rápida   lenta *(slow)*

2. Go back to your list of associations for spring. Did any of the words appear in the song? If so, what words?

Comunidad

Find a native Spanish speaker in your community who is open to answering a few questions. Remember to use **usted** forms if you don't know the person. Ask the person where he/she is from, and what words from the lexical variations shown in **Investiguemos el vocabulario** on page 78 are most used in that country. Ask questions such as these:

¿De dónde eres? / ¿De dónde es usted?

En Puerto Rico, ¿cómo se dice…?

En Granada, España

Comparaciones

Clothing in different regions of the Spanish-speaking world varies widely depending on a number of factors such as age, socioeconomic status, community size, and rural versus urban locations. The photographs below show two groups of college students. Read the information, study the photos, and answer the questions that follow.

1. ¿Qué ropa llevan los estudiantes en las fotos? ¿Es similar a la ropa que llevan los estudiantes en tu universidad? ¿Piensas que *(Do you think that)* los españoles y los latinoamericanos usan ropa similar a la tuya *(yours)*? Describe las similitudes *(similarities)* y diferencias.

2. La segunda foto es de una celebración. ¿Hay diferencias entre *(between)* la ropa que llevan a la universidad y la ropa que llevan a la fiesta? ¿Tu ropa es diferente cuando *(when)* estás en una fiesta? ¿Cuáles son las diferencias?

Courtesy of Fernando Casas, ITESO

Dmitriy Shironosov/Shutterstock

Conexiones... a la redacción

With a partner, choose a season and write a list of adjectives, activities, and expressions that you associate with it. Then, write a stanza of four lines dedicated to that season. Remember that poems normally don't have complete sentences and that it isn't necessary to have a rhyme.

LianeM/iStockphoto

A analizar

Nicolás is going to introduce himself and talk about his likes and dislikes. Watch the video, then read his introduction, paying particular attention to the verb **gustar,** and answer the questions that follow.

> **Me gusta** la universidad y también **me gustan** las clases... son muy interesantes y mis profesores son buenos. ¡Pero no **me gusta** el frío en el invierno! ¡Tampoco **me gusta** caminar en la nieve ni llevar abrigo, gorro, guantes, bufanda, botas... ¡uy! **Me gustan** más el sol y el calor de Puerto Rico.

© Cengage Learning

1. The verb **gustar** is used to express likes and dislikes. What do you think **me gusta** means?
2. Notice that **gusta** and **gustan** are both used. Now find the words that follow **gustan** each time it is used. How are these words different from the ones that follow **gusta**?

A comprobar

The verb **gustar**

1. The Spanish equivalent of *I like* is **me gusta,** which literally means *it pleases me.* The expression **me gusta** is followed by singular nouns.

   > **Me gusta** *tu vestido.*
   > *I like your dress. (Your dress **pleases me.**)*

   > **Me gusta** *el verano.*
   > *I like summer. (Summer **pleases me.**)*

2. When followed by a plural noun or multiple nouns, it is necessary to use **gustan.**

   > **Me gustan** los zapatos negros.
   > *I like black shoes. (Black shoes **please me.**)*

   > **Me gustan** el otono y la primavera.
   > *I like spring and fall. (Spring and fall **please me**).*

3. When followed by a verb or a series of verbs, the singular form **gusta** is always used.

   > Me **gusta** nadar y esquiar. *I **like** to swim and ski.*
   > No me **gusta** llevar lentes. *I don't **like** wearing glasses.*

4. **Gustar** can also be used to ask about or indicate what other people like.

me gusta(n)	*I like*	nos gusta(n)	*we like*
te gusta(n)	*you like*	os gusta(n)	*you like (plural, Spain)*
le gusta(n)	*he/she likes*	les gusta(n)	*they, you (plural) like*

> ¿**Te gustan** mis botas?
> *Do you like my boots?*

> **Nos gusta** el otoño.
> *We like fall.*

5. Contrary to English, when using **gustar** with a noun, you must use the definite article as well.

   > Le gustan **los bluyines.**
   > *He likes **blue jeans**.*

   > ¿Les gusta **el invierno?**
   > *Do you (all) like **winter**?*

6. When clarifying who *he, she* or *they* are, it is necessary to use **a** in front of the name.

   > **A Mario** le gustan los pantalones cómodos.
   > *Mario likes comfortable pants.*

7. To express different degrees, use the terms **mucho** *(a lot),* **un poco** *(a little),* and **para nada** *(not at all).*

   > Me gusta **mucho** el color rojo.
   > *I like the color red **a lot**.*

   > A Alba le gustan **un poco** las sandalias.
   > *Alba likes the sandals **a little bit**.*

   > ¡No nos gusta el frío **para nada!**
   > *We don't like the cold **at all!***

INVESTIGUEMOS EL VOCABULARIO

When using **gusta** with people, it has a romantic implication. In **Capítulo 8** you will learn the expression **caer bien,** which is used to say that you like a person.

> **Me gusta Juan.**
> *I like Juan (as a romantic interest).*

A practicar

3.6 **Me gusta el verano** Renata loves everything about summer in her home country, Argentina, but doesn't like anything about winter. Listen to her statements and decide if they are logical or not by replying **lógico** or **ilógico**.

1-17

3.7 **Combinaciones lógicas** Decide which phrases in the second column best complete those in the first column.

1. En el restaurante me gustan...
2. En el restaurante no me gusta...
3. En la universidad me gusta...
4. En la universidad no me gustan...
5. En casa me gusta...
6. En casa no me gustan...

a. la clase de inglés.
b. los menús variados.
c. ayudar a mis hijos con su tarea.
d. el servicio malo.
e. los exámenes difíciles.
f. las tareas domésticas (chores).

3.8 **¿Qué te gusta?** Complete the following mini-dialogues with **me** or **te** and **gusta** or **gustan.**

1. Elena: Sonia, ¿ _____ _____ comprar zapatos?
   Sonia: Sí, _____ _____ mucho comprar zapatos.
   Elena: ¿ _____ _____ los tenis?
   Sonia: No, _____ _____ más las sandalias.

2. Hugo: ¿ _____ _____ esquiar, Raúl?
   Raúl: No, para nada. No _____ _____ el frío.
   Hugo: ¿ _____ _____ practicar deportes en verano?
   Raúl: Sí, _____ _____ el golf y el tenis.

3.9 **¿Te gusta... ?** Circulate throughout the classroom and talk with 10 different students about their likes and dislikes. Be sure to use some of the following expressions: **mucho, un poco,** and **para nada.**

Modelo bailar
   Estudiante 1: ¿Te gusta bailar?
   Estudiante 2: Sí, me gusta (mucho) bailar. No, no me gusta bailar (para nada).

1. el color azul
2. las clases de ciencias
3. llevar tenis
4. la música rock
5. los caballos
6. hablar por teléfono y mandar mensajes
7. los chocolates
8. las novelas románticas
9. el invierno
10. ¿?

¿Te gusta el invierno?

3.10 **Nuestros gustos** Look at the pictures below and, using the expression **le(s) gusta(n)**, tell what Octavio and Olivia like and don't like.

Modelo *A Octavio no le gusta estudiar.*

1.

2.

3.

4.

5.

6.

© Cengage Learning

3.11 **En común** Choose four of the following items that you like. Then circulate throughout the classroom and interview your classmates to find out if they like the same things. For each of the items you chose, find at least one other classmate who shares your opinion.

Modelo Estudiante 1: *¿Te gusta cantar?*
Estudiante 2: *Sí, me gusta (mucho) cantar. / No, no me gusta cantar.*

____ los colores pastel   ____ la primavera

____ esquiar   ____ los deportes de invierno

____ la ropa de verano   ____ el fútbol y el béisbol

____ los bluyines de marca *(name brand)*   ____ nadar y tomar el sol

____ llevar pantalones cortos   ____ ¿?

3.12 **La universidad** You are going to find out what both you and your partner like about your school.

Paso 1 Write a list of 6 items or activities that you like at your school.

Paso 2 With a partner, take turns asking if the other likes the items or activities on the list and check the items that you both like.

Paso 3 Using **Nos gusta(n)...** report to the class the items you have in common.

Modelo *Nos gustan la historia, la geografía y el español.*

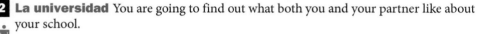

A analizar

Now watch again as Nicolás introduces himself and talks about his likes and dislikes. Then read his introduction and this time pay attention to the forms of the verb **vivir** that he uses.

> Me llamo Nicolás y soy de Puerto Rico. Mi familia **vive** en San Juan, bueno, mis padres **viven** en San Juan con mi hermana, pero yo **vivo** en Nueva York con mis tíos porque estudio en la Universidad de Nueva York. Nosotros **vivimos** en un apartamento en el Bronx.

Vivir is an **-ir** verb. Use what you have learned about **-ar** verbs on page 48 and the examples in the paragraph above to complete the chart.

yo _____	nosotros(as) _____
tú _____	vosotros(as) vivís
él, ella, usted _____	ellos, ellas, ustedes _____

A comprobar

Regular -er and -ir verbs

1. In **Capítulo 2** we learned the forms of verbs whose infinitives end in **-ar**. The following are regular **-er** and **-ir** verbs:

Los verbos *-er*

aprender (a + *infinitive*)	to learn (to do something)	creer	to believe
		deber (+ *infinitive*)	should (do something)
beber	to drink		
comer	to eat	leer	to read
comprender	to understand	vender	to sell
correr	to run		

Los verbos *-ir*

abrir	to open	escribir	to write
asistir (a)	to attend	recibir	to receive
decidir	to decide	vivir	to live

2. Regular **-er** and **-ir** verbs follow a pattern very similar to regular **-ar** verbs.

beber					
yo	**-o**	beb**o**	nosotros(as)	**-emos**	beb**emos**
tú	**-es**	beb**es**	vosotros(as)	**-éis**	beb**éis**
él, ella, usted	**-e**	beb**e**	ellos, ellas, ustedes	**-en**	beb**en**

escribir					
yo	**-o**	escrib**o**	nosotros(as)	**-imos**	escrib**imos**
tú	**-es**	escrib**es**	vosotros(as)	**-ís**	escrib**ís**
él, ella, usted	**-e**	escrib**e**	ellos, ellas, ustedes	**-en**	escrib**en**

Remember the following rules:

a. To form negative sentences, the word **no** is placed in front of the conjugated verb.

Los niños **no comprenden** inglés. *The children **don't understand** English.*

b. When using two verbs together, the second verb stays in the infinitive.

Debemos **estudiar** en la biblioteca. *We should **study** in the library.*

Los estudiantes aprenden a **hablar** español. *The students are learning **to speak** Spanish.*

c. To form simple questions, place the subject after the conjugated verb and add the question marks at the beginning and end of the question.

¿Vive Alfredo en Bogotá? *Does Alfredo live in Bogota?*

A practicar

3.13 **¿Qué tienen?** Choose the most logical verb to complete the sentence.

1. Cuando tengo hambre, yo _____ un sándwich.

    a. como   **b.** creo   **c.** corro

2. Vanesa y Nelson tienen prisa y _____ a clase.

    a. comprenden   **b.** escriben   **c.** corren

3. Cuando tienen calor, mis padres _____ las ventanas.

    a. deciden   **b.** asisten a   **c.** abren

4. Belinda y yo tenemos éxito en la clase de cálculo y _____ buenas notas.

    a. vendemos   **b.** recibimos   **c.** aprendemos

5. Cuando Leopoldo tiene sed, _____ agua.

    a. debe   **b.** come   **c.** bebe

3.14 **Mis amigos y yo** Complete the sentences with the forms of the verbs indicated.

1. **(leer)** Mi amigo Gustavo y yo **(a.)** _____ muchos libros. Yo **(b.)** _____ novelas de ciencia ficción y él **(c.)** _____ novelas de suspenso.

2. **(vender)** Mi amiga Patricia y yo trabajamos en una tienda *(store)* y nosotros **(a.)** _____ ropa para mujeres. Yo **(b.)** _____ vestidos y Patricia **(c.)** _____ zapatos.

3. **(abrir)** En clase, la profesora **(a.)** _____ su libro. Los estudiantes **(b.)** _____ sus libros también. A Elena no le gusta estudiar y no desea **(c.)** _____ su libro.

3.15 **Un día en la vida de Antonio** With a partner, take turns describing Antonio's activities. Use the **-er** and **-ir** verbs from this lesson as well as other verbs you have learned.

© Cengage Learning

3.16 **En busca de…** Find classmates who do the following activities. Be sure to find a different person for each activity.

1. leer novelas románticas
2. recibir buenas notas
3. correr en la mañana
4. beber mucho café

5. vivir en un apartamento
6. escribir muchos mensajes de texto
7. asistir a conciertos
8. comer en la cafetería

3.17 **¿Qué hacen?** Tell your partner about the things you and others do. Choose a subject from the first column and combine it with a verb from the second column. Be sure to add a phrase from the parentheses to complete your sentence. **¡OJO!** Pay attention to the form of the verb.

yo
mis compañeros de clase
mis amigos y yo
mi mejor amigo
mi profesor de español
mi familia

deber (estudiar, escribir la tarea, leer el libro)
recibir (buenas notas, muchos mensajes, cartas)
asistir a (clase de español, muchos conciertos, muchas fiestas)
vivir en (una casa, un apartamento, el campus)
comprender (el español, las matemáticas, el inglés)
comer (en restaurantes, en la cafetería, mucha pizza)

3.18 **Entrevista** Take turns asking and answering the following questions.

1. Normalmente ¿asistes a clases en el verano?
2. ¿Comprendes al profesor de español?
3. ¿Lees mucho? ¿Lees novelas o revistas *(magazines)*?
4. ¿Dónde vives? ¿Vives con otra persona?
5. ¿Bebes mucho café?
6. ¿Recibes muchos mensajes? ¿De quién? *(From whom?)*
7. ¿Debes escribir muchas composiciones para *(for)* tus clases? ¿Para qué clases?
8. ¿Crees que *(that)* aprender español es fácil o difícil? ¿Por qué?

3.19 **¿Qué debe hacer?** With a partner, come up with recommendations for what the following people should do. Use the verb **deber** and one of the following verbs.

| aprender | asistir | buscar | comer | correr | decidir |
| estudiar | hablar | practicar | ser | trabajar | viajar |

Modelo Carla tiene problemas con su novio.
   Ella debe hablar con su novio.

1. Julio y Claudia tienen malas notas en sus clases.
2. A Mónica no le gusta su ropa pero no tiene dinero para comprar ropa nueva.
3. Me gusta el frío pero vivo en Puerto Rico.
4. El señor Ortíz desea estar más sano *(healthy)*.
5. Pablo y yo no tenemos muchos amigos.
6. La señorita García desea ser doctora.

3.20 **Yo también** Using some of the verbs below, tell your partner what you do. Your partner will tell you if he or she does the same activities or not. Then report to the class the activities that you and your partner both do.

| abrir | aprender | asistir | beber | comer | comprender |
| correr | deber | decidir | leer | recibir | vender |

Modelo correr
   Estudiante 1: *Yo corro en el gimnasio.*
   Estudiante 2: *¡Yo también! / Yo no corro. No me gusta correr.*

Estrategia

Understand before moving on

Do you feel comfortable using **gustar** as well as **-er** and **-ir** verbs? If there is anything you're still not sure about, now is a good time to check in with your instructor for help. For more support, you can also view the tutorials for **gustar, -er** verbs and **-ir** verbs in iLrn.

© ArtmannWitte/Shutterstock

En vivo 🔊

Entrando en tema

¿Te gusta ir de compras *(to go shopping)*? ¿Dónde prefieres comprar ropa? ¿Por qué?

De compras

🔊 You are going to hear a commercial. Listen carefully and then answer the comprehension
1-18 questions.

Estrategia

Before you listen, look at the
Vocabulario útil and anticipate
what the commercial might be
about.

Vocabulario útil

ahora mismo	*right now*	**el precio**	*price*
barato(a)	*cheap*	**¿Vienes conmigo?**	*Would you come with me?*
de moda	*fashionable*		

Comprensión

1. ¿De qué es el comercial?
2. ¿Qué ropa lleva puesta la chica? ¿Le gusta esa *(that)* ropa a su amigo?
3. ¿Qué otros artículos de ropa compró *(bought)* la chica?
4. ¿Cuánto cuesta *(costs)* la blusa?

🖥 Más allá

Write your own commercial for a store. Keep it simple! Just give the name of the store, a
couple of reasons to buy there, and three or four examples of items they sell. Once you
are satisfied with your commercial, record it and post to Share It! and find out what your
classmates are advertising.

© Dmitry Kalinovsky/Shutterstock

Lectura

Reading Strategy: Skimming

Skim through the text before reading it thoroughly. You can skim by reading the first sentence of each paragraph and also by looking only for the most important information in the text such as names, places, and events. You will notice certain key ideas. Without looking up any words, try to identify three main ideas.

Antes de leer

The people in the photos below are wearing traditional clothing. With a classmate match the photos with the country where you think they are from (**Argentina, Perú,** or **Cuba**). Then answer the questions below based on your own experience.

© Don Tremain/JupiterImages © Kobby Dagan/Shutterstock © Joel Shawn/Shutterstock

1. ¿Qué factores consideran para relacionar las fotografías con los países?
2. ¿Hay ropa tradicional en el estado / la región donde vives? ¿Cómo es?

A leer

La ropa tradicional

show

Muchas regiones del mundo hispano tienen una gran variedad de trajes tradicionales que **muestran** su cultura y sus tradiciones, y también reflejan su historia y su clima. En muchas culturas es posible determinar de qué región o comunidad es una persona solamente por el traje y los colores que lleva, como es el caso de Guatemala.

> En muchas culturas es posible determinar de dónde es una persona solamente por el traje

Nevertheless
cities

Sin embargo, no todas las personas llevan sus trajes tradicionales todo el tiempo. En las **ciudades** las personas prefieren usar ropa moderna como camisas, faldas, vestidos y bluyines. Muchos indígenas que van a vivir a las ciudades prefieren no usar su ropa tradicional para **evitar** la discriminación.

avoid

Sin embargo, es posible ver la **belleza** de la ropa tradicional en muchas partes. Por ejemplo, a muchas mujeres en la región andina de Bolivia y Ecuador les gusta llevar puesta su ropa tradicional: una pollera (falda) larga, una blusa en color **llamativo** y un **sombrero de bombín**. Este **conjunto** es un signo

beauty

flashy
bowler hat
outfit

de distinción y elegancia. Gracias a esta ropa, estas mujeres, **conocidas como** Cholitas, se identifican como un grupo, **fomentando** la solidaridad y su identidad cultural.

known as
promoting

Otro ejemplo de ropa tradicional es el de las blusas de las mujeres Kuna Yala, en la costa de Panamá. Sus blusas se llaman molas y están decoradas con **motivos** geométricos del océano y de animales, pero las molas **están cambiando** y ahora muchos **diseños** reflejan la interacción con el mundo moderno.

La ropa indígena refleja las **creencias** y los valores de una comunidad, y muchas veces el estado civil o social de una persona. Para muchos indígenas, la ropa tradicional es una parte vital de su identidad, y una conexión a sus **antepasados**. ¿Qué valores refleja tu ropa?

motifs
are changing
designs

beliefs

ancestors

Comprensión

1. ¿Qué reflejan los trajes tradicionales?
2. ¿Qué ropa prefieren llevar las personas en las ciudades?
3. ¿Qué ropa llevan las Cholitas de Bolivia?
4. ¿Qué son las molas? ¿Quiénes usan las molas?

Después de leer

With a partner, describe a traditional outfit that reflects the climate, culture, and history of a region of your country. What would the men wear? And the women? What colors are the outfits? What do the colors represent?

¿Cuál es la fecha? ¿Qué día es hoy?

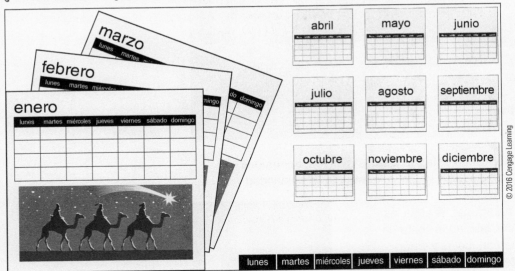

marzo

febrero

enero

lunes	martes	miércoles	jueves	viernes	sábado	domingo

abril   mayo   junio

julio   agosto   septiembre

octubre   noviembre   diciembre

© 2016 Cengage Learning

lunes	martes	miércoles	jueves	viernes	sábado	domingo

Estrategia

Understand before moving on Be sure to make an appointment to see your instructor or a tutor right away in order to get some extra help if you don't understand something.

Palabras adicionales

ahora	now	**la fecha**	date	**por la tarde**	in the afternoon
el Año Nuevo	New Year	**hoy**	today	**por la noche**	in the evening
el día feriado	holiday	**mañana**	tomorrow	**Navidad**	Christmas
el cumpleaños	birthday	**por la mañana**	in the morning		

terminar	to end
todos los días	every day

1. To tell time, the verb **ser** is used. Use **es la** with **una** and **son las** with all other hours.

   ¿Qué hora es? *What time is it?*

   Son las tres. *It's three o'clock.*   **Es** la una. *It's one.*

2. To tell time from the hour to the half hour (1–30 minutes), use **y** between the hour and the minutes. To tell time after the half hour (31–59 minutes), use **menos** and the minutes until the next hour.

   Son las siete **y** cinco.   Son las tres **menos** veinte.

   It's 7:05.   *It's 2:40.*

3. Use **cuarto** to express a quarter before or after the hour, and use **media** to express half past the hour.

   Son las diez y **cuarto**.   Son las once menos **cuarto**.   Son las ocho y **media**.

   It's 10:15.   *It's 10:45.*   *It's 8:30.*

4. It is also common to express time as read on a digital clock.

   Es la una y cincuenta. *It's 1:50.*   **Son las seis y quince.** *It's 6:15.*

5. To ask or tell at what time something is done, use the preposition **a**.

   ¿A qué hora trabajas?   *At what time do you work?*

   Trabajo **a** las cuatro de la tarde. *I work at 4:00 in the afternoon.*

6. To express that an event goes from a certain time to another specific time, use **de las... a las...**

   Trabajo **de las** 2:00 **a las** 5:00 de la tarde. *I work from 2:00 to 5:00 in the afternoon.*

7. To express A.M. or P.M., use the following expressions: **de la mañana** (*in the morning*), **de la tarde** (*in the afternoon*), and **de la noche** (*in the evening*). To express *noon* use **mediodía** and to express *midnight* use **medianoche**.

8. When talking about dates, use the phrase:

   Es (*number*) **de** (*month*).

   Hoy **es** once **de** julio.   *Today is the eleventh of July.*

9. To talk about the first of the month use **primero**.

   Es **primero** de julio.   *It is the first of July.*

Notice that the names of the months and days of the week are not capitalized in Spanish.

INVESTIGUEMOS EL VOCABULARIO

When talking about days and dates:

- use the definite article (**el** or **los**) to talk about something that happens on a particular day or days.

  El examen es **el** miércoles.
  The test is on Wednesday.

  Trabajo **los** viernes y sábados.
  I work on Fridays and Saturdays.

- other than **sábado** and **domingo**, the plural form for other days of the week is the same as the singular form.

el sábado	**los sábados**
el lunes	**los lunes**

  In some Spanish-speaking countries, calendars show the first day of the week as Monday (**lunes**).

A practicar

3.21 **Escucha y responde** Escribe la palabra **mes** en un papel y **día** en otro. Escucha la lista de meses y días. Si escuchas un mes, levanta el papel que dice **mes**. Si escuchas un día, levanta el papel que dice **día**. (*Write the word* **mes** *on one piece of paper and* **día** *on another. Listen to a list of months and days. If you hear a month hold up* **mes**; *if you hear a day of the week, hold up* **día**.)

1-19

3.22 **En orden** Completa las secuencias con la palabra que falta. (*Complete the following sequences with the missing word.*)

1. enero, febrero, marzo, _____
2. viernes, sábado, _____
3. lunes, miércoles, _____
4. septiembre, octubre, _____
5. lunes, martes, _____
6. junio, julio, _____
7. jueves, sábado, _____
8. mayo, agosto, noviembre, _____

3.23 **¿Qué hora es?** Mira los celulares y di qué hora es. (*Look at the cell phones and tell what time it is.*)

1. 2. 3. 4. 5. 6.

3.24 **Entrevista** En parejas túrnense para preguntar y responder las siguientes preguntas. (*Working with a partner, take turns asking and answering the following questions.*)

1. ¿Cuándo es tu cumpleaños? Y el cumpleaños de tu mejor (*best*) amigo?
2. ¿Cuál es tu día feriado (*holiday*) favorito? ¿En qué mes es?
3. ¿Cuál es tu mes favorito? ¿Por qué?
4. ¿Qué días tienes clases? ¿A qué hora es tu primera clase de la semana?
5. ¿Trabajas? ¿Qué días trabajas? ¿A qué hora trabajas normalmente?

> **INVESTIGUEMOS LA CULTURA**
>
> Here are some holidays that are commonly celebrated in most Spanish-speaking countries: **el Día de los Muertos** (*Day of the Dead*), **el Día de los Reyes Magos** (*Three Kings Day*), **la Pascua** (*Easter, Passover*), **la Navidad** (*Christmas*), **la Nochebuena** (*Christmas Eve*), **la Semana Santa** (*Holy Week*).

3.25 **La tele** En parejas túrnense para preguntar a qué hora son los programas y en qué canal son. Uno mira la programación y las preguntas aquí y el otro mira el **Apéndice B**. (*With a partner, take turns asking what times the shows are on and on what channel. One will look at the guide and questions here, and the other will look at Appendix B.*)

Modelo Estudiante 1: *¿A qué hora es* Veredicto final*?*
Estudiante 2: Veredicto final *es a las dos de la tarde.*
Estudiante 1: *¿En qué canal es?*
Estudiante 2: *Es en Canal 5.*

> **INVESTIGUEMOS EL VOCABULARIO**
>
> In Spain and in many parts of Latin America, the 24-hour clock is used when posting hours for businesses and for schedules, such as school schedules, flight schedules, and movie and television schedules. To convert the 24-hour clock, subtract 12:00 from 13:00 and later, so that 14:30 would be 2:30 in the afternoon.

PROGRAMACIÓN ● Películas ● Especiales ● Deportes ● Nuevos

		14:00	14:30	15:00	15:30	16:00	16:30	17:00	17:30	18:00	18:30	19:00
Jueves 10 de agosto	Galavisión	Cable 10	Héroe		El Amor no	El Chapulín Colorado		Laura en América			La Oreja		
	Canal 22	Cable 22	TV UNAM	De Cine	Película se Anunciará			México	La Magia de la Naturaleza		Ciencia Cierta		
	Movie City	Digital 480	(1:40) ★★"Dos Ilusiones" (2004)			(:35) "A los 30 Años" (Francia, 2004)			(:20) ★ "Gritos del Más Allá (2005)				
	Canal 5		Veredicto final		Será anunciada				Difícil de creer		Quiero amarte		

© Cengage Learning

¿A qué hora es... ?

1. *Los Archivos del FBI*
2. *Adictos*
3. *Aprendiendo a vivir*
4. *Durmiendo con el enemigo*

Conexiones culturales

Las celebraciones

Cultura

José Guadalupe Posada was a Mexican artist who produced numerous engravings depicting skeletons in everyday scenes, usually having fun. Although Posada's intention originally was satirical, as his work dealt with political and social issues, his art has been consistently used by Mexicans to decorate and celebrate **el Día de los Muertos.**

Find out when *El Día de los Muertos* is celebrated and learn more about Mexico in **Exploraciones del Mundo Hispano** in Appendix A.

© Giraudon/Art Resource, NY

INVESTIGUEMOS LA MÚSICA

"La Llorona" is a well-known Mexican legend associated with the Day of the Dead. Listen to the song "La Llorona" sung by Lila Downs, a Mexican-American artist whose music is influenced by the music of Mixtec, Zapotec, Maya, and Nahuatl cultures. What is the tone of the song? What words can you understand?

 Explore other works by José Guadalupe Posada. Choose a favorite, then post to Share It! with a caption. Tell the class what you like about it in Spanish. Here are some keywords to help with your search: **grabado** *(engraving)*, **ilustración**, **caricatura**.

Comparaciones

The following are celebrations in Spain or Latin American countries. Are there similar celebrations in the United States? If so, when are they celebrated? Can you think of holidays that are unique to the United States?

San Fermín	el 7 de julio	Los españoles corren con los toros.
El Día de los Muertos	el 1 y 2 de noviembre	Los mexicanos honran *(honor)* a sus antepasados.
El Día de los Inocentes	el 28 de diciembre	Los hispanos hacen bromas *(jokes).*
El Carnaval	la semana antes *(before)* del Miércoles de Cenizas *(Ash Wednesday)*	Los hispanos cantan y bailan en las calles.
San Juan	el 24 de junio	Los paraguayos juegan *(play)* con fuego *(fire).*
El Año Nuevo	el 1° de enero	Los latinos celebran la llegada del nuevo año.
La Tomatina	el último *(last)* miércoles de agosto	Los españoles pelean *(fight)* con tomates.
El Día del Estudiante	el 21 de septiembre	Los estudiantes argentinos tienen fiestas en el parque y juegan al fútbol.

Conexiones... a la religión

Another Catholic tradition widely observed throughout the Spanish-speaking world is the celebration of **el santo.** Each day of the year is attributed to a particular saint, and it is common practice to give a baby the name of the saint of the day when he or she was born. For babies who do not share the name of the patron saint of their birthday, their **santo** is celebrated like a second birthday. For example, suppose a child born on October 31 is named Fernando. Fernando will always celebrate his birthday on October 31 as well as his **santo** on May 30, **día de San Fernando.**

Look at the calendar and determine when these people would celebrate their **santo.**

Óscar de la Renta (diseñador *[designer]*, República Dominicana, 1932)
Rómulo Gallegos (autor, Venezuela, 1884–1969)
Gilberto Santa Rosa (cantante, Puerto Rico, 1962)
Marta Sánchez (cantante, España, 1966)
Rufino Tamayo (pintor, México, 1899–1991)

If someone in your family has a Christian name, find out when you would celebrate his/her **santo.**

Óscar de la Renta

Febrero

1. San Cecilio
2. San Cornelio
3. San Óscar
4. San Gilberto
5. Santa Felicia
6. Santa Dorotea
7. Santa Juliana
8. San Lucio
9. San Abelardo
10. San Jacinto
11. Nuestra Sra. de Lourdes
12. San Damián
13. Santa Maura
14. San Valentín
15. San Faustino
16. San Elías
17. San Rómulo
18. San Eladio
19. San Gabino
20. San Eugenio
21. San Pedro Damián
22. Santa Leonor
23. Santa Marta de Astorga
24. San Sergio
25. San Valerio
26. San Alejandro
27. San Basilio
28. San Rufino
29. Santa Emma

Comunidad

 Find a native Spanish speaker in your community who is willing to answer your questions. Ask him/her what holidays are celebrated in his/her country of origin and which are his/her favorites. Post your findings on Share It!

Ask questions such as these:

¿Qué días festivos celebran en su país?
¿Cuál es su favorito? / ¿Cuáles son sus favoritos?

3

Exploraciones gramaticales

A analizar ▶

Rosa y Paula hablan de su día. Después de ver el video, lee su conversación y observa las formas del verbo **ir.** Luego contesta las preguntas que siguen. *(Rosa and Paula talk about their day. After watching the video, read their conversation and observe the forms of the verb **ir.** Then answer the questions that follow.)*

Rosa:	¡Hola Paula! ¿Cómo estás?
Paula:	Bien, ¿y tú Rosa?
Rosa:	Bien. ¿Adónde **vas**?
Paula:	**Voy** a clase ahora. Después **voy** a la biblioteca porque tengo que estudiar para un examen de historia...
Rosa:	¿Y si tú y yo **vamos a comer** al Café Rústico? Tienen muy buenas pizzas.
Paula:	¡Qué buena idea... **vamos**!
Rosa:	¡Excelente! ¡Hasta luego!

1. The forms **voy, vas,** and **vamos** in the conversation are forms of the verb **ir.** Is the verb regular like **vivir** or irregular like **ser**? Explain why.

2. Using the forms presented in the conversation and what you already know about verbs, complete the chart.

   ir

   yo _____ nosotros _____

   tú _____ vosotros vais

   él, ella, usted _____ ellos, ellas, ustedes _____

3. Why do you think the verb **ir** is not conjugated in the phrase **necesito ir?**

A comprobar
The verb **ir**

ir *(to go)*			
yo	**voy**	nosotros(as)	**vamos**
tú	**vas**	vosotros(as)	**vais**
él, ella, usted	**va**	ellos, ellas, ustedes	**van**

1. The verb **ir** is used to tell where someone goes and often requires the preposition **a** *(to)*. When asking where someone goes, the preposition **a** is added to the word **dónde** *(adónde)*.

   ¿Adónde van ustedes después de la clase?
   Where do you go after class?
   Vamos a la biblioteca. *We go to the library.*

2. Just as there are contractions in English *(can't, don't)*, there are also contractions in Spanish. In Spanish, however, these contractions are not optional. Similar to the contraction **del,** when using the preposition **a** in front of a masculine definite article, it combines with **el** to form the contraction **al (a + el = al).** The **a** does not contract with the other articles.

   Los sábados yo voy **al** estadio con mis amigos.
   Saturdays I go to the stadium with my friends.

   Al mediodía mis amigos van **a la** cafetería.
   At noon my friends go to the cafeteria.

3. It is common to use the verb **ir** in the present tense to tell where someone is going at that moment.

> Mi amiga **va** a la universidad ahora.
> *My friend **is going** to the university now.*

> Nosotros **vamos** al gimnasio.
> *We **are going** to the gym.*

4. The verb **ir** is used in a variety of expressions.

ir de compras	*to go shopping*
ir de excursión	*to go hiking*
ir de paseo	*to go for a walk*
ir de viaje	*to take a trip*

A practicar

3.26 Las vacaciones de verano Todos viajan este verano. Lee las siguientes oraciones y di qué países van a visitar. Sigue el modelo. *(Everyone is traveling this summer. Read the following sentences and tell which countries they will visit. Follow the model.)*

> Modelo Adriana va a Santiago.
> *Adriana va a Chile.*

Argentina	**Costa Rica**	**España**
Perú	**Puerto Rico**	**la República Dominicana**

1. Yo voy a San Juan.
2. Manuela va a Buenos Aires.
3. Jorge y Horacio van a San José.
4. Marina y yo vamos a Santo Domingo.
5. La familia Montalvo va a Lima.
6. Los hermanos Castro van a Madrid.

INVESTIGUEMOS LA MÚSICA

Julieta Venegas is a popular Mexican singer, songwriter, and musician. Listen to her song "Me voy." Why do you think she is leaving?

3.27 Después de las clases Completa el párrafo con la forma apropiada del verbo **ir.** *(Complete the paragraph with the appropriate form of the verb **ir**.)*

Después de *(After)* las clases, mis compañeros (1) _____ a casa,

y yo (2) _____ a la biblioteca con mi amigo Fernando. Nosotros

(3) _____ al café después para tomar algo. Luego, él (4) _____

a su casa, y yo (5) _____ al centro estudiantil para trabajar. ¿Adónde

(6) _____ tú después de las clases?

3.28 A clase Usando el vocabulario de las clases del **Capítulo 2** y el verbo **ir,** explica adónde van las siguientes personas para hacer las actividades indicadas. *(Using class subject vocabulary from **Capítulo 2** and the verb **ir**, explain where the following people go to do the indicated activities.)*

> Modelo Tú aprendes a escribir bien.
> *Vas a la clase de redacción.*

1. Yo estudio los mapas y aprendo las capitales.
2. Elisa tiene que hablar enfrente de sus compañeros de clase hoy.
3. Gael y Damián leen una novela de Mario Vargas Llosa.
4. Tú estudias los elementos y haces experimentos.
5. Valentín y yo aprendemos de las plantas y los animales.
6. La profesora Arango enseña las teorías de Freud.
7. Paolo es actor en el nuevo drama de la universidad.
8. Tú estudias los eventos importantes del pasado *(past)*.
9. Yo tengo que analizar figuras como el triángulo.
10. Germán y tú aprenden de Sócrates y Platón.

3.29 **¿Adónde van?** Usando la forma apropiada del verbo **ir,** di adónde van las siguientes personas. **¡OJO!** Usa la contracción **al** cuando sea necesario. *(Using the appropriate form of the verb **ir,** tell where the following people are going. **¡OJO!** Remember to use the contraction **al** when necessary.)*

1. yo

2. el profesor Rosales

3. Ricardo y yo

4. tu amigo y tú

5. mis amigos

6. tú

© Cengage Learning

3.30 **¿Adónde vas?** Escribe adónde vas para hacer las siguientes actividades. Usa palabras del vocabulario o el nombre del lugar. Luego busca compañeros que vayan a los mismos lugares. *(Write down where you go to do the following activities. Use vocabulary words or the name of the place. Then find classmates who go to the same places.)*

Modelo   para *(in order to)* nadar
　　　　　Estudiante 1: *¿Adónde vas para nadar?*
　　　　　Estudiante 2: *Yo voy a City Fitness. / Yo voy al gimnasio. / Yo no nado.*

1. para comer

2. para estudiar

3. para tomar un café

4. para leer

5. para mirar la tele

6. para escuchar música

7. para caminar o correr

8. para bailar

A analizar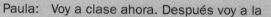

Rosa y Paula hablan de sus actividades. Después de ver el video, lee su conversación y observa las expresiones en negritas. Luego contesta las preguntas que siguen. *(Rosa and Paula are talking about their activities. Watch the video again. Then read their conversation and look at the boldface expressions. Then answer the questions that follow.)*

Paula: Voy a clase ahora. Después voy a la biblioteca porque tengo que estudiar para un examen de historia.

Rosa: Yo también tengo que ir a la bibioteca hoy. **Voy a buscar** unos libros para una investigación. ¿Qué **vas a hacer** después?

Paula: Nada. **Voy a comer** en la cafetería.

Rosa: ¿Y si tú y yo **vamos a comer** al Café Rústico? Tienen muy buenas pizzas.

Paula: ¡Qué buena idea... vamos!

1. Do the phrases in bold express past, present, or future?
2. What patterns do you notice?

© Cengage Learning

A comprobar

Ir + a + *infinitive*

1. Similar to the English verb *to go*, the verb **ir** can be used to talk about the future. To tell what someone is *going to do*, use the following structure:

ir	+	a	+	*infinitive*
Voy		a		viajar.
Van		a		trabajar.

Vamos a estudiar esta noche.
*We **are going** to study tonight.*

Juan **va a ir** al café con Elena.
*Juan **is going to go** to the café with Elena.*

2. To ask what someone is going to do, use the verb **hacer** in the question. When responding, the verb **hacer** is not necessary.

¿Qué vas a hacer (tú)?
What are you going to do?

(Yo) Voy a estudiar (trabajar, comer, etcétera).
I am going to study (work, eat, etc.).

Note: You will learn the forms of the verb **hacer** in **Capítulo 5.**

A practicar

3.31 **Un poco de lógica** Varias personas van a diferentes lugares en el campus. Selecciona la respuesta apropiada de la segunda columna para indicar lo que van a hacer cuando llegan. *(Various people are going to different places on campus. Select the appropriate answer from the second column to tell what they are going to do when they get there.)*

1. Yo voy a la librería.
2. Raquel va al gimnasio.
3. Mis amigos van a la cafetería.
4. Sergio va a clase.
5. Paloma y yo vamos al estadio.
6. Agustina y Octavio van a la biblioteca.

a. Van a comer.
b. Vamos a mirar fútbol
c. Voy a comprar un libro.
d. Va a tomar un examen.
e. Van a estudiar.
f. Va a correr.

3.32 **El cumpleaños de Merche** Hoy es el cumpleaños de Merche y tiene un día muy ocupado. Usando **ir** + **a** + infinitivo, explica lo que va a hacer hoy y a qué hora. *(Today is Merche's birthday, and she has a busy day. Using **ir** + **a** + infinitive, tell what she is going to do today and what time she is going to do it.)*

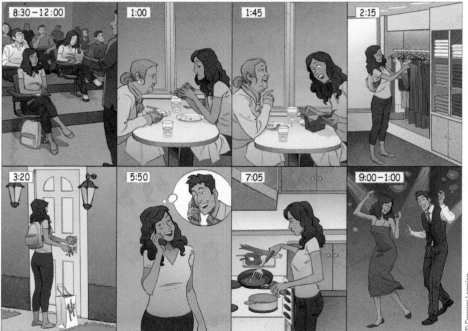

© Cengage Learning

3.33 **¿Qué vas a hacer mañana?** Pregúntale a tu compañero qué va a hacer mañana a las siguientes horas. *(Ask your partner what he/she is going to do tomorrow at the following times.)*

Modelo 2:00 P.M.
Estudiante A: *¿Qué vas a hacer mañana a las dos de la tarde?*
Estudiante B: *(Yo) Voy a correr en el parque.*

1. 8:00 A.M.
2. 10:30 A.M.
3. 12:00 P.M.
4. 1:15 P.M.

5. 3:30 P.M.
6. 6:45 P.M.
7. 8:15 P.M.
8. 10:00 P.M.

3.34 **¿Qué vas a hacer?** Trabaja con un compañero para preguntarse sobre sus planes. *(Work with a partner asking about each others' plans.)*

Modelo ahora

> Estudiante 1: *¿Qué vas a hacer ahora?*
> Estudiante 2: *Voy a comer en la cafetería, ¿y tú?*
> Estudiante 1: *Voy a estudiar.*

1. esta *(this)* noche
2. mañana por la mañana
3. mañana por la noche
4. el sábado
5. el domingo
6. la próxima *(next)* semana
7. este verano
8. el próximo semestre

3.35 **De vacaciones** El curso de primavera terminó y vas a ir de vacaciones con un amigo. Mira el anuncio y con un compañero decidan cómo van a contestar las siguientes preguntas. *(The spring semester is ending and you are going to go on vacation with a friend. With a classmate, look at the advertisement and decide how you will answer the following questions.)*

Modelo Estudiante 1: *¿Adónde vamos a ir?*
> Estudiante 2: *Vamos a Puerto Rico.*
> Estudiante 1: *No me gusta el calor. Vamos a...*

1. ¿Adónde van a ir?
2. ¿Cuándo van a viajar?
3. ¿Qué ropa van a necesitar?
4. ¿Qué van a hacer?
5. ¿Cuándo van a regresar?

Agencia de Viajes Vagabundo

San Juan, Puerto Rico (5 días) $650
Hotel Miramar ★ ★ ★ ★
Playa *(beach)* privada

Bariloche, Argentina (7 días) $1850
Hotel Nevada ★ ★ ★
Estación de esquí a 5 kilómetros

Cuzco, Perú (8 días) $1475
Hotel Tierra Andina ★ ★ ★ ★
En el centro, cerca del *(near)* mercado y tiendas *(stores)*

Madrid, España (9 días) $1995
Hotel Príncipe ★ ★ ★
Cerca de museos y teatros

3.36 **Tiempo libre** En parejas túrnense para preguntar lo que van a hacer en las siguientes situaciones. *(In pairs take turns asking what you are going to do in the following situations.)*

Modelo Es domingo y no tienes mucha tarea.
> Estudiante 1: *¿Qué vas a hacer?*
> Estudiante 2: *Voy a tomar un café con mi amiga.*

1. Mañana no hay clases y no necesitas trabajar.
2. La clase de español termina a las diez y tu siguiente *(next)* clase es a las doce.
3. Son las vacaciones de primavera y vas a recibir un cheque de $800 de los impuestos *(taxes)*.
4. Es sábado y hace buen tiempo.
5. Recibes un cheque de 50 dólares por tu cumpleaños.
6. Es viernes por la noche.

Lectura

Antes de leer

In many countries there are important celebrations and holidays that are unique to the country. Make a list of the holidays that are important in the United States. Which ones do you celebrate and why? Look back at the celebrations mentioned in **Conexiones culturales.** Do you know other celebrations from a Spanish-speaking country? The following reading is about Christmas, a particularly important celebration because the majority of the population in Spain and Latin America is Catholic.

A leer

La Navidad en algunos países hispanos

© Fer Gregory/Shutterstock

Muchas de las tradiciones en Latinoamérica son religiosas y tienen sus orígenes en tradiciones españolas. Una de estas tradiciones es la de la Navidad. Para muchos, la celebración de la Navidad se inicia **antes** del 25 de diciembre. Desde noviembre es posible escuchar **villancicos** en los comerciales de televisión y de la radio. En varios países las fiestas inician el 16 de diciembre y continúan todas las noches hasta el 24 de diciembre. Estas fiestas se llaman *posadas*. En las posadas muchas personas visitan otras casas en la comunidad.

before

Christmas carols

[...les gusta cantar villancicos, comer comida tradicional y romper piñatas.]

Durante estas fiestas, a las personas les gusta cantar villancicos y comer **comida** tradicional. A los niños les gusta mucho romper piñatas. A veces también hay *pastorelas*, que son similares a pequeñas **obras de teatro** con lecciones religiosas o morales.

food

plays

En muchos países las personas van a la **iglesia** el 24 de diciembre (Nochebuena), comen con su familia y, a la medianoche, abren los regalos de Navidad. Las celebraciones de Navidad terminan el 6 de enero, el Día de los Reyes Magos. En algunos países los niños reciben regalos de los **Tres Reyes Magos,** y todos comen la famosa **rosca** de reyes.

Rosca de reyes

church

the Three Kings
ring-shaped bread

Comprensión

Decide si las siguientes afirmaciones son ciertas o falsas. Corrige las oraciones falsas. *(Decide whether the following statements are true or false. Correct any false statements.)*

1. En toda Latinoamérica las celebraciones de Navidad inician el 25 de diciembre.
2. Las pastorelas son fiestas en las que las personas cantan villancicos.
3. Es tradicional ir a la iglesia en Nochebuena.
4. En algunos países, los niños reciben regalos el Día de los Reyes Magos.
5. La rosca de reyes es una comida tradicional.

INVESTIGUEMOS LA MÚSICA

"Los peces en el río" is a simple Christmas carol. Find the version by the Gipsy Kings on the Internet and listen to it.

Después de leer

En el Diccionario personal al final del capítulo escribe una lista de 5 palabras en inglés que asocias con Navidad, Jánuca, Kuanza, otra celebración del solsticio invernal o el Año Nuevo. Después, usa un diccionario para saber cómo se dice en español y comparte tu vocabulario nuevo en Share It! y lee las palabras de tus compañeros. *(In the personal dictionary at the end of the chapter, write 5 words in English that you associate with Christmas, Hanukkah, Kwanzaa, another winter solstice celebration or the New Year. After, use a dictionary to look up how to say the words in Spanish and share your new vocabulary words on Share It! and read your classmates' words.)*

En Jánuca, celebramos con la familia.

Redacción

An international student from a Spanish-speaking country is going to attend your university. Write an e-mail to the student explaining what the climate in your area is like, what people often do, and advise him/her as to what clothing he or she will need.

Paso 1 Write down the current season. Then write a list of the types of weather you experience in your area during that time.

Paso 2 Jot down things people do in your area during that time.

Paso 3 Decide whether you are writing to a male or a female student. Then write down a list of clothing items that people wear in your area. Think about what they would wear to school, to go out, and to do any of the activities you wrote down in **Paso 2.**

Paso 4 Start your e-mail by writing the date in Spanish and greeting the student using the expression **Querido(a)** *(Dear).* Remember to use **Querido** if it is a male student and **Querida** if it is a female student.

Paso 5 Begin your first paragraph by introducing yourself to the international student and telling him or her where you study. Then, using the information you generated in **Pasos 1** and **3,** tell him or her what season it is, what the weather is like in your area, and what particular clothing items he/she needs for that climate.

Paso 6 Using the information you generated in **Pasos 2** and **3,** begin a second paragraph and tell him or her what students usually wear to class. Then explain what kinds of activities people do in their free time and any particular clothing items he or she would need.

Paso 7 Conclude your letter with **Hasta pronto** or **Tu nuevo(a) amigo(a).**

Paso 8 Edit your e-mail:

1. Do your sentences use a friendly, inviting, and conversational tone?
2. Are your paragraphs logically organized or do you skip from one idea to the next?
3. Are there any short sentences you can combine by using **y** or **pero**?
4. Are there any spelling errors?
5. Do adjectives agree with the objects they describe?
6. Does each verb agree with its subject?

En vivo

Entrando en materia

¿En qué meses hay muchos anuncios de agencias de viajes?

Un anuncio de una agencia de viajes

Lee el anuncio y contesta las preguntas que siguen.

VUELO+HOTEL | VUELO | HOTELES | CRUCEROS | VACACIONES | DISNEYLAND PARIS

VACACIONES DE SEMANA SANTA

Muy pronto van a comenzar las vacaciones de Semana Santa. ¿Ya tiene usted reservaciones? ¿no? **¡No se preocupe!**[1] En la Agencia de Viajes Araucana tenemos paquetes familiares con todo incluído, **para que usted y su familia disfruten**[2] sus vacaciones. Nuestros precios son **los más bajos**[3] y nuestro servicio es **el mejor**[4]. Usted solo tiene que decidir adónde ir. Tenemos paquetes para destinos nacionales e internacionales para todos los **presupuestos**[5].

Opción 1: El Calafate, Argentina
(4 días/3 noches), desde 300,000 CLP (pesos chilenos)
Incluye:
Pasaje aéreo[6] desde Santiago
Traslados[7]
3 noches de **alojamiento**[8] en el Hotel Alto Calafate, con desayunos
Excursión Parque Nacional Perito Moreno

Opción 2: Viña del Mar, paquete **de lujo**[9]
(4 días/3 noches), desde 150,000 CLP (pesos chilenos)
Incluye:
Autobús desde Santiago
Traslados
3 noches de alojamiento en el Hotel del Mar, con desayunos
Entrada[10] al Casino Viña del Mar y a la discoteca del hotel

Opción 3: Patagonia Chilena (Punta Arenas)
(4 días/3 noches), desde 250,000 CLP (pesos chilenos)
Incluye:
Pasaje aéreo desde Santiago
3 noches de alojamiento en el Hotel Punta Arenas
Excursión de un día completo al Parque Nacional Torres del Paine

Opción 4: Machu Picchu, Perú
(6 días/5 noches), desde 430,000 CLP (pesos chilenos)
Incluye:
Pasaje aéreo Santiago-Cusco-Santiago
Tren a Aguascalientes y autobús a Machu Picchu
3 noches de alojamiento en el Hotel Cusco,
2 noches en el Hotel Machu Picchu
Tenemos descuentos para grupos de 3 personas o más

[1]*Don't worry!* [2]*so that you and your family enjoy* [3]*the lowest* [4]*the best* [5]*budgets*
[6]*airfare* [7]*transfers* [8]*lodging* [9]*luxury* [10]*admittance*

Comprensión

1. ¿Cómo se llama la Agencia de Viajes?
2. ¿A qué lugares *(places)* sugiere viajar la agencia?
3. ¿Cuál es el viaje más barato *(least expensive)*?
4. De los cuatro destinos ¿cuál te gusta más y por qué?

Más allá

Investiga otro destino turístico interesante en Sudamérica. ¿En qué país está? ¿Qué atracciones turísticas hay? ¿Cuántos días recomiendas para visitarlo? ¿En qué mes o estación es mejor ir? Comparte tus recomendaciones en Share It! *(Explore another interesting tourist destination in South America. What country is it in? What attractions are there? How many days do you you recommend visiting? What month or season is best to go? Share your recommendations on Share It!)*

© Left: FXEGS Javier Espuny/Shutterstock; Right: Dan Breckwoldt/Shutterstock

Vocabulario

Sustantivos

el clima	*climate*
el descuento	*discount*
la devolución	*return*
el ecosistema	*ecosystem*
el ecoturismo	*ecotourism*
el medio ambiente	*environment*
la naturaleza	*nature*
el pago	*payment*
la reserva	*reservation*
el seguro	*insurance*
la temporada	*season*

Adjetivos

caluroso(a)	*hot*
diligente	*diligent*
educado(a)	*polite*
húmedo(a)	*humid*
lluvioso(a)	*rainy*
responsable	*responsible*
seco(a)	*dry*

Verbos

averiguar	*to find out*
cobrar	*to charge*
confirmar	*to confirm*
devolver	*to return*
pagar	*to pay*
recorrer	*to go through*

Frases útiles

Tenemos descuento para grupos familiares.
We have family discount plans.

Es temporada alta/baja.
This is high/low season.

¿Me da su número de tarjeta de crédito?
May I have your credit card number?

Este es su número de confirmación.
This is your confirmation number.

© Andresr/Shutterstock

DATOS IMPORTANTES

Educación: Estudios secundarios. Certificación de agente de turismo por escuelas privadas o universidades. Algunas universidades ofrecen licenciatura en viajes y turismo. Se requieren conocimientos *(knowledge)* de computación y se prefieren estudios complementarios en negocios.

Salario: Promedio *(Average)* de $50 000, comisiones de hasta 25% y bonos

Dónde se trabaja: Agencias de viaje, corporaciones, hoteles y oficinas nacionales de turismo

Vocabulario nuevo Completa las oraciones con la palabra apropiada de la lista de vocabulario. *(Complete the sentences with the appropriate vocabulary word from the list.)*

1. Muchos turistas visitan España en el verano porque es _____ alta.
2. Debes tener un paraguas porque España tiene un clima _____.
3. No llueve mucho en esa parte de México porque tiene un clima _____.
4. Costa Rica tiene una gran diversidad de plantas y animales y por eso _____ es muy popular.
5. Si pagas antes de ir, recibes _____ del 10%.

▶ Marcela Díaz, agente de turismo

Marcela Díaz trabaja en una importante agencia de turismo. Vende paquetes de ecoturismo a distintos lugares de Latinoamérica. En el video vas a ver a Marcela preparando un viaje por teléfono para un nuevo cliente. *(Marcela works at an important travel agency. She sells ecotorism packages to different places in Latin America. In the video you are going to see Marcela on the phone planning a trip with a new client.)*

Antes de ver

Muchos vendedores trabajan por comisión y reciben dinero extra por cada venta que hacen. Para ellos, los clientes son muy importantes. Necesitan ser educados y diligentes con ellos. Según tu experiencia si una persona habla con una agente de viajes, ¿qué tipo de preguntas específicas hace? *(Many salespeople work on commission and receive extra money for each sale they make. For them, clients are very important and salespeople must be polite and diligent with them. Based on your experience, what specific questions does the agent ask?)*

Comprensión

1. ¿Qué mira Carlos en la televisión normalmente?
2. ¿Qué país le recomienda Marcela?
3. ¿Qué animal especial vive en El Yunque?
4. ¿Cómo es el clima en Puerto Rico en esa temporada?
5. ¿Qué hacen en Luquillo?
6. ¿Adónde van el último *(last)* día?

Después de ver

En parejas, representen a un agente de viajes y a un cliente que quiere hacer ecoturismo por un país de Latinoamérica. El agente recomienda un lugar de acuerdo con los gustos del cliente. Consideren el clima y hagan recomendaciones de ropa para llevar. *(In pairs, role-play a travel agent and a client that wants to do ecotourism in a Latin American country. The agent should recommend a place according to the client's tastes. Think about the climate and make recommendations of what clothing to wear.)*

3.37 **Un día en el centro** Escoge el verbo apropiado y completa los párrafos con la forma necesaria. *(Choose the appropriate verb and complete the paragraphs with the necessary form.)*

A Teresa le (**1.**) _____ (gusta/gustan) mucho comprar ropa y

(**2.**) _____ (tener/ser) que buscar un vestido porque ella

(**3.**) _____ (abrir/deber) asistir a un evento importante el viernes. Ella

(**4.**) _____ (ir/vivir) a una tienda *(store)* con ropa bonita. A Teresa le

(**5.**) _____ (gusta/gustan) los zapatos y al final compra unos zapatos y

un vestido elegante.

Después de sus compras, Teresa (**6.**) _____ (tener/ser) hambre. Ella y

su amiga van a (**7.**) _____ (comer/beber) en el restaurante Río Grande.

Ellas (**8.**) _____ (correr/creer) que el restaurante (**9.**) _____

(vende/leer) los mejores *(best)* tacos. Las dos chicas (**10.**) _____ (decidir/

recibir) comer tacos y (**11.**) _____ (deber/beber) agua.

3.38 **¿Qué van a hacer?** Di lo que van a hacer estas personas según el tiempo que hace donde viven. Debes usar el futuro (**ir** + **a** + infinitivo). *(Indicate what the following people are going to do according to the weather where they live. You should use the future [**ir** + **a** + infinitive].)*

1. Yo vivo en Antigua y hoy llueve.
2. Carla vive en Santo Domingo y hoy hace buen tiempo.
3. Yago y Matilde viven en Granada y hoy nieva.
4. Zoila y yo vivimos en Tegucigalpa y hoy hace calor.
5. Hugo y Marisabel viven en Caracas y hoy hace mal tiempo.
6. Cándido vive en Asunción y hoy hace mucho frío.
7. Yo vivo en Bogotá y hoy hace fresco.
8. Ulises vive en La Paz y hoy hace viento.
9. Renata y yo vivimos en San Juan y hoy hace sol.
10. ¿Dónde vives tú? ¿Qué tiempo hace? ¿Qué vas a hacer hoy?

3.39 **Explicaciones** Lee las oraciones y usa **gustar** para explicar por qué estas personas no hacen ciertas actividades. *(Read the sentences and then, using the verb* **gustar,** *explain why these people don't do certain activities.)*

Modelo Frank no estudia. → *No le gustan sus clases.*
           Miguel y Ofelia no miran la tele. → *Les gusta leer en la noche.*

1. Yo no como chocolates.
2. Tú no comes en restaurantes.
3. Laura y Ángel no limpian su casa.
4. Tomasa no lleva pantalones cortos.
5. Felipe no recibe muchos mensajes electrónicos.
6. Nuria y yo no estudiamos en la biblioteca.

Exploraciones de repaso: comunicación

3.40 **Descripción de fotos** Escoge una de las fotos y contesta las siguientes preguntas. *(Choose one of the photos and answer the following questions.)*

1. ¿Qué estación es?
2. ¿Qué tiempo hace?
3. ¿Cuál es la relación entre las personas?
4. ¿Qué ropa llevan?
5. ¿Qué hacen? *(What are they doing?)*

Estrategia

Understand before moving on

When did you use this strategy in Chapter 3? Go to Share It! and explain how it helped you.

3.41 **Ocho diferencias** Trabaja con un compañero. Uno mira la ilustración aquí y el otro mira la ilustración en el Apéndice B. Túrnense para describir su ilustración y buscar las ocho diferencias. *(Work with a partner. One of you will look at the illustration on this page and the other will look at the illustration in Appendix B. Take turns describing the illustrations to find the eight differences.)*

3.42 **Mi agenda** Tu compañero y tú tienen que encontrar una hora para estudiar español. *(You and your partner have to find a time to study Spanish.)*

Paso 1 On a piece of paper write down your schedule for the week (Monday through Friday). You should include your classes, work, and other activities.

Paso 2 Work with a partner to find a time to study Spanish together. Using the expression **¿Qué tal...?** *(How about...?)*, take turns asking if a free time will work for the other. Continue until you find a time.

Paso 3 Share with the class the day and time you will study together.

🔊 Vocabulario 1
1-20

La ropa y los accesorios

el abrigo	*coat*
la blusa	*blouse*
los bluyines	*blue jeans*
la bolsa	*purse*
las botas	*boots*
la bufanda	*scarf*
los calcetines	*socks*
la camisa	*shirt*
la camiseta	*T-shirt*
la chaqueta	*jacket*
la corbata	*tie*
la falda	*skirt*
el gorro	*cap*
los guantes	*gloves*
el impermeable	*raincoat*
los lentes	*glasses*
los pantalones	*pants*
los pantalones cortos	*shorts*
el paraguas	*umbrella*
la pijama	*pajamas*
las sandalias	*sandals*
el sombrero	*hat*
el suéter	*sweater*
los tenis	*tennis shoes*
el traje	*suit*
el traje de baño	*swimming suit*
el vestido	*dress*
los zapatos	*shoes*

El tiempo

Está despejado.	*It is clear.*
Está nublado.	*It is cloudy.*
Hace buen tiempo.	*The weather is nice.*
Hace calor.	*It's hot.*
Hace fresco.	*It is cool.*
Hace frío.	*It's cold.*
Hace mal tiempo.	*The weather is bad.*
Hace sol.	*It's sunny.*
Hace viento.	*It is windy.*
Llueve.	*It rains. / It is raining.*
Nieva.	*It snows. / It is snowing.*

Las estaciones

el invierno	*winter*
el otoño	*fall*
la primavera	*spring*
el verano	*summer*

Los verbos

abrir	*to open*
aprender (a + infinitive)	*to learn (to do something)*
asistir (a)	*to attend*
beber	*to drink*
comer	*to eat*
comprender	*to understand*
correr	*to run*
creer	*to believe*
deber	*should, ought to*
decidir	*to decide*
escribir	*to write*
leer	*to read*
recibir (un regalo)	*to receive (a gift)*
vender	*to sell*
vivir	*to live*

Los colores see p. 78

Los colores see p. 78

Expresiones importantes

me gusta	*I like*
te gusta	*you like*
le gusta	*he/she likes*
nos gusta	*we like*
os gusta	*you (plural) like (Spain)*
les gusta	*they, you (plural) like*

Palabras adicionales

cómodo(a)	*comfortable*
llevar	*to wear, to carry; to take*
llevar puesto(a)	*to be wearing*

🔊 Vocabulario 2

Los días de la semana

el lunes	*Monday*		el viernes	*Friday*
el martes	*Tuesday*		el sábado	*Saturday*
el miércoles	*Wednesday*		el domingo	*Sunday*
el jueves	*Thursday*			

Los meses

enero	*January*		julio	*July*
febrero	*February*		agosto	*August*
marzo	*March*		septiembre	*September*
abril	*April*		octubre	*October*
mayo	*May*		noviembre	*November*
junio	*June*		diciembre	*December*

Los verbos

ir	*to go*		terminar	*to finish*

Palabras adicionales

ahora	*now*		la medianoche	*midnight*
el Año Nuevo	*New Year*		el mediodía	*noon*
el cumpleaños	*birthday*		Navidad	*Christmas*
el día	*day*		la semana	*week*
el día feriado	*holiday*		por la mañana /	*in the morning*
la fecha	*date*		tarde / noche	*/ afternoon /*
el fin de semana	*weekend*			*evening*
hoy	*today*		todos los días	*every day*
mañana	*tomorrow*			

Diccionario personal

_____

_____

_____

_____

_____

_____

_____

Learning Strategy

Participate

Participate in class. You cannot learn another language simply by observing. You must be willing to use the language actively, and to learn from the mistakes you make.

In this chapter you will learn how to:

- Describe your town or city
- Describe your home
- Tell where things are located
- Request information about the cost of things
- Use question words to ask for specific information

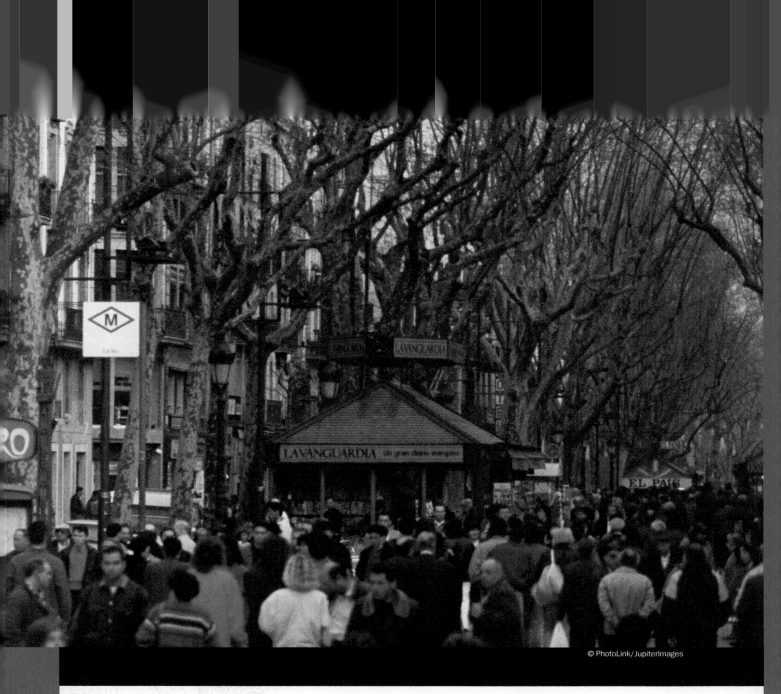

© PhotoLink/JupiterImages

El señor Ramírez tiene media hora para ir al banco y hacer otras diligencias *(errands)*. ¿Qué más puede hacer en el centro de la ciudad?

Otros lugares	Other places			Los verbos	
el aeropuerto	*airport*	**el negocio**	*business*	**depositar dinero**	*to deposit money*
el bar	*bar*	**la oficina**	*office*	**mandar una carta /**	*to send a letter /*
el café	*cafe*	**la playa**	*beach*	**un paquete**	*a package*
el club	*club*	**el templo**	*temple*	**mirar una película**	*to watch a movie*
el edificio	*building*	**el zoológico**	*zoo*	**rezar**	*to pray*
el mercado	*market*				

INVESTIGUEMOS EL VOCABULARIO

The suffix **-ería** is often used to indicate stores where certain products are sold. What is sold in the following stores?

chocolatería   **frutería**   **papelería**   **tortillería**

INVESTIGUEMOS EL VOCABULARIO

In the Spanish-speaking world, there are variations in the words that describe places to shop. For example, a department store could be referred to as **el almacén** or **la tienda de departamentos.** A supermarket could be **la bodega, el supermercado,** or **la tienda de autoservicio.**

A practicar

4.1 **Escucha y responde** Vas a escuchar una lista de lugares. Indica con el pulgar hacia arriba si es posible comprar un producto en el lugar. Si no es posible, indica con el pulgar hacia abajo.

1-22

4.2 **¿Cierto o falso?** Decide si las oraciones son ciertas o falsas. Corrige las oraciones falsas.

1. En la playa compramos ropa.
2. En la discoteca miramos animales.
3. Nadamos en la piscina.
4. Miramos películas en el cine.

5. En el parque compramos medicinas.
6. Estudiamos y aprendemos en la tienda.
7. En la plaza rezamos.
8. Mandamos cartas en el banco.

4.3 **¿Con qué frecuencia... ?** Para cada actividad, habla con un compañero diferente y pregúntale con qué frecuencia hace la actividad.

Modelo ir a la playa
    Estudiante 1: *¿Con qué frecuencia vas a la playa?*
    Estudiante 2: *Voy a la playa una vez al año.*

1. comprar comida en el mercado
2. rezar en el templo
3. caminar en el parque
4. mirar películas en el cine

5. enviar cartas en el correo
6. depositar cheques en el banco
7. ir al zoológico
8. bailar en una discoteca

> **INVESTIGUEMOS EL VOCABULARIO**
>
> When saying how often you do something, use the word **vez.**
>
> **una vez a la semana**
> *once a week*
>
> **dos veces al mes**
> *two times a month*
>
> To say you never do something, use the word **nunca** in front of the conjugated verb.
>
> Yo **nunca** voy al museo.
> *I **never** go to the museum.*

4.4 **Conversemos** Entrevista a tu compañero. Túrnense con las siguientes preguntas.

1. ¿Cuál es tu supermercado favorito?
2. ¿Hay un banco cerca de *(nearby)* tu casa? ¿Cómo se llama?
3. ¿Te gusta ir al cine?
4. ¿Cuál es tu restaurante favorito?
5. ¿En qué tienda prefieres comprar tu ropa?
6. ¿Adónde prefieres ir con tus amigos?
7. ¿Te gusta ir a museos? ¿Cómo se llama tu museo favorito?
8. ¿Te gusta ir al parque? ¿Por qué?

Estrategia

Participate in class.

The activities on this page offer many opportunities to use Spanish actively in class and to learn from your mistakes instead of worrying about making one.

4.5 **Planes para el fin de semana** Trabaja con un compañero. para descubrir cuáles son las actividades de Jazmín, Lila y Arturo durante el fin de semana y dónde las hacen. Uno de ustedes va a ver la información en esta página, y el otro va a ver la información en el **Apéndice B.**

Modelo Estudiante 1: *¿Qué hace Jazmín el sábado por la mañana?*
    Estudiante 2: *Jazmín compra fruta.*
    Estudiante 1: *¿Dónde compra fruta?*
    Estudiante 2: *En el mercado.*

	Jazmín	Lila	Arturo
sábado por la mañana	comprar fruta (mercado)		rezar (la sinagoga)
sábado por la tarde		comprar ropa (el centro comercial)	
sábado por la noche			mirar una película (el cine)
domingo por la mañana	nadar (la playa)	visitar a un amigo (el hospital)	

Conexiones culturales
Ciudades fuera de lo común

Cultura

Las grandes ciudades del mundo generalmente tienen museos muy importantes. Dos museos de fama internacional son El Prado en Madrid, España, y el Museo del Oro *(Gold)* en Bogotá, Colombia. El Museo del Prado tiene una de las colecciones de arte más importantes del mundo, especialmente de pintores europeos de los siglos *(centuries)* XVI al XIX. El Museo del Oro tiene una colección impresionante de artículos prehispánicos hechos de *(made of)* oro y otros metales, con instalaciones modernas y exposiciones con multimedia.

© Pat_Hastings/Shutterstock

Courtesy of Margarita Casas

¿De qué artistas crees que hay cuadros en El Prado?
¿Qué civilizaciones prehispánicas crees que están representadas en el Museo del Oro?
¿Qué otros museos de todo el mundo son muy famosos y por qué?

 Busca los nombres de artistas españoles y colombianos en **Exploraciones del mundo hispano** en el **Apéndice A.**

Investiga en Internet los sitios web oficiales del Museo del Prado y del Museo del Oro. Identifica una obra que te guste de uno de los museos. Sube *(Upload)* a Share It! la obra que te gusta y comparte *(share)* el nombre del artista y de la obra.

Comunidad

Busca a una persona de un país donde se habla español y haz una entrevista con las siguientes preguntas: **¿Dónde compras comida generalmente? ¿Dónde prefieres comprar ropa? ¿Son diferentes las tiendas en tu país?** Repórtale la información a la clase.

© Claudiu Marius Pascalina/Dreamstime.com

Comparacio...

Las ciudades pequeñas ...ntes a las grandes ciudades no solo por su tamaño (size). Observa el ma... una pequeña ciudad al lado del lago Titicaca, en Perú. ¿Hay algún edifi...bes...n tu ciudad? ¿Cuál? ¿Cuáles son los lugares turísticos principales? Si llegas a...bes caminar mucho para ver los lugares de interés?

AEROPUERTO A JULIACA

PUNO

Jr. Ilave 06
Lemus
Tarapaca
Jr. Avacucho 12 16
Jr. Cajamarca
Jr. Puno
Jr. Arequipa
Jr. Libertad
Jr. Alfonso Ugarte
Jr. Oquendo
09
Jr. Deza
Jr. Pardo
Jr. Independencia
05
03
19
10
17
Jr. Lampa
Santuario Dos de Mayo
Av. La Torre
Tren al Cusco y Arequipa
Av. Los Incas
Urb. San Juan
Jr. Deustua
Jr. Tacna
Jr. Melgar
15
Jr. Moquegua
Jr. Tacna
Av. Titicaca
Av. Pineda Arce
14
Av. Los Incas
Jr. Arequipa
Av. El Sol
Av. Simón Bolívar
Parque Ramón Castilla
Jr. El Sol
Jr. Carabaya
Av. Simón Bolívar
...Cultura
...Popular
...onde de Lemos
Hospital Regional Manuel Nuñes Butron 04
Av. Acota
Jr. Tacna
18
LAGO TITICACA
Islas flotantes de los Uros.
Puerto Lacustre
Salida a la Frontera (Yunguyo - Desaguadero)
Av. Echenique
...kacota
Isla Taquile

© Cengage Learning

Conexiones... a las relaciones internacionales

Muchas ciudades del mundo participan en un programa de ciudades hermanas. La Asociación Internacional de Ciudades Hermanas es una organización que promueve el respeto mutuo, la comprensión y la cooperación. Por ejemplo, Miami, Florida, es ciudad hermana de Managua, Nicaragua. El objetivo del programa es conectar a dos ciudades semejantes *(similar)* en superficie que están en diferentes zonas del mundo para fomentar *(to encourage)* el contacto humano. ¿Cuál es la ciudad hermana de la capital de tu estado? ¿Qué actividades y eventos tienen?

Image Source/Getty Images

Managua, la capital de Nicaragua, es ciudad hermana de Miami.

A analizar

Nicolás y Santiago hablan de sus planes. Después de ver el video, lee parte de su conversación y observa las formas del verbo **poder.**

> Nicolás: ¿**Puedes** ir conmigo? Como está cerca del restaurante cubano, **podemos** comer después.
>
> Santiago: Uy, me gustaría, pero no **puedo.** Tengo que ir a la biblioteca ahora. Voy a estudiar con Paula para el examen de ciencias políticas.

1. Using your knowledge of verb conjugation and the forms in the conversation, complete the chart with the correct forms of the verb **poder.**

   poder

   yo _____   nosotros(as) _____

   tú _____   vosotros (as) podéis

   él, ella, usted _____   ellos, ellas, ustedes _____

2. Now look at the conjugated forms of **poder** above. Which forms have a stem (the first part of the verb) that is different from the infinitive? How do they change?

A comprobar

Stem-changing verbs (o → ue)

1. There are a number of verbs that have changes in the root or stem. They are called stem-changing verbs. Notice in the verbs below, that the **o** changes to **ue** in all forms except the **nosotros** and **vosotros** forms. The endings are the same as other -**ar**, -**er**, and -**ir** verbs.

almorzar *(to eat lunch)*

yo	alm**ue**rzo	nosotros(as)	almorzamos
tú	alm**ue**rzas	vosotros(as)	almorzáis
él, ella, usted	alm**ue**rza	ellos, ellas, ustedes	alm**ue**rzan

volver *(to return)*

yo	**vue**lvo	nosotros(as)	volvemos
tú	**vue**lves	vosotros(as)	volvéis
él, ella, usted	**vue**lve	ellos, ellas, ustedes	**vue**lven

dormir *(to sleep)*

yo	**due**rmo	nosotros(as)	dormimos
tú	**due**rmes	vosotros(as)	dormís
él, ella, usted	**due**rme	ellos, ellas, ustedes	**due**rmen

Los niños **duermen** en este dormitorio.
*The children **sleep** in this bedroom.*

Gloria y yo **almorzamos** en la cafetería.
*Gloria and I **eat lunch** in the cafeteria.*

The verbs listed below are also **o → ue** stem-changing verbs.

costar	to cost
devolver	to return (something)
encontrar	to find
llover	to rain
morir	to die
poder	to be able to
recordar	to remember
soñar (con)	to dream (about)

2. The verb **jugar** is conjugated similarly to the **o → ue** stem-changing verbs, changing the **u** of its stem to **ue**.

jugar *(to play)*

yo	**jue**go	nosotros(as)	jugamos
tú	**jue**gas	vosotros(as)	jugáis
él, ella, usted	**jue**ga	ellos, ellas, ustedes	**jue**gan

A practicar

4.6 **Un poco de lógica** ¿Qué verbo completa mejor la oración?

1. Matilde siempre _____ a la casa después de trabajar.
   a. llueve   **b.** vuelve   **c.** almuerza

2. Los niños _____ con el perro en el parque.
   a. juegan   **b.** sueñan   **c.** encuentran

3. Nosotros _____ en el café.
   a. dormimos   **b.** volvemos   **c.** almorzamos

4. Renata no _____ un vestido bonito en la tienda.
   a. sueña   **b.** encuentra   **c.** vuelve

5. Mis amigos _____ mirar una película en el cine.
   a. juegan   **b.** cuestan   **c.** pueden

6. Mi esposo y yo _____ en un hotel en Montevideo.
   a. dormimos   **b.** podemos   **c.** encontramos

7. Yo _____ el libro a la biblioteca.
   a. encuentro   **b.** vuelvo   **c.** devuelvo

8. La ciudad es confusa y no _____ dónde está el hotel.
   a. recuerdo   **b.** puedo   **c.** duermo

La ciudad es confusa.

Peter Bernik/Shutterstock

4.7 **Nuestros sueños** Completa el siguiente párrafo con las formas necesarias del verbo **soñar**.

Todos tienen sueños *(dreams)* para el año nuevo. Yo (1) _____ con un trabajo y mi esposo (2) _____ con comprar un auto nuevo. Nosotros también (3) _____ con comprar una casa nueva. Mis hermanos (4) _____ con unas vacaciones en la playa. Y tú ¿con qué (5) _____?

¿Sueñas con comprar un auto?

© Monkey Business Images/Shutterstock

4.8 **¿Cuánto cuesta?** Estás en una tienda de ropa en España. Con un compañero, túrnense para preguntar cuánto cuestan los objetos.

> **Modelo** Estudiante 1: *¿Cuánto cuesta el sombrero negro?*
> Estudiante 2: *Cuesta treinta y cinco euros.*

1.

2.

3.

4.

© Cengage Learning

4.9 **¿Quién puede?** Usando el verbo **poder,** explícale a tu compañero quién puede o no puede hacer las siguientes actividades.

> **Modelo** viajar este verano
> *Yo puedo viajar este verano.*
> *Mi esposo no puede viajar este verano.*

1. tocar el piano
2. bailar bien
3. jugar al golf

4. hablar francés
5. nadar
6. ir a bares

7. votar *(to vote)*
8. comer mucho
9. cocinar bien

4.10 **En busca de...** Busca a ocho compañeros diferentes que hagan una de las siguientes actividades.

1. Normalmente (dormir) ocho horas.
2. (Volver) a casa después de las clases.
3. (Almorzar) en un restaurante una vez a la semana.
4. (Jugar) al tenis.
5. (Soñar) con un auto nuevo.
6. (Poder) cantar muy bien.
7. (Devolver) ropa a la tienda con frecuencia.
8. (Encontrar) a amigos en el cine.

> **INVESTIGUEMOS LA MÚSICA**
>
> Rakim y Ken-Y es un grupo de reggaetón de Puerto Rico. Escucha su éxito "Un sueño" en Internet. ¿Cuál es el sueño del que hablan?

A analizar ▶

Santiago le explica a Nicolás dónde está el correo. Mira el video otra vez. Después lee parte de su conversación y observa las formas del verbo **estar.**

Nicolás: ¡Hola Santiago! ¿Cómo **estás**?

Santiago: **Estoy** muy bien, ¿y tú?

Nicolás: Bien, pero no sé dónde **está** el correo y tengo que mandar este paquete a mis padres.

Santiago: No **está** muy lejos. Mira, **estamos** en la calle San Pedro y el correo **está** en la calle Santa Rosa, enfrente del restaurante cubano.

1. You learned some of the forms of the verb **estar** in **Capítulo 1.** The boldfaced verbs are also forms of the verb **estar.** From what you have already learned and by looking at the examples above, fill in the following chart.

estar

yo _____   nosotros(as) _____

tú _____   vosotros(as) _____

él, ella, usted _____   ellos, ellas, ustedes _____

2. **Estar** is used in the conversation for two different purposes. Can you identify them?

A comprobar

The verb **estar** with prepositions of place

Las preposiciones de posición

a la derecha de	to the right of	**dentro de**	inside	**enfrente de**	in front of, facing
a la izquierda de	to the left of	**detrás de**	behind	**entre**	between
al lado de	beside, next to	**en**	in, on, at	**fuera de**	outside
cerca de	near	**encima de**	on top of	**lejos de**	far from
debajo de	below				

1. Notice that most of the prepositions include the word **de** (of).

You will remember from **Capítulo 2** that the **de** in front of a masculine noun combines with **el** to become **del (de + el = del),** and that it does not contract with the other articles.

Mi casa está al lado **del** café.
My house is next to the café.

El cine está a la derecha **de** la tienda.
The movie theater is to the right of the store.

2. The verb **estar** is used to express position; therefore, it is used with all prepositions of place.

estar *(to be)*

yo	estoy	nosotros(as)	estamos
tú	estás	vosotros(as)	estáis
él, ella, usted	está	ellos, ellas, ustedes	están

A practicar

4.11 **Actividades en la ciudad** Lee las oraciones. ¿Qué actividades pueden hacer (do) las personas en el lugar donde están?

1. Yo estoy en la plaza.

2. Mis hijos están en la escuela.

3. Tú estás en el aeropuerto.

4. Mi esposa está en la oficina.

5. Mis amigos están en el café.

6. Mi hermano está en el correo.

7. Mi madre y yo estamos en el parque.

8. Tú estás en el banco.

4.12 **En la capital** Completa las oraciones con la forma necesaria del verbo **estar**. Luego identifica los países donde están las ciudades.

Modelo   Mario ____está____ en Santiago. *Está en Chile.*

1. Yo _____ en Lima.

2. Usted _____ en San José.

3. Gloria y yo _____ en La Habana.

4. Joaquín y Héctor _____ en San Juan.

5. Hugo _____ en Caracas.

6. Tú _____ en Tegucigalpa.

7. Cristina _____ en Quito.

8. Los Gardel _____ en Buenos Aires.

4.13 **¿Dónde están?** Usa la forma apropiada del verbo **estar** y el vocabulario para explicar dónde están las diferentes personas. Luego explica qué hacen (they do) allí.

Modelo   los niños
   Los niños están en el zoológico. Miran los animales.

1. Ricardo

2. mis amigos

3. la señora Montero

4. mis amigos y yo

5. tú

6. tu perro y tú

© Cengage Learning

4.14 **En la ciudad** Mira el plano, escucha la descripción de la ciudad y decide si cada oración es cierta o falsa. Corrige las oraciones falsas.

1-23

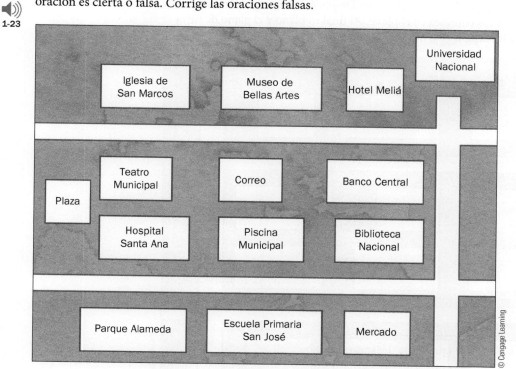

Iglesia de San Marcos
Museo de Bellas Artes
Hotel Meliá
Universidad Nacional

Plaza
Teatro Municipal
Correo
Banco Central

Hospital Santa Ana
Piscina Municipal
Biblioteca Nacional

Parque Alameda
Escuela Primaria San José
Mercado

© Cengage Learning

4.15 **El plano** En parejas inventen tres oraciones más sobre el plano. Las oraciones pueden ser ciertas o falsas y deben incluir las preposiciones. Después van a leer las oraciones para la clase y los otros compañeros van a decidir si son ciertas o falsas.

4.16 **¿Dónde está... ?** En parejas túrnense para hacer y contestar preguntas sobre el dibujo. Usen todas las preposiciones posibles para cada pregunta.

Modelo el café

Estudiante 1: *¿Dónde está el café?*
Estudiante 2: *El café está al lado de la librería.*

1. el banco	**3.** el automóvil	**5.** el gimnasio	**7.** el parque
2. la librería	**4.** la bicicleta	**6.** el perro	**8.** la tienda

BANCO · FARMACIA · TIENDA · Café · Librería Libertad · Gimnasio Musculoso

© Cengage Learning

4.17 **Creando una ciudad** Con un compañero túrnense para decidir dónde están los edificios en la ciudad en el plano *(city map)* abajo. Después de describir dónde están, escriban los nombres de los edificios en el plano. Al final tu plano y el plano de tu compañero deben ser idénticos.

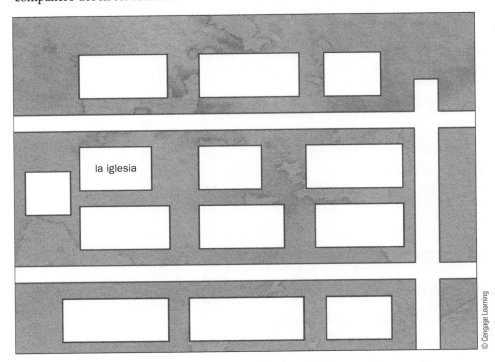

la iglesia

4.18 **¿Es cierto?** En parejas túrnense para hacer oraciones ciertas o falsas sobre las posiciones de los edificios, los coches y la piscina en la ilustración. El otro estudiante debe decidir si la afirmación es cierta y corregir las afirmaciones falsas.

Modelo Estudiante 1: *Hay un coche detrás del banco.*
Estudiante 2: *Falso, está enfrente del banco.*

Entrando en materia

¿Adónde te gusta ir en la ciudad o pueblo donde vives?

Turismo local en Ecuador

◀)) Escucha el reportaje *(news report)* sobre los esfuerzos *(efforts)* para promover el turismo
1-24 local en Ecuador.

Vocabulario útil

la comida	*food*	**los eventos**	*events*
compartir	*to share*	**las noticias**	*news*
disfrutar	*to enjoy*	**el portal**	*web page*

Comprensión

Decide si las afirmaciones son ciertas o falsas. Corrige las oraciones falsas.

1. Según las noticias, a muchos habitantes de Quito les gusta pasar tiempo en las calles de la ciudad.
2. La Compañía de Turismo de Ecuador tiene un nuevo portal en Internet.
3. En el portal las personas pueden compartir recomendaciones.
4. El fin de semana hay un concierto en el cine frente a la plaza principal.
5. El locutor *(announcer)* piensa que el portal es una mala idea.

© Naamfein/Dreamstime.com

Más allá

Escribe una reseña *(review)* de un lugar que te gusta visitar en tu ciudad. ¿Qué tipo de lugar es? ¿Cómo se llama? ¿Dónde está? ¿Por qué es bueno?

Comparte tu reseña en Share It! y, si es posible, incluye fotos. Luego lee las recomendaciones de los otros estudiantes.

Antes de leer

¿Qué cosas hay en todas las grandes ciudades? ¿Cómo imaginas que son las capitales de España y los países latinoamericanos?

A leer

Algunas ciudades únicas de Latinoamérica

were / before

La mayoría de las grandes ciudades latinoamericanas combina lo moderno con lo histórico. Algunas de las ciudades **fueron** fundadas mucho **antes** de la llegada de los españoles, como es el caso de Cuzco, la capital del imperio Inca en Perú, y de la Ciudad de México, fundada por los aztecas con el nombre de Tenochtitlán. Hoy día en las dos ciudades se pueden ver ruinas de civilizaciones indígenas al lado de edificios coloniales de hasta 400 años de antigüedad. Por supuesto, en España y Latinoamérica también hay muchas ciudades modernas, con **rascacielos** y otras maravillas de la ingeniería, como **puentes** y avenidas de circulación rápida.

skyscrapers
bridges

> [Un elegante ejemplo de modernidad se encuentra en Buenos Aires...]

as

was

subdivisions

Un elegante ejemplo de modernidad se encuentra en Buenos Aires, la capital de Argentina y su ciudad más importante. Con más de doce millones de habitantes. "Baires", **como** la llaman los argentinos, **fue** fundada en 1536 con el nombre original de "Puerto de Nuestra Señora Santa María del Buen Aire". Los **barrios** de la ciudad reflejan su pasado de inmigrantes. Es una ciudad cosmopolita y llena de cultura. Es famosa por sus monumentos, como

Puerto Madero, en Buenos Aires

el Obelisco, y por tener la avenida **más ancha** del mundo: la Avenida 9 de julio.

widest

Otra ciudad moderna y de **hermosa** arquitectura es Bogotá. La ciudad de Bogotá es la capital de Colombia y en 2006 fue declarada "capital del libro del mundo" por la UNESCO, gracias a las increíbles bibliotecas de la ciudad.

beautiful

La ciudad de Bogotá

Cada una de estas ciudades es especial por su arquitectura, sus monumentos, parques, restaurantes, cafés, tiendas y boutiques. Sin duda, como muchas otras ciudades latinoamericanas, son muy atractivas para el turismo.

Comprensión

Contesta las preguntas.

1. ¿Qué combinan muchas de las ciudades de Latinoamérica?
2. ¿Cómo se llamaba la capital del imperio Inca en Perú?
3. ¿Cómo llaman los argentinos a su capital?
4. ¿Por qué es famosa Buenos Aires?
5. ¿Por qué fue declarada "la capital del libro del mundo" Bogotá?

Después de leer

Busca una página en Internet con información para turistas en una ciudad de España o Latinoamérica. Después contesta las preguntas.

1. ¿Qué actividades puedes hacer?
2. ¿Te gustaría visitar la ciudad? ¿Por qué?

La ciudad de Cuenca, en Ecuador, es famosa por sus iglesias.

Esta es la casa de Lola. ¿Qué hay en su casa?

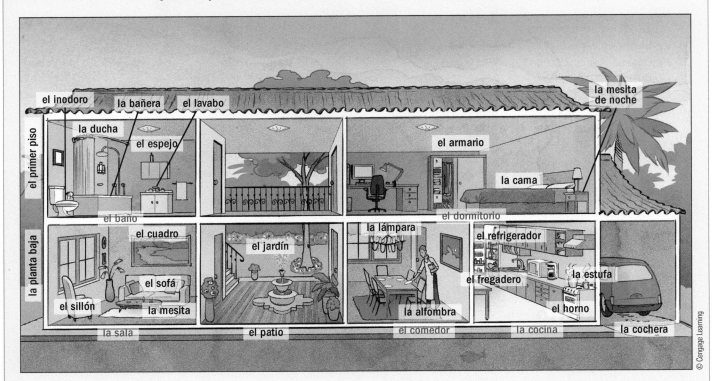

el inodoro · la bañera · el lavabo · la mesita de noche · la ducha · el espejo · el primer piso · el armario · la cama · el baño · el dormitorio · la planta baja · el cuadro · la lámpara · el refrigerador · el jardín · el sofá · el fregadero · la estufa · el sillón · la mesita · la alfombra · el horno · la sala · el patio · el comedor · la cocina · la cochera

© Cengage Learning

alquilar	to rent	el (horno de) microondas	microwave (oven)
el apartamento	apartment	la lavadora	washer
la cafetera	coffee maker	el lavaplatos	dishwasher
las cortinas	curtains	los muebles	furniture
la dirección	address	las plantas	plants
el electrodoméstico	appliance	la secadora	dryer
la flor	flower		
la habitación	room		

INVESTIGUEMOS LA GRAMÁTICA

You learned in **Capítulo 2** that adjectives that express quantity, such as **mucho, poco,** and **varios,** are placed in front of the noun they describe. **Primero** is another adjective that precedes nouns. Notice that in the masculine singular form it becomes **primer** when in front of a noun.

Mi dormitorio está en el **primer** piso.
*My bedroom is on the **first** floor.*

Es la **primera** casa en la calle.
*It is the **first** house on the street.*

INVESTIGUEMOS EL VOCABULARIO

Notice that **el primer piso** refers to what people in the United States would call the second floor. In many Spanish-speaking countries the first floor is referred to as the ground floor, or **la planta baja.**

A practicar

4.19 **Escucha y responde** Vas a escuchar algunas oraciones. Indica con el pulgar hacia arriba si la oración es lógica. Si no es lógica, indica con el pulgar hacia abajo.

CD 1-25

4.20 **¿Dónde están?** ¿En qué habitación de la casa están los siguientes muebles o aparatos?

1. el horno
2. el sillón
3. el lavabo
4. el lavaplatos
5. el armario
6. la cafetera
7. la mesita de noche
8. la cama
9. el inodoro

4.21 **¡Qué desastre!** La casa es un desastre y no puedes encontrar nada. Con un compañero, túrnense para preguntar dónde están los objetos perdidos *(lost)*.

Modelo la corbata
Estudiante 1: *¿Dónde está la corbata?*
Estudiante 2: *Está encima de la cama.*

1. el teléfono
2. el libro
3. la bota
4. el suéter

5. el paraguas
6. el cuaderno
7. los peces
8. el gato

> **INVESTIGUEMOS EL VOCABULARIO**
>
> While **el dormitorio** is a standard word for *bedroom*, there are many other terms:
>
> **el cuarto** (Latin America)
> **la habitación** (Mexico, Spain)
> **la pieza** (Mexico, Chile)
> **la alcoba** (South America)
> **la recámara** (Latin America)
>
> **La sala** is the most commonly used term for *living room*, but in Argentina and Chile it is called **el living**. In other countries it is called **el recibidor** or **el cuarto de estar**.
>
> A refrigerator is **la nevera** or **la heladera** in South America but **el frigorífico** in Spain.

4.22 **Adivinanza** Mira el dibujo al inicio de la lección. Vas a elegir y a describir tres objetos en dos o tres oraciones. No debes mencionar el objeto en tu descripción. Usa **es para** para describir la función del aparato. Con un compañero túrnense para adivinar el objeto que el otro describe.

Modelo Estudiante 1: *Está en la cocina. Está debajo de la estufa. Es para cocinar.*
Estudiante 2: *¡Es el horno!*

4.23 **Comparemos** Trabaja con un compañero. Uno de ustedes mira la casa en esta página mientras el otro mira la casa en el **Apéndice B.** Túrnense para describir las casas y busquen las seis diferencias.

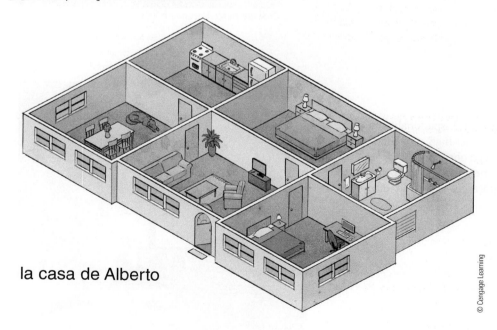

la casa de Alberto

Cultura

Entre las atracciones turísticas de cada ciudad, es común que haya alguna casa en donde vivió *(lived)* una persona destacada para la historia o la cultura de ese país. Muchas de las casas de personas famosas son transformadas en *(are converted into)* museos. Por ejemplo, Pablo Neruda, el famoso poeta de Chile, tuvo casas en Santiago de Chile, en Valparaíso y en Isla Negra. Hoy en día todas sus casas son museos que se pueden visitar. En ellas hay muchas obras de arte y objetos que pertenecieron a *(belonged to)* Neruda.

Otra casa muy visitada es la de Ernesto "Ché" Guevara, famoso revolucionario que participó en la Revolución Cubana. Al igual que Neruda el Che vivió en varias casas que ahora lo homenajean *(pay tribute to him)*. Una de las más populares es el Museo Casa del Ché en Alta Gracia, Argentina donde vivió de niño *(as a child)*.

La siguiente es una lista de otras casas de personas famosas. Busca en Internet para decir quiénes fueron *(were)* estas personas y dónde están sus casas.

La Casa-Museo de Federico García Lorca

El Museo Casa natal de Rubén Darío

La Casa-Museo Quinta de Simón Bolívar

 Busca a un escritor colombiano en **Exploraciones del mundo hispano** en el **Apéndice A** y después investiga si tiene una casa-museo.

Casa de Pablo Neruda en Valparaíso

Comunidad

Entrevista a una persona de un país hispanohablante acerca de su casa. ¿Qué habitaciones hay? ¿Qué hay en las habitaciones? Toma notas y luego observa qué variaciones léxicas de la página 129 usa la persona que entrevistas. ¿Notas otras variaciones? Repórtale a la clase la información más relevante.

Casa de Ernesto Guevara

Comparaciones

Una expresión común en la cultura hispana es una que se usa para dar la bienvenida a un visitante: "Está usted en su casa", o "Mi casa es su casa". Hay muchas expresiones en español que hablan de la casa. Otro ejemplo es "Candil (*lamp*) de la calle, obscuridad de su casa", una expresión que se usa para hablar de una persona que es muy amable con las personas fuera de su casa, pero no con las de su familia. Los siguientes son otros refranes (*proverbs*) que se refieren a la casa. ¿Cuál de las fotos asocias con cada refrán? ¿Por qué? ¿Qué valores reflejan? ¿Estás de acuerdo con ellos? ¿Hay equivalentes en inglés?

Casa sin hijos, higuera (*fig tree*) sin higos (*figs*).

Cuando de casa estamos lejanos, más la recordamos.

En la casa en que hay un viejo, no faltará (*lack*) un buen consejo (*advice*).

La ropa sucia (*dirty*) se lava en casa.

¿Cuáles son algunos refranes en inglés que hablan de la casa? ¿Qué valores reflejan? ¿Reflejan valores semejantes o diferentes a los refranes en español?

Conexiones... a la arquitectura

Algunos de los arquitectos más famosos del mundo son españoles. Un ejemplo histórico es el de Antonio Gaudí (1852–1926) y un ejemplo moderno es el de Santiago Calatrava (1951– ...). Gaudí era un hombre muy sencillo y religioso. Su obra maestra (*masterpiece*) es la Catedral de la Sagrada Familia, en Barcelona, que todavía está en construcción. Su arquitectura es considerada modernista, pero su estilo es único en el mundo. Por otra parte está Santiago Calatrava. Aunque no es arquitecto sino (*but*) ingeniero, sus edificios se caracterizan por conjuntar (*bring together*) la ingeniería y la arquitectura. Calatrava es particularmente famoso por sus puentes (*bridges*), estaciones de trenes y estadios. ¿Qué estilo prefieres? ¿Tienes un arquitecto o un estilo arquitectónico favorito? ¿Quién o cuál?

Casa Milá en Barcelona, una obra de Gaudí

Museo diseñado por Santiago Calatrava, Valencia, España

A analizar ▶

Santiago habla con una señora sobre un apartamento que ella desea alquilarle. Después de ver el video, lee parte de su conversación y contesta las preguntas que siguen.

Santiago:	¿Cómo es el apartamento?
Señora:	Bueno, la sala es bonita y muy grande. Hay un dormitorio con una cama matrimonial y un escritorio donde puede estudiar. También hay una cocina pequeña y un cuarto de baño con ducha y lavabo.
Santiago:	¿Qué electrodomésticos hay en la cocina?
Señora:	Hay una estufa, un refrigerador y una lavadora.
Santiago:	¿Cuánto cuesta al mes?
Señora:	$750 e incluye el gas pero no el agua.
Santiago:	Y ¿cuál es la dirección?
Señora:	Está en la calle 8, número 53, cerca del hospital.

© Cengage Learning

1. Punctuation for questions is different in Spanish and English. What is the difference?
2. Identify the interrogatives (question words) in the conversation. What do all of the question words have in common?

A comprobar

Interrogatives

¿cómo?	how?	¿adónde?	to where?	¿quién(es)?	who?	¿cuántos(as)?	how many?
¿cuándo?	when?	¿de dónde?	from where?	¿qué?	what?	¿cuánto(a)?	how much?
¿dónde?	where?	¿por qué?	why?	¿cuál(es)?	which?		

*Notice that all question words have an accent.

1. In most questions:
   - the subject is placed after the verb.
   - the question word is often the first word of the question.
   - it is not necessary to have a helping word such as *do* or *does.*
   - it is necessary to have an inverted question mark at the beginning of the question and another question mark at the end.

interrogative + verb + subject		
¿Cuál	es	tu casa?
¿Dónde	vives	tú?

2. Prepositions (**a, con, de, en, por, para,** etc.) cannot be placed at the end of the question as is often done in English. They *must* be in front of the question word.

   ¿Con quién vives?
   Who (Whom) do you live with?

3. **Quién** and **cuál** must agree in number with the noun that follows, and **cuánto** and **cuántos** must agree in gender.

   ¿Cuántas habitaciones tiene la casa?
   How many rooms does the house have?

   ¿Quiénes son tus compañeros de casa?
   Who are your roommates?

4. There are two ways to express *What?* or *Which?*

When asking *which*, use **qué** in front of a noun and **cuál** in front of a verb or with the preposition **de**.

> **¿Qué** electrodomésticos necesitas?
> *What (Which) appliances do you need?*

> **¿Cuáles** son sus camas?
> *Which (ones) are their beds?*

> **¿Cuál** de estos apartamentos te gusta?
> *Which of these apartments do you like?*

When asking *what*, use **cuál** with the verb **ser** with the exception of the question **¿Qué es?** *(What is it?)*. Use **qué** with all other verbs.

> **¿Cuál** es tu número de teléfono?
> *What is your phone number?*

> **¿Qué** buscas en la sala?
> *What are you looking for in the living room?*

A practicar

4.24 **La respuesta lógica** Lee las preguntas y decide cuál es la respuesta más lógica.

1. _____ ¿Cómo es la casa?
2. _____ ¿Cuántos baños hay?
3. _____ ¿Dónde está la casa?
4. _____ ¿Qué hay en la cocina?
5. _____ ¿Quién vive en la casa ahora?
6. _____ ¿Por qué venden la casa?

    a. Uno.
    b. Hay una estufa y un refrigerador.
    c. Ella tiene un nuevo trabajo en otra ciudad.
    d. Es pequeña, pero muy cómoda.
    e. Una madre con sus dos hijos.
    f. Está en el centro.

4.25 **¿Qué o cuál?** Decide si debes usar **¿Qué?** o **¿Cuál(es)?** para completar las preguntas.

1. ¿_____ dormitorio te gusta más?
2. ¿En _____ calle está el apartamento?
3. ¿_____ es tu casa, la casa blanca o la casa azul?
4. ¿_____ muebles hay en la sala?
5. ¿_____ son los electrodomésticos que necesitas?
6. ¿En _____ piso están los dormitorios?
7. ¿_____ de los apartamentos está más cerca?
8. ¿_____ es la dirección de la casa?

4.26 **Una conversación por teléfono** Escuchas parte de una conversación telefónica entre el señor Ruiz y Magdalena sobre un apartamento que él tiene para alquilar. Completa la conversación telefónica con las preguntas lógicas de ella. Inventa la última pregunta y la respuesta.

Señor Ruiz:	¿Bueno?
Magdalena:	Buenos días. 1. ¿ _____?
Señor Ruiz:	Estoy bien, gracias.
Magdalena:	2. ¿ _____?
Señor Ruiz:	El apartamento está en la calle Montalvo.
Magdalena:	3. ¿ _____?
Señor Ruiz:	Hay tres dormitorios.
Magdalena:	4. ¿ _____?
Señor Ruiz:	Cuesta 2000 pesos al mes.
Magdalena:	5. ¿ _____?
Señor Ruiz:	Usted puede visitar el apartamento hoy mismo.
Magdalena:	6. ¿...?
Señor Ruiz:	_____ Bueno, adiós.

¿Bueno?

© toocanimages/Shutterstock

4.27 **Una casa** Trabaja con un compañero. Mira la foto e inventa preguntas sobre la casa y las personas que viven allí. Luego inventa respuestas para las preguntas de tu compañero.

Modelo *¿Cuántas personas viven aquí?*

Las casas en Valaparaíso, Chile, son famosas por sus colores.

4.28 **Información, por favor** Imagínate que trabajas en una oficina dónde alquilan apartamentos y necesitas completar el formulario con la información de un cliente nuevo. Debes hacerle algunas preguntas a tu compañero para completar el formulario. En donde dice preferencias, el cliente debe imaginar dos o tres características que quiere en una casa, por ejemplo **Necesita tener dos baños.** Cuando terminen, cambien de papel *(change roles)*.

Modelo Nombre
       Estudiante A: *¿Cómo se llama Ud.?*
       Estudiante B: *Me llamo…*

FORMULARIO PARA ALQUILAR UN APARTAMENTO	
Nombre	
Edad *(Age)*	
Dirección	
Origen	
Nombre de esposo(a)	
Número de hijos	
Trabajo	
Preferencias	

A analizar

Santiago habla con una señora sobre un apartamento que ella tiene para alquilar. Después de ver el video lee esta parte de su conversación y observa las formas del verbo **preferir**.

Santiago:	Me gustaría ver *(see)* el apartamento.
Señora:	Bueno, mi esposo y yo **preferimos** recibir a las personas interesadas durante el fin de semana. ¿Qué día **prefiere** usted, el sábado o el domingo?
Santiago:	**Prefiero** el sábado por la mañana si es posible.
Señora:	Bueno, ¿qué tal el sábado a las once?
Santiago:	¡Perfecto! Hasta el sábado.

© Cengage Learning

1. Using the examples from the conversation and your knowledge of conjugating stem-changing verbs, complete the table with the verb **preferir**.

   preferir

   yo _____   nosotros(as) _____

   tú _____   vosotros(as) _____

   él, ella, usted _____   ellos, ellas, ustedes _____

2. How do the **nosotros** and **vosotros** forms of the verb differ from the other forms?

A comprobar

Stem-changing verbs e → ie and e → i

1. In **Exploraciones gramaticales 1** you learned that some verbs have changes in the stem. Notice that in the verbs below the **e** changes to **ie** and that the endings are the same as other **-ar, -er,** and **-ir** verbs.

cerrar *(to close)*

yo	cierro	nosotros(as)	cerramos
tú	cierras	vosotros(as)	cerráis
él, ella, usted	cierra	ellos, ellas, ustedes	cierran

querer *(to want)*

yo	quiero	nosotros(as)	queremos
tú	quieres	vosotros(as)	queréis
él, ella, usted	quiere	ellos, ellas, ustedes	quieren

mentir *(to lie)*

yo	miento	nosotros(as)	mentimos
tú	mientes	vosotros(as)	mentís
él, ella, usted	miente	ellos, ellas, ustedes	mienten

The verbs listed below are also **e → ie** stem-changing verbs.

comenzar (a)	to begin (to do something)
nevar	to snow
empezar (a)	to begin (to do something)
pensar	to think
encender	to turn on
perder	to lose
entender	to understand
preferir	to prefer

2. **Pensar en** means *to think about* and **pensar de** means *to think of* (opinion). **Pensar** + an infinitive means *to plan to do something.*

> Ella **piensa** mucho **en** sus hijos.
> *She thinks about her children a lot.*

> ¿Qué **piensas de** la casa?
> *What do you think of the house?*

> Yo **pienso** buscar un apartamento.
> *I plan to look for an apartment.*

3. There are some **-ir** verbs in which the **e** in the stem changes to **i**. As with the **e → ie** stem-changing verbs, these verbs also change in all forms except **nosotros** and **vosotros,** and the endings are the same as regular **-ir** verbs.

repetir *(to repeat)*

yo	repito	nosotros(as)	repetimos
tú	repites	vosotros(as)	repetís
él, ella, usted	repite	ellos, ellas, ustedes	repiten

The verbs listed below are **e → i** stem-changing verbs like **repetir.**

competir	to compete	servir	to serve
pedir	to ask for	sonreír	to smile
reír	to laugh		

4. Notice that the verb **reír** requires an accent mark on the **i** when it is conjugated. The same rule applies for **sonreír.**

reír *(to laugh)*

yo	**río**	nosotros(as)	**reímos**
tú	**ríes**	vosotros(as)	**reís**
él, ella, usted	**ríe**	ellos, ellas, ustedes	**ríen**

5. **Pedir** means *to ask for (something)* and **preguntar** means *to ask (a question).* The preposition *for* is part of the verb **pedir,** so you should not use **por** or **para** with it.

> Los niños **piden** permiso de sus padres.
> *Children ask permission from their parents.*

> Él **pregunta** si van a vender su casa.
> *He is asking if they are going to sell their house.*

A practicar

4.29 **En la tienda de muebles** Todos quieren comprar algo nuevo. ¿Para qué habitación son los objetos que quieren comprar?

1. Mi esposo y yo queremos comprar una cama.

2. Raúl quiere comprar un auto.

3. Carlota y Esteban quieren comprar una mesa con cuatro sillas.

4. Jimena quiere comprar un sofá.

5. Yo quiero comprar un horno de microondas.

4.30 **¿Qué piensan hacer más tarde?** Usando el verbo **pensar,** explica qué piensan hacer las personas, cuándo y dónde.

Modelo mi hermana
Mi hermana piensa leer un libro en el patio a las dos y media.

1. yo

2. mi esposa

3. mis hijos

4. mi esposa y yo

5. mi abuelo

6. Y tú ¿qué piensas hacer más tarde?

© Cengage Learning

4.31 **Somos iguales** Marca cuatro de las siguientes oraciones que sean ciertas *(are true)* para ti. Después, busca cuatro diferentes compañeros para quienes una de las oraciones también sea cierta.

__ Sirvo la comida en mi casa.

__ Quiero viajar a otro país.

__ Sonrío en las fotos.

__ No miento.

__ Enciendo la radio cuando estudio.

__ Normalmente empiezo a estudiar después de *(after)* las ocho de la noche.

__ A veces *(Sometimes)* pierdo la tarea.

__ Pienso comer en un restaurante hoy.

__ Entiendo otra lengua.

__ Pido ayuda con la tarea de español.

4.32 **Entrevista** Con un compañero túrnense para entrevistarse con las siguientes preguntas.

Los estudios

1. ¿Dónde prefieres estudiar?

2. Normalmente ¿a qué hora empiezas a estudiar?

3. ¿Entiendes al profesor de español?

4. ¿A veces pides ayuda con la tarea de español? ¿A quién?

El tiempo libre

5. ¿Enciendes la tele en la noche? ¿Qué te gusta mirar?

6. ¿Compites en un deporte? ¿Cuál?

7. ¿Qué piensas hacer este fin de semana?

8. ¿Quieres viajar en el verano? ¿Adónde?

¿Adónde quieres viajar?

herjua/Shutterstock

Lectura

Antes de leer

¿Cómo crees que van a ser las casas en el futuro?

A leer

Soluciones a la vivienda

Debido a las diferencias en el clima y la cultura de los diferentes países, las viviendas pueden ser muy diferentes. A continuación aparecen algunos ejemplos.

Los palafitos

of rivers

Los palafitos (casas hechas sobre pilares) se pueden ver en países como Argentina, Chile, Colombia, Perú y Venezuela. Son comunes en zonas **fluviales** de corrientes tranquilas, donde el nivel del agua varía notablemente durante el año. En el caso de Venezuela, los palafitos son unas de las viviendas más antiguas del país. De hecho, el nombre de este país viene del

Chile

nombre Venecia, ya que el descubridor Alonso de Ojeda observó este tipo de casa a su llegada a la región, en 1499.

wood
steel/life

Las columnas sobre las que se construyen las casas generalmente están hechas de **madera,** aunque en algunos lugares se usan ahora materiales sintéticos prefabricados y **acero,** para alargar la **vida** de las casas. La arquitectura de estas casas permite habitar regiones que de otra forma serían inhabitables. Sin embargo, existen algunas desventajas, como problemas de

health

salud a causa de la contaminación del agua o la humedad.

La ruca mapuche

Los mapuches son los habitantes originales del territorio que hoy es Chile. La Ruca es la construcción más importante dentro de la arquitectura mapuche y está fabricada con materiales de la región. Las rucas

round

tradicionales son **redondas** u ovaladas, aunque también pueden ser rectangulares. Son muy grandes, pero tienen solo una habitación. A los

Ruca en Chile

lados están las camas y provisiones y en el centro se pone un fogón para cocinar; algunos utensilios **cuelgan del techo.** *hang from the ceiling*
En la actualidad se están **desarrollando** *developing* programas de etno-turismo que permitirán conocer la cultura mapuche conviviendo y **hospedándose** con ellos. *lodging*

Las islas flotantes de los uros
Este tipo de vivienda es única de los uros, un grupo étnico del Perú que vive en el lago Titicaca. Puede decirse que estas casas son una combinación de palafitos y rucas. Desde hace cientos de años los uros viven en islas flotantes construidas a base de una planta de la región (la totora). Encima de las islas están sus casas, una especie de cabañas similares a las rucas mapuches (con una habitación solamente), pero mucho más pequeñas. Estas viviendas también se construyen con la totora. Sin embargo, los uros cocinan fuera de sus casas para **evitar incendios.** Una desventaja de este tipo de casa es *to avoid fires* la alta humedad, la cual ocasiona problemas de reumas entre la población.

La casa cueva
Una casa **cueva** es una vivienda que tiene *cave* al menos una parte en la **tierra** o en una *land* estructura natural, como una cueva. Su mayor ventaja es su carácter ecológico y su temperatura agradable: fresca en el verano y cálida en el invierno. Gracias a sus características, **ahorra** energía y protege *saves* mejor de vientos o lluvias fuertes. Las casas cueva son muy flexibles y pueden

adaptarse a las necesidades de familias diferentes. Mucha gente piensa que son viviendas **obscuras,** pero no es verdad: se distinguen por su luminosidad. Las *dark* casas cueva nos acercan al **medio ambiente** proporcionando al mismo tiempo *environment* todas las comodidades de la vida moderna.

En España las casas cueva se utilizan desde hace **miles** de años. *thousands* Probablemente las más famosas sean las que están cerca de la ciudad de Granada, que **hoy en día** funcionan como hoteles. La mayor **desventaja** de *nowadays/disadvantage* estas viviendas es que requieren de más espacio para **albergar** a una familia, a *to house* diferencia de otras soluciones como los edificios de apartamentos.

Comprensión

Decide si las oraciones son ciertas o falsas. Corrige las oraciones falsas.

1. Gracias a los palafitos, algunas personas pueden vivir en zonas fluviales.
2. Las rucas son un tipo de vivienda que se usa en el lago Titicaca.
3. En las rucas hay múltiples habitaciones.
4. La totora es la casa de los uros.
5. Las casas cueva son viviendas obscuras.
6. Las casas cueva ahorran energía.

Después de leer

¿Te gustaría *(Would you like)* vivir en una de las casas en el artículo? ¿Cuál? ¿Por qué?

Redacción

You are going to write an email to a new friend in which you tell him or her about where you live. One approach to descriptive writing is to begin with a general idea and to then become more specific. That is what you will do in this email. In the first paragraph, you will discuss the town or city where you live; in the second paragraph you will describe your home in general, and in the last paragraph you will discuss your favorite room.

Paso 1 Jot down as many adjectives as you can think of that you would use to describe the town or city where you live. Write a list of the things your town or city has to offer: businesses, museums, etc.

Paso 2 Jot down as many phrases as you can about your home in general. Think about the following questions: Do you live in an apartment or a house? Whom do you live with? How would you describe your home (color, big, old, comfortable, etc.)? What rooms does it have?

Paso 3 Decide which room you like best. Jot down as many phrases as you can about that room. Think about the following questions: Why is it your favorite room? What items do you like in that room? How much time do you spend there? What do you do there?

Paso 4 After your greeting, begin your first paragraph by telling where you live. Then develop the paragraph in which you describe your city or town using the ideas you generated in **Paso 1.**

Paso 5 Write a transition sentence in which you tell where your home is located, such as the street you live on or what you live near. Then, develop the rest of the paragraph in which you describe your home using the information you generated in **Paso 2.**

Paso 6 Begin your third paragraph with a transition sentence that connects the second paragraph with the new idea to be discussed (your favorite room).

> **Modelo** *Hay muchas habitaciones en mi casa, pero mi habitación favorita es la sala.*

Paso 7 Develop the rest of the paragraph using the ideas you generated in **Paso 3.** Be sure to have a concluding statement at the end of the third paragraph. At the end of your email, ask your new friend two or three questions about where he/she lives.

Paso 8 Edit your essay:

1. In each paragraph, do all of your sentences support the topic sentence?
2. Are your paragraphs logically organized or do you skip from one idea to the next?
3. Are there any short sentences you can combine by using **y** or **pero**?
4. Are there any spelling errors?
5. Do adjectives agree with the objects they describe?
6. Do verbs agree with their subjects?

En vivo

Entrando en materia

¿Qué información hay en la sección de anuncios para apartamentos y casas en el periódico (*newspaper*)?

Casas en venta

Estos son anuncios para unas casas en venta en Ponce, Puerto Rico.

URBANIZACIÓN COLINAS DEL VALLE

CASAS EN VENTA

En una de las mejores zonas de Ponce, cerca de parques y un centro comercial

Modelo Bugambilia
- 3 habitaciones
- 2 baños y medio
- cocina integral
- sala-comedor amplia
- acabados de lujo
- estacionamiento cubierto para un auto

Modelo Rosal
- 4 habitaciones
- 2 baños
- cocina con desayunador
- sala
- comedor
- acabados de lujo
- terraza
- estacionamiento para un auto

Todo lo que necesita para vivir cómodamente.

Visite nuestras casas modelos todos los días de 9:00 A.M. a 9:00 P.M.

Comprensión

1. ¿Qué crees que es un "medio baño"?
2. ¿Qué piensas que significa "estacionamiento cubierto"?
3. ¿Cuál de las dos casas prefieres? ¿Por qué?

 Más allá

Imagina que encuentras el anuncio de tu casa ideal en el periódico. Escribe el anuncio incluyendo dónde está y la lista de todo lo que tiene la casa. Comparte tu anuncio en Share It! y lee los anuncios de tus compañeros. ¿Irías a ver *(Would you go to see)* una de las casas de los anuncios?

Vocabulario

Sustantivos

la calefacción central	*central heat*
los cimientos	*foundation*
el (la) dueño(a)	*owner*
la entrada	*entrance*
la fecha de inicio	*starting date*
la finalización	*completion*
el frente	*façade*
la grúa	*crane*
el ladrillo	*brick*
la maqueta	*scale model*
el plano	*blueprint*

Adjetivos

apurado(a)	*in a hurry*
construido(a)	*built*
creativo(a)	*creative*
preparado(a)	*ready, prepared*
retrasado(a)	*late*

Verbos

cavar	*to dig*
conectar	*to connect*
demoler	*to demolish*
diseñar	*to design*
instalar	*to install*
construir	*to built*

Frases útiles

Con vista a...
With a view to . . .

Les presento el nuevo proyecto.
I'm pleased to introduce the new project.

¿Cuántos pisos tiene el edificio?
How many stories are in the building?

El edificio tiene cien unidades.
The building has one hundred units.

Estas son las dimensiones.
These are the dimensions.

Usamos materiales de primera calidad.
We use top-quality materials.

¡Manos a la obra!
Let's get to work!

¡Manos a la obra!

DATOS IMPORTANTES

Educación: Estudios universitarios completos en arquitectura; Experiencia en compañías constructoras; Capacidad de trabajo en equipo

Salario: Entre $100 000 y $200 000, dependiendo de la responsabilidad del proyecto de construcción

Dónde se trabaja: Compañías constructoras, Departamento de Obras Públicas del gobierno, contratistas, consultorías

Vocabulario nuevo Completa las oraciones con la palabra apropiada de vocabulario.

1. Si vives en un clima frío es necesario tener _____.

2. _____ es donde está la puerta de la casa.

3. _____ es un modelo en tres dimensiones.

4. Es necesario ser _____ para diseñar una casa.

5. Estamos _____ y no vamos a completar la construcción a tiempo (*on time*).

▶ Briana Vásquez, Arquitecta

Briana Vásquez es arquitecta y trabaja para una importante compañía constructora. Ella es responsable de la obra de construcción de edificios de apartamentos. También debe comunicarse con los dueños del edificio. En el video vas a ver a la arquitecta Vásquez mientras habla con uno de los dueños.

© Sandra Gligorijevic/Shutterstock

Antes de ver

Los arquitectos desarrollan *(develop)* los proyectos de construcción. Luego supervisan a los trabajadores de la construcción para realizar los planos a la perfección.

1. ¿En qué tipo de proyectos trabaja un arquitecto?
2. Imagínate que quieres construir un edificio. ¿Qué preguntas le haces al arquitecto?

Comprensión

1. ¿Qué tipo de apartamentos quiere ofrecer el Sr. Sierra?

2. ¿Qué vista tienen los apartamentos de tres habitaciones?

3. ¿Cómo son los apartamentos de dos habitaciones?

4. ¿Cuántos pisos va a tener el edificio?

5. ¿Qué va a estar al lado de la entrada principal del edificio?

6. ¿Cuándo es la fecha de finalización de la construcción?

Después de ver

En grupos pequeños, representen una reunión entre un arquitecto asociado, un trabajador que es el jefe de construcción y un dueño. El dueño piensa construir un edificio de apartamentos. Hagan un diálogo entre las tres personas. Deben explicarle al arquitecto lo que quieren tener en su apartamento. El arquitecto puede hacer preguntas específicas.

4.33 **En casa** Completa el párrafo con la forma apropiada del verbo entre paréntesis.

Toda la familia (**1.**) _____ (estar) en casa hoy. Mi esposa y yo (**2.**) _____
(estar) en la cocina. Nosotros siempre (**3.**) _____ (almorzar) a esta hora, y hoy
yo (**4.**) _____ (pensar) preparar unos sándwiches. Los niños (**5.**) _____
(estar) en casa también. Ellos no (**6.**) _____ (poder) jugar en el jardín porque
(**7.**) _____ (llover) hoy. Vicente (**8.**) _____ (dormir) en su habitación,
y Marisa (**9.**) _____ (jugar) unos videojuegos en la sala. Después de *(After)*
comer, mis hijos (**10.**) _____ (querer) ir al cine con sus amigos. Mi esposa y yo
(**11.**) _____ (preferir) mirar una película aquí en casa.

4.34 **En tu salón de clase** Usando las preposiciones, identifica donde están las
personas y objetos en tu salón de clase.

Modelo al lado de
   La pizarra está al lado de la ventana.

1. enfrente de
2. cerca de
3. encima de
4. a la derecha de
5. dentro de
6. debajo de
7. entre
8. detrás de

La pizarra está cerca de la ventana.

4.35 **Comprensión de lectura** Imagínate que eres profesor y tienes que escribir
cinco preguntas de comprensión para los estudiantes sobre este párrafo. ¡**OJO**! Las
respuestas a las preguntas deben estar en el párrafo.

Soy Rómulo y vivo en Montevideo, Uruguay.
Vivo en un apartamento en el centro de
la ciudad con mi amigo Pablo. Nuestro
apartamento no es muy grande pero es
cómodo. Tiene dos dormitorios y un baño.
También tiene una sala pequeña donde Pablo
y yo miramos la tele. Mi habitación favorita es
mi dormitorio. Allí *(there)* me gusta escuchar
música y leer.

Me gusta leer en mi dormitorio.

4.36 **¡Adivina dónde estoy!** Vas a trabajar con un compañero. Uno de ustedes debe imaginar que está en un lugar en la casa o en la ciudad. El otro debe hacer hasta *(up to)* diez preguntas para adivinar *(to guess)* dónde está, pero la respuesta debe ser solo **sí** o **no**. Túrnense para contestar.

Modelo Estudiante 1: *¡Adivina dónde estoy!*
Estudiante 2: *¿Comes en este lugar?*
Estudiante 1: *No.*

Estudiante 2: *¿Hay libros y mesas?*
Estudiante 1: *Sí.*
Estudiante 1: *¿Estás en la biblioteca?*
Estudiante 2: *Sí.*

4.37 **Seis diferencias** Trabaja con un compañero. Uno mira el dibujo aquí y el otro mira el dibujo en el **Apéndice B.** Túrnense para describirlos y buscar seis diferencias.

© Cengage Learning

4.38 **Buscando un apartamento** Con un compañero van a decidir dónde quieren vivir.

Paso 1 Escribe una lista de lo que es importante para ti a la hora de decidir dónde quieres vivir. Luego mira los anuncios y decide cuál de los apartamentos prefieres.

Paso 2 Tu compañero y tú necesitan escoger *(choose)* uno de los apartamentos. Convence a tu compañero de que tu selección es donde deben vivir.

Paso 3 Tomen una decisión y compártenla *(share it)* con la clase. Deben explicar por qué seleccionaron el apartamento.

Apartamento amueblado, un dormitorio grande con dos camas, baño con bañera y ducha, sala-comedor, cocina con lavadora, en la línea del autobús, $750 al mes	Cerca de la universidad, apartamento con dos dormitorios, baño con ducha, medio baño, sala amplia, cocina con espacio para comer, $950 al mes	Apartamento en tercer piso con balcón, dos dormitorios, baño con ducha, sala, comedor, cocina con lavaplatos, aire acondicionado, $875 al mes	Apartamento en planta baja, tres dormitorios, dos baños con ducha, sala-comedor, acceso a piscina y gimnasio, $1050 al mes	Apartamento muy céntrico con acceso a restaurantes y tiendas, dos dormitorios, un baño con bañera, sala, cocina grande, espacio reservado para un coche, $900 al mes

🔊 Vocabulario 1

1-26

Los lugares	**Places**
el aeropuerto	*airport*
el banco	*bank*
el bar	*bar*
el café	*cafe*
la calle	*street*
el centro comercial	*mall, shopping center*
el cine	*movie theater*
el club	*club*
el correo	*post office*
la discoteca	*nightclub*
el edificio	*building*
la escuela	*school*
la farmacia	*pharmacy*
el hospital	*hospital*
el hotel	*hotel*
la iglesia	*church*

el mercado	*market*
la mezquita	*mosque*
el museo	*museum*
el negocio	*business*
la oficina	*office*
el parque	*park*
la piscina	*swimming pool*
la playa	*beach*
la plaza	*city square*
el restaurante	*restaurant*
la sinagoga	*synagogue*
el supermercado	*supermarket*
el teatro	*theater*
el templo	*temple*
la tienda	*store*
el zoológico	*zoo*

Los verbos

almorzar (ue)	*to have lunch*
alquilar	*to rent*
costar (ue)	*to cost*
depositar	*to deposit*
devolver (ue)	*to return (something)*
dormir (ue)	*to sleep*
encontrar (ue)	*to find*
estar	*to be*

jugar (ue)	*to play*
llover (ue)	*to rain*
morir (ue)	*to die*
poder (ue)	*to be able to*
recordar (ue)	*to remember*
rezar	*to pray*
soñar (ue) (con)	*to dream (about)*
volver (ue)	*to come back*

Palabras adicionales

la carta	*letter*
el dinero	*money*

el paquete	*package*
la película	*movie*

Las preposiciones

a la derecha de	*to the right of*
al lado de	*beside, next to*
a la izquierda de	*to the left of*
cerca de	*near*
debajo de	*under*
dentro de	*inside*
detrás de	*behind*

en	*in, on, at*
encima de	*on top of*
enfrente de	*in front of*
entre	*between*
fuera de	*outside*
lejos de	*far from*

Diccionario personal

_____

_____

🔊 Vocabulario 2

Habitaciones de la casa

el baño	*bathroom*		el dormitorio	*bedroom*
la cochera	*garage*		el jardín	*garden*
la cocina	*kitchen*		el patio	*patio*
el comedor	*dining room*		la sala	*living room*

Muebles, utensilios y aparatos electrodomésticos

la alfombra	*carpet*		el (horno de) microondas	*microwave (oven)*
el armario	*closet, armoire*		el inodoro	*toilet*
la bañera	*bathtub*		la lámpara	*lamp*
la cafetera	*coffee maker*		el lavabo	*bathroom sink*
la cama	*bed*		la lavadora	*washer*
las cortinas	*curtains*		el lavaplatos	*dishwasher*
el cuadro	*painting, picture*		la mesita	*coffee table*
la ducha	*shower*		las plantas	*plants*
el espejo	*mirror*		el refrigerador	*refrigerator*
la estufa	*stove*		la secadora	*dryer*
la flor	*flower*		el sillón	*armchair*
el fregadero	*kitchen sink*		el sofá	*couch*
el horno	*oven*			

Los verbos

cerrar (ie)	*to close*		pedir (i)	*to ask for*
comenzar (ie) (a)	*to begin (to do something)*		pensar (ie)	*to think*
			perder	*to lose*
competir (i)	*to compete*		preferir (ie)	*to prefer*
empezar (ie) (a)	*to begin (to do something)*		reír (i)	*to laugh*
			repetir (i)	*to repeat*
encender	*to turn on*		querer (ie)	*to want*
entender (ie)	*to understand*		servir (i)	*to serve*
mentir (ie)	*to lie*		sonreír (ie)	*to smile*
nevar (ie)	*to snow*			

Palabras adicionales

el apartamento	*apartment*		el mueble	*furniture*
la dirección	*address*		la planta baja	*ground floor*
la habitación	*room*		el (primer) piso	*(first) floor*

Palabras interrogativas

¿adónde?	*to where?*		¿de dónde?	*from where?*
¿cómo?	*how?*		¿dónde?	*where?*
¿cuál(es)?	*which?*		¿por qué?	*why?*
¿cuándo?	*when?*		¿qué?	*what?*
¿cuánto(a)?	*how much?*		¿quién(es)?	*who?*
¿cuántos(as)?	*how many?*			

Juan Ramón Jiménez:

Biografía

Juan Ramón Jiménez (1881–1958) nace (*born*) en Moguer, España. Estudia derecho (*law*) en la Universidad de Sevilla, pero decide no practicar. Con la ayuda del poeta modernista Rubén Darío, Jiménez publica su primer libro en 1900, a la edad (*age*) de 10 años. Durante su carrera trabaja como crítico literario y editor de varias revistas (*magazines*) literarias y pasa (*spends*) tiempo en diferentes países como Francia, Portugal y Estados Unidos. Cuando empieza la Guerra (*War*) Civil, viaja a las Américas. Vive en Cuba, los Estados Unidos y más tarde en Puerto Rico donde muere en 1958. Su poesía es muy visual, y el verde y el amarillo son los colores dominantes.

Antes de leer

1. ¿Qué colores asocias con el otoño?
2. Examina el poema. ¿Qué palabras (*words*) se refieren a elementos de la naturaleza?

Departure

path/gold/blackbirds

Ida* de otoño

Por un **camino** de **oro** van los **mirlos**... ¿Adónde?
Por un camino de oro van las rosas... ¿Adónde?
Por un camino de oro voy...
¿Adónde, otoño? ¿Adónde, pájaros y flores?

Después de leer

A. Comprensión

1. ¿Qué color es dominante en el poema?
2. ¿Qué acción hay en el poema?
3. ¿Qué quiere saber (*to know*) la voz poética?
4. Si las estaciones del año son símbolos para las fases de la vida ¿qué representan las cuatro estaciones?

B. Conversemos

Habla con un compañero para compartir (*share*) sus respuestas a las preguntas.

1. ¿Qué colores asocian con el verano? ¿y con la primavera y el invierno?
2. ¿Cuál es su estación favorita? ¿Por qué?

Antes de leer

1. ¿Con qué estación se asocian las canciones *(songs)* de los pájaros?
2. ¿Adónde van los pájaros en el invierno?

Canción de invierno

Cantan. Cantan.
¿Dónde cantan los pájaros que cantan?

It has rained/branches   **Ha llovido**. Aún las **ramas**
without/leaves   están **sin hojas** nuevas. Cantan. Cantan
los pájaros. ¿En dónde cantan
los pájaros que cantan?

cages   No tengo pájaros en **jaulas**.
No hay niños que los vendan. Cantan.
valley/Nothing   El **valle** está muy lejos. **Nada**...

know   Yo no **sé** dónde cantan
los pájaros-cantan, cantan-
los pájaros que cantan.

Juan Ramón Jiménez, "Canción de Invierno," *Juan Ramón Jiménez para niños y niñas—y otros seres curiosos*. Ediciones de la Torre, 2010.
By permission of the Herederos de Juan Ramón Jiménez.

Después de leer

A. Comprensión

1. ¿Piensas qué la voz poética escucha las canciones de los pájaros? ¿Por qué?
2. ¿Qué piensas que representan los pájaros?
3. La voz poética pregunta dónde cantan los pájaros que cantan. ¿Dónde están los pájaros que cantan?
4. El poema es repetitivo. ¿Qué efecto creen que el autor quiere transmitir con la repetición?
5. ¿Cuál es el tono del poema?

B. Conversemos

 Habla con un compañero para compartir sus respuestas a las siguientes preguntas.

1. ¿Te gusta el poema? ¿Por qué?
2. ¿Qué estación crees que inspira más a los poetas? ¿Por qué?
3. ¿Conoces *(Do you know)* un poema en inglés o en español sobre una estación? ¿Cuál?

Investiguemos la literatura: El tono

The tone of a work refers to the attitude that a writer communicates toward a particular subject through the work. It can be playful, formal, angry, loving, etc. You can often identify the tone of a work by paying attention to the author's word choice. Does the author use words or expressions that are positive, negative, or neutral?

CAPÍTULO **5**

Learning Strategy

Guess intelligently

When you are listening to audio recordings or your instructor, or when watching a video, make intelligent guesses as to the meaning of words you do not know. Use context, intonation, and if possible, visual clues such as gestures, facial expressions and images to help you figure out the meaning of words.

In this chapter you will learn how to:

- Describe your feelings, emotions, and physical states
- Talk about ongoing actions
- Discuss abilities needed for certain jobs and professions

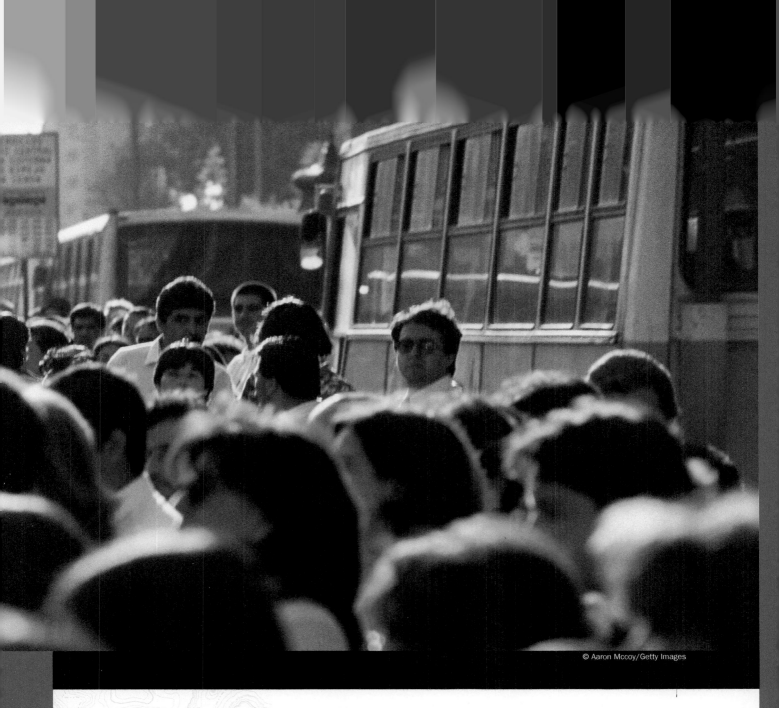

© Aaron Mccoy/Getty Images

Laura trabaja en el Café Simón. Es un lugar muy popular en el centro histórico de la ciudad. ¿Cómo están las personas en el café?

Los estados de ánimo

estar alegre	to be happy	**estar divertido(a)**	to be entertained, to be in a good mood	**estar frustrado(a)**	to be frustrated
estar celoso(a)	to be jealous			**estar interesado(a)**	to be interested
estar contento(a)	to be happy, to be content			**estar ocupado(a)**	to be busy
		estar enfermo(a)	to be sick	**estar sano(a)**	to be healthy
estar deprimido(a)	to be depressed	**estar equivocado(a)**	to be wrong	**estar seguro(a)**	to be sure
		estar feliz	to be happy		

A practicar

5.1 Escucha y responde Escucha los adjetivos de emoción. Indica con el pulgar hacia arriba *(thumbs up)* si es una emoción positiva o con el pulgar hacia abajo *(thumbs down)* si es una emoción negativa.

1-28

5.2 ¿Lógica o ilógica? Indica si las siguientes oraciones son lógicas o ilógicas.

1. Vamos a tener un examen difícil y estamos felices.
2. Tus amigos te preparan una fiesta sorpresa y estás celoso.
3. Nuestro hijo está muy enfermo. Estamos preocupados.
4. Después de correr 15 kilómetros estás cansado.
5. Estás sano porque tienes una F en matemáticas.

5.3 **¿Cómo estás?** Con un compañero, túrnense para expresar sus reacciones ante estas situaciones.

Modelo Tienes tres exámenes y recibes una A en todos.
Estudiante 1: *¡Estoy contento! ¿Y tú?*
Estudiante 2: *¡Yo estoy sorprendido!*

1. Vas de vacaciones a las islas Canarias y pierdes tu pasaporte.
2. Tú y tu novio se casan (*get married*) hoy.
3. Recibes un kilo de chocolates y los comes todos en un día.
4. Necesitas trabajar pero no puedes encontrar un trabajo.
5. Llegas tarde al aeropuerto y pierdes tu vuelo (*flight*).
6. Hay una persona que no conoces (*that you don't know*) en la sala de tu casa.

Estamos enamorados.

5.4 **Asociaciones** Habla con un compañero para explicar la emoción que asocian con las situaciones de la lista. Explica por qué.

Modelo Estoy en la clase de matemáticas.
Estoy frustrado porque no comprendo los problemas de matemáticas. / Estoy feliz porque me gustan las matemáticas.

1. Es lunes.
2. Es verano.
3. Estoy en la clase de historia.
4. Tengo un examen final.
5. Es el Día de San Valentín.
6. Llueve.
7. Estoy en el templo.
8. Estoy en la universidad.

5.5 **¿Y tú?** Con un compañero, túrnense para completar las oraciones con mucha información. En la última (*last*) oración, ustedes deciden el estado de ánimo.

Modelo Cuando estoy cansado yo... ¿y tú?
Estudiante 1: *Cuando estoy cansada, yo duermo en mi sofá con mi gato ¿y tú?*
Estudiante 2: *Yo también duermo, pero prefiero tomar una siesta en mi cama.*

1. Cuando estoy enamorado, yo... ¿y tú?
2. Cuando estoy triste, yo... ¿y tú?
3. Cuando estoy aburrido, yo... ¿y tú?
4. Cuando estoy enojado, yo... ¿y tú?
5. Cuando estoy enfermo, yo... ¿y tú?
6. Cuando estoy ___¿?___ , yo... ¿y tú?

5.6 **Los chismes (gossip)** Imagina que tu compañero y tú están intercambiando información sobre cómo están todos sus amigos. Pregúntense para completar la información. Uno de ustedes va a ver la información en esta página, y el otro en el **Apéndice B**. ¡OJO! ¡Presta atención a la concordancia (*agreement*)!

Modelo Estudiante 1: *¿Cómo está Ramira?*
Estudiante 2: *Está contenta.*
Estudiante 1: *¿Por qué?*
Estudiante 2: *Porque va a ir de vacaciones a Venezuela.*

Nombre	¿Cómo está(n)?	¿Por qué?
Ramira	contento	Va a ir de vacaciones a Venezuela.
Emanuel y Arturo	ocupado	
Gisela	enojado	Sus amigas no hablan con ella.
Alex		Su hijo es agresivo con otros niños de su escuela.
Karina e Iliana		
Gerardo	preocupado	
Javier y Manuel		No tienen actividades para el fin de semana.

Conexiones culturales

Las emociones y el bienestar

Cultura

Emociones fuertes como la tristeza, la depresión o la alegría pueden resultar en obras *(works)* de arte en las manos *(in the hands)* de una artista talentosa como la pintora mexicana Frida Kahlo (1907–1954). Kahlo es famosa por sus autorretratos *(self-portraits)*, los que muestran su sufrimiento. Cuando tenía 17 años, sufrió un accidente en un tranvía *(streetcar)* y se fracturó la espina dorsal *(spinal cord)* y varios huesos *(bones)*. Como resultado, pasó mucho tiempo en el hospital, nunca pudo tener hijos y sufrió de dolor *(pain)* por el resto de su vida *(life)*.

Observa el cuadro de Frida Kahlo. ¿Qué emociones produce? ¿Por qué? ¿Qué colores usa?

Pensando en la muerte, de Frida Kahlo

Muchas de las obras del pintor ecuatoriano Osvaldo Guayasamín también muestran sufrimiento. Investiga en Internet obras de Osvaldo Guayasamín. Sube a Share It! una pintura que te gusta y explica: ¿Cómo se llama la pintura? ¿Qué emociones produce?

Comunidad

Entrevista a una persona de un país hispanohablante. Pregúntale quién es su artista favorito, de dónde es y cómo son sus pinturas. Después repórtale la información a la clase.

¿Quién es tu artista favorito?

Busca una pintura del artista favorito de la persona que entrevistaste. Sube la pintura a Share it! y explica: **¿Quién es el artista? ¿Qué hay en la pintura? ¿Qué emociones produce? ¿Cuál es el mensaje de la pintura? ¿Te gusta?**

Comparaciones

Con un compañero, hagan *(make)* una lista de cinco supersticiones populares en la cultura de ustedes. Después lean la lista de supersticiones del mundo hispano. ¿Hay supersticiones similares a las que mencionaron?

1. Pasar por debajo de una escalera *(ladder)* trae mala suerte.

2. Abrir un paraguas dentro de una casa trae mala suerte.

3. Romper un espejo trae siete años de mala suerte.

4. Cruzarse con un gato negro trae mala suerte.

5. Sentir comezón *(itch)* en la mano es señal de que se va a recibir dinero.

6. Para tener un buen año con el dinero, uno debe usar calzoncillos *(underwear)* amarillos para recibir el año nuevo.

Si encontraste *(If you found)* supersticiones parecidas *(similar)*, ¿cómo puedes explicar la similitud?

Conexiones... a la literatura

Generalmente, ¿qué emociones puede provocar la poesía? Piensa en un poema que conoces. ¿Qué emociones te provoca?

Alfonsina Storni (1892–1938), poeta argentina, fue *(was)* la primera mujer reconocida entre los grandes escritores de su época. Uno de los temas más frecuentes en sus poemas es el feminismo.

El siguiente es un poema en el cual una mujer habla con el hombre con quien tiene una relación.

Hombre pequeñito

Hombre pequeñito, hombre pequeñito,
Suelta a tu canario que quiere **volar**...   *release / to fly*
Yo soy el canario, hombre pequeñito,
Déjame saltar.   *Let me jump*

Estuve en tu **jaula**, hombre pequeñito,   *cage*
Hombre pequeñito que jaula me das.
Digo pequeñito porque no me entiendes,   *I say*
Ni me entenderás.

Tampoco te entiendo, pero mientras tanto
Ábreme la jaula que quiero escapar;
Hombre pequeñito, **te amé** media hora,   *I loved you*
No me pidas más.

> **INVESTIGUEMOS LA MÚSICA**
>
> Listen to the song "La Negra Tomasa" by Los Caifanes. What emotions are mentioned in the song?

¿Qué emoción te produce este poema? Da ejemplos concretos de las palabras o frases que producen la emoción.

 Busca el nombre de otro poeta argentino y aprende más sobre Argentina en **Exploraciones del mundo hispano** en el **Apéndice A.**

A analizar

Mira el video. Después lee parte de la conversación entre Camila y Vanesa y observa los verbos en negritas. Luego contesta las preguntas que siguen.

Vanesa:	¡Hola Camila! ¿Cómo estás?
Camila:	Bien, pero estoy muy ocupada hoy.
Vanesa:	¿Por qué? ¿Qué **estás haciendo**?
Camila:	Mis suegros van a llegar de Colombia esta noche y **estoy preparando** comida. Afortunadamente no tengo que limpiar la casa. Rodrigo está en casa hoy y **está limpiando** la sala y los baños.
Vanesa:	¿Y los niños?
Camila:	**Están escribiendo** su tarea... Bueno, ¿y cómo estás tú, Vanesa?
Vanesa:	¡Estoy muy feliz!

1. How are the verbs in bold formed?
2. In **Capítulo 4,** you learned to use the verb **estar** to indicate location. Look at the conversation again. In what other two ways is the verb **estar** used here?

A comprobar

Estar with adjectives and the present progressive

1. Remember that **estar** is an irregular verb:

estar *(to be)*

yo	**estoy**	nosotros	**estamos**
tú	**estás**	vosotros	**estáis**
él, ella, usted	**está**	ellos, ellas ustedes	**están**

2. In addition to indicating location as you learned in **Capítulo 4,** the verb **estar** is also used to express an emotional, mental, or physical condition.

> Mis padres están felices.
> *My parents **are** happy.*
>
> Yo estoy cansado hoy.
> *I **am** tired today.*
>
> Nosotros estamos muy ocupados.
> *We **are** very busy.*

3. The verb **estar** is also used with present participles to form the present progressive. The present progressive is used to describe actions in progress at the moment.

To form the present participle, add **-ando** (**-ar** verbs) or **-iendo** (**-er** and **-ir** verbs) to the stem of the verb.

> hablar → habl**ando**
> comer → com**iendo**
> vivir → viv**iendo**

> El profesor **está hablando** con Tito ahora.
> *The professor **is talking** to Tito now.*

4. The present participle of the verb **ir** is **yendo.** However, it is much more common to use the present tense of the verb when the action is in progress.

> **Voy** a la iglesia. / **Estoy yendo** a la iglesia.
> *I'm going to church.*

You will recall from **Capítulo 4** that to say where someone is going in the future, it is necessary to use the verb **ir** in the present tense or to use the structure **ir** + **a** + *infinitive.*

> **Vamos (a ir)** a una fiesta mañana.
> *We **are going (to go)** to a party tomorrow.*

5. When the stem of an **-er** or an **-ir** verb ends in a vowel, **-yendo** is used instead of **-iendo.**

> leer – le**yendo**   oír *(to hear)* – o**yendo**
> traer *(to bring)* – tra**yendo**

6. Stem changing **-ir** verbs have an irregular present participle. An **e** in the stem becomes an **i,** and an **o** in the stem becomes a **u.**

> mentir – m**i**ntiendo   pedir – p**i**diendo
> repetir – rep**i**tiendo   servir – s**i**rviendo
> dormir – d**u**rmiendo   morir – m**u**riendo

7. In the present progressive, the verb **estar** must agree with the subject; however, you will notice that there is only one form for each present participle. It does NOT agree in gender (masculine/feminine) or number (singular/plural) with the subject.

> Mis hijos están estudiando inglés.
> *My children are studying English.*

> Sandra está leyendo su libro de química.
> *Sandra is reading her chemistry book.*

A practicar

5.7 **¿Cierto o falso?** Escucha las oraciones sobre el dibujo y decide si cada oración es cierta o falsa.

1-29

© Cengage Learning

5.8 **La fiesta** Estás en una fiesta en la casa de Dalia. Un amigo llama por teléfono y tú describes lo que está pasando en la fiesta. Usa los verbos entre paréntesis en la forma del presente progresivo para explicar lo que están haciendo todos.

Modelo yo (hablar por teléfono)
>   *Estoy hablando por teléfono.*

1. Dalia (servir la comida)
2. Luis y Alfonso (comer pizza)
3. María Esther (beber una soda)
4. Felicia, Marciano y Mateo (jugar a las cartas)
5. Fernando (bailar con su novia)
6. los padres de Dalia (dormir)
7. la hermana de Dalia (leer una novela)
8. el hermano de Dalia (¿?)

5.9 **¿Qué están haciendo?** Con un compañero de clase, decidan dos actividades que las personas de la lista están haciendo.

Miguel Cabrera, jugador de béisbol

Modelo Los estudiantes están en la biblioteca.
Están estudiando.
Están buscando libros.

1. El chef Pepín está en la cocina.
2. El presidente está en Camp David.
3. Juanes y Shakira están en el estudio.
4. El profesor de español está en la oficina.
5. Miguel Cabrera está en el parque.
6. Tú estás en la clase de biología.
7. Isabel Allende está en su oficina.
8. Sonia Sotomayor está en Washington, D.C.

5.10 **En la oficina** Usando el presente progresivo, describe lo que están haciendo en la oficina.

5.11 **Un amigo curioso** Trabaja con un compañero. Imaginen que uno de ustedes llama por teléfono a las siguientes horas y pregunta **¿Qué estás haciendo?** Túrnense para ser el amigo curioso y para responder.

Modelo 8:00 de la mañana
Estudiante 1: *¿Qué estás haciendo?*
Estudiante 2: *Estoy tomando café.*

1. 9:00 de la mañana
2. mediodía
3. 2:00 de la tarde
4. 5:00 de la tarde
5. 8:00 de la noche
6. medianoche

¿Qué estás haciendo?

A analizar ▶

Mira el video otra vez. Después lee parte de la conversación entre Camila y Vanesa y observa los usos de los verbos **ser** y **estar**.

Camila:	Mis suegros van a llegar de Colombia esta noche y **estoy** preparando comida. Afortunadamente no tengo que limpiar la casa. Rodrigo **está** en casa hoy y **está** limpiando la sala y los baños…
Vanesa:	¿Y cómo **son** tus suegros? ¿Tienes una buena relación con ellos?
Camila:	Pues, sí, nos llevamos bien. **Son** simpáticos, en particular mi suegra. Ella también **es** maestra. Mi suegro **es** un poco difícil con la comida. Él **es** de Uruguay y no le gusta mucho la comida colombiana. Bueno, ¿y cómo **estás** tú, Vanesa?
Vanesa:	¡**Estoy** muy feliz! ¡Carlos Vives viene a dar un concierto!
Camila:	¿De veras? ¿Cuándo?
Vanesa:	Va a **estar** en el auditorio municipal el once de mayo. ¿Quieres ir?
Camila:	¡Por supuesto! **Es** mi artista favorito. Oye, ¿qué hora **es**?
Vanesa:	**Son** las tres y media.

1. What are the uses of **estar** you have learned so far? Find examples in the paragraph.
2. Look at the verb **ser** in the paragraph. What are the different ways in which it is used?

A comprobar

Ser and estar

1. The verb **ser** is used in the following ways:

    a. to describe characteristics of people, places, or things

      La profesora **es** inteligente.
      The professor is intelligent.

      Mi coche **es** muy viejo.
      My car is very old.

    b. to identify a relationship, occupation, or nationality

      Esta **es** mi novia; **es** peruana.
      This is my girlfriend; she is Peruvian.

      Ellos **son** mecánicos.
      They are mechanics.

    c. to express origin

      Yo **soy** de Cuba.
      I am from Cuba.

    d. to express possession

      Este libro **es** de Álvaro.
      This book belongs to Álvaro.

    e. to tell time and give dates

      Es tres de marzo y **son** las dos.
      It is the third of March, and it is two o'clock.

2. The verb **estar** is used in the following ways:

    a. to indicate location

      El perro **está** enfrente de la casa.
      The dog is in front of the house.

    b. to express an emotional, mental, or physical condition

      Estoy muy feliz.
      I am very happy.

      Mi madre **está** enferma hoy.
      My mother is sick today.

      Las secretarias **están** ocupadas.
      The secretaries are busy.

    c. in the present progressive

      Estoy estudiando.
      I am studying.

3. It is important to realize that the use of **ser** and **estar** with some adjectives can change the meaning of those adjectives. The use of **ser** indicates a characteristic or a trait, while the use of **estar** indicates a condition. Here are some common adjectives that change meaning:

estar aburrido(a) *to be bored*

ser aburrido(a) *to be boring*

estar alegre (feliz) *to be happy (emotion)*

ser alegre (feliz) *to be a happy person*

estar bueno(a)/ malo(a) *to be (taste) good/bad (condition)*

ser bueno(a)/malo(a) *to be good/bad (general quality)*

estar guapo(a) *to look handsome/pretty (condition)*

ser guapo(a) *to be handsome/pretty (characteristic)*

estar listo(a) *to be ready*

ser listo(a) *to be clever*

estar rico(a) *to be delicious*

ser rico(a) *to be rich*

> **INVESTIGUEMOS LA GRAMÁTICA**
>
> While **estar** is generally used to indicate location, if you want to say where an event takes place, use **ser**.
> La fiesta **es** en la casa de Alejandro.
> *The party **is** at Alejandro's house.*

Carlos **es** alegre.

Carlos is happy. (a happy person) (personality)

Graciela **está** alegre.

Graciela is happy. (emotion)

La fruta **es** buena.

Fruit is good. (general quality)

Los tomates **están** buenos.

The tomatoes are (taste) good. (present condition)

A practicar

5.12 **¿Es posible?** Mira la foto y lee las oraciones. Decide si son posibles o no.

1. Son amigos.
2. Están enojados.
3. Están en la universidad.
4. Son muy viejos.
5. Están hablando.
6. Son de Puerto Rico.

© Alberto L. Pomares G./iStockphoto

5.13 **¿Cómo son o cómo están?** Decide qué expresiones pueden completar las oraciones correctamente. Hay más de una posibilidad para cada oración.

1. Yo estoy…

   a. cansada   b. en clase ahora   c. estudiante   d. enamorado

2. Javier y Marta son…

   a. mis amigos   b. enfermos   c. colombianos   d. enfrente de la clase

3. Madrid es…

   a. en Europa   b. cosmopolita   c. muy bonita   d. la capital de España

4. El profesor de español está…

   a. en la oficina   b. interesante   c. rubio   d. ocupado

5. Nosotros somos…

   a. inteligentes   b. de Chile   c. hermanos   d. preocupados

6. Mis primos son…

   a. profesores   b. cerca de la casa   c. guapos   d. estudiando

7. Tú estás…

   a. mi amigo   b. contenta   c. inteligente   d. detrás del hotel

8. Mi hermano está…

   a. hablando   b. listo   c. peruano   d. simpático

5.14 **Una foto** En parejas, contesten las preguntas sobre la foto. Inventen la información que no es evidente. **¡OJO!** Atención al uso de los verbos **ser** y **estar**.

1. ¿Quiénes son las personas en la foto?
2. ¿Cómo están hoy?
3. ¿Cómo son?
4. ¿De dónde son?
5. ¿Dónde están?
6. ¿Qué están haciendo?

© StockLite/Shutterstock

5.15 **¿Ser o estar?** Completa el párrafo con la forma apropiada del presente del indicativo de **ser** o **estar.**

Hoy **(1)** _____ primero de septiembre, el primer día de clases. **(2)** _____ las once y media y yo **(3)** _____ en la clase de inglés. Yo **(4)** _____ un poco nervioso porque es mi primera clase de inglés. Laura **(5)** _____ mi amiga y ella **(6)** _____ en la clase también. Nosotros **(7)** _____ muy interesados en aprender inglés. El profesor de la clase **(8)** _____ el señor Berg. Él **(9)** _____ alto, delgado y moreno. Es evidente que él **(10)** _____ simpático. Creo que va a **(11)** _____ un buen semestre.

5.16 **¿Cómo eres y cómo estás?** Decide cuáles de los siguientes adjetivos te describen a ti. Después pregúntale a tu compañero si esos adjetivos también lo describen a él. Atención al uso de **ser** y **estar,** y a las formas de los adjetivos.

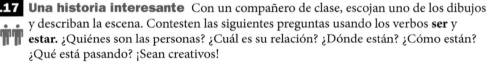

Modelo   contento   Estudiante 1: *¿Estás contento?*
                     Estudiante 2: *Sí, estoy contento. /*
                     No, no estoy contento.
         rico   Estudiante 1: *¿Eres rica?*
                     Estudiante 2: *Sí, soy rica. / No, no soy rica.*

1. enamorado   6. romántico
2. triste   7. enfermo
3. inteligente   8. atlético
4. tímido   9. preocupado
5. cansado   10. optimista

© schwarzhana/Shutterstock

5.17 **Una historia interesante** Con un compañero de clase, escojan uno de los dibujos y describan la escena. Contesten las siguientes preguntas usando los verbos **ser** y **estar.** ¿Quiénes son las personas? ¿Cuál es su relación? ¿Dónde están? ¿Cómo están? ¿Qué está pasando? ¡Sean creativos!

Modelo   *El hombre es Tomás y la mujer es Graciela. Son buenos amigos.*
         Están en la sala de espera (waiting room) *del hospital porque la madre de Graciela*
         está enferma.
         Ellos están muy preocupados...

© Cengage Learning

Entrando en materia

¿Quién es tu actor favorito y cómo es su personalidad? ¿Qué le preguntarías
(would you ask) si pudieras *(if you could)* hablar con él o ella?

Entrevista de un actor

🔊 Vas a escuchar un fragmento de una entrevista *(interview)* con el actor Francisco Méndez.
1-30 Escucha con atención y después responde las preguntas.

Vocabulario útil

las admiradoras	*fans*
conociéndonos	*getting to know each other*
el maquillaje	*makeup*
los milagros	*miracles*
parecer	*to seem*

Estrategia

Guess intelligently

Make intelligent guesses as to the meaning of words you do not know, and use context and intonation to help you figure out the meanings of words.

Comprensión

1. ¿En qué evento están? ¿dónde?
2. ¿Cómo es la personalidad de Francisco, según él *(according to him)*?
3. ¿Cómo está Francisco cuando debe hablar frente a muchas personas?
4. ¿Cómo es la novia de Francisco?
5. ¿Francisco está enamorado de su novia?

🖧 Más allá

Imagina que puedes entrevistar a un actor, a una actriz o a un artista que te gusta mucho.
Piensa en cinco preguntas que harías *(that you would ask)* en tu entrevista. Comparte
el nombre del actor o del artista y tus preguntas en Share it! Lee las preguntas de tus
compañeros. ¿Conoces a todos los actores y artistas?

Tengo muchos admiradores.

© wassiliy-architect/Shutterstock

Lectura

Antes de leer

Contesta las preguntas.

1. En general ¿qué necesitas para ser feliz?

2. ¿En qué países piensas que las personas son más felices? ¿Por qué?

A leer

¿Quiénes son más felices?

research
it is known
but rather

Gracias a muchas **investigaciones**
se sabe que la felicidad no depende
del dinero, **sino** de la calidad de las
relaciones entre las personas. Aunque
hay muchos estudios sobre la felicidad
con resultados diferentes, en la mayoría
de estos estudios los latinos **aparecen**

appear

entre las personas más felices del
planeta. En estas páginas hablaremos
sobre los resultados de tres estudios
sobre la felicidad.

El primero fue publicado por la
revista *Forbes.* En este estudio no
hay ningún país latinoamericano y
los Estados Unidos aparecen en el
10º lugar. Los primeros puestos son
todos para países europeos y para
Canadá, Australia y Nueva Zelandia.
Sin embargo, este estudio se basa
solamente en estadísticas económicas

© Monkey Business Images/Shutterstock

salaries

[los latinos aparecen entre las
personas más felices del planeta]

como **sueldos** altos
y oportunidades de
empleo, y no en la
opinión de las personas

it has been proven

entrevistadas. Un problema con este criterio es que **se ha comprobado**
experimentalmente que la economía no tiene relación con el nivel de la felicidad

once

una vez que se pueden satisfacer las necesidades básicas.

El segundo estudio lo publica el índice del Planeta Felíz *(Happy Planet Index)*, que da periódicamente sus resultados según criterios de **sustentabilidad** y de la percepción (subjetiva) de felicidad de los encuestados. En sus resultados del 2012, Costa Rica está en el primer lugar y 17 de los 25 países más felices del mundo están en Latinoamérica. Otros países en la lista son Colombia, todos los países centroamericanos, Venezuela, Cuba, Argentina, Chile y México. Los Estados Unidos están en el puesto 114, cerca del final de la lista.

sustainability

© Jacob Wackerhausen/iStockphoto

El tercer estudio, **hecho** por Global Research en 2012, está basado completamente en preguntarles a las personas si son muy felices, felices, poco felices o infelices. De acuerdo

done

a las respuestas obtenidas, entre los primeros 25 países hubo 3 países latinoamericanos (Venezuela, Argentina y Uruguay). España está también entre esos países. Chile y México siguen de cerca. Esta investigación **concluyó** que Latinoamérica es la región más felíz del mundo, mientras que Europa está en el **último** lugar (solo el 15% dijo ser muy felíz). Los Estados Unidos están en el lugar 13° en la lista, a pesar de que otro estudio *(Harris Poll*, 2013) encontró que en los Estados Unidos solo el 33% de las personas piensa que es feliz.

concluir to conclude

last

Curiosamente, de entre todas las estadísticas demográficas, el único factor que parece afectar la felicidad es estar casado: las personas que están casadas **dicen** ser más felices.

claim

Sources: http://www.nationmaster.com/graph/lif_hap_net-lifestyle-happiness-net
Nationmaster.com; Ipsos-na.com; *El Ciervo*

Comprensión

1. ¿Cuál es el tema del artículo?
2. Según el artículo ¿de qué depende la felicidad?
3. Según *Forbes* ¿qué condiciones son necesarios para ser felíz?
4. Según el índice del Planeta Felíz, ¿cuál es el país más felíz? ¿Qué países latinoamericanos están en la lista de los más felices según el índice del Planeta Felíz?
5. ¿Hay similitudes en los tres estudios?

Después de leer

Con un compañero, escriban una lista de cuatro o cinco cosas que pueden hacer para ser más felices.

Luisa es fotógrafa y asiste a una reunión de aniversario de su graduación para ver a sus compañeros. ¿Qué profesiones tienen ellos?

REUNIÓN DE LA GENERACIÓN DEL 98

la enfermera · el músico · el médico · la mesera · el mecánico · la fotógrafa · la cocinera · el pintor · el actor · el asistente de vuelo · el piloto · el policía · el científico · el deportista

© Cengage Learning

Las profesiones

el (la) abogado(a)	lawyer
la actriz	actress
el (la) agente de viajes	travel agent
el amo(a) de casa	homemaker
el (la) arquitecto(a)	architect
el bailarín/la bailarina	dancer
el (la) cantante	singer
el (la) contador(a)	accountant
el (la) consejero(a)	counselor
el (la) dependiente	store clerk
el (la) diseñador(a)	designer
el (la) escritor(a)	writer
el (la) ingeniero(a)	engineer
el jefe/la jefa	boss
el (la) maestro(a)	teacher
el (la) modelo	model

el (la) periodista	reporter
el (la) político(a)	politician
el (la) psicólogo(a)	psychologist
el (la) secretario(a)	secretary
el (la) trabajador(a) social	social worker
el (la) vendedor(a)	salesperson
el (la) veterinario(a)	veterinarian

Palabras adicionales

el (la) cliente	client
la entrevista	interview
ganar	to earn; to win
la solicitud	application; want ad
el sueldo	salary
el trabajo	job

A practicar

5.18 **Escucha y responde** Vas a escuchar una lista de profesiones. Levanta la mano si una persona que tiene la profesión mencionada lleva uniforme.

1-31

5.19 **¿Dónde trabajan?** Relaciona a la persona con su lugar de trabajo.

1. _____ un dependiente   **a.** un hospital

2. _____ un cocinero   **b.** un teatro

3. _____ un pintor   **c.** un restaurante

4. _____ un actor   **d.** una tienda

5. _____ un médico   **e.** un estudio

5.20 **¿Qué hacen?** Con un compañero escriban una actividad que hacen las siguientes personas en su trabajo.

Modelo   mesero
> *Un mesero sirve café.*

1. maestro   **4.** policía

2. secretario   **5.** ama de casa

3. enfermero   **6.** deportista

5.21 **¿Cuál es su profesión?** ¿Puedes identificar las profesiones de las siguientes personas? Identifica las que sabes *(the ones you know)* y después pregunta a tus compañeros para completar la información. Incluye toda la información adicional posible.

Modelo   Jennifer López
> Estudiante 1: *¿Cuál es la profesión de Jennifer López?*
> Estudiante 2: *Es cantante. También es actriz en las películas* Selena, Gigli *y* El cantante. *Ella es de Puerto Rico.*

1. Albert Pujols   **5.** Esmeralda Santiago

2. Carolina Herrera   **6.** Fernando Botero

3. Isabel Allende   **7.** Carlos Santana

4. Antonio Banderas   **8.** Michelle Bachelet

5.22 **Consejero** Imagina que eres consejero y debes recomendarles una profesión a algunos estudiantes, según sus clases favoritas y sus intereses. Túrnense con un compañero.

Modelo   las matemáticas y la química
> Estudiante 1: *Me gustan las matemáticas y la química. ¿Qué profesión debo estudiar?*
> Estudiante 2: *Debes ser científico o ingeniero.*

1. los deportes y la clase de español   **4.** la biología y los animales

2. las clases de historia y de arte   **5.** las fiestas y cocinar

3. la música y bailar   **6.** las leyes *(law)* y la política

> **INVESTIGUEMOS LA MÚSICA**
> Listen to the Spanish classic "Cuando seas grande" by Argentinian rocker Miguel Mateos. What does the teenager in the song want to be when he grows up?

5.23 **Personas famosas** Trabaja con un compañero para completar la información. Uno de ustedes debe ver la tabla en esta página, y el otro debe ver la tabla en el **Apéndice B.** Túrnense para preguntar y responder.

Nombre	Profesión	País de origen
Alicia Alonso	bailarina	
Óscar de la Renta		República Dominicana
Andrea Serna	periodista, modelo	Colombia
Baruj Benacerraf		
Gabriela Mistral	escritora, maestra	
Luis Federico Leloir		Argentina

Cultura

Las profesiones relacionadas con el arte deben enfrentar un reto *(challenge)* adicional: además de crear su arte, deben también crear un mercado para su arte, es decir, deben encontrar compradores, o empleadores que necesiten bailarines, actores, escritores, etcétera.

Según un estudio publicado en los Estados Unidos, casi la mitad *(almost half)* de los artistas pasan la mayor parte de su tiempo en el sector comercial, buscando oportunidades de darse a conocer *(to make themselves known)* en su comunidad. Uno de los mejores ejemplos de un genio artístico que aprendió a promover *(to promote)* su arte con éxito fue Salvador Dalí, el pintor surrealista, quien usaba su excentricidad para vender su arte. Además, Dalí supo rodearse *(knew how to surround himself)* de personas influyentes. Sin embargo, se debe mencionar que Dalí contó con un mecenas *(sponsor)* muy rico, Edward James. Dalí terminó por romper con *(break away from)* el grupo de artistas surrealistas. Lo acusaron de amar demasiado el dinero y también lo condenaron por no proclamarse contra el fascismo porque Dalí pensaba que el arte puede ser apolítico. Cuando lo expulsaron del grupo surrealista, Dalí respondió simplemente: "El surrealismo soy yo". El tiempo le dio la razón: Salvador Dalí se conoce como el padre del surrealismo.

Observa la obra de Dalí de la fotografía. ¿Te gusta? ¿Por qué?

Persistencia de la memoria, de Salvador Dalí

© Digital Image © The Museum of Modern Art/Licensed by SCALA/Art Resource, NY.
© 2014 Artists Rights Society (ARS), New York.

Busca en Internet más pinturas de Salvador Dalí. Sube a Share It! una pintura que te gusta. Luego mira las pinturas de tus compañeros. ¿Cuál te gusta más? ¿Por qué?

Comunidad

Entrevista a una persona de un país hispanohablante acerca de su ocupación. Puedes preguntarle en qué y dónde trabaja, si le gusta su trabajo y si quiere tener una ocupación diferente en el futuro. Repórtale a la clase la información.

© Xavier Subias/age fotostock

Comparaciones

¿Piensas que en los Estados Unidos la gente trabaja mucho? ¿Crees que trabajan más en otros países? Mira la información en el cuadro y contesta las preguntas.

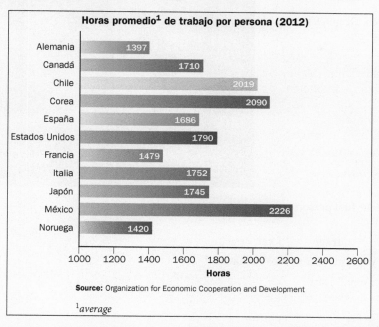

Horas promedio[1] de trabajo por persona (2012)

País	Horas
Alemania	1397
Canadá	1710
Chile	2019
Corea	2090
España	1686
Estados Unidos	1790
Francia	1479
Italia	1752
Japón	1745
México	2226
Noruega	1420

Horas

Source: Organization for Economic Cooperation and Development

[1]average

En promedio (*On average*), ¿cuántas horas trabajan al año en Chile y en México? ¿Quiénes trabajan más: los españoles o los estadounidenses? ¿Cómo puedes explicar las diferencias?

Conexiones... a la economía y al comercio

Hay muchas compañías de los Estados Unidos que tienen fábricas (*factories*) en países en vías de desarrollo (*developing*). Estas industrias se llaman **maquiladoras,** y hacen todo tipo de productos, como ropa, zapatos, muebles, productos químicos y electrónicos.

Habla con un compañero sobre las siguientes preguntas. Luego investiga qué compañías de los Estados Unidos tienen maquiladoras en otros países y repórtaselo a la clase.

1. ¿Cuáles son las ventajas (*advantages*) y las desventajas para la compañía? ¿y para los empleados?
2. ¿Qué efectos tienen las maquiladoras en la economía de los Estados Unidos? ¿y en la economía de los países donde se establecen?

© Ragne Kabanova/Shutterstock

Investiga en Internet y aprende más sobre los países latinoamericanos donde los Estados Unidos tienen maquiladoras en el **Apéndice A: Exploraciones del mundo hispano.**

A analizar

Vanesa habla de su profesión. Mira el video. Después lee el párrafo y observa las formas de los verbos.

> Yo soy fotógrafa y trabajo para esta revista. ¡Me gusta mucho mi trabajo! Siempre llego a la oficina a las ocho y **pongo** todo en orden. Durante el día **conduzco** a diferentes lugares y **veo** a personas interesantes. Además tengo suerte porque **salgo** de viaje con frecuencia. **Traigo** la cámara si la quieren ver.

1. Look at the paragraph again and find the first person **(yo)** form of the following verbs.

   conducir   poner   salir   traer   ver

2. Do you notice a pattern in any of the **yo** forms of the verbs? What is it?

A comprobar

Verbs with changes in the first person

1. Some verbs in the present tense are irregular only in the first person **(yo)** form. You have already seen the verb **hacer.**

   hacer *(to do; to make)*

hago	hacemos
haces	hacéis
hace	hacen

2. The following verbs also have irregular first person forms:

   poner *(to put; to set)*   **pongo,** pones, pone, ponemos, ponéis, ponen

   salir *(to go out, to leave)*   **salgo,** sales, sale, salimos, salís, salen

   traer *(to bring)*   **traigo,** traes, trae, traemos, traéis, traen

   conducir *(to drive)*   **conduzco,** conduces, conduce, conducimos, conducís, conducen

   dar *(to give)*   **doy,** das, da, damos, dais, dan

   ver *(to see)*   **veo,** ves, ve, vemos, veis, ven

> **INVESTIGUEMOS A LA GRAMÁTICA**
>
> When telling where someone is leaving from, it is necessary to use the preposition **de**.
>
> Salgo **de** la casa a las 7:00.
> *I leave the house at 7:00.*

3. The following verbs are not only irregular in the first person form, but also have other changes:

decir *(to say, to tell)*

digo	decimos
dices	decís
dice	dicen

venir *(to come)*

vengo	venimos
vienes	venís
viene	vienen

seguir *(to follow; to continue)*

sigo	seguimos
sigues	seguís
sigue	siguen

oír *(to hear)*

oigo	oímos
oyes	oís
oye	oyen

A practicar

5.24 **¿Quién soy?** Decide quién hace las siguientes actividades.

> **Modelo** Les doy inyecciones a las mascotas.
> *el veterinario*

1. Hago las reservaciones para personas que quieren viajar.
2. Conduzco un coche con luces *(lights)* rojas y azules. No quieres conducir muy rápido cuando yo estoy cerca.
3. Les traigo la comida a los clientes en el restaurante.
4. Veo a muchas personas enfermas.
5. Escribo artículos, entrevisto a personas famosas y digo la verdad *(truth)*.
6. Oigo los problemas de muchas personas.
7. Muchas personas vienen a mi estudio y yo tomo fotos de ellas.
8. Pongo todo en orden en casa y salgo para comprar comida.

5.25 **Un día ocupado** Completa el párrafo usando los verbos de la lista en la primera persona singular (**yo**).

Soy ama de casa.

conducir	hacer	poner	salir	tener	venir

Soy ama de casa y (**1**) _____ que hacer mucho trabajo todos los días.

Primero (**2**) _____ el almuerzo para mis hijos. A las 7:45 ellos suben al

(get into) auto y (**3**) _____ a la escuela. Después, voy al supermercado,

(**4**) _____ a casa y (**5**) _____ la comida en el refrigerador. Más tarde

(**6**) _____ otra vez a la escuela para recoger a mis hijos.

5.26 **¿Qué hace Rocío?** Rocío es agente de viajes. Con un compañero, describan lo que hace Rocío. Incluyan todos los detalles posibles y usen verbos que conocen (know) y los siguientes verbos : **poner, oír, hacer, decir, salir, conducir.**

© Cengage Learning

5.27 **¿Con qué frecuencia...?** Habla con seis compañeros de clase y pregúntale a cada uno con qué frecuencia hace una de las siguientes actividades. Después, comparte la informacíon con la clase.

siempre (always)   **a veces** (sometimes)   **casi nunca** (almost never)
nunca (never)

Modelo   hacer la cama
        Estudiante 1: *¿Con qué frecuencia haces la cama?*
        Estudiante 2: *Siempre (A veces/Casi nunca/Nunca) hago la cama.*

1. seguir las recomendaciones de tus amigos
2. salir los fines de semana
3. ver la televisión por la noche
4. venir tarde a la clase
5. dar respuestas correctas en clase
6. hacer la tarea para la clase de español

5.28 **Los estudios** Entrevista a un compañero de clase para saber (to know) más sobre sus hábitos.

1. ¿Qué coche conduces? ¿Tienes que conducir a la universidad?
2. ¿A qué hora vienes a la universidad? ¿A qué hora regresas a casa?
3. ¿Cuántos libros tienes en tu mochila? ¿Siempre (Always) traes el libro de español a clase?
4. ¿Cuándo haces la tarea? ¿Dónde prefieres hacer la tarea?
5. ¿Pones música cuando estudias? ¿Qué tipo de música escuchas cuando estudias?
6. ¿Sales con compañeros de clase? ¿Con quiénes?

¿Dónde prefieres hacer la tarea?

© wavebreakmedia/Shutterstock

Exploraciones gramaticales

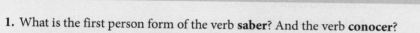

A analizar

Óscar habla de su profesión. Mira el video. Después lee la información y observa el uso de los verbos **saber** y **conocer**.

> **Camila:** Ahora, vamos a **conocer** al señor Fuentes.
>
> **Óscar:** Muchas gracias. ¿**Saben** cuál es mi profesión?
>
> **Niños:** ¡Policía!
>
> **Óscar:** ¡Exacto! Probablemente ustedes **saben** que mi trabajo es muy importante. **Conozco** a muchas personas que viven aquí y trabajo para protegerlos. Yo **conozco** muy bien la ciudad y las calles. Tengo un coche blanco y azul, y **sé** conducir muy bien. Puedo correr muy rápido si es necesario, y también **sé** hacer karate. ¡Es un trabajo muy interesante!

1. What is the first person form of the verb **saber**? And the verb **conocer**?
2. The verbs **saber** and **conocer** both mean *to know*. Explain the difference in their uses above.

A comprobar

Saber and conocer

1. As with the other verbs in this chapter, **saber** and **conocer** are irregular in the first person form.

saber	**sé**, sabes, sabe, sabemos, sabéis, saben
conocer	**conozco**, conoces, conoce, conocemos, conocéis, conocen

2. While the verbs **saber** and **conocer** both mean *to know*, they are used in different contexts.
   - **Saber** is used to express knowledge of facts or information as well as skills.
   - **Conocer** is used to express acquaintance or familiarity with a person, place, or thing.

   Notice the difference in meaning in the following sentences:

   > Ana **conoce** Chile. *(familiarity)*
   > Ana **sabe** dónde está Chile. *(fact)*

   > Paco **conoce** a Diego. *(acquainted with)*
   > Paco **sabe** dónde vive Diego. *(information)*

   > **Conozco** la poesía de Neruda. *(familiarity)*
   > **Sé** que Neruda es un poeta famoso. *(fact)*

3. When using **saber** to mean *to know how to do something*, it is followed by the infinitive.

   > El ingeniero **sabe diseñar** edificios.
   > The engineer **knows how to design** buildings.

   > El cantante **sabe cantar**.
   > The singer **knows how to sing**.

4. When expressing some knowledge or familiarity with general concepts or subjects, the verb **conocer** is used.

   > El artista **conoce** el arte prehispánico.
   > The artist **knows** (is familiar with) *pre-Hispanic art*.

   > La enfermera **conoce** la medicina.
   > The nurse **knows** (is familiar with) *medicine*.

5. When the recipient of the action (direct object) is a person or a pet, an **a** is used in front of the object. This is known as the **a personal** and is not translated into English. It is not necessary to use it with the verb **tener**; however when using the verb **conocer** to tell that someone knows a person, it is necessary to use the **a personal**.

   > La profesora **conoce a** los estudiantes.
   > The professor **knows** her students.

   > El jefe **conoce a** sus empleados.
   > The boss **knows** his employees.

A practicar

5.29 **¿Lógica o ilógica?** Decide si las siguientes descripciones de profesiones son lógicas. Corrige las oraciones ilógicas.

1. La bailarina sabe jugar al fútbol.
2. El periodista conoce a muchas personas famosas.
3. El médico sabe dónde está la farmacia.
4. El contador sabe cantar bien.
5. El veterinario conoce a unos criminales.
6. La secretaria sabe usar la computadora.
7. El psicólogo conoce bien la cocina del restaurante.
8. El escritor conoce las obras *(works)* más importantes de la literatura.

5.30 **Oraciones incompletas** Decide qué opciones pueden completar las siguientes oraciones. Hay más de una posibilidad para cada oración.

1. El médico conoce...
   - **a.** a sus pacientes.
   - **b.** la medicina.
   - **c.** dar inyecciones.
   - **d.** el hospital.

2. El arquitecto sabe...
   - **a.** al ingeniero.
   - **b.** diseñar casas.
   - **c.** dónde está la casa.
   - **d.** la ciudad.

3. El científico conoce...
   - **a.** las ciencias.
   - **b.** cómo hacer el experimento.
   - **c.** el laboratorio.
   - **d.** que su trabajo es importante.

4. El consejero sabe...
   - **a.** los problemas de sus clientes.
   - **b.** escuchar bien.
   - **c.** a sus clientes.
   - **d.** a qué hora vienen los clientes.

5.31 **¿Saber o conocer?** Primero completen individualmente las siguientes oraciones con las formas necesarias de los verbos **saber** y **conocer.** Después, túrnense para leer las definiciones y decir cuál es una profesión lógica.

Modelo Estudiante 1: Yo ____sé____ tocar el piano.
Estudiante 2: Un músico.

1. Yo _____ bien la ley *(law).*
2. Julio _____ pintar bien.
3. Matilde y Simón _____ a muchos médicos.
4. Fabio _____ al presidente.
5. Daniela y yo _____ tomar buenas fotos.
6. Yo _____ dónde están los buenos hoteles.
7. Mario y Luisa _____ bien a los animales en el zoológico donde trabajan.
8. Tú _____ cocinar muy bien.
9. Yo _____ bailar tango.
10. El señor Montero _____ a sus estudiantes.

© Sandra Gligorijevic/Shutterstock

5.32 **Puerto Rico** Con un compañero, túrnense para preguntar si saben o conocen las siguientes cosas.

Modelo Puerto Rico

> Estudiante 1: *¿Conoces Puerto Rico?*
> Estudiante 2: *Sí, conozco Puerto Rico. / No, no conozco Puerto Rico.*

> hablar español bien
> Estudiante 1: *¿Sabes hablar español bien?*
> Estudiante 2: *Sí, sé hablar español bien. / No, no sé hablar español bien.*

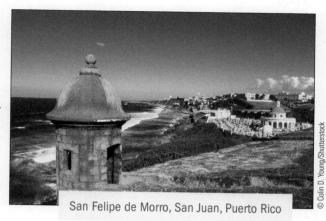

San Felipe de Morro, San Juan, Puerto Rico

© Colin D. Young/Shutterstock

1. dónde está Puerto Rico
2. un puertorriqueño
3. la comida puertorriqueña
4. quién es el gobernador de Puerto Rico
5. San Juan
6. la historia de Puerto Rico
7. cuándo es el día de la independencia de Puerto Rico
8. bailar salsa

5.33 **¿Qué saben? ¿Qué conocen?** En parejas, túrnense para completar las siguientes oraciones.

1. a. Nosotros conocemos…
   b. Nosotros sabemos…
2. a. Los periodistas conocen…
   b. Los periodistas saben…
3. a. Un jefe conoce…
   b. Un jefe sabe…
4. a. El presidente conoce…
   b. El presidente sabe…

5.34 **En busca de...** Decide qué verbo necesitas usar en cada oración y después busca a ocho compañeros diferentes que respondan positivamente a una de las siguientes preguntas. Después de responder, deben contestar la pregunta adicional. Luego, comparte las respuestas con la clase.

1. ¿(sabes/conoces) a una persona famosa? (¿Quién?)
2. ¿(sabes/conoces) un buen restaurante? (¿Cuál?)
3. ¿(sabes/conoces) hablar otra lengua (¿Cuál?)
4. ¿(sabes/conoces) a una persona de otro país *(country)*? (¿Qué país?)
5. ¿(sabes/conoces) el nombre del presidente de Argentina? (¿Cómo se llama?)
6. ¿(sabes/conoces) cocinar? (¿Cuál es tu especialidad?)
7. ¿(sabes/conoces) muy bien la ciudad donde vives? (¿Cuál es tu lugar favorito?)
8. ¿(sabes/conoces) cuál es la capital de Venezuela? (¿Cuál es?)

Lectura

Antes de leer

Menciona dos profesiones que te parecen poco comunes. ¿Por qué piensas que son poco comunes? ¿Conoces a alguien con una profesión poco común?

A leer

Profesiones poco comunes

cambiar: *to change*

En un mundo que está **cambiando** muy rápidamente, los trabajos de la gente también cambian a gran velocidad y muchos trabajos ya casi no existen, pero también aparecen nuevos empleos. Aquí te presentamos algunos trabajos poco comunes y muy modestos. Algunos están desapareciendo, y otros son relativamente nuevos.

thief
law

Ladrón profesional: Este novedoso trabajo es para ladrones que no roban más y están del lado de la **ley**. Muchas tiendas de departamentos contratan a estas personas para descubrir vulnerabilidades con la seguridad y corregirlas para **evitar** robos.

> [los trabajos de la gente también cambian a gran velocidad]

to avoid

La lavandera: Para las personas que no están contentas con su lavadora de ropa, o no tienen una, la lavandera es una gran ayuda. Va a la casa de una persona para lavar **a mano** toda la ropa **sucia.**

by hand / dirty

El organillero: En raras ocasiones, puedes encontrar al organillero en un parque de la ciudad, tocando música con su organillo. No es muy común pero a veces es posible ver a un chimpancé bailando a la música del organillero, y pidiéndole dinero a la gente en la calle. Esta profesión originada en Europa ya es casi algo del pasado.

© John Mitchell / Alamy

dice
losses

Inspector de dados: Es muy importante para los casinos no tener dados defectuosos, pues pueden ocasionar muchas **pérdidas.** Por eso los fabricantes de dados y los casinos necesitan personas para probar los dados antes de usarlos en el casino.

El adivinador: Va por el parque con un pajarito en una **jaula.** Cuando el cliente le paga al adivinador, el pájaro selecciona un papel que dice su suerte, igual que un horóscopo.

cage

Repartidores: Van por toda la ciudad y llevan artículos de gran importancia a las casas de la gente. Hay muchos tipos de repartidores, pero los

más importantes son los repartidores de agua potable y los que reparten el gas para cocinar. Otros repartidores llevan **refrescos** o periódicos a las casas.

soft drinks

Limpiador de chicles: Un trabajo relativamente moderno es el de limpiar los chicles de las calles. Aunque, en el caso de Chile **intentaron** limpiar con

gum

tried

agua a presión, y productos químicos, nada funciona tan bien como una vieja espátula. En otros países no existe este trabajo tan expecializado, sino que emplean un vehículo especial para limpiar las calles. Esta labor de limpieza es importante porque el chicle (o goma de mascar) es un foco de bacterias y enfermedades: una sola goma puede tener hasta 70 mil bacterias y hongos. Otra consecuencia es que los pájaros mueren después de comer un chicle. Además **afean** la ciudad ¿y a quién le gusta **pisar** uno?

makes it ugly / step on

Sources: Trabajo.about.com; Diario.latercera.com; Eluniversal.com.mx; 3djuegos.com

Comprensión

1. ¿Cuáles de estos trabajos están desapareciendo? ¿Cuáles son relativamente modernos?
2. ¿Quiénes usan los servicios de los ladrones profesionales?
3. ¿Qué hace la lavandera?
4. ¿Dónde trabaja el adivinador y por qué necesita un pájaro?
5. ¿Qué artículos llevan a las casas los repartidores?
6. ¿Por qué es importante limpiar los chicles de las calles?

Después de leer

En grupos de tres, hablen sobre los trabajos que tienen o los trabajos que consideren interesantes. Incluyan lo siguiente: las habilidades *(skills)* necesarias, la preparación necesaria, el sueldo, lo que les gusta del trabajo y lo que no les gusta del trabajo.

Redacción

Write an email to a friend telling him/her about a new job.

Paso 1 Brainstorm a list of jobs that you think are fun or exciting.

Paso 2 Pick one of the jobs from your list of interesting jobs. Jot down as many things as you can about that job: Why do you find it interesting? Where do professionals in that field work? What do they do? What do they have to know? Who do they work with? How much do they work?

Paso 3 Write a list of emotions that you might feel if you were to have a job like the one you described in **Paso 2.**

Paso 4 Imagine that you have the job you described in **Paso 2.** Begin the email to your friend and ask how he/she is doing. Then say how you are feeling.

Paso 5 Continue your email telling your friend that you have a new job. Then write a paragraph in which you discuss various aspects of the job using the information you generated in **Paso 2.** Also describe how you are feeling about the job using the list you created in **Paso 3.**

Paso 6 Conclude your email.

Paso 7 Edit your email:

1. Is your email logically organized with smooth sentence transitions?
2. Are there any short sentences you can combine by using **y** or **pero**?
3. Do verbs agree with the subjects?
4. Do adjectives agree with the nouns they describe?
5. Did you use **ser** and **estar** properly?
6. Are there any spelling errors?

Entrando en materia

Cuando buscas un trabajo y lees solicitudes de trabajo, ¿qué tipo de requisitos *(requirements)* es común encontrar?

Solicitudes de trabajo

Aquí hay algunas solicitudes de empleo de un periódico de Colombia.

EMPLEO

ARQUITECTO. Empresa solicita Arquitecto o Diseñador. Hombres o mujeres, 25 a 35 años, experiencia programas 3d autocad, etc. Excelente presentación, disponibilidad de horario y para viajar. Interesados comunicarse al 3636-1111 (de 10:00 a 18:00 hrs).

DEPENDIENTE. Mujer honesta y responsable para trabajar en una óptica en Plaza Fancy, turno completo, sin experiencia y preparatoria terminada. Interesadas enviar curriculum vitae a: plazafancy@empleos.com. Sueldo base $4,000 + Comisión.

CAJERO. Administrador de pizzería, hombre, edad máxima 30 años, zona Ciudad Bugambilias. Contratación Inmediata. Comunicarse al: 3693-9393.

SUPERVISOR. Empresa en expansión ofrece oportunidad de trabajo de medio tiempo, de lunes a viernes. Buscamos personas mayores de 17 años para supervisar personal y atender líneas telefónicas. Para mayor información comunicarse al número 467676767 o enviar hoja de vida al correo electrónico empleo@gmail.com preguntar por la señorita Marciano.

SE Solicita Ama de Casa. Para atender señor solo. Tardes libres. Informes al 345-0900- 2636.

CHOFER. Hotel solicita chofer de camioneta. Requisitos: Inglés indispensable, disponibilidad de horario para rotar turnos, actitud de servicio. Interesados presentar solicitud en Avenida Bolívar 7002, en horario de oficina.

ABOGADA. Bufete de abogados e inversionistas requiere abogada titulada. Responsabilidades: Examinar procesos civiles. Informes al 900 800-7000.

DENTISTA o pasante para trabajo en clínica dental de Ortodoncia. Turno completo, sexo femenino. Informes al 987- 5567-8133 a mandar curriculum o: ortodoncia@ortomax.com.

EJECUTIVO(A) de ventas con experiencia, auto compacto y disponibilidad para viajar, 25–35 años. Ofrecemos producto de primera necesidad para la industria hotelera, sueldo base más comisión, y prestaciones de ley. Interesados enviar c.v con foto a: gerencia@ hotelería.com.

ENFERMERA(O). General/técnica, indispensable cédula profesional. Edad: 25–45 años, estado civil indistinto, experiencia comprobable de tres años. Sueldo según aptitudes. Enviar curriculum a: recursoshumanos@ hospitalSanJose.com.

MESEROS y cantineros. Ambos sexos. Requisitos: experiencia mínima de 3 años, excelente presentación, disponibilidad de horario. Presentarse con curriculum o solicitud elaborada en Restaurante Bar Arcoiris, centro histórico, teléfono 987-6543- 4571.

RECEPCIONISTA. Empresa nacional solicita personal mixto para trabajar medio tiempo. Requisitos: responsable y con iniciativa, disponibilidad de horario. Buena presentación, edad 23 a 35 años, manejo de PC, paquete Office. Citas al Tel: 541-5959-6283, extensión 345.

SE solicita Instructor de Yoga. Experiencia mínima de un año, de 20 a 35 años, interesados llamar al cel: 044-33 3403-3466.

Comprensión

1. ¿Qué tipo de trabajos ofrecen las solicitudes de empleo?
2. ¿Qué tipo de requisitos tienen?
3. ¿Qué diferencias hay entre estos anuncios y los de los Estados Unidos?

Más allá

Escribe un anuncio de empleo para una profesión no representada en estos anuncios. Compártela en Share It! y lee los anuncios de tus compañeros. ¿Te interesa alguno de los anuncios?

Vocabulario

Sustantivos

el abuso	*abuse*
el alcohol	*alcohol*
la autoestima	*self-esteem*
la custodia	*custody*
la droga	*drug*
la rehabilitación	*rehabilitation*
la violencia	*violence*

Adjetivos

agresivo(a)	*aggressive*
obsesionado(a)	*obsessed*
violento(a)	*violent*

Verbos

dejar de + *infinitive*   *to stop doing something*

Frases útiles

¿En qué puedo ayudarle?
How can I help you?

¿Tiene problemas de salud?
Do you have any health problems?

¿Cuál es su número de seguridad social?
What is your Social Security number?

¿Cómo se llama la persona encargada de su caso?
What is the name of your case worker?

Voy a referirlo a...
I am going to refer you to . . .

Necesitamos hacer una cita con...
We need to make an appointment with . . .

Estrategia

Guess intelligently.

Use context, intonation as well as visual clues such as body language, gestures, facial expressions, and images to help you figure out the meaning of words.

DATOS IMPORTANTES

Educación: Licenciatura en trabajo social o carrera relacionada, aunque muchos puestos requieren una maestría

Salario: Entre $38 000 y $60 000

Dónde se trabaja: Escuelas primarias y secundarias, hospitales, asilos para ancianos, centros para el tratamiento de abuso, agencias para individuos y familias, el gobierno local o estatal

Vocabulario nuevo Completa las oraciones con la palabra apropiada de la lista de vocabulario.

1. Para un alcohólico es difícil _____ beber.
2. La cocaína y la heroína son _____ ilegales.
3. Una persona que no tiene un buen concepto de sí mismo *(himself)* tiene _____ baja.
4. Si los padres son violentos, no pueden tener _____ de sus hijos.
5. Muchas veces es necesario ir a un centro de _____ para poder controlar una adicción.

▶ Ana Correa, trabajadora social

Ana Correa es trabajadora social y ayuda a personas con diferentes problemas, como la falta de *(lack of)* trabajo, las drogas y la violencia doméstica. En el video vas a ver una entrevista entre Ana y una persona que necesita ayuda.

© Cengage Learning

Antes de ver

1. ¿Cuáles son los problemas sociales más comunes en los Estados Unidos? Existen esos problemas en tu comunidad?
2. ¿Qué tipo de ayuda crees que puede ofrecer un trabajador social para los problemas mencionados en la pregunta número 1?
3. ¿Hay lugares en tu comunidad donde puedes hablar con un trabajador social?

Comprensión

1. ¿Cómo se llama el hombre que habla con Ana Correa y qué problema tiene?

2. ¿Cómo está el hombre en el momento de la entrevista?

3. ¿Qué datos le pide la trabajadora social?

4. ¿Con quién vive el Sr. Gómez?

5. ¿Qué dice la Sra. Correa sobre el alcohol?

6. ¿Es el Sr. Gómez agresivo?

7. ¿Qué debe hacer el Sr. Gómez?

Después de ver

 En grupos de tres, representen a una pareja o dos amigos que van a ver a un trabajador social por primera vez. Uno perdió *(lost)* su trabajo y no puede encontrar un nuevo trabajo. El trabajador social debe hacer preguntas y dar consejos.

El consejero debe preguntar sobre:

Nombre de la persona

Dirección y teléfono

Educación

Habilidades y talentos

Preferencias

Preguntas posibles para el consejero:

¿En qué les puedo ayudar?

¿Cómo están ahora?

5.35 **Un día en la vida** Completa el siguiente párrafo con la forma necesaria de la palabra entre paréntesis. A veces debes escoger entre dos palabras. **¡OJO!** Algunos de los verbos requieren el uso del presente progresivo.

Me llamo Romina. **(1)** _____ (Ser/Estar) de Cuzco, Perú, pero

(2) _____ (ser/estar) en Nueva York. **(3)** _____ (Ser/Estar) cocinera ¡y

me encanta mi trabajo! Ahora estoy **(4)** _____ (trabajar) en un restaurante

con un cocinero francés. Estoy **(5)** _____ (aprender) mucho con él.

Yo **(6)** _____ (saber/conocer) a mis clientes muy bien. Ellos **(7)** _____

(venir) al restaurante con frecuencia y **(8)** _____ (decir) que mi comida es la

mejor en Nueva York. Algún día quiero **(9)** _____ (ser/estar) dueña *(owner)*

de un restaurante andino. Yo **(10)** _____ (saber/conocer) cocinar muy bien...

¡yo **(11)** _____ (hacer) unos platos deliciosos! **(12)** _____ (Ser/Estar)

segura de que puedo tener éxito.

5.36 **Descripción personal** Conjuga el verbo en la primera persona (**yo**), y completa la oración de una forma original para escribir una descripción personal.

1. (Ser)...
2. Hoy (estar)...
3. (Venir) a la clase de...
4. Los fines de semana (salir)...

5. Yo no (saber)...
6. (Conocer) a...
7. No (hacer)...
8. (Conducir)...

5.37 **Mensajes de texto** Estás visitando la ciudad de Barcelona, en España, y escribes varios mensajes en tu teléfono celular para decirles a tus amigos lo que estás haciendo en ese momento. Usa el presente progresivo para hablar de tus actividades.

1. 10:30 A.M. – caminar por el parque Güell
2. 1:00 P.M. – comprar recuerdos en las Ramblas
3. 2:00 P.M. – almorzar en el Café 4Gats
4. 4:00 P.M. – visitar el mercado
5. 6:00 P.M. – ver cuadros en el Museo de Picasso
6. 8:00 P.M. – beber y comer en un restaurante de tapas

5.38 **En el trabajo** Explica lo que las siguientes personas saben o conocen según *(according to)* la profesión que tienen.

Modelo Isabel es veterinaria.
Ella conoce a las mascotas de sus clientes. Sabe cómo ayudar a los animales.

1. Leticia es mesera.
2. Ernesto es secretario.
3. Esmeralda es mujer policía.
4. Mario es deportista.
5. Alicia es ama de casa.
6. Marcelo es maestro.

5.39 **Descripción de fotos** Con un compañero describan las siguientes fotos. Deben determinar quiénes son las personas en las fotos, qué relación tienen, cuáles son sus profesiones, qué están haciendo y qué emociones se muestran en las fotos. ¡OJO con los verbos **ser** y **estar**!

Modelo *Marta no está contenta. Es escritora y está hablando por teléfono con el editor. Él necesita el libro en dos semanas.*

5.40 **Información, por favor** Trabaja con un compañero. Uno debe mirar el gráfico en esta página y el otro debe mirar el gráfico en el **Apéndice B.** Túrnense para preguntarse y completar el gráfico con la información necesaria. Necesitan identificar sus profesiones, sus orígenes, dónde están ahora y cómo están. Atención al uso de **ser** y **estar.**

Nombre	Profesión	Origen	Localización	Emoción
Carlota		Madrid	la casa	
Éric			el banco	frustrado
César	periodista	San Juan		cansado
Paloma	abogada		el correo	
Samuel		Managua	la oficina	
Camila	diseñadora			divertida

5.41 **¿Estás feliz?** Tú y tu compañero trabajan para una revista y deben escribir un test de felicidad para los lectores *(readers)*.

Paso 1 Escribe una lista de 5–7 actividades que hace una persona feliz.

Paso 2 Comparte *(Share)* tu lista con tu compañero y decidan 6 actividades que deben incluir en el test.

Paso 3 Tomen el test y descubran si son felices. Después compartan los resultados con el resto de la clase.

Vocabulario 1

Los estados de ánimo y otras expresiones con el verbo *estar*

aburrido(a)	*bored*	enojado(a)	*angry*
alegre	*happy*	equivocado(a)	*wrong*
asustado(a)	*scared*	feliz	*happy*
avergonzado(a)	*embarrassed*	frustrado(a)	*frustrated*
borracho(a)	*drunk*	interesado(a)	*interested*
cansado(a)	*tired*	loco(a)	*crazy*
celoso(a)	*jealous*	nervioso(a)	*nervous*
confundido(a)	*confused*	ocupado(a)	*busy*
contento(a)	*happy*	preocupado(a)	*worried*
deprimido(a)	*depressed*	sano(a)	*healthy*
divertido(a)	*entertained; in a good mood*	seguro(a)	*sure*
enamorado(a) (de)	*in love (with)*	sorprendido(a)	*surprised*
enfermo(a)	*sick*	triste	*sad*

Palabras adicionales

la salud   *health*

Diccionario personal

_____

_____

_____

_____

_____

_____

_____

_____

_____

_____

🔊 Vocabulario 2

1-33

Las profesiones

el (la) abogado(a)	*lawyer*		el (la) ingeniero(a)	*engineer*
el actor	*actor*		el jefe/la jefa	*boss*
la actriz	*actress*		el (la) maestro(a)	*elementary/ high school teacher*
el (la) agente de viajes	*travel agent*			
el amo(a) de casa	*homemaker*		el (la) mecánico(a)	*mechanic*
el (la) arquitecto(a)	*architect*		el (la) médico(a)	*doctor*
el (la) asistente de vuelo	*flight attendant*		el (la) mesero(a)	*waiter*
			el (la) modelo	*model*
el bailarín/la bailarina	*dancer*		el (la) músico(a)	*musician*
			el (la) periodista	*journalist*
el (la) cantante	*singer*		el (la) piloto	*pilot*
el (la) científico(a)	*scientist*		el (la) pintor(a)	*painter*
el (la) cocinero(a)	*cook*		el policía/la mujer policía	*police officer*
el (la) consejero(a)	*adviser*			
el (la) contador(a)	*accountant*		el (la) político(a)	*politician*
el (la) dependiente	*clerk*		el (la) psicólogo(a)	*psychologist*
el (la) deportista	*athlete*		el (la) secretario(a)	*secretary*
el (la) diseñador(a)	*designer*		el (la) trabajador(a) social	*social worker*
el (la) enfermero(a)	*nurse*			
el (la) escritor(a)	*writer*		el (la) vendedor(a)	*salesperson*
el (la) fotógrafo(a)	*photographer*		el (la) veterinario(a)	*veterinary*

Palabras adicionales

el (la) cliente	*client*		el sueldo	*salary*
la entrevista	*interview*		el trabajo	*job*
la solicitud	*application; want ad*			

Los verbos

conducir	*to drive*		saber	*to know (facts; how to do something)*
conocer	*to know, to be acquainted with*			
			salir	*to go out, to leave*
dar	*to give*		seguir (i)	*to follow*
decir (i)	*to say, to tell*		traer	*to bring*
ganar	*to earn*		venir (ie)	*to come*
hacer	*to do, to make*		ver	*to see*
oír	*to hear*			
poner	*to put; to set*			

Learning Strategy

Study with a partner

Study with a friend or form a study group. Not only will you benefit when someone in your group understands a concept that you may have difficulty with, but you can also increase your own understanding by teaching others who need extra help. Group study will provide you with more opportunities to speak and listen to Spanish as well.

In this chapter you will learn how to:

- Talk about your daily routine
- Discuss your hobbies and pastimes
- Talk about when and how often you do things
- Talk about sports
- Discuss events that occurred in the past

¿Cómo pasas el día?

© Caroline Webber/age fotostock

Es temprano por la mañana y la familia Cervantes comienza su día.

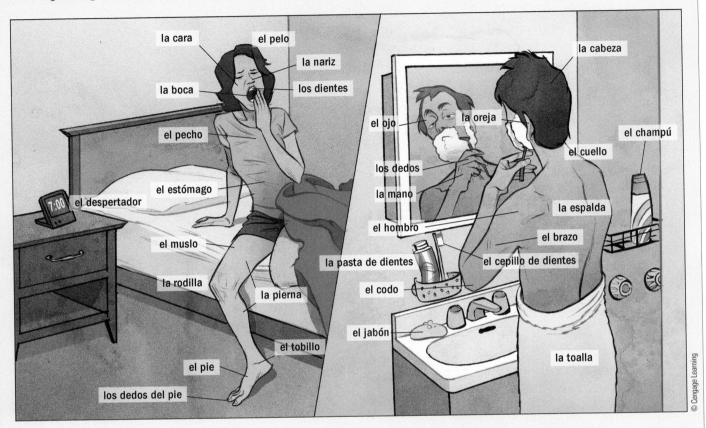

Verbos

acostarse (ue)	to go to bed, to lie down	**ducharse**	to shower	**verse**	to look at oneself
afeitarse	to shave	**estirarse**	to stretch	**vestirse (i)**	to get dressed
arreglarse	to fix oneself up; to get ready	**lavarse**	to wash		
		levantarse	to get up	**Palabras adicionales**	
bañarse	to bathe, to take a bath	**maquillarse**	to put on make-up	**tarde**	late
cepillarse	to brush	**peinarse**	to comb or style one's hair	**temprano**	early
cortarse	to cut				
despertarse (ie)	to wake up	**ponerse (la ropa)**	to put on (clothing)		
divertirse (ie)	to have fun	**quitarse (la ropa)**	to take off (clothing)		
dormirse (ue)	to fall asleep	**secarse**	to dry oneself		
		sentarse (ie)	to sit down		

> **INVESTIGUEMOS EL VOCABULARIO**
>
> In addition to **el pelo, el cabello** can also be used to refer to hair.

A practicar

6.1 **Escucha y responde** Vas a escuchar varias partes del cuerpo. Señala la parte del cuerpo que escuches.

🔊 1-34

6.2 **Asociaciones** ¿Qué ropa asocias con las siguientes partes del cuerpo?

1. los pies
2. las piernas
3. la cabeza
4. las manos
5. el cuello
6. la espalda y el pecho

6.3 ¿Qué parte del cuerpo es? Completa las descripciones.

1. _____ está entre la cabeza y los hombros y sirve para mover la cabeza.

2. Tenemos dos _____, y cada uno tiene cinco dedos. Sirven para caminar y bailar.

3. Usamos _____ para hablar y para comer.

4. Tenemos dos _____ en la cara para ver.

5. _____ está en el brazo, entre la mano y el hombro.

6. Tenemos dos _____. Una está en el lado izquierdo de la cabeza, y la otra en el lado derecho.

7. Yo tengo _____ largo, rubio y rizado *(curly)*.

8. _____ es una parte que conecta la pierna con el pie.

6.4 No corresponde Trabaja con un compañero. Observen los grupos de palabras y túrnense para decidir cuál es diferente. Expliquen por qué.

Modelo la pierna   la toalla   el pie
        la toalla porque no sirve para caminar

1. los pies	las manos	el cuello
2. los dedos	la boca	la nariz
3. el pelo	el codo	la rodilla
4. el estómago	el diente	la espalda
5. el muslo	la oreja	el tobillo
6. el despertador	la pasta de dientes	el jabón

6.5 ¿Cuándo? Con un compañero, túrnense para explicar en qué situaciones una persona tiene que hacer las siguientes actividades.

Modelo ducharse con agua fría
        Estudiante 1: *¿Por qué una persona tiene que ducharse con agua fría?*
        Estudiante 2: *La persona tiene mucho calor.*

1. sentarse al frente de la clase
2. acostarse muy tarde
3. vestirse con ropa muy vieja
4. estirarse

5. levantarse muy temprano
6. afeitarse las piernas
7. cortarse el pelo
8. cepillarse los dientes

> **INVESTIGUEMOS EL VOCABULARIO**
> In some Latin American countries, **el dentífrico** is used rather than **la pasta de dientes** to say *toothpaste.*
> In Mexico **rasurarse** is used to say *to shave* rather than **afeitarse,** and **bañarse** refers to both showering and bathing.

6.6 Unos monstruos Trabaja con un compañero. Uno debe mirar el dibujo en esta página, y el otro va a mirar el dibujo en el **Apéndice B.** Túrnense para describir los monstruos y encontrar las cinco diferencias.

© Cengage Learning

Conexiones culturales

La vida diaria

Cultura

Antonio López García (1936–) es un famoso artista español. Comenzó a pintar influenciado por su tío, quien era pintor. López García escribió: "Una obra nunca se acaba *(is finished)*, sino que se llega al límite de las propias *(own)* posibilidades". Con esta idea describe su propio proceso como pintor, ya que *(since)* a veces toma muchos años para terminar un cuadro. Varias de sus obras reflejan momentos de la vida diaria. Algunos críticos definen su estilo como hiperrealista porque sus cuadros parecen casi fotografías.

Observa su cuadro *Lavabo y espejo*. ¿Qué objetos reconoces? ¿Te gusta? ¿Por qué? ¿Qué sentimientos *(feelings)* te inspira?

> Investiga en Internet otras obras de Antonio López García. Sube una que te guste en Share It! con el título de la pintura. Identifica qué hay en la pintura y explica por qué te gusta.

Antonio López García, *Lavabo y espejo*

Comparaciones

Cada país tiene frases y refranes que reflejan la cultura popular. Las siguientes frases populares se relacionan con las partes del cuerpo. Por ejemplo, la frase "cuesta un ojo de la cara" significa que algo cuesta mucho dinero. Si una persona dice "¡Hoy en día *(Nowadays)* la gasolina cuesta un ojo de la cara!" significa que la gasolina es muy costosa. ¿Puedes adivinar el significado de los refranes después de leer los ejemplos? ¿Conoces alguna frase que signifique lo mismo en inglés?

1. **ser codo**
   ¡Mi novio es muy codo! Nunca me invita a cenar.

2. **hacérsele (a uno) agua la boca**
   Mi mamá hace un flan delicioso. ¡Se me hace agua la boca!

3. **tomar el pelo**
   ¿No hay exámenes en la clase de matemáticas? ¿Me estás tomando el pelo?

4. **no tener pies ni cabeza**
   No entiendo la explicación. No tiene ni pies ni cabeza.

5. **no tener pelos en la lengua**
   Mi hermana no tiene pelos en la lengua y siempre dice lo que piensa.

> **INVESTIGUEMOS LA MÚSICA**
>
> Listen to "Mis Ojos" by the Mexican rock group Maná. Write all the parts of the body mentioned in the song. Listen a second time. What is the tone of the song? Why?

Conexiones... a la música

Pin Pon fue originalmente un programa de televisión de Chile en el que un personaje *(character)* llamado Pin Pon le enseña a los niños buenos hábitos y valores *(values)*. La siguiente es una canción infantil de este programa. Pin Pon se conoce en todos los países latinoamericanos.

© Carlos Restrepo/Shutterstock

Pin Pon es un **muñeco**   *doll*
con cara de cartón
se lava la carita
con agua y con jabón.

Se peina los cabellos
con peines de **marfil**   *ivory*
y aunque le den **tirones**   *tugs*
no **llora** ni hace así.   *cry*

Como siempre **obedece**   *obeys*
lo que manda mamá
estudia las lecciones
antes de irse a acostar.

Y cuando las **estrellas**   *stars*
empiezan a **brillar**   *to shine*
Pin Pon se va a la cama
reza y se echa a soñar.

¿Conoces alguna canción en inglés con el mismo propósito *(goal)*? ¿Qué dice la canción?

Busca el nombre de una película chilena y aprende más sobre Chile en **Exploraciones del mundo hispano** en el **Apéndice A.**

Comunidad

Como la canción de Pin Pon, existen muchos libros para niños que enseñan a tener buenos hábitos de higiene. Pregunta en la biblioteca de tu comunidad si tienen un programa para leerles en español a los niños. Si tu biblioteca no tiene un programa, puedes ser voluntario en un programa bilingüe en un jardín de niños o en una escuela primaria. ¡Leer es una magnífica manera de practicar español!

© Rob Marmion/Shutterstock

Exploraciones **gramaticales**

A analizar ▶

Camila habla con su consejera sobre su rutina. Después de ver el video, lee lo que Camila dice y observa las estructuras de los verbos.

> Todos los días **me despierto** a las seis, **me peino** rápidamente y **me visto**. Después de **arreglarme**, despierto a mi hijo y preparo su cereal... Acuesto al niño y después mi esposo y yo vemos la tele un poco. Antes **de acostarme**, me baño. Prefiero **bañarme** en la noche porque no tengo mucho tiempo en la mañana. **Me acuesto**, leo y **me duermo**.

1. What is the subject of the verbs in bold in the examples above?
2. What do you notice about the verbs in bold in the paragraph above?
3. Notice the different structures of the verbs **acostar** and **despertar** in the examples below. How are they different? Why do you think the structures are different?

   Todos los días **me despierto** a las seis... / **despierto** a mi hijo y preparo su cereal...

   Acuesto al niño... / **Me acuesto,** leo y me duermo.

A comprobar

Reflexive verbs

1. Many verbs used to discuss daily routines (**bañarse, despertarse, vestirse,** etc.) are known as reflexive verbs. Reflexive verbs are used to indicate that the subject performing the action also receives the action of the verb. In other words, these verbs are used to describe actions we do to ourselves.

   Ella **se pone** un vestido azul.
   *She **puts on** (herself) a blue dress.*

   Yo **me levanto** temprano.
   *I **get** (myself) **up** early.*

2. Reflexive verbs are conjugated in the same manner as other verbs; however, they must have a reflexive pronoun. The reflexive pronoun agrees with the subject of the verb.

   lavarse *(to wash oneself)*

yo	**me** lavo	nosotros	**nos** lavamos
tú	**te** lavas	vosotros	**os** laváis
él, ella, usted	**se** lava	ellos, ellas, ustedes	**se** lavan

The following verbs from the **Vocabulario** section are verbs with reflexive pronouns:

acostarse* (ue)	divertirse* (ie)	ponerse
afeitarse	dormirse* (ue)	quitarse
arreglarse	ducharse	secarse
bañarse	estirarse	sentarse* (ie)
cepillarse	lavarse	verse
despertarse* (ie)	levantarse	vestirse* (i)

*stem-changing verbs

3. The reflexive pronoun is placed in front of a conjugated verb.

   Nosotros **nos** acostamos tarde.
   We go to bed late.

   Yo **me** estoy durmiendo.
   I am falling asleep.

> **INVESTIGUEMOS LA GRAMÁTICA**
>
> **Dormirse** has a reflexive pronoun, but it is slightly different from the other reflexive verbs. The pronoun indicates a change of state rather than a subject doing something to himself/herself.

4. When using an infinitive, attach the reflexive pronoun to the end. Note that even in the infinitive form, the pronoun agrees with the subject. The pronoun can also be attached to the present participle, but you must add an accent to maintain the original stress.

> ¿Vas a bañar**te** ahora?
> *Are you going to bathe now?*

> Estoy lavánd**ome** la cara.
> *I am washing my face.*

5. Many verbs can be used reflexively or nonreflexively, depending on who (or what) receives the action.

> Gerardo **se lava** las manos.
> *Gerardo **washes** his (own) hands.*

> Felipe **lava** el coche.
> *Felipe **washes** the car.*

> (Felipe does not receive the action; the car does.)

> Rebeca **se mira** en el espejo.
> *Rebeca **looks at herself** in the mirror.*

> Los niños miran a la maestra.
> *The children **look at** the teacher.*

> (The children do not receive the action; the teacher does.)

6. When using reflexive verbs, do not use possessive adjectives.

> Silvia se lava **el** pelo.
> *Silvia washes **her** hair.*

7. Some verbs have a slightly different meaning when used with a reflexive pronoun, such as **irse** *(to go away, to leave)* and **dormirse** *(to fall asleep).*

> Liz **se duerme** a las diez todas las noches.
> *Liz falls asleep at ten o'clock every night.*

> Liz **duerme** ocho horas cada noche.
> *Liz sleeps eight hours each night.*

A practicar

6.7 **Conclusiones lógicas** Empareja las columnas para hacer oraciones lógicas.

1. El despertador suena a las ocho y tú...
2. No hay agua caliente y por eso yo...
3. Empieza la clase de aeróbic y la profesora...
4. Son las once de la noche y nosotros...
5. Tengo que ir a una fiesta formal y yo...
6. Después de comer ellos...

a. me pongo un vestido elegante.
b. se estira.
c. se cepillan los dientes.
d. te levantas y te vistes.
e. nos acostamos.
f. prefiero no ducharme.

6.8 **Mis hábitos** Habla con un compañero sobre tus hábitos. Conjuga el verbo en la forma apropiada y completa las oraciones.

Modelo Yo (lavarse) el pelo...
> Estudiante 1: *Yo me lavo el pelo con Champú Reina, ¿y tú?*
> Estudiante 2: *Yo me lavo el pelo con Champú Brillo.*

1. Los fines de semana yo (acostarse)...
2. Yo (estirarse) cuando...
3. A veces yo (dormirse) cuando...
4. Yo nunca (ponerse)...
5. En clase de español prefiero (sentarse)...
6. Yo (divertirse) cuando...

NotarYES/Shutterstock

6.9 **Entrevista** Entrevista a un compañero con estas preguntas.

1. ¿A qué hora te despiertas de lunes a viernes? ¿y los sábados o domingos?
2. Generalmente, ¿cuánto tiempo necesitas para arreglarte?
3. ¿En qué ocasiones te pones ropa elegante?
4. ¿A veces te duermes en clase? ¿En qué clase?
5. ¿Qué haces para divertirte?
6. ¿Prefieres bañarte o ducharte?

6.10 **Una mañana muy apurada** Completa el siguiente párrafo con la forma necesaria del verbo apropiado. Después, compara tus respuestas con las de un compañero. **¡OJO!** Unos verbos son reflexivos y otros no.

Carmen **(1.)** _____ (despertar/despertarse) y **(2.)** _____ (mirar/mirarse) el reloj. ¡Las siete de la mañana! Los niños deben estar en la escuela a las ocho. Rápidamente va al cuarto de sus hijos y **(3.)** _____ (despertar/despertarse) a Carlos y Víctor. Ellos **(4.)** _____ (levantar/levantarse) y van al baño. Mientras los niños **(5.)** _____ (bañar/bañarse), Carmen **(6.)** _____ (preparar/prepararse) el desayuno *(breakfast)* para ellos. Cuando Carlos y Víctor entran en la cocina para desayunar, Carmen corre al baño y empieza a **(7.)** _____ (arreglar/arreglarse). Ella **(8.)** _____ (maquillar/maquillarse) y **(9.)** _____ (vestir/vestirse). Después Carmen **(10.)** _____ (llamar/llamarse) a sus hijos. Carlos y Víctor van al baño y **(11.)** _____ (cepillar/cepillarse) los dientes. Carmen **(12.)** _____ (peinar/peinarse) a los chicos y todos salen de la casa a las ocho menos diez.

6.11 **Las rutinas** ¿Qué están haciendo estas personas?

1.

2.

3.

4.

5.

6.

6.12 **En busca de...** Busca a compañeros que hagan las siguientes actividades. Habla con una persona diferente para cada actividad de la lista. **¡OJO!** Tienes que decidir si debes usar la forma reflexiva del verbo o no y conjugarlo para preguntarles a tus compañeros. Luego comparte *(share)* la información con la clase.

Modelo (duchar/ducharse) en la noche
    Estudiante 1: *¿Te duchas en la noche?*
    Estudiante 2: *Sí, me ducho en la noche.*

1. (levantar/levantarse) temprano los fines de semana
2. preferir (vestir/vestirse) con ropa cómoda
3. (lavar/lavarse) la ropa una vez a la semana
4. normalmente (dormir/dormirse) siete horas
5. preferir (sentar/sentarse) al frente de la clase
6. (poner/ponerse) la mesa antes de comer
7. (afeitar/afeitarse) todos los días
8. (cepillar/cepillarse) a una mascota

A analizar

Camila habla con su consejera. Mira el video otra vez. Después lee lo que dice Camila y observa las expresiones de tiempo en negritas.

Todos los días me despierto a las seis, me peino rápidamente y me visto. **Después de** arreglarme, despierto a mi hijo y preparo su cereal. Mi mamá **siempre** llega a las siete y media y yo salgo para la escuela. Paso el día en la escuela enseñando y **a veces** tengo reuniones con los otros maestros o con los padres de los niños en la tarde. Normalmente llego a casa **a las cinco** y empiezo a preparar la comida. **Después** mi esposo limpia la cocina mientras yo juego con mi hijo. Acuesto al niño y **después** mi esposo y yo vemos la tele un poco. **Antes de** acostarme, me baño.

1. What form of the verb is used after the expressions **antes de** and **después de**?
2. What form of the verb is used with the other expressions of time?

A comprobar

Adverbs of time and frequency

1. One of the functions of an adverb is to tell when an action occurs. The following are common adverbs of time, some of which you have already learned:

a menudo	*often*
ahora	*now*
hoy	*today*
luego	*later*
mañana	*tomorrow*
más tarde	*later*
pronto	*soon*
todos los días	*every day*

Más tarde ellos van a arreglarse para salir.
Later they are going to get ready to go out.

Carmina está duchándose **ahora**.
Carmina is showering now.

Notice that it is possible to use the adverb either before or after the action.

2. The following adverbs of time usually come before the verb:

a veces*	*sometimes*
mientras*	*while*
normalmente	*normally, usually*
(casi) nunca	*(almost) never*
(casi) siempre	*(almost) always*
todavía	*still*
ya	*already*
ya no	*no longer*

*If using a subject in the sentence, these adverbs are placed in front of the subject.

A veces mi hermana se acuesta después de la medianoche.
Sometimes my sister goes to bed after midnight.

Mi padre **nunca** se afeita los fines de semana.
My father never shaves on the weekend.

3. To say what someone does before or after another activity, use the expressions **antes de** + *infinitive* and **después de** + *infinitive*.

> **Antes de acostarse, mi hijo lee un libro.**
> *Before going to bed, my son reads a book.*

> **Los niños necesitan cepillarse los dientes después de comer.**
> *The children need to brush their teeth after eating.*

When using a verb after a preposition (**a, con, de, para,** etc.), it is necessary to use the infinitive. **Antes** and **después** can also be used without the preposition **de**; however, the meaning changes slightly and they are translated as *beforehand* and

afterwards, respectively. They are followed by the conjugated verb.

> **Normalmente tomo un café y después voy a la universidad.**
> *Normally I have coffee and afterwards I go to the university.*

4. When saying how often you do something, use the word **vez** *(time)*.

> **Él se corta las uñas una vez a la semana.**
> *He cuts his nails **once a week**.*

> **Me cepillo los dientes tres veces al día.**
> *I brush my teeth **three times a day**.*

Notice that this adverbial expression comes after the activity.

A practicar

6.12 **¿Cierto o falso?** Habla con un compañero y dile *(tell him/her)* si las oraciones son ciertas o falsas para ti. Corrige las oraciones falsas para que sean *(so that they are)* ciertas.

1. Normalmente me seco el pelo con una secadora.
2. Me cepillo los dientes diez veces al día.
3. Me afeito todos los días.
4. Me ducho y luego me acuesto.
5. Escucho música mientras me arreglo.
6. Me visto después de cepillarme los dientes.
7. A menudo me despierto antes de escuchar el despertador.
8. Nunca me maquillo.

6.13 **¿Qué haces?** Completa las oraciones con las actividades que haces con la frecuencia indicada.

Modelo Siempre... *tomo café antes de la clase de español.*

1. Todos los días...
2. Una vez al día...
3. A veces...
4. Una vez al mes...
5. Una vez al año...
6. Ya no...
7. Casi nunca...
8. Nunca...

Siempre tomo café antes de la clase de español.

© beginwithaspin/Shutterstock

6.14 **¿Cuándo?** Mira las ilustraciones y explica cuándo las personas hacen una de las actividades en relación a la otra.

Modelo *Antes de ponerse un sombrero, se peina. / Después de peinarse, se pone un sombrero.*

1.

2.

3.

4.

5.

6.

© Cengage Learning

6.15 **¿Con qué frecuencia?** Con un compañero, pregúntense con qué frecuencia hacen las actividades de la lista.

Modelo cepillarse los dientes
　　　　 Estudiante 1: *¿Con qué frecuencia te cepillas los dientes?*
　　　　 Estudiante 2: *Me cepillo los dientes tres veces al día.*

1. levantarse antes de las ocho
2. bañarse (en la bañera)
3. ponerse ropa elegante
4. cortarse el pelo
5. lavarse la cara
6. dormirse con la tele encendida *(turned on)*
7. afeitarse
8. acostarse tarde

6.16 **¿Qué haces antes?** Con un compañero, túrnense para contestar las preguntas sobre sus actividades anteriores.

Modelo antes de levantarse
　　　　 Estudiante 1: *¿Qué haces antes de levantarte?*
　　　　 Estudiante 2: *Antes de levantarme apago* (turn off) *el despertador y escucho un poco de música.*

1. antes de salir para la universidad
2. antes de tomar un examen
3. antes de hacer ejercicio
4. antes de comer
5. antes de salir con amigos
6. antes de acostarse
7. antes de hacer un viaje
8. antes de comprar un coche

6.17 Opuestas Elisa y Florencia son muy diferentes y comparten *(share)* un apartamento. Con un compañero, túrnense para comparar sus hábitos. Usen algunos de los adverbios de tiempo.

Modelo Elisa lava la ropa todas las semanas pero Florencia casi nunca lava la ropa.

Elisa

Florencia

6.18 Entrevista Con un compañero, túrnense para responder las preguntas y describir sus rutinas. Usen los adverbios de tiempo para explicar la secuencia de actividades.

1. ¿Cómo es tu rutina por la mañana?
2. ¿Cómo es tu rutina por la noche?
3. ¿Cómo es un día típico en la universidad?
4. ¿Cómo es un día típico en el trabajo?
5. ¿Cómo es un sábado típico?
6. ¿Cómo es un domingo típico?
7. ¿Cómo es una cita romántica típica?
8. ¿Cómo es una típica celebración de Año Nuevo?

6.19 Una vida sana En un grupo de 3–4 estudiantes van a decidir quién tiene la vida más sana.

Paso 1 Escribe una lista de 7–8 hábitos y actividades que consideras sanas.

Paso 2 Comparte tu lista con los otros de tu grupo. Luego decidan 6 o 7 hábitos y actividades que piensan que son las más importantes para mantener una vida sana.

Paso 3 Pregúntense *(Ask each other)* con qué frecuencia hacen las actividades de la lista. Luego repórtenle a la clase quién tiene la vida más sana y por qué.

Entrando en materia

¿Qué le puedes decir a un niño que te pregunta por qué debemos lavarnos las manos?

Cómo mantenernos sanos

◀)) Vas a escuchar un fragmento de un programa para niños en donde hablan sobre buenos
1-35 hábitos de higiene personal. Escucha con atención y responde las preguntas que siguen.

Vocabulario útil

contagiarse	*to become infected*	**frotar**	*to rub*
enfermarse	*to become sick*	**los gérmenes**	*germs*
la enfermedad	*illness*	**la higiene**	*hygiene*
estornudar	*to sneeze*	**los resfriados**	*colds*
la época	*era, time*	**toser**	*to cough*

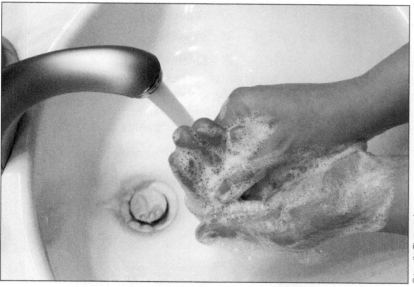
© topseller/Shutterstock

Comprensión

1. ¿Quién es el invitado *(guest)* al programa de hoy?
2. ¿Cuál es el tema del programa?
3. ¿Cómo llegan al cuerpo los gérmenes y bacterias?
4. ¿Qué significa "lavarse bien las manos"?
5. ¿Qué debe (o no) hacer una persona enferma para no contagiar a otros?

🔲 Más allá

Escoge una de las siguientes opciones, escribe una explicación para niños y compártela en
Share It!

1. por qué deben lavarse los dientes
2. por qué deben lavarse el pelo y peinarse

Lectura

Antes de leer

1. ¿Qué personas crees que toman siestas más frecuentemente y por qué?

2. ¿En qué países piensas que se toman siestas y por qué?

A leer

La siesta

La costumbre de dormir durante el día por media hora se originó en Roma, donde se usaba la expresión "hora sexta" para hablar del tiempo dedicado a dormir y descansar después de cinco horas de mucho trabajo. En España *became* "la hora sexta" **se convirtió** en *la siesta*. En el horario tradicional, exportado después a los países latinoamericanos, la gente come con su familia al mediodía y después descansa un poco antes de volver a trabajar.

Este tiempo es importante porque la comida al mediodía es la comida principal en muchos de

[recomiendan la siesta como algo positivo]

estos países, y es saludable tomar tiempo para digerir. Además, en los meses cuando hace mucho calor, nadie quiere salir a la calle durante *the warmest* estas horas, **las más calurosas** del día. Muchos estudios científicos recomiendan la siesta como algo positivo para la salud *as* **ya que** previene problemas cardiacos, ayuda a la digestión y

Casi nadie sale durante la hora de la siesta.

disminuye el estrés. Aún más, aunque las personas no siempre usan la siesta para dormir, la interrupción de las labores permite a las familias reunirse y pasar más tiempo juntas.

En algunos países hay empresas que entienden el valor de la siesta, y dan a sus trabajadores un espacio donde pueden descansar por algunos minutos para incrementar su productividad. Desafortunadamente, la hora dedicada a la siesta es una costumbre que está desapareciendo en muchos países. La gente ya casi nunca tiene tiempo para descansar debido principalmente a la presión de la vida en las ciudades, en donde el tiempo es poco, el tráfico y las distancias son grandes, y los negocios prefieren no cerrar, para tener algunos clientes más.

La siesta coincide con las horas de más calor.

Comprensión

1. ¿Cuál es el origen de la palabra *siesta*?
2. ¿Qué hacen las personas durante la hora de la siesta?
3. ¿Cuáles son los beneficios de tomar una siesta?
4. ¿Por qué está desapareciendo esta costumbre?
5. En tu opinión ¿crees que la costumbre de la siesta va a desaparecer por completo? ¿Por qué?

Después de leer

Habla con un compañero para responder las preguntas.

1. ¿Duermes una siesta a veces? ¿Por qué?
2. ¿Piensas que es una buena idea dormir siestas?
3. ¿Cuáles son las ventajas y las desventajas de dormir la siesta?

¡Es verano! Hace buen tiempo y algunas personas de la ciudad salen a disfrutar del buen tiempo.

esquiar en agua

la tienda de campaña

jugar al fútbol

el fútbol americano

la pelota

pescar

la raqueta

la red

bucear

el bádminton

patinar

andar en bicicleta

los patines

jugar al golf

montar a caballo

© Cengage Learning

Los deportes

el atletismo	track and field
el básquetbol	basketball
el béisbol	baseball
la natación	swimming
el tenis	tennis
el voleibol	volleyball

Los pasatiempos

acampar	to camp
esquiar en tabla	to snowboard
hacer alpinismo	to go mountain climbing
ir de excursión	to go hiking
jugar al ping-pong	to play ping-pong

levantar pesas	to lift weights
patinar en hielo	to ice skate

Palabras adicionales

el (la) aficionado(a)	fan (of a sport)
el campo	field
la cancha	court
el equipo	team; equipment
la entrada	ticket
el lago	lake
el partido	game (sport), match
el saco de dormir	sleeping bag

INVESTIGUEMOS EL VOCABULARIO
Here are two lexical variations:

el baloncesto	basketball
el (la) fanático(a)	fan

A practicar

6.20 **Escucha y responde** Vas a escuchar una lista de actividades. En un papel escribe **deporte** y en otro **equipo**. Si escuchas el nombre de un deporte, levanta el papel que dice **deporte,** y si es equipo para jugar, levanta el papel que dice **equipo.**

1-36

6.21 ¿Qué actividad es? Identifica el nombre del deporte que se necesita para completar las oraciones.

1. Es necesario tener dos equipos de seis personas, una pelota y una red para jugar al _____.

2. Jugamos _____ con raquetas, una mesa, una red y pelotas pequeñas.
3. Cuando vamos a acampar dormimos en_____.
4. Para jugar al fútbol necesitamos dos _____ de once personas.
5. Es necesario tener una _____ para jugar tenis.
6. El deporte más popular en Europa y Latinoamérica es _____.

> **INVESTIGUEMOS LA GRAMÁTICA**
>
> In Spanish it is possible to say both **juego fútbol** and **juego al fútbol.** Also, volleyball can be spelled as **volibol** or **voleibol.**

6.22 Relaciones Con un compañero, túrnense para relacionar las palabras de las dos columnas y explicar la relación.

1. la raqueta	**a.** el básquetbol
2. esquiar	**b.** la entrada
3. el partido	**c.** patinar en el hielo
4. el voleibol	**d.** el equipo
5. la cancha	**e.** la red
6. el aficionado	**f.** el campo

6.23 ¿Qué palabra no corresponde al grupo? Encuentra la palabra que no corresponda *(belong)*, y después compara tus respuestas con las de un compañero. Expliquen por qué no corresponde.

1. pescar	nadar	acampar	bucear
2. la raqueta	la tienda de campaña	la pelota	la red
3. patinar en hielo	jugar al golf	esquiar	esquiar en tabla
4. el fútbol	ir de excursión	el béisbol	el básquetbol
5. el aficionado	el saco de dormir	el partido	la cancha

6.24 En busca de... Busca a compañeros en tu clase que hacen las siguientes actividades en su tiempo libre. Deben dar información adicional al responder. Después repórtenle la información a la clase.

Modelo jugar al ping-pong
      Estudiante 1: *¿Juegas al ping-pong?*
      Estudiante 2: *Sí, juego al ping-pong en casa de mis amigos.*

1. jugar al fútbol	**5.** jugar bien al básquetbol
2. levantar pesas	**6.** estar en un equipo deportivo
3. acampar en el verano	**7.** patinar en hielo
4. ver golf en televisión	**8.** gustar ver fútbol americano

6.25 Actividades de verano Los organizadores de los eventos de verano para una pequeña ciudad están intercambiando información sobre el equipo que necesitan y las actividades que tienen planeadas. Trabaja con un compañero para completar la información. Uno de ustedes debe ver la información en esta página, y el otro debe ver la información en el **Apéndice B.**

Evento	Lugar del evento	Equipo que tienen	Equipo/recursos que necesitan
1.		cancha	pelotas
2. Excursión a la playa	Playa Bonita		
3.	la piscina del parque		instructores
4. Torneo de ping-pong		seis mesas	
5.	el estadio universitario	red	

Conexiones culturales
Los deportes en España y Latinoamérica

Cultura

El béisbol es muy popular en todos los países de la región del Caribe. Cuba, la República Dominicana y Venezuela son famosos por aportar excelentes jugadores de béisbol a las grandes ligas de los Estados Unidos, como el dominicano David Ortíz. San Pedro de Macorís, en la República Dominicana, es un pequeño pueblo que tiene una gran importancia para el béisbol, pues un gran número de jugadores de la MLB provienen de aquí. Uno de los jugadores más conocidos de este pueblo es Sammy Sosa.

Descubre el nombre de la isla que la República Dominicana comparte con Haití y aprende más sobre el país en **Exploraciones del mundo hispano** en el **Apéndice A.**

Busca en Internet quiénes son otros beisbolistas famosos de San Pedro de Macorís y para quién juegan. ¿Cómo crees que afecta a un pueblo pequeño tener tantos deportistas famosos? ¡Comparte tu respuesta y los nombres de los beisbolistas en Share It!

INVESTIGUEMOS LA MÚSICA
Similar to the Olympic Games, the FIFA World Cup soccer matches are played every four years. "We Are One" (Ola Ola) was selected as the official song of the 2014 World Cup and was performed by Jennifer López at the opening ceremony. The official anthem "Dar um Jeito" (We Will Find a Way) was performed at the closing ceremony by Carlos Santana, Wyclef Jean, Avicii and Alexandre Pires. Listen to both songs. Which do you like better? Why?

Comunidad

Muchos deportistas en los Estados Unidos vienen de países hispanohablantes. Investiga si hay jugadores de países hispanohablantes en tu universidad y escribe una entrevista para ese deportista. Las siguientes son algunas ideas para la entrevista:

¿Por qué le gusta jugar?

¿Con qué frecuencia practica?

¿Quiere ser profesional? ¿Por qué?

¿Cuándo empezó a jugar?

¿Jugó en un equipo de la escuela secundaria?

¿El deporte le ayudó a llegar a la universidad? ¿Cómo?

Comparaciones

En muchos países de habla hispana se practican deportes en las universidades, pero juegan un papel diferente de los deportes en los Estados Unidos, donde los estudiantes obtienen créditos por practicar deportes. En Latinoamérica los deportes son considerados un entretenimiento y generalmente las personas no mencionan sus actividades deportivas en su curriculum vitae *(résumé)*, excepto los deportistas. Sin embargo, la mayoría de las universidades tienen equipos deportivos que representan a su alma mater con orgullo.

¿Son importantes las actividades deportivas en tu universidad?

¿Hay becas *(scholarships)* para deportistas en tu universidad?

¿Son importantes las actividades deportivas en tu vida en general?

¿Cuántas horas a la semana practicas deportes?

Busca una universidad en España o en Latinoamérica en Internet y compara las actividades deportivas que se ofrecen con las actividades de una universidad en los Estados Unidos. Después, comparte los resultados de tu comparación en Share It!

Conexiones... a la antropología

Muchas civilizaciones antiguas practicaban deportes como juegos de pelota, pero el objetivo no era solamente el entretenimiento ya que el juego tenía significados religiosos. Entre las culturas anteriores a los incas, en los Andes, se usaban pelotas de goma *(rubber)* para jugar juegos parecidos al hockey y al tenis de hoy en día. También llenaban un pequeño saco con arena *(sand)* y lo decoraban con plumas *(feathers)* para practicar un juego similar al bádminton de hoy.

En el juego de pelota azteca (Tlachtli) la cancha representaba el mundo, y la pelota el sol o la luna. En este juego, la pelota debía atravesar el aro hecho de piedra *(stone)*. El juego de pelota azteca tenía una gran semejanza *(similarity)* con el juego Pok-a-tok de los mayas, juego en el que los jugadores debían tocar la pelota solamente con los codos, las rodillas o las caderas *(hips)*.

¿Conoces el origen de otros deportes o juegos?

Juego de pelota de los mayas, en Tikal

Source: http://www.efdeportes.com/efd90/juego.htm

A analizar

Rodrigo habla con Óscar sobre el fin de semana. Mira el video. Después lee lo que dice Rodrigo y observa las formas de los verbos en negritas.

> **Óscar:** (Yo) Te **llamé** el sábado para invitarte al partido de fútbol, pero no **contestaste.**
>
> **Rodrigo:** Camila y yo **pasamos** el fin de semana en la casa de sus padres. Viven cerca de un lago, entonces mi suegro y yo salimos en el bote y **pescamos.** A mi suegra no le gusta pescar, así que Camila y ella **nadaron** y **tomaron** el sol. ¡Pero lo mejor del fin de semana fue la comida! ¡Mi suegra es muy buena cocinera y **preparó** unas comidas muy ricas!

1. The boldfaced verbs are in the preterite tense. Do they refer to events that have already happened or that are going to happen in the future?

2. All the boldfaced words are **-ar** verbs. Using the verbs in the paragraph as a model, fill in the blanks with the appropriate verb endings .

-ar

yo	_____	nosotros(as)	_____
tú	-aste	vosotros(as)	-asteis
él, ella, usted	_____	ellos, ellas, ustedes	_____

A comprobar

The preterite

INVESTIGUEMOS LA GRAMÁTICA

Notice that the endings for regular **-er** and **-ir** verbs are identical in the preterite.

1. The preterite is used to discuss actions completed in the past.

> ¿**Jugaste** al tenis ayer?
> *Did you **play** tennis yesterday?*
>
> No, **nadé** en la piscina.
> *No, I **swam** in the pool.*

2. To form the preterite of regular **-ar, -er,** and **-ir** verbs, add these endings to the stem of the verb.

hablar *(to speak, to talk)*

yo	habl**é**	nosotros(as)	habl**amos**
tú	habl**aste**	vosotros(as)	habl**asteis**
él, ella, usted	habl**ó**	ellos, ellas, ustedes	habl**aron**

comer *(to eat)*

yo	com**í**	nosotros(as)	com**imos**
tú	com**iste**	vosotros(as)	com**isteis**
él, ella, usted	com**ió**	ellos, ellas, ustedes	com**ieron**

escribir *(to write)*

yo	escrib**í**	nosotros(as)	escrib**imos**
tú	escrib**iste**	vosotros(as)	escrib**isteis**
él, ella, usted	escrib**ió**	ellos, ellas, ustedes	escrib**ieron**

3. **-ar** and **-er** verbs that have stem changes in the present tense do not have a stem change in the preterite. You will learn about **-ir** stem-changing verbs later in this chapter.

cerrar *(to close)*

yo	cerré	nosotros(as)	cerramos
tú	cerraste	vosotros(as)	cerrasteis
él, ella, usted	cerró	ellos, ellas, ustedes	cerraron

volver *(to return)*

yo	volví	nosotros(as)	volvimos
tú	volviste	vosotros(as)	volvisteis
él, ella, usted	volvió	ellos, ellas, ustedes	volvieron

4. Verbs ending in **-car, -gar,** and **-zar** have spelling changes in the first person singular (**yo**) in the preterite. Notice that the spelling changes preserve the original sound of the infinitive for **-car** and **-gar** verbs.

-car	c → **qué**
tocar	yo **toqué,** tú tocaste, él tocó,...
-gar	g → **gué**
jugar	yo **jugué,** tú jugaste, él jugó,...
-zar	z → **cé**
empezar	yo **empecé,** tú empezaste, él empezó,...

5. The third person singular and plural of **leer** and **oír** also have spelling changes. An unaccented **i** always changes to **y** when it appears between two vowels. Notice the use of accent marks on all forms except the third person plural.

leer *(to read)*

yo	leí	nosotros(as)	leímos
tú	leíste	vosotros(as)	leísteis
él, ella, usted	**leyó**	ellos, ellas, ustedes	**leyeron**

oír *(to hear)*

yo	oí	nosotros(as)	oímos
tú	oíste	vosotros(as)	oísteis
él, ella, usted	**oyó**	ellos, ellas, ustedes	**oyeron**

6. The following expressions are helpful when talking about the past:

anoche	last night
ayer	yesterday
la semana pasada	last week

A practicar

6.26 **El orden lógico** Héctor y Gustavo pasaron un muy buen fin de semana. Lee las oraciones sobre sus actividades y ponlas en un orden lógico.

_____ Héctor invitó a Gustavo a ir a la playa por el fin de semana.

_____ Los dos salieron para la playa.

_____ Héctor llamó a su mejor amigo, Gustavo.

_____ Gustavo llegó a la casa de Héctor a las siete.

_____ El viernes Héctor volvió a casa después de trabajar.

_____ Gustavo aceptó la invitación con mucho entusiasmo.

_____ Cuando llegaron a la playa, buscaron un hotel.

6.27 **El sábado pasado** Usa la información de los dibujos para describir lo que Beatriz hizo *(did)* el sábado pasado con su novio Arturo. Pueden usar los siguientes verbos u otros:

| aceptar | beber | comer | comprar | ducharse | encontrarse *(to meet)* | ganar |
| hablar | invitar | lavarse | llamar | llegar | mirar | perder |

6.28 **¿Qué hiciste?** Con un compañero, completen las siguientes oraciones para hablar de su fin de semana. Usen el pretérito. Pueden usar los siguientes verbos u otros verbos.

Modelo Estudiante 1: *Anoche yo comí en un restaurante, ¿y tú?*
Estudiante 2: *Anoche yo cociné para mi familia.*

| levantarse | trabajar | salir | estudiar | pasar bien/mal |
| limpiar | jugar | mirar | escribir | hablar por teléfono |

1. El fin de semana pasado yo...
2. El viernes por la noche yo...
3. El sábado yo...
4. El sábado por la noche yo...
5. El domingo yo...
6. El domingo por la noche yo...

6.29 **El verano pasado** Con un compañero, túrnense para preguntar y contestar las preguntas sobre lo que hicieron *(you did)* el verano pasado.

1. ¿Trabajaste? ¿Dónde? ¿Cuántas horas a la semana?
2. ¿Viajaste? ¿Adónde? ¿Con quién?
3. ¿Tomaste clases? ¿Cuáles?
4. ¿Asististe a un evento (concierto, deporte, etc.)? ¿De qué? ¿Te gustó?
5. ¿Conociste a una persona? ¿A quién?
6. ¿Jugaste un deporte? ¿Cuál?

6.30 **La semana pasada** Escribe tres actividades que hiciste *(you did)* la semana pasada. Luego busca a tres compañeros diferentes que hicieron una de esas tres actividades también. **¡OJO!** Usa el pretérito.

A analizar

Rodrigo habla con Óscar sobre su fin de semana. Mira el video otra vez. Después lee lo que Rodrigo dice y observa las formas de los verbos.

Fernando **consiguió** unas entradas para el partido de los Toros el sábado pasado. Nos invitó a Vicente y a mí. Fernando y Vicente son grandes aficionados de los Toros y **se vistieron** de rojo, pero yo **me vestí** de los colores de las Chivas, ya sabes, soy gran aficionado de ellos. Después de llegar al estadio y sentarnos, **pedimos** algo de comer. Ellos **pidieron** perros calientes, pero yo pedí nachos. Cuando empezó el partido nos levantamos y gritamos por nuestros equipos. Todos **nos divertimos,** pero creo que ellos **se divirtieron** más porque al final ganaron los Toros.

1. Write out the verb forms you see in bold in the paragraph above and identify how their stems are different from the present tense forms.

2. **Conseguir, vestirse, pedir,** and **divertirse** all have stem changes in the present as well as in the preterite. How are the stem changes different in the preterite?

A comprobar

Stem-changing verbs in the preterite

-ir verbs that have stem changes in the present tense also have stem changes in the preterite. The third person singular and plural (**él, ella, usted, ellos, ellas,** and **ustedes**) change e → i and o → u.

pedir *(to ask for, to request)*

yo	pedí	nosotros(as)	pedimos
tú	pediste	vosotros(as)	pedisteis
él, ella, usted	pidió	ellos, ellas, ustedes	pidieron

Yo **pedí** una quesadilla durante el partido.
Mis amigos **pidieron** tacos.

dormir *(to sleep)*

yo	dormí	nosotros(as)	dormimos
tú	dormiste	vosotros(as)	dormisteis
él, ella, usted	durmió	ellos, ellas, ustedes	durmieron

Other common stem-changing verbs:

conseguir (i)	repetir (i)
divertirse (i)	seguir (i)
morir (u)	servir (i)
preferir (i)	vestirse (i)

¿Se **divirtieron** ustedes?
Sí, nos **divertimos** mucho.

Todos **dormimos** en la tienda de campaña.
Mi hermano **durmió** en una hamaca.

A practicar

6.31 **Un poco de lógica** Decide si las siguientes oraciones son lógicas o no. Si no son lógicas, explica por qué.

1. Alfonso es aficionado al béisbol y consiguió entradas para un partido de su equipo favorito.
2. La mañana del partido se levantó, se vistió y después se bañó.
3. Como prefirió llegar antes de la primera entrada *(inning)*, salió de la casa muy tarde.
4. Sirvieron comida en el estadio y él pidió un taco y una soda.
5. Su equipo ganó y no se divirtió.
6. Cuando volvió a casa estaba cansado y se durmió inmediatamente.

6.32 **En los Juegos Panamericanos** Tomás, un entrenador, viajó con su equipo de voleibol a Guadalajara, México, para competir en los Juegos Panamericanos. Completa el siguiente párrafo con la forma apropiada del pretérito del verbo indicado. **¡OJO!** No todos los verbos tienen cambio en el radical.

El equipo de Tomás Guitiérrez (**1.**) _____ (competir) en los Juegos Panamericanos de verano. Antes de salir, Tomás llamó al Hotel Bahía y (**2.**) _____ (pedir) habitaciones para todos los jugadores. (**3.**) Las _____ (conseguir) a un buen precio. Cuando llegaron, estaban muy cansados. (**4.**) _____ (pedir) servicio a la habitación y (**5.**) _____ (acostarse). Todos (**6.**) _____ (dormir) bien y (**7.**) _____ (despertarse) temprano para ir al estadio. (**8.**) Ellos _____ (jugar) bien y al final ganaron. Después del partido (**9.**) _____ (volver) al hotel. Tomás decidió quedarse en la habitación leyendo, pero los jugadores (**10.**) _____ (preferir) relajarse en el sauna. Luego se bañaron y (**11.**) _____ (vestirse) para salir a celebrar. Salieron a comer y después a bailar; (**12.**) _____ (divertirse) mucho.

6.33 **Un día de fútbol** Isabel y Mónica son aficionadas al fútbol. En parejas describan el día que fueron a un partido. Incluyan los siguientes verbos: **acostarse, conseguir, divertirse, dormirse, preferir, sentarse, vestirse** y **volver.**

6.34 **En el pasado** Con un compañero, túrnense para conjugar el verbo en el pretérito y completar las oraciones de una forma original. Reporten la información a la clase.

Modelo Ayer yo (jugar)...

Estudiante 1: *Ayer jugué al voleibol con mis amigas, ¿y tú?*
Estudiante 2: *Yo no jugué nada, pero mi hermano jugó al básquetbol.*

1. Anoche yo (dormir)...
2. La última vez *(last time)* que fui a mi restaurante favorito, yo (pedir)...
3. El fin de semana pasado yo (almorzar)...
4. Una vez que cociné, yo (servir)...
5. Esta mañana yo (preferir)...
6. El semestre pasado, yo (conseguir)...
7. Este semestre yo (comenzar)...
8. Una vez yo (perder)...

6.35 **Un evento** Entrevista a un compañero sobre la última vez que asistió a un evento (un partido, una obra de teatro, etcétera).

1. ¿A qué evento asististe?
2. ¿Con quién asististe al evento?
3. ¿Quién consiguió las entradas?
4. ¿Cómo se vistieron para el evento?
5. ¿Sirvieron comida? ¿Qué comida?
6. ¿Se divirtieron en el evento?
7. ¿A qué hora te acostaste?

6.36 **En busca de...** Pregúntales a ocho compañeros si hicieron las siguientes actividades. Habla con un compañero diferente para cada actividad. Tu compañero debe dar información adicional. Después reporten la información a la clase.

Modelo reír mucho el fin de semana (¿Por qué?)

Estudiante 1: *¿Reíste mucho el fin de semana?*
Estudiante 2: *Sí, reí mucho el fin de semana.*
Estudiante 1: *¿Por qué?*
Estudiante 2: *Porque miré una película cómica.*

1. almorzar en un restaurante la semana pasada (¿Cuál?)
2. divertirse durante el fin de semana (¿Dónde?)
3. vestirse elegante recientemente (¿Por qué?)
4. dormir bien anoche (¿Cuántas horas?)
5. pedir ayuda en una clase este semestre (¿Qué clase?)
6. conseguir un trabajo nuevo durante el año pasado (¿Dónde?)
7. servir la cena esta semana (¿Cuándo?)
8. perder algo recientemente (¿Qué?)

Lectura

Antes de leer

¿Qué deportes piensas que son muy populares en España y Latinoamérica? ¿Sabes el nombre de un deportista famoso de estos lugares?

A leer

Deportistas famosos

pride

A veces un deportista es más que un deportista; a veces los atletas son símbolos de **orgullo** nacional y le dan a la juventud un ejemplo positivo. Tal es el caso de uno de los jugadores más famosos de fútbol, Lionel Messi.

Lionel Messi (1987–) es probablemente el jugador de fútbol argentino más conocido en el mundo desde la época de Diego Maradona. Messi juega para el Club FC Barcelona y el equipo nacional de Argentina. Tiene también la nacionalidad española desde el año 2005. La FIFA nombró a Messi como el mejor jugador del mundo en 2009 y en 2013.

© Maxisport/Shutterstock

> [a veces los atletas son símbolos de orgullo nacional]

Leo, como se le conoce, nació en Rosario, Argentina. Su carrera como futbolista comenzó a los cinco años, cuando empezó a jugar en un club local. A los once años

growth

le diagnosticaron una deficiencia en la hormona del **crecimiento.** Aunque el River Plate —uno de los equipos más populares de la Argentina— estaba interesado en Messi, no quisieron pagar su tratamiento médico. En cambio, FC Barcelona se interesó en él de inmediato. Pagaron el tratamiento médico y

moved

Lionel y su familia **se mudaron** a Barcelona, donde Messi empezó a jugar para las categorías inferiores a los 13 años, jugando su primer partido con el equipo oficial a los 16 años.

Además de ganar el título del mayor número de goles en numerosas ocasiones, la revista *Time* lo nombró una de las 32 personas más influyentes en el año 2011 (fue el único deportista de la lista). Messi también es embajador oficial de la UNICEF y tiene una fundación (Fundación Leo Messi) cuyo objetivo es

risk

ayudar a los niños y adolescentes en situación de **riesgo** a realizar sus sueños.

© AFP/Getty Images

Mariana Pajón (1991–) es una deportista colombiana que practica el ciclismo. Aunque su **hazaña** más conocida es haber ganado una medalla en los Juegos Olímpicos de Londres 2012, la trayectoria de Pajón inició cuando ganó una **carrera** a los cuatro años, compitiendo contra niños de cinco y seis años. Mariana viene de una familia de deportistas, ya que su padre practicaba el automovilismo y su madre la **equitación**.

feat

race

horseback riding

Además de la medalla de **oro** en Londres, entre sus **logros**, Mariana ganó medallas de oro en los Juegos Olímpicos Panamericanos (2011), los Juegos Centroamericanos y del Caribe (2010) y los Juegos Sudamericanos (2010). Fue nombrada la atleta del año en Colombia en 2011. En el año 2010, tan solo en los Estados Unidos, Pajón ganó el primer lugar en el *North American Continental Championship* y en la competencia de *Gator Nationals*. Con estos trios Mariana ascendió al segundo **puesto** en la clasificación mundial.

gold
successes

place

Aunque Mariana todavía no tiene una fundación, es conocida en Colombia por dedicar tiempo a labores sociales, especialmente con fundaciones que trabajan para los niños.

Finalmente hay que mencionar a Jefferson Pérez (1974–), un deportista que hizo historia en Ecuador cuando ganó la primera medalla de oro olímpica para este país en el año 1996, en la caminata de 20 kms. Después de ganarla, Jefferson completó un **peregrinaje** de casi 500 kms., desde Quito hasta Cuenca, su ciudad natal. Jefferson volvió a ganar una medalla olímpica de **plata** en 2008, para la misma carrera de 20 kms. Además ganó medallas en los Campeonatos Mundiales de Atletismo de 1999, 2003, 2005 y 2007. Jefferson fue reconocido como el mejor deportista de Ecuador en 2008. Aunque en la actualidad Pérez ya está retirado de las competencias, **dirige** una compañía que se dedica a promover y **apoyar** el talento deportivo en Ecuador y en toda Latinoamérica.

pilgrimage
silver

directs
to support

Comprensión

1. ¿Quiénes son los tres deportistas de los que habla la lectura? ¿De dónde son?
2. ¿Por qué Messi se fue a vivir a Barcelona? ¿Cuál es uno de sus logros?
3. ¿Qué causas promueve *(promotes)* Messi con la UNICEF y con su fundación?
4. ¿Qué deporte practica Mariana Pajón? ¿Qué labor social promueve?
5. ¿Cuál es uno de los logros de Jefferson Pérez?
6. ¿A qué se dedica Pérez ahora?

Después de leer

Con un compañero de clase, escriban una lista de atletas hispanos que conocen y los deportes que juegan. Escojan uno de la lista y busquen detalles interesantes sobre esa persona para compartirlos con la clase.

© Neale Cousland/Shutterstock

Write an email to a friend telling him or her about a sporting event.

Paso 1 Think of a sporting event you participated in, attended, or watched on TV. Then jot down a list of things you did. Think about the following questions: What was the event? When was it? Did you have to get tickets or make arrangements? Did you have to get up early or stay up late? What did you do before the event? What happened during the event? Did your team win or lose? What did you do after the event?

Paso 2 Begin your email with a greeting and ask how your friend is. Then, write a topic sentence using an expression of time to tell your friend when you participated in, attended, or watched the sporting event.

El 30 de julio yo...
La semana pasada yo...

Paso 3 Using the information you generated in **Paso 1,** recount the events of the day. In order to connect your ideas, use some of the expressions you learned in **Exploraciones gramaticales 2** in this chapter.

Paso 4 Write a concluding statement in which you tell how you felt at the end of the day. Then close your email.

Paso 5 Edit your email:

1. Do all of the sentences in each paragraph support the topic sentence?
2. Is the paragraph logically organized with smooth transitions between sentences?
3. Are there any short sentences you can combine with **y** or **pero**?
4. Do verbs agree with the subject? Are they conjugated properly?
5. Are there any spelling errors? Do the preterite verbs that need accents have them?

Entrando en materia

¿Por qué es importante el deporte? ¿Cuáles son algunas cualidades que la gente (en general) admira de los deportistas?

Un reportaje biográfico

Vas a leer un segmento de un reportaje autobiográfico del deportista Javier Gadano. Lee con atención y después responde las preguntas.

Nací en el seno de una familia modesta. Mi papá y mi mamá trabajaron muy duro para **sacarnos adelante** a mis hermanos y a mí. Nunca nos **faltó** comida sobre la mesa, pero no teníamos mucho más de lo necesario. Mis tres hermanos y yo, todos **varones,** dormíamos en una habitación. Desde chico me gustaron mucho los deportes, pero la escuela no me atraía y tuve que repetir el **quinto** año. Debo de confesar que me **saltaba** la escuela cuando tenía la oportunidad.

provide for / lacked
boys

fifth / skipped

Así pasó el tiempo hasta que un día, cuando tenía unos doce años, un entrenador de educación física de nuestro colegio me vio jugar en un partido con mis amigos, después de las clases ese día. Recuerdo que **anoté** dos goles en ese partido, y estaba listo para volver a casa cuando don Genaro —así se llamaba el entrenador—, me alcanzó y me preguntó cómo me llamaba y qué año cursaba. Primero no lo tomé en serio, pero don Genaro comenzó a venir a nuestros juegos regularmente.

scored

Al final de cada partido me buscaba y me preguntaba sobre mi familia, sobre la escuela, sobre mi **vida.** Un día me puse a estudiar matemáticas para salir bien en una **prueba** solo para reportárselo a don Genaro. Fue la primera vez que sentí ganas de triunfar porque alguien más estaba interesado en mí. Me fue muy bien en esa prueba, mis notas empezaron a mejorar.

life
quiz

Un día don Genaro llegó a ver el juego con otro **caballero,** y después hablaron conmigo para invitarme a jugar en una de las ligas de su club deportivo. Me fue bien, y con el **apoyo** de don Genaro seguí estudiando y practicando el fútbol todos los días. Con esta disciplina estaba ocupado todos los días. Nunca me metí en problemas con **la ley** y, como todos saben, llegué a jugar en la primera división muy, muy joven. ¡Todo iba fabuloso! ...Hasta que la fama se me subió a la cabeza. En esos días yo perdí contacto con don Genaro. Con el dinero y la fama empecé a cometer errores graves, como asistir a demasiadas fiestas, emborracharme y... en fin. Empecé a faltar a los entrenamientos. Al final de la temporada el club no extendió mi contrato. Perdí mi casa, mi coche y hasta a mis amigos. Y bueno, pasó un año entero antes de entender la causa de mis problemas. Regresé a entrenar. La disciplina del deporte es algo que me salvó de la ruina y le da dirección a mi vida, además de la oportunidad de ayudar a otros.

gentleman

support

law

Comprensión

Decide si las ideas son ciertas o falsas. Corrige las falsas.

1. Javier Gadano creció en una familia con mucho dinero.
2. A Javier siempre le gustó mucho la escuela.
3. Don Genaro motivó a Javier a pasar sus exámenes de matemáticas.
4. Javier perdió su contrato con un equipo de fútbol porque se fracturó una pierna.
5. Javier tiene la oportunidad de ayudar a otros gracias al deporte.

Más allá

¿Admiras a algún deportista? Sube información del deportista a Share It! y explica por qué lo admiras.

La educación física ▶

© iofoto/Shutterstock

Vocabulario

Sustantivos

el (la) adolescente	*teenager*
los aparatos	*exercise machines*
la autoestima	*self-esteem*
el calambre	*cramp*
el calentamiento	*warm-up*
la dieta	*diet*
los ejercicios aeróbicos	*aerobics*
el (la) entrenador(a)	*trainer*
el masaje	*massage*
el músculo	*muscle*
la serie	*series/set*
el sobrepeso	*overweight*

Adjetivos

agotado(a)	*exhausted*
disciplinado(a)	*disciplined*
extenuante	*exhausting*

Verbos

entrenar(se)	*to train oneself*
respirar	*to breathe*
sudar	*to sweat*

Expresiones útiles

estar en buena forma
to be in good shape

Descanse.
Take a break.

Haga abdominales.
Do sit-ups.

Haga flexiones.
Do push-ups.

Haga tres series de...
Do three series of . . .

Tome agua.
Drink some water.

DATOS IMPORTANTES

Educación: Certificación de entrenador personal. Se prefieren profesores de educación física. Otros requisitos adicionales importantes: estudios terciarios y universitarios relacionados con medicina; por ejemplo, asistencia médica, técnica en primeros auxilios, enfermería, etcétera.

Salario: Entre $20 000 y $100 000

Dónde se trabaja: Gimnasios, clubes privados, clubes comunitarios, clubes deportivos profesionales (fútbol, béisbol, boxeo, etcétera)

Vocabulario nuevo ¿Qué palabra o expresión mejor completa cada oración?

1. Para tener brazos fuertes (haga flexiones / tome agua).
2. Para estar en buena forma es importante (respirar / entrenarse).
3. Si usted está agotado, (haga ejercicios aeróbicos / descanse).
4. Es necesario hacer (calentamientos / calambres) antes de hacer ejercicios aeróbicos.
5. Después de hacer mucho ejercicio, estoy muy (agotado/extenuante).

▶ Ricardo Melo, entrenador personal

Ricardo Melo es entrenador personal. Trabaja en un club privado y entrena a personas que quieren bajar de peso o estar en buena forma. En el video vas a ver una entrevista entre Ricardo y la madre de una joven que necesita ir al gimnasio.

Antes de ver

Los entrenadores personales ayudan a personas con diferentes necesidades. ¿Qué tipo de necesidades crees que puede tener una persona que va a un gimnasio? ¿Qué preguntas iniciales le hacen al entrenador? ¿Consideras que el entrenamiento individual es mejor que el entrenamiento en grupo? Explica.

Comprensión

1. ¿Por qué la hija de la Sra. Matos necesita ir al gimnasio?
2. ¿Cuántos años tiene la hija?
3. ¿Dónde hace gimnasia la hija de la Sra. Matos?
4. ¿Qué tipo de ejercicios recomienda el entrenador para empezar a trabajar las piernas?
5. ¿Qué otros ejercicios recomienda el entrenador?
6. Según el entrenador ¿con qué debe combinar el programa de ejercicio?

Después de ver

En parejas, representen a un entrenador personal y a una persona que necesita su ayuda. Expliquen por qué la persona busca al entrenador. ¿Quiere estar en buena forma? ¿Desea fortalecer una parte del cuerpo? ¿Tiene algún problema físico? ¿El médico le recomendó hacer ejercicio? ¿Hay algo que no puede hacer? El entrenador le explica un plan para esa situación.

6.37 **¿Quién lo hace?** Explica quién hace las actividades de la lista.

Modelo cepillarse los dientes tres veces al día
Mi abuela se cepilla los dientes tres veces al día.

1. siempre levantarse temprano
2. vestirse a la moda (*in style*)
3. cortarse el pelo una vez al mes
4. sentarse al frente de la clase
5. a veces dormirse en clase
6. maquillarse en el coche
7. afeitarse la cabeza
8. normalmente acostarse tarde

Las personas famosas se visten a la moda.

6.38 **El órden lógico** Explica el orden lógico de las dos actividades.

Modelo ponerse el pantalón / ponerse los zapatos
Debes ponerte el pantalón antes de ponerte los zapatos. / Debes ponerte los zapatos después de ponerte el pantalón.

1. hacer ejercio / bañarse
2. maquillarse / lavarse la cara
3. comer / cepillarse los dientes
4. acostarse / ponerse la pijama
5. despertarse / levantarse
6. vestirse / ducharse
7. lavarse el pelo / secarse el pelo
8. arreglarse / salir

6.39 **De pesca** Completa la historia con la forma apropiada del pretérito del verbo entre paréntesis.

Esta mañana yo (**1.**) _____ (despertarse) temprano para ir de pesca con mis amigos Alfredo y César. (Yo) (**2.**) _____ (vestirse), (**3.**) _____ (comer) un poco de fruta, (**4.**) _____ (tomar) un café y (**5.**) _____ (salir) de casa. En media hora (**6.**) _____ (llegar) al lago y mis amigos (**7.**) _____ (llegar) un poco después.

   Nosotros (**8.**) _____ (pasar) toda la mañana en el agua. Alfredo y yo (**9.**) _____ (pescar) unos peces bonitos. ¡Pobre César! Él no (**10.**) _____ (conseguir) pescar nada, pero (**11.**) _____ (divertirse) mucho. A las dos nosotros (**12.**) _____ (decidir) ir a comer. (**13.**) _____ (comer) en un restaurante cerca del lago; luego mis amigos (**14.**) _____ (volver) a sus casas y yo a la mía (*mine*).

6.40 **Un pasado interesante** Trabaja con un compañero. Túrnense para hacer y contestar las preguntas sobre las fotos. Deben usar el pretérito en todas las respuestas.

1.

© Vladimir Mucibabic/Shutterstock

a. ¿Qué hizo *(What did he do)* anoche?
b. ¿Por qué durmió en el coche?
c. ¿Qué pasó cuando se despertó?

2.

© Jaimie Duplass/Shutterstock

a. ¿Quién llamó?
b. ¿Qué pasó?
c. ¿Qué hizo la mujer después?

3.

© Surkov Vladimir/Shutterstock

a. ¿Adónde viajaron?
b. ¿Qué hicieron allí *(What did they do there)*?
c. ¿Qué pasó cuando regresaron?

6.41 **¿Qué hizo?** Dante es estudiante de secundaria pero no es muy aplicado. Con un compañero, túrnense para completar la información sobre lo que hizo *(what he did)* esta mañana. Uno de ustedes va a mirar la información en esta página y el otro va a mirar en el **Apéndice B.**

Modelo Estudiante 1: *¿Qué hizo a medianoche?*
Estudiante 2: *Se acostó.*

12:00	acostarse
7:00	
7:30	terminar de escribir la tarea
7:40	afeitarse en la ducha
8:00	
8:55	sentarse en la clase de geografía
9:35	
9:58	
10:10	pedir ir al baño
10:30	
11:00	levantar pesas en el gimnasio

6.42 **La semana pasada** Con un compañero, van a ver si le dedicaron más tiempo a la diversión o a las obligaciones.

Paso 1 Decidan si las siguientes actividades son divertidas u obligatorias. Añadan *(Add)* 4 o 5 otras actividades que hacen en una semana típica y decidan si son divertidas u obligatorias.

asistir a clases	estudiar	practicar un deporte
cocinar	leer	salir con amigos
escribir un ensayo	mirar la tele	trabajar

Paso 2 Averigüen *(Find out)* cuánto tiempo pasaron la semana pasada haciendo las actividades de su lista. ¿Dedicaron más tiempo a la diversión o a las obligaciones?

Paso 3 Repórtenle a la clase sus resultados dando algunos ejemplos.

🔊 Vocabulario 1

1-37

Los verbos reflexivos

acostarse (ue)	to lie down; to go to bed
afeitarse	to shave
arreglarse	to fix oneself up; to get ready
bañarse	to bathe; to shower (Mex.)
cepillarse	to brush
cortarse	to cut
despertarse (ie)	to wake up
divertirse (ie)	to have fun
dormirse (ue)	to fall asleep
ducharse	to shower

estirarse	to stretch
irse	to leave, to go away
lavarse	to wash
levantarse	to get up
maquillarse	to put on make-up
peinarse	to comb or style one's hair
ponerse (la ropa)	to put on (clothing)
quitarse (la ropa)	to take off (clothing)
secarse	to dry oneself
sentarse (ie)	to sit down
verse	to look at oneself
vestirse (i)	to get dressed

Las partes del cuerpo

la boca	mouth
el brazo	arm
la cabeza	head
la cara	face
el codo	elbow
el cuello	neck
el dedo	finger
el dedo (del pie)	toe
el diente	tooth
la espalda	back
el estómago	stomach
el hombro	shoulder

la mano	hand
el muslo	thigh
la nariz	nose
el ojo	eye
la oreja	ear
el pecho	chest
el pelo	hair
el pie	foot
la pierna	leg
la rodilla	knee
el tobillo	ankle

Adverbios

a menudo	often
a veces	sometimes
ahora	now
antes de + infinitive	before (doing something)
después de + infinitive	after (doing something)
hoy	today
luego	later
mañana	tomorrow

más tarde	later
mientras	while
normalmente	normally, usually
(casi) nunca	(almost) never
pronto	soon
(casi) siempre	(almost) always
todavía	still
todos los días	every day
ya	already
ya no	no longer

Palabras adicionales

el champú	shampoo
la pasta de dientes	toothpaste
el despertador	alarm clock
el jabón	soap

tarde	late
temprano	early
la toalla	towel

Vocabulario 2

Los deportes

el alpinismo	*mountain climbing*
el atletismo	*track and field*
el bádminton	*badminton*
el básquetbol	*basketball*
el béisbol	*baseball*
el fútbol	*soccer*
el fútbol americano	*American football*
el golf	*golf*
la natación	*swimming*
el tenis	*tennis*
el voleibol	*volleyball*

El equipo

el equipo	*equipment, team*
el patín	*skate*
la pelota	*ball*
la raqueta	*racquet*
la red	*net*
el saco de dormir	*sleeping bag*
la tienda de campaña	*camping tent*

Verbos

acampar	*to go camping*
andar en bicicleta	*to ride a bicycle*
bucear	*to scuba dive*
esquiar en el agua	*to water-ski*
esquiar en tabla	*to snowboard*
hacer alpinismo	*to climb mountains*
ir de excursión	*to hike*
ir de pesca	*to go fishing*
jugar al ping-pong	*to play ping-pong*
levantar pesas	*to lift weights*
montar a	*to ride (an animal)*
patinar	*to skate*
patinar en hielo	*to ice skate*
pescar	*to fish*

Palabras adicionales

el (la) aficionado(a)	*fan (of a sport)*
anoche	*last night*
ayer	*yesterday*
el campo	*field*
la cancha	*court*
la entrada	*ticket*
el lago	*lake*
el partido	*game*
la semana pasada	*last week*

Diccionario personal

_____

_____

_____

_____

_____

_____

_____

_____

© Used by permission of Donato Ndongo

Donato Ndongo

Biografía

Donato Ndongo-Bidyogo (1950–) es un escritor, político y periodista de Guinea Ecuatorial. Su trabajo profesional ha incluido varios puestos en universidades españolas, y más de diez años trabajando para la agencia de noticias *(news)* EFE en África central. También trabajó como director adjunto del Centro Cultural Hispano-Guineano en Malabo. Dentro de su labor política, destaca como fundador del Partido del Progreso de Guinea Ecuatorial en 1984.

Como escritor, Ndongo es autor de libros de ficción, ensayos y poesía. Algunas de sus obras más destacadas incluyen *Historia y Tragedia de Guinea Ecuatorial* (1977), y la antología de literatura ecuatoguineana titulada *Las tinieblas de tu memoria negra.*

Ndongo ha vivido en el exilio desde 1994, cuando se marchó a España debido a su oposición al gobierno de Teodoro Obiang. Entre 2005 y 2009, Ndongo trabajó como profesor visitante de la Universidad de Missouri en Columbia. Después de su estancia en los Estados Unidos, regresó a España.

Antes de leer

1. El título del poema que vas a leer es "Cántico". ¿Qué piensas que significa esta palabra?

2. El poema habla de lo que un poeta debe hacer. En tu opinión ¿cuáles son los deberes u objetivos de un poeta?

Cántico

Yo no quiero ser poeta
para cantar a África.
Yo no quiero ser poeta
para glosar lo negro.
5   Yo no quiero ser poeta así.

El poeta no es cantor de
beauties — **bellezas.**
flaunts — El poeta no **luce** la
brillante piel negra.
10   El poeta, este poeta no tiene
voz
undulating gait — para **andares ondulantes** de
hermosas damas
curly / hips — de pelos **rizados** y **caderas**
15   redondas.
land — El poeta llora su **tierra**
inmensa y pequeña
dura y frágil

© Borderlands/Alamy

luminosa y oscura
20   rica y pobre.
Este poeta tiene su mano
atada   — *tied*
a las **cadenas** que atan a   — *chains*
su gente.
25   Este poeta no siente
nostalgia
de glorias pasadas.
Yo no canto al sexo
exultante

thick lips	30	que huele a jardín de rosas.
		Yo no adoro **labios gruesos**
		que saben a mango fresco.
		Yo no pienso en la mujer
stooped		**encorvada**
basket	35	bajo su **cesto** cargado de
wood		**leña**
		con un niño chupando la
empty breast		**teta vacía.**
		Yo describo la triste historia
	40	de un mundo poblado de
		blancos
		negros
		rojos y
		amarillos
pool	45	que saltan de **charca** en
		charca
		sin hablarse ni mirarse.
		El poeta llora a los muertos
kill		que **matan** manos negras
	50	en nombre de la Negritud.
		Yo canto con mi pueblo
		una vida pasada bajo
cacao tree		**el cacaotero**

		para que ellos
	55	**merienden**	have a snack
		cho-co-la-te.
		Si su pueblo está triste,
		el poeta está triste.
		Yo no soy poeta por
	60	**voluntad** divina.	will
		El poeta es poeta por
		voluntad humana.
		Yo no quiero la poesía
		que solo deleita los
	65	oídos de los poetas.
		Yo no quiero la poesía
		que se lee en noches de
		vino tinto
		y mujeres **embelesadas.**	spellbound
	70	Poesía, sí.
		Poetas, sí.
		Pero que sepan lo que
		es el hombre
		y por qué sufre el
	75	hombre
		y por qué **gime** el	groans
		hombre.

Courtesy of the author, Donato Ndongo.

Después de leer

A. Comprensión

1. Según la voz narrativa, ¿qué es importante decir en las poesías?
2. ¿Cuál es el mensaje del poema?
3. ¿Cuál es el tono? ¿Por qué?
4. ¿Cuál es el tema?
5. Encuentra dos descripciones que hablan de la vida en Guinea Ecuatorial. ¿Qué emoción te producen?

B. Conversemos

1. En tu opinión ¿se debe mezclar (to mix) la poesía con la política y los problemas sociales? ¿Por qué?
2. ¿Conoces otros autores que piensan que la poesía debe tener un elemento social? ¿Quiénes?
3. Escribe una lista de temas políticos o sociales que piensas que son buen tema para una poesía.

Investiguemos la literatura: El tema

The theme of a literary text refers to the underlying ideas, what the piece is really about. To find it, look for patterns and ideas that are restated in different parts of the work. It is not the subject of the work, but more of a view of the human experience and attitude. Some common themes include growing up, love, death, and nature.

Learning Strategy

Try a variety of memorization techniques

Use a variety of techniques to memorize vocabulary and verbs until you find the ones that work best for you. Some students learn better when they write the words, others learn better if they listen to recordings of the words while looking over the list, and still others prefer to rely on flashcards.

In this chapter you will learn how to:

- Talk about food
- Order meals at a restaurant
- Use numbers above 100

© Stuart Pearce/age fotostock

La señora Montero escoge frutas y verduras frescas y baratas en el mercado.

el brócoli | los pepinos | las piñas | los plátanos | el cereal | la mermelada | la mayonesa | la catsup | la mostaza | las zanahorias | la sandía | la leche | los huevos | el melón | las naranjas | los champiñones | las papas | el queso | el pan | la lechuga | el jamón | las cebollas | los duraznos | la mantequilla | las manzanas | la crema | las uvas | las fresas | los pepinillos

© Cengage Learning

En la cocina

el aceite	*oil*
la fruta	*fruit*
el maíz	*corn*
el tomate	*tomato*
la verdura	*vegetable*
el yogur	*yogurt*

Verbos

hornear	*to bake*

Los números mayores de cien

cien	*100*
ciento uno	*101*
doscientos	*200*
trescientos	*300*
cuatrocientos	*400*
quinientos	*500*
seiscientos	*600*
setecientos	*700*

ochocientos	*800*
novecientos	*900*
mil	*1000*
dos mil	*2000*
un millón	*1 000 000*

Palabras adicionales

la rebanada	*slice*

INVESTIGUEMOS EL VOCABULARIO

The names of foods often vary throughout the Spanish-speaking world. Here are some of the variations:

el maíz (Spain; general term) = **el elote** (Mexico), **el choclo** (Argentina, Chile, Paraguay, Peru, and most South American countries)

la fresa (Spain, Mexico) = **la frutilla** (Argentina, Bolivia, Chile, Paraguay, Uruguay)

el plátano (Spain, Mexico) = **la banana** (el Caribe); **el banano** (Central America, Colombia)

la piña (Spain, Mexico) = **el ananá(s)** (Argentina, Paraguay, Uruguay)

la papa (Latin America) = **la patata** (Spain)

el durazno (Latin America) = **el melocotón** (Spain)

la mantequilla (most Spanish-speaking countries) = **la manteca** (Argentina, Paraguay, Uruguay)

A practicar

7.1 **Escucha y responde** Vas a escuchar algunas afirmaciones sobre diferentes frutas, verduras y otras palabras del vocabulario. Indica con el pulgar hacia arriba si la afirmación es cierta, y con el pulgar hacia abajo si es falsa.

2-2

7.2 Relaciona las columnas ¿Qué fruta o verdura corresponde a la descripción?

1. _____ Es una fruta roja, verde o amarilla. Es un regalo típico para los profesores.
2. _____ Es verde y la comemos en ensaladas.
3. _____ Es anaranjada y larga. Tiene vitamina A.
4. _____ Es una fruta tropical que se produce mucho en Hawaii.
5. _____ Es una fruta amarilla que crece en un árbol.
6. _____ Las usamos para hacer vino.
7. _____ Es un condimento que ponemos en los sándwiches.
8. _____ Es una fruta pequeña y roja.

a. la zanahoria
b. el plátano
c. la fresa
d. las uvas
e. la mostaza
f. la lechuga
g. la manzana
h. la piña

7.3 Los ingredientes Trabaja con un compañero para decidir los ingredientes que se necesitan para preparar estas comidas.

Modelo un sándwich
Para preparar un sándwich necesitamos pan, mayonesa, mostaza, queso y jamón.

1. una ensalada verde
2. una sopa de verduras
3. una quesadilla

4. un omelet
5. unos nachos
6. una ensalada de frutas

7.4 Descripciones Trabaja con un compañero. Túrnense para escoger una fruta, un vegetal o un ingrediente de la ilustración en la página 226 y describirlo. No deben decir el nombre de la comida.

Modelo Estudiante 1: *No es una fruta. Es para hacer sándwiches.*
Estudiante 2: *El pan.*

7.5 ¿Con qué frecuencia? Trabaja en un grupo de 3 o 4 compañeros y pregúntense con qué frecuencia hacen las actividades. Después deben reportar a la clase.

1. comer huevos
2. almorzar en la cafetería de la escuela
3. poner catsup en su comida
4. comer cereal

5. pedir papas fritas en un restaurante
6. comer un sándwich con queso
7. beber leche
8. comer verduras

7.6 ¿Cuánto cuesta? Trabaja con un compañero. Uno de ustedes va a ver la información en esta página, y el otro debe ver el **Apéndice B**. Imagínense que están en dos supermercados diferentes en Chile. Llámense por teléfono para preguntar cuánto cuestan los productos de cada ilustración. Los precios que tu compañero necesita están abajo, en el papel. Tomen notas y sumen *(add)* los precios. ¿Quién va a pagar más?

Tu compañero quiere comprar...

un melón, un kilo $620
una lechuga $155
huevos, una docena $899
queso, 500 gramos $867

jamón, 250 gramos $1,743
pepinos, 500 gramos $476
naranjas, 3 kilos $1,634
zanahorias, un kilo $469

Tú quieres comprar...

un kilo

un kilo

un kilo

un litro

© Cengage Learning

La comida como cultura

Algo muy particular de cada cultura es su comida. Hoy en día, gracias a los eficientes medios de transporte y a tecnologías para preservar los alimentos, podemos comer productos que se producen o cultivan en cualquier parte del mundo. Sin embargo, a pesar de esta globalización de la comida, existen hábitos muy diferentes en las diversas regiones. Hay diferencias en cómo se prepara la comida, en los productos que se usan, dónde se compran y hasta dónde se come, con quién y a qué hora. Identifica las costumbres de la lista con el país o la región donde se hace. Puedes repetir respuestas.

El ceviche es popular en muchos países. Esta foto muestra un plato de ceviche como se prepara en Perú.

Argentina	**Chile**	**Perú**
Bolivia	**España**	**Uruguay**
Centroamérica	**México**	**toda Latinoamérica**

1. Se come más carne que en cualquier otro país.
2. Producen vinos excelentes.
3. Consumen muchos más refrescos *(sodas)* que leche.
4. Son famosos por sus jamones.
5. La comida más importante es por la tarde, entre la 1:00 y las 3:00 PM.
6. Su cocina está muy influenciada por la cocina italiana.
7. Tienen una gran variedad de papas y son muy importantes en su dieta.
8. Prefieren comer con la familia y generalmente encuentran tiempo para hacerlo.
9. Producen y comen una gran variedad de frutas tropicales. El maíz es también importante en su dieta.

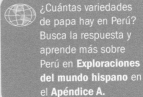

¿Cuántas variedades de papa hay en Perú? Busca la respuesta y aprende más sobre Perú en **Exploraciones del mundo hispano** en el **Apéndice A.**

   Observa la lista nuevamente. ¿Son algunas de estas afirmaciones verdaderas para los Estados Unidos? ¿Cuáles?

Comparaciones

En la mayoría de los países donde se habla español la dieta varía por región. Por ejemplo:

- En Sudamérica no se comen chile ni tortillas.
- Los frijoles negros son un alimento básico en Cuba, la República Dominicana, partes de México y Centroamérica.
- En Bolivia se come un cereal muy nutritivo llamado quinoa.
- En Chile y en Argentina frecuentemente se bebe vino con la comida.
- En España, en promedio se comen 7 kilos de queso por persona al año. En Argentina se consumen unos 12 kilos por persona, y en México 3 kilos.
  [Source: CDIC cheese consumption data, 2013]

   ¿Cómo se comparan tus hábitos alimenticios con los de las personas de los países que se mencionan arriba?

La carne es muy popular en países como Argentina, Paraguay y Uruguay.

Conexiones... a la gastronomía

La comida es una parte muy importante de las tradiciones y cultura de cada país. Los siguientes son algunos ejemplos.

En Argentina, Paraguay y Uruguay se bebe un té que se hace con una yerba llamada mate. Hay varias formas de prepararlo y beberlo, pero en la más tradicional se hace con hojas secas de mate y agua caliente. Se prepara y se bebe en un recipiente hecho con el fruto de la calabaza *(gourd)*, y se bebe con una bombilla *(straw)*. El té se pasa de persona a persona, así que beber mate es una actividad social.

La paella

Gallo Pinto

Un platillo tradicional de Costa Rica es el Gallo Pinto. Este plato se prepara con arroz, pollo, frijoles y otros ingredientes que le dan un sabor *(flavor)* especial, como cebolla y cilantro. Hay muchas variaciones de este platillo. De hecho, el arroz y los frijoles son la base para platillos importantes de otros países, como el platillo Moros y Cristianos, típico de Cuba.

Abajo hay una lista de otros platillos. Escoge cuatro de ellos e investiga qué son y qué ingredientes se necesitan para prepararlos.

Bolivia: chicha
Chile: empanadas
Colombia: buñuelos
Ecuador: ceviche
España: paella

Honduras: baleada
Panamá: chocao panameño
Paraguay: sopa paraguaya
República Dominicana: tostones
Venezuela: hallacas

 En **Exploraciones del mundo hispano** del **Apéndice A** puedes encontrar más platillos tradicionales de cada uno de los países donde se habla español.

Comunidad

Entrevista a una persona de un país donde se habla español. Pregúntale acerca de las comidas típicas de su país, su comida favorita y los ingredientes necesarios. Pregúntale también a qué hora son las comidas en su país y si es común comprar comida rápida.

Un plato típico del Perú es el lomo saltado.

A analizar ▶

Camila y Vanesa van a un café para hablar. Mira el video.
Después lee parte de su conversación y observa las formas
de los verbos en negritas.

Camila: (Yo) **Fui** al supermercado para comprar
la comida para la fiesta de mi hija. Por
ser sábado, había mucha gente y **fue**
imposible entrar y salir muy rápido. Y
los precios... ¡todo **fue** muy caro, en
particular la carne! Un kilo de jamón por
veinte dólares...

Vanesa: ¡Guau! ¡Qué caro!... mi día **fue** tranquilo.
Por la mañana **fui** de compras y por la
tarde un amigo y yo **fuimos** al nuevo restaurante para comer.
La comida **fue** excelente y los precios **fueron** muy razonables.

1. The verbs **ser** and **ir** are irregular in the preterite and they have the same conjugated forms.
   Look at the paragraph above and decide which of the verbs is a form of **ser** and which is a form of **ir.**

2. Using the forms in the paragraph above and what you learned about the preterite in **Capítulo 6,**
   complete the chart below with the appropriate forms of **ser / ir** in the preterite.

   yo _____   nosotros _____

   tú _____   vosotros _____

   él, ella, usted _____   ellos, ellas, ustedes _____

A comprobar

Irregular verbs in the preterite

1. There are a number of verbs that are irregular in the
   preterite. The verbs **ser** and **ir** are identical in this tense.

ir *(to go)* / **ser** *(to be)*			
yo	**fui**	nosotros(as)	**fuimos**
tú	**fuiste**	vosotros(as)	**fuisteis**
él, ella, usted	**fue**	ellos, ellas, ustedes	**fueron**

   #### Estrategia

   Try different memorization techniques

   Try some of these techniques to help memorize
   the verbs and see what works best for you:
   write out the conjugations, say the conjugations
   out loud while looking over the list, or make
   flashcards.

2. The verbs **dar** and **ver** are conjugated similarly.

dar *(to give)*			
yo	**di**	nosotros(as)	**dimos**
tú	**diste**	vosotros(as)	**disteis**
él, ella, usted	**dio**	ellos, ellas, ustedes	**dieron**

ver *(to see)*			
yo	**vi**	nosotros(as)	**vimos**
tú	**viste**	vosotros(as)	**visteis**
él, ella, usted	**vio**	ellos, ellas, ustedes	**vieron**

3. Other irregular verbs can be divided into three groups. Notice that there are no accents on these verbs and that they all take the same endings (with the exception of the 3rd person plural of the verbs with **j** in the stem).

Verbs with *u* in the stem: poner			
yo	puse	nosotros(as)	pus**imos**
tú	pus**iste**	vosotros(as)	pus**isteis**
él, ella, usted	puso	ellos, ellas, ustedes	pus**ieron**

Other verbs with the same pattern			
andar	**anduv-**	saber	**sup-**
estar	**estuv-**	tener	**tuv-**
poder	**pud-**		

Verbs with *i* in the stem: hacer			
yo	hice	nosotros(as)	hic**imos**
tú	hic**iste**	vosotros(as)	hic**isteis**
él, ella, usted	hizo	ellos, ellas, ustedes	hic**ieron**

Other verbs with the same pattern	
querer	**quis-**
venir	**vin-**

Verbs with *j* in the stem: decir			
yo	dije	nosotros(as)	dij**imos**
tú	dij**iste**	vosotros(as)	dij**isteis**
él, ella, usted	dijo	ellos, ellas, ustedes	dij**eron**

Other verbs with the same pattern			
conducir	**conduj-**	traducir	**traduj-**
producir	**produj-**	traer	**traj-**

4. The preterite of **hay** is **hubo** *(there was, there were)*.

Hubo un accidente en la cocina.   ***There was** an accident in the kitchen.*

Hubo problemas en el restaurante.   ***There were** problems in the restaurant.*

> **INVESTIGUEMOS LA GRAMÁTICA**
> As with the present tense of **haber (hay)**, there is only one form in the preterite **(hubo)** regardless of whether it is used with a plural or singular noun.

A practicar

7.7 **En el restaurante** Lee las oraciones y observa los verbos subrayados *(underlined)* que están en el pretérito. Decide cuál es el infinitivo del verbo.

1. La familia Martínez <u>fue</u> al restaurante Buen Gusto para comer.
2. El mesero <u>vino</u> a la mesa para darnos los menús.
3. El mesero <u>puso</u> el pan en la mesa.
4. Poco después el mesero <u>trajo</u> la comida.
5. El mesero le <u>dio</u> la cuenta *(bill)* al señor Martínez.

7.8 **Fechas importantes** Con un compañero, decidan en qué año ocurrieron los siguientes acontecimientos históricos y después túrnense para hacer oraciones completas con la información.

Modelo Manuel de Falla (componer *to compose) El amor brujo.*   1915
Manuel de Falla compuso El amor brujo en 1915.

1. Hernán Cortés (estar) en México.   **a.** 1492
2. (Haber) una revolución en Cuba.   **b.** 1808
3. Napoleón (querer) conquistar España.   **c.** 1959
4. Cristóbal Colón (hacer) su primer viaje a las Américas.   **d.** 1519
5. Miguel Hidalgo (dar) el grito *(shout)* de independencia en México.   **e.** 1810

7.9 **La semana pasada** Primero, conjuga el verbo en el pretérito y luego completa la oración de una manera lógica. Después compara tu semana con la de un compañero de clase.

Modelo yo (hacer)...

Estudiante 1: *La semana pasada hice una fiesta. ¿Qué hiciste tú?*
Estudiante 2: *La semana pasada yo hice la cena para mi familia.*

La semana pasada…

1. yo (conducir)…
2. mi amigo (estar)…
3. mis amigos y yo (ir)…
4. yo (tener) que…
5. uno de mis profesores (decir) que *(that)*…
6. mis compañeros y yo (poder)…
7. yo (ver)…
8. mis compañeros de clase (traer)…

7.10 **¿Qué pasó?** Con un compañero, túrnense para describir lo que pasó en las escenas. Deben usar los siguientes verbos en el pretérito.

conducir   decir   hacer   ir   poner   querer   traer

1.

2.

3.

4.

© Cengage Learning

7.11 **En busca de…** Pregúntales a ocho compañeros diferentes si hicieron una de las actividades de la lista. Si responden afirmativamente debes perdirles más información.

1. conducir a la universidad hoy (¿A qué hora?)
2. estar en una fiesta durante el fin de semana (¿Dónde?)
3. ir de compras recientemente (¿Qué compró?)
4. traer su almuerzo de la casa hoy (¿Qué comida preparó?)
5. tener un examen la semana pasada (¿En qué clase?)
6. poder hacer la tarea anoche (¿Para qué clase?)
7. ver una buena película recientemente (¿Cuál?)
8. hacer un viaje el año pasado (¿Adónde?)

INVESTIGUEMOS LA MÚSICA

Look online for the song "La fuerza del destino" by the Spanish pop group Mecano and listen to it. What preterite verbs do you recognize? What is the theme of the story told in the song?

A analizar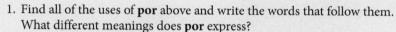

Camila y Vanesa van a un café para hablar. Mira el video otra vez. Después lee parte de su conversación y observa los usos de **por** y **para.**

Camila: Fui al supermercado **para** comprar la comida **para** la fiesta de mi hija. **Por** ser sábado, había mucha gente y fue imposible entrar y salir muy rápido. Y los precios... ¡todo fue muy caro, en particular la carne! Un kilo de jamón **por** veinte dólares...

Vanesa: ¡Guau! ¡Qué caro!... mi día fue tranquilo. **Por** la mañana fui de compras y **por** la tarde un amigo y yo fuimos al nuevo restaurante **para** comer. La comida fue excelente y los precios fueron muy razonables.

Camila: ¡Qué bueno! A ver si Rodrigo y yo vamos a ese restaurante **para** celebrar su cumpleaños.

Mesera: Aquí tengo sus cafés. ¿**Para** quién es el capuchino?

Camila: Es **para** mí. Gracias.

Mesera: Y el moca **para** usted.

1. Find all of the uses of **por** above and write the words that follow them. What different meanings does **por** express?
2. Now find all of the uses of **para** and write the words that follow them. What different meanings does **para** express?

A comprobar

Por and para and prepositional pronouns

1. Por is used to indicate:

a. cause, reason, or motive *(because of, on behalf of)*

Por la lluvia, no vamos a la piscina hoy.
***Because of** the rain, we are not going to the pool today.*

Hicieron sacrificios **por** sus hijos.
*They made sacrifices **on behalf of** their children.*

b. duration, period of time *(during, for)*

Van a estar en el restaurante **por** dos horas.
*They will be in the restaurant **for** two hours.*

c. exchange *(for)*

Él compró las piñas **por** 15 pesos.
*He bought the pineapples **for** 15 pesos.*

Gracias **por** el regalo de cumpleaños.
*Thank you **for** the birthday gift.*

d. general movement through space *(through, around, along, by)*

Pedro caminó **por** el mercado.
*Pedro walked **through** (**by**) the market.*

Para llegar a la piscina, tienes que pasar **por** el gimnasio.
*To get to the pool, you have to pass **by** the gym.*

e. expressions

por ejemplo	*for example*	**por** fin	*finally*
por eso	*that's why*	**por** supuesto	*of course*
por favor	*please*		

2. Para is used to indicate:

  a. goal, purpose *(in order to, used for)*

  Vamos al mercado **para** comprar fruta.
  *We are going to the market (**in order**) **to** buy fruit.*

  El pan es **para** hacer sándwiches.
  *The bread is **for** making sandwiches.*

  b. recipient *(for)*

  Ella compró un regalo **para** su amiga.
  *She bought a gift **for** her friend.*

  c. destination *(to)*

  Salen **para** las montañas el sábado.
  *They are going **to** the mountains Saturday.*

  d. deadline *(for, due)*

  La tarea es **para** mañana.
  *The homework is **for** (**due**) tomorrow.*

  e. contrast to what is expected *(for)*

  Para estar a dieta, él come mucho.
  ***For** being on a diet, he eats a lot.*

  f. expressions

para colmo	*to top it all off*	**para** siempre	*forever*
para nada	*not at all*	**para** variar	*for a change*

3. In **Capítulo 1**, you learned to use subject pronouns (**yo, tú, él**, etc.). Except for **yo** and **tú**, these same pronouns are used after prepositions.

mí	nosotros(as)
ti	vosotros(as)
él	ellos
ella	ellas
usted	ustedes

El regalo es para **ti.**
A **mí** me gustan las fresas. (emphasis)

4. Instead of using **mí** and **ti** with **con, conmigo** and **contigo** are used.

  Vamos a comer **contigo.**
  *We'll go to eat **with you.***

> **INVESTIGUEMOS LA GRAMÁTICA**
> The negative of **con** is **sin** *(without)*, and it takes the same personal pronouns as the other prepositions.
> No quiero comer sin **ti.**

A practicar

7.12 **Una fiesta de cumpleaños** Jacinto llama a un proveedor de comida *(caterer)*. Lee las preguntas del proveedor y decide cuál es la respuesta más lógica.

1. ¿Por qué organiza la fiesta?
2. ¿Para cuándo necesita la comida?
3. ¿Para cuántas personas necesita comida?
4. ¿Cuándo van a llegar los invitados?
5. ¿Cuánto tiempo va a durar *(to last)* la fiesta?
6. ¿Cómo prefiere pagar por la comida?

a. El 15 de abril.
b. Con tarjeta de crédito.
c. Por la tarde.
d. Veinticinco.
e. Es el cumpleaños de mi esposa.
f. Por cuatro horas.

¿Para cuándo necesita la comida?

© Champiofoto/Shutterstock

7.13 **En el supermercado** Completa el siguiente párrafo con **por** y **para.**

Ayer fui al supermercado **(1.)** _____ comprar la comida de la semana.

Siempre me gusta ir **(2.)** _____ la mañana porque hay menos personas, pero

ayer hubo mucha gente en el supermercado **(3.)** _____ un evento especial

(4.) _____ celebrar los 20 años del negocio. Tenían grandes especiales,

(5.) _____ ejemplo, queso manchego a 100 pesos **(6.)** _____ kilo.

Decidí comprar 2 kilos **(7.)** _____ hacer sándwiches durante la semana. A mi

esposo no le gusta el queso, **(8.)** _____ eso compré jamón **(9.)** _____

él. Al final compré toda la comida **(10.)** _____ la semana y ahorré *(saved)*

mucho dinero.

7.14 **Planes para el día** Fernando llama a su amiga Verónica. Completa la conversación con **por** o **para** o el pronombre preposicional apropiado. **¡OJO!** También es posible usar **conmigo** o **contigo**.

Vamos a tener un picnic.

Fernando: Hola, Verónica. Voy a ir a la playa mañana. ¿Quieres ir **(1.)** _____?

Verónica: ¡A **(2.)** _____ me gusta mucho la playa! ¡**(3.)** _____ (Por/Para) supuesto que voy **(4.)** _____!

Fernando: Vamos a salir temprano **(5.)** _____ (por/para) la mañana **(6.)** _____ (por/para) pasar *(to spend)* todo el día en la playa. También van a ir José, Pablo y Catarina con **(7.)** _____.

Verónica: ¡Qué bueno! ¿Qué quieres que lleve *(take)*?

Fernando: Vamos a tener un picnic, entonces puedes llevar algo **(8.)** _____ (por/para) comer.

Verónica: ¿A **(9.)** _____ te gusta el jamón?

Fernando: Sí, me gusta mucho, pero Catarina es vegetariana.

Verónica: Bueno, voy a llevar jamón y también puedo llevar queso **(10.)** _____ (por/para) **(11.)** _____. No tengo coche hoy. ¿Puedes venir **(12.)** _____ (por/para) **(13.)** _____?

Fernando: No hay problema. Paso **(14.)** _____ (por/para) **(15.)** _____ a las ocho.

Verónica: Bueno, voy a estar lista. ¡Hasta entonces!

7.15 **En la caja** Imagínense que están en la caja *(cash register)* para pagar sus compras en el supermercado. Uno de ustedes es el cliente y el otro es el dependiente que quiere vender una tarjeta con minutos para el celular. Respóndanse las preguntas que aparecen a continuación.

Estudiante 1 (el cliente):

1. ¿Puedo conseguir descuentos por ser mayor de 55 años?
2. ¿Por cuánto tiempo es la oferta del jamón?
3. ¿Puedo usar la tarjeta de crédito para pagar?

Estudiante 2 (el dependiente):

4. ¿Necesita minutos para su teléfono?
5. ¿Para qué compañía telefónica quiere la tarjeta?
6. ¿Por cuántos minutos quiere la tarjeta?

¿Puedo usar la tarjeta de crédito para pagar?

7.16 Oraciones incompletas Con un compañero, completen las oraciones. Deben pensar en los usos diferentes de **por** y **para.**

1. **a.** Voy al supermercado por…
   b. Voy al supermercado para…

2. **a.** El chef prepara la comida por…
   b. El chef prepara la comida para…

3. **a.** Por ser un buen chef,…
   b. Para ser un buen chef,…

4. **a.** Quiero los huevos por…
   b. Quiero los huevos para…

5. **a.** El mesero fue a la cocina por…
   b. El mesero fue a la cocina para…

6. **a.** Tenemos una reservación por…
   b. Tenemos una reservación para…

INVESTIGUEMOS LA MÚSICA

Carlos Ponce is a Puerto Rican singer and actor. One of his hit songs is called "Rezo." What do you think the song will be about? Search online, listen to the song and compare your answers. What phrases do you hear with **por**? And with **para**?

7.17 En la recepción Con un compañero, túrnense para explicar lo que hicieron Manuel y las otras personas según *(according to)* los dibujos. **¡OJO!** Deben usar el pretérito y **por** o **para.**

© Cengage Learning

7.18 Una foto Con un compañero, escojan una de las fotos e inventen una historia basada en la foto. Deben incluir varios usos de **por** y **para** en su historia.

© Monkey Business Images/Shutterstock

© Lewis Tse Pui Lung/Shutterstock

En vivo 🔊

Entrando en materia

¿Qué comidas compras con frecuencia en el supermercado? Si alguien quiere ahorrar dinero en el supermercado ¿qué debe hacer?

Las compras en el supermercado

🔊 Vas a escuchar un programa de radio producido por una organización de protección al
2-3 consumidor. Después de escuchar, responde las preguntas que siguen.

Vocabulario útil

ahorrar	*to save*	los derechos	*rights*
el azúcar	*sugar*	la envoltura	*wrappers, packaging*
caducar	*to expire*	la lata	*can (of food)*
congelado(a)	*frozen*	el sodio	*sodium*
congelar	*to freeze*	la temporada	*season*
dejarse llevar por impulsos	*to impulse buy*		

Es importante comprar frutas y verduras de la temporada.

© Matthew Dixon/Shutterstock

Comprensión

1. En general ¿de qué hablan en este programa de radio?
2. ¿Cuál es la segunda estrategia?
3. ¿Por qué es buena idea hacer un menú para la semana?
4. ¿Por qué recomiendan comprar productos congelados y no en lata?

🖥️ Más allá

Escribe una estrategia que usas para ahorrar en el supermercado. Comparte tu estrategia en Share It! y lee las recomendaciones de otros estudiantes.

Lectura

Antes de leer

Escribe una lista de comidas que se consumen durante el Día de Acción de Gracias. ¿Qué ingredientes se necesitan para prepararlas? ¿Conoces una comida típica de algún país latinoamericano? ¿Qué comida? ¿Qué ingredientes se necesitan para prepararla?

A leer

Los alimentos del Nuevo Mundo

people

where they used to live

Es obvio que en épocas anteriores **la gente** comía los alimentos que estaban disponibles en la zona **donde habitaban.** Debido a las diferencias climáticas y geográficas, los animales y plantas del Nuevo Mundo (el continente americano) eran muy diferentes a los que existían en Europa.

[¿puedes imaginar el resto del mundo sin chocolate...?]

Hoy en día, gracias al avance en las comunicaciones del mundo y a las nuevas técnicas de transporte y preservación de los alimentos,

were harvested

es posible comer productos que se **cosecharon** o produjeron a miles de kilómetros de distancia. Nuestro

used to be

mundo **era** muy diferente antes de la llegada de los europeos al Nuevo Mundo.

¿Puedes imaginar tu dieta sin leche, sin queso, sin carne de res o sin naranjas ni plátanos? Estos son solo algunos de los productos

were not available

que **no había** en el Nuevo Mundo. Por otra parte, ¿puedes imaginar el resto del mundo sin chocolate, vainilla, tomates, maíz,

turkeys

papas, chiles o **pavos**? La lista de productos americanos es

goes well beyond

larga y su importancia **va mucho más allá** del gusto por estos productos. Un buen ejemplo es el

© Jill Battaglia/iStockphoto

Las papas son originarias de Sudamérica.

de las papas, las cuales les salvaron la vida a millones de europeos durante el período de escasez que siguió a la Segunda Guerra Mundial en Europa.

Si se piensa en la identidad cultural de algunos países ¿puedes imaginar a Suiza o a Bélgica sin chocolates? ¿Puedes imaginar las típicas pizzas

El cacao y la vainilla son originarios de Mesoamérica.

italianas sin tomate? ¿o la **picante** comida de la India sin chile?

spicy

Tanto el tomate como el maíz, la vainilla y el cacao se originaron en Mesoamérica, el territorio que hoy es parte de México y de Centroamérica. De hecho, las palabras *tomate* y *chocolate* vienen de las palabras del náhuatl *tomatl* y *xocolatl*. *Ahuacatl* y *chilli* son palabras náhuatl para **aguacate** y chile, otras plantas nativas de las Américas.

avocado

Un poco más al sur se originan la papa y la quinoa, un cereal que aunque no es muy conocido en los Estados Unidos, se considera que puede ser la solución al problema del hambre en el mundo, debido a su gran valor nutritivo.

Dos ingredientes centrales en muchos países en Asia son los chiles y los **cacahuates.** Los helados europeos son populares gracias al chocolate y la vainilla, y las papas a la francesa no pueden existir sin papas. Estos productos son solo una pequeña parte de las aportaciones del Nuevo Mundo para el resto del planeta.

peanuts

Comprensión

1. ¿Cuáles son cuatro productos originarios de las Américas que son importantes en las celebraciones culturales de los Estados Unidos?

2. ¿Qué frutos tomaron su nombre del idioma náhuatl, el idioma de los aztecas?

3. ¿Qué es la quinoa y por qué es importante?

4. En tu opinión ¿cuáles son tres productos de América que tienen mucha importancia en la economía mundial? ¿Por qué?

5. ¿Qué productos muy importantes en tu dieta personal no había en América antes de la llegada de los europeos?

Después de leer

Cada región o país tiene su comida típica. Piensa en los factores externos que ayudan a determinar la comida típica de una región. Despúes considera la comida típica donde vives. Con un compañero, explíquenle al resto de la clase cómo preparar una comida típica de su estado o su región.

El señor Buenrostro y su familia salen a comer en un restaurante para celebrar su cumpleaños.

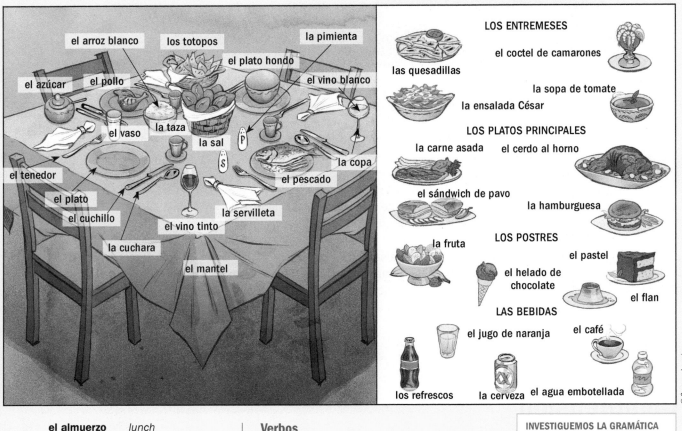

LOS ENTREMESES
las quesadillas
el coctel de camarones
la sopa de tomate
la ensalada César

LOS PLATOS PRINCIPALES
la carne asada   el cerdo al horno
el sándwich de pavo
la hamburguesa

LOS POSTRES
la fruta
el pastel
el helado de chocolate
el flan

LAS BEBIDAS
el jugo de naranja   el café
los refrescos   la cerveza   el agua embotellada

el arroz blanco · los totopos · la pimienta · el plato hondo · el azúcar · el pollo · el vino blanco · el vaso · la taza · la sal · la copa · el tenedor · el pescado · el plato · el cuchillo · la servilleta · el vino tinto · la cuchara · el mantel

© Cengage Learning

el almuerzo	lunch
la cena	dinner
la cuenta	bill
el desayuno	breakfast
la orden	order
el tazón	serving bowl

Verbos

cenar	to eat dinner
dejar (una propina)	to leave (a tip)
desayunar	to eat breakfast

INVESTIGUEMOS LA GRAMÁTICA

The word **agua** is feminine, and therefore any adjectives need to be in the feminine form; however, it takes the masculine article for pronunciation purposes.

A practicar

7.19 **Escucha y responde** Vas a escuchar los nombres de varias comidas y bebidas. En un papel dibuja un vaso y en otro un tenedor. Si escuchas una bebida, levanta el vaso y si escuchas una comida levanta el tenedor.

2-4

7.20 **¿Cuál es?** Contesta con la opción más lógica.

1. ¡Tengo mucha sed! Quiero _____.
   a. arroz   **b.** un pastel   **c.** un refresco   **d.** un pollo
2. Mi entremés favorito es _____.
   a. fruta   **b.** pimienta   **c.** un café   **d.** una quesadilla
3. Mi café necesita más _____.
   a. taza   **b.** azúcar   **c.** cucharita   **d.** sal
4. Mi postre favorito es _____.
   a. la cerveza   **b.** la leche con chocolate   **c.** el helado   **d.** el azúcar
5. Para cortar la carne necesito _____.
   a. un cuchillo   **b.** una cuchara   **c.** una servilleta   **d.** la sal

INVESTIGUEMOS EL VOCABULARIO

In Spain, a cake is called **una torta**; however, in Mexico **una torta** is a type of sandwich.
Sándwich, borrowed from English, is commonly used throughout the Spanish-speaking world. The less commonly used Spanish equivalent is **el emparedado**.

7.21 **Relaciones** Relaciona las siguientes palabras con una palabra de la lista. Después, trabaja con un compañero para decir qué relación hay entre las palabras.

la carne   la copa   la cuchara   el plato principal   el postre   la sal   la taza   el vaso

Modelo   el café... la bebida → *El café es una bebida.*

1. el cerdo
2. el pastel
3. el vino
4. la sopa
5. el jugo
6. la pimienta
7. las enchiladas
8. el té

7.22 **Encuesta** Encuentra a seis personas que hacen las siguientes actividades. Contesta con oraciones completas y después reporta a la clase.

Modelo   desayunar cereal todos los días
Estudiante 1: *¿Desayunas cereal todos los días?*
Estudiante 2: *Sí, siempre desayuno cereal todos los días.*

1. pedir postre siempre cuando come en un restaurante
2. su comida favorita es el desayuno
3. saber hacer flan
4. comer carne más de tres veces a la semana
5. no tomar cerveza nunca
6. cenar frente al televisor

INVESTIGUEMOS EL VOCABULARIO
In some countries, **la comida** is used to refer to the noon meal, which is the main meal of the day.

7.23 **En un restaurante** En parejas, túrnense para hacer el papel *(play the role)* de mesero y de cliente.

Mesero: Buenas tardes, (señor/señorita/señora). ¿Prefiere la sección de fumar o de no fumar?
Cliente: _____
Mesero: ¿Desea una bebida?
Cliente: _____
Mesero: ¿Qué prefiere como plato principal?
Cliente: _____
Mesero: ¿Le gustaría *(Would you like)* un postre?
Cliente: _____
Mesero: ¿Necesita algo más *(something else)*?
Cliente: _____
Mesero: ¡Buen provecho! *(Enjoy!)*

¿Desean una bebida?

© Photos To Go

7.24 **Comparemos** Trabaja con un compañero. Uno va a mirar el dibujo en esta página y el otro va a mirar el dibujo en el **Apéndice B.** Túrnense para describir los dibujos y encontrar cinco diferencias.

© Cengage Learning

Cultura

A veces un lugar para comer se vuelve casi tan importante como un monumento para una ciudad debido a su comida y a la historia del lugar. Por ejemplo, 4Gats en Barcelona fue un lugar de reunión para muchos artistas famosos, como Pablo Picasso.

Otro ejemplo famoso es La Cabaña, en Buenos Aires. La Cabaña es el restaurante especializado en carnes más viejo de la capital argentina. Su libro de visitas tiene la firma de visitantes muy famosos, entre ellos Charles de Gaulle, Henry Kissinger, Richard Nixon, el Rey Juan Carlos, Joan Crawford y Walt Disney, para mencionar solo a algunos.

En La Habana, Cuba, se distingue un restaurante llamado La Bodeguita del Medio. En parte es famosa por las personas importantes que la han visitado, como Pablo Neruda, Salvador Allende, Marlene Dietrich y Ernest Hemingway. El poeta nacional de Cuba, Nicolás Guillén, le dedicó un verso. Más allá de su fama, la Bodeguita se distingue por ser una especie de museo, ya que de sus paredes cuelgan (hang) fotos y artefactos que cuentan la historia de Cuba. Este restaurante también parece ser el lugar donde se inventó el mojito. Aún quienes no se interesan por la historia se sentirán atraídos a un menú con algunas de las mejores especialidades criollas cubanas, como frijoles negros, pierna de puerco asada, yuca con mojo y plátanos fritos.

Piensa en una ciudad de un país hispano que te interesa conocer y busca información sobre algún restaurante o café famoso de esa ciudad.

La Bodeguita del Medio es uno de los restaurantes más conocidos de La Habana.

Busca en Internet otros restaurantes importantes en el mundo hispanohablante. Para buscar, usa palabras como **restaurante**, **café**, **pub**, **taberna**, **famoso**, **histórico** y el nombre de un país o una ciudad hispanohablante. Escoge uno y sube la información o el menú a Share It! Explica por qué te gustaría comer en ese restaurante.

Comunidad

Visita un supermercado de tu comunidad y busca la sección de comida de otras partes del mundo. Luego prepara un reporte y usa las siguientes preguntas para guiarte.

¿Hay comida latinoamericana o española?

¿Qué productos encuentras?

Mira las etiquetas (labels). ¿Dónde están hechos (made)?

¿Te sorprende la cantidad de productos de otros países? ¿Por qué?

¿Hay otras tiendas con comida de otros países? ¿De qué países?

¿Hay comida latinoamericana o española en tu supermercado?

Conexiones... a la salud

Muchas personas piensan que somos lo que comemos *(we are what we eat)*. En estos tiempos modernos mucha gente no tiene tiempo para preparar comida y esto puede afectar negativamente los hábitos alimenticios. Además, muchas personas compran comidas procesadas que son muy económicas, pero también tienen un alto contenido de calorías, azúcares y sodio. Una consecuencia de estos cambios es la gran cantidad de personas obesas que hay en muchos países. Entre los países industrializados con un mayor porcentaje de obesidad aparecen los Estados Unidos, México, Chile y Australia. El caso de México puede explicarse, en parte, por el dramático consumo de refrescos. Los mexicanos consumen en promedio 149 litros de refrescos por año.

Escribe una lista de productos que piensas que tienen un impacto negativo en la salud *(health)* de las personas. Después entrevista a tres compañeros de la clase para saber si también piensan que estos productos son malos para la salud. Reporta la información a la clase.

La comida rápida no siempre es la más saludable.

Comparaciones

¿Dónde compras la comida? ¿Vas a tiendas especializadas? En España y Latinoamérica siempre ha sido *(it has been)* muy común comprar la comida en diferentes tiendas pequeñas en vez del supermercado. La siguiente es una lista de diferentes tipos de tiendas. ¿Qué productos crees que venden en los siguientes lugares?

1. una tortillería
2. una heladería
3. una panadería
4. una frutería
5. una lechería
6. una carnicería
7. una chocolatería

En una alfajorería se venden alfajores, un postre típico de Argentina.

¿Cuáles son las ventajas *(advantages)* de ir a las tiendas especializadas? ¿y las desventajas? ¿Dónde compras tú esos *(those)* productos? ¿Puedes encontrar estas tiendas especializadas donde vives?

A analizar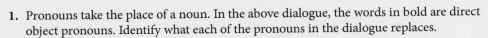

Rosa y Santiago salen a comer en un restaurante. Mira el video. Después lee parte de su conversación y observa los pronombres de objeto directo en negritas. Después contesta las preguntas que siguen.

Mesero:	Buenas tardes. ¿Están listos?
Rosa:	Sí. Me gustarían los tacos de pescado, por favor.
Mesero:	Lo siento, no **los** tenemos ahora. Ya no hay más pescado.
Rosa:	¡Ay, qué lástima! Bueno, en ese caso quiero las enchiladas suizas. ¿Vienen con salsa verde o salsa roja?
Mesero:	Con salsa verde.
Rosa:	Perfecto, **las** voy a pedir.
Mesero:	¿Y para usted, caballero?
Santiago:	Tengo una pregunta, ¿**la** sopa de pollo tiene chile?
Mesero:	No, no **lo** tiene.
Santiago:	Bien, **la** voy a pedir entonces.

© Cengage Learning

1. Pronouns take the place of a noun. In the above dialogue, the words in bold are direct object pronouns. Identify what each of the pronouns in the dialogue replaces.

2. What do **lo** and **la** mean in the dialogue above? And **los** and **las**?

3. Where are the pronouns in bold placed?

4. What pronoun would you use to replace **el arroz**? And **las cervezas**?

A comprobar

Direct object pronouns 1

1. A direct object is a person or a thing that receives the action of the verb. It tells to whom or to what something is being done.

   Juan pide **pollo**.
   Juan is ordering chicken. (The chicken is what is being ordered.)

   Elena invita a **Natalia** a comer.
   Elena is inviting Natalia to eat. (Natalia is who is being invited.)

2. In order to avoid repetition, the direct object can be replaced with a pronoun. In Spanish, the pronoun must agree in gender and number with the direct object it replaces.

¿Tienes **las tazas**?   *Do you have **the cups**?*

Sí, **las** tengo.   *Yes, I have **them**.*

In answering the question, it is not necessary to repeat the direct object, **las tazas**; instead it is replaced with the pronoun **las**.

3. The following are the third person direct object pronouns:

	singular		plural	
masculino	**lo**	*it, him, you (formal)*	**los**	*them, you*
femenino	**la**	*it, her, you (formal)*	**las**	*them, you*

4. The direct object pronoun is placed in front of the conjugated verb.

> ¿Comes carne?
> *Do you eat meat?*
>
> No, no **la** como.
> *No, I don't eat it.*

5. When using a verb phrase that has an infinitive or a present participle (**-ando, -iendo**), the pronoun can be placed in front of the conjugated verb, or it can be attached to the infinitive or the present participle. Notice that an accent is necessary when adding the pronoun to the end of the present participle.

> **La** voy a invitar. / Voy a invitar**la**.
> *I am going to invite **her**.*
>
> ¿**Lo** quieres comer? / ¿Quieres comer**lo**?
> *Do you want to eat **it**?*
>
> Él **lo** está sirviendo. / Él está sirviéndo**lo**.
> *He is serving **it**.*

A practicar

7.25 **En el restaurante** Lee la siguiente conversación e identifica el objeto o la persona que el pronombre reemplaza *(replaces)*.

Sr. Ortega: ¿Quieres el menú?

Sra. Ortega: No, no <u>lo</u> (**1.**) necesito. Ya sé qué quiero.

Sr. Ortega: ¿Sí? ¿Vas a pedir el pollo como siempre?

Sra. Ortega: No, no <u>lo</u> (**2.**) quiero comer hoy. Voy a pedir la carne asada.

Sr. Ortega: Yo voy a pedir<u>la</u> (**3.**) también. ¿Pedimos una botella de vino?

Sra. Ortega: Sí, <u>la</u> (**4.**) podemos pedir.

Sr. Ortega: Bueno, estamos listos. ¿Dónde está el mesero? No <u>lo</u> (**5.**) veo.

Sra. Ortega: Allí está. ¿Por qué no <u>lo</u> (**6.**) llamas?

Sr. Ortega: ¡Señor!

7.26 **La semana pasada** Habla con un compañero sobre quién hizo las siguientes actividades en sus casas la semana pasada. Deben usar los pronombres de objeto directo y el pretérito cuando contesten las preguntas. Es posible responder con **nadie** *(no one)*.

Modelo ¿Quién tomó leche?
> Estudiante 1: *¿Quién tomó leche?*
> Estudiante 2: *Yo la tomé. ¿Y en tu casa?*
> Estudiante 1: *Nadie la tomó.*

1. ¿Quién compró la comida?
2. ¿Quién preparó el desayuno?
3. ¿Quién puso la mesa?
4. ¿Quién cocinó la cena?

5. ¿Quién sirvió la comida?
6. ¿Quién comió postre?
7. ¿Quién lavó los platos?
8. ¿Quién limpió la cocina?

¿Quién comió postre?

© luxmilita/Shutterstock

7.27 **¿Quién lo hace?** Mira los dibujos. Con un compañero, túrnense para hacer y responder preguntas con las palabras. Usen pronombres de objeto directo para responder.

Modelo *(Look at drawing #1)* comer/ensalada
Estudiante 1: *¿Quién come la ensalada?*
Estudiante 2: *Eva **la** come.*

1.

a. tomar/sopa   **b.** comer/pan

2.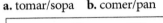

a. servir/tacos   **b.** servir/hamburguesas

3.

a. necesitar/tenedor   **b.** necesitar/cuchara

4.

a. tomar/cerveza   **b.** tomar/refresco

7.28 **Entrevista** Túrnense para hacer y contestar las siguientes preguntas. **¡OJO!** Deben usar pronombres de objeto directo para reemplazar *(replace)* las palabras subrayadas *(underlined)* cuando contesten para evitar la repetición.

1. ¿Desayunaste esta mañana? ¿Tomaste <u>café</u>?
2. ¿Trajiste <u>el almuerzo</u> a la universidad? ¿Qué trajiste?
3. ¿A qué hora cenaste anoche? ¿Quién preparó <u>la cena</u>?
4. ¿Cocinaste esta semana? ¿Preparaste <u>verduras</u>?
5. ¿Comiste <u>postre</u> después de la cena anoche? ¿Qué comiste?
6. ¿Tomaste <u>refrescos</u> con el almuerzo? ¿Qué tomaste?
7. ¿Quién limpió <u>la cocina</u> en tu casa después de la cena anoche? ¿Lavó <u>los platos</u> a mano?
8. ¿Compraste <u>comida</u> en el supermercado esta semana? ¿Qué compraste?

7.29 **¿Para qué es?** Con un compañero, túrnense para explicar lo que hacemos con las siguientes cosas. Deben usar los pronombres de objeto directo y verbos diferentes en las respuestas y dar explicaciones completas.

Modelo el arroz
Estudiante 1: *¿Qué hacemos con el arroz?*
Estudiante 2: *Lo servimos con frijoles. / Lo ponemos en la paella. / Lo cocinamos en agua.*

1. el refresco   3. la ensalada   5. el cuchillo   7. la sopa
2. el helado   4. las enchiladas   6. los totopos   8. los tomates

A analizar

Rosa y Santiago salen a comer en un restaurante. Después de ver el video otra vez, lee parte de su conversación y observa los pronombres de objeto directo en negritas.

> Rosa: Gracias por invitar**me** a cenar aquí. **Me** conoces y sabes que este es mi restaurante favorito.
>
> Santiago: Sí, **te** conozco muy bien, Rosa.

1. To whom do the pronouns **me** and **te** refer?
2. How would you translate the sentences above?

© Cengage Learning

A comprobar

Direct object pronouns 2

In the last **Exploraciones gramaticales** section, you learned about third person direct object pronouns. The following are all of the direct object pronouns.

	singular		plural	
first person	**me**	*me*	**nos**	*us*
second person	**te**	*you*	**os**	*you (plural)*
third person	**lo, la**	*it, him, her, you (formal)*	**los, las**	*they, you (plural)*

1. As with the third person direct object pronouns, these pronouns are placed in front of the conjugated verb. They can also be attached to an infinitive or a present participle. Remember that an accent is necessary when adding the pronoun to the present participle.

El mesero **nos** ve.
*The waiter sees **us**.*

Te quiero invitar a cenar. / Quiero invitar**te** a cenar.
*I want to invite **you** to dinner.*

Ana **me** está llamando. / Ana está llamánd**ome**.
*Ana is calling **me**.*

2. The following are some of the verbs that are frequently used with these direct object pronouns:

ayudar	felicitar *(to congratulate)*	querer *(to love)*
buscar		saludar
conocer	invitar	*(to greet)*
creer	llamar	ver
encontrar	llevar *(to take along)*	visitar
escuchar		

A practicar

7.30 **¿Qué significa?** Decide cuál es la traducción correcta.

1. No te entiendo.
    a. I don't understand you.   **b.** You don't understand me.

2. Mi madre me llama todos los días.
    a. My mother calls me every day.   **b.** I call my mother every day.

3. ¿Te esperan tus amigos?
    a. Are you waiting for your friends?   **b.** Are your friends waiting for you?

4. No nos ven.
    a. They don't see us.   **b.** We don't see them.

7.31 **Algunas preguntas** Decide cuál es la respuesta correcta.

1. ¿Quién me llama?
   a. Héctor te llama.   b. Héctor me llama.

2. ¿Te comprenden tus padres?
   a. Sí, te comprenden.   b. Sí, me comprenden.

3. ¿Me ayudas con la tarea?
   a. Sí, te ayudo.   b. Sí, me ayudas.

4. ¿Cuándo te invitan a comer?
   a. Te invitan a comer hoy.   b. Me invitan a comer hoy.

5. ¿Vas a visitarnos mañana?
   a. Sí, voy a visitarnos.   b. Sí, voy a visitarlos.

6. ¿El profesor los vio a ustedes?
   a. Sí, nos vio.   b. Sí, los vio.

7.32 **En clase** Contesta las preguntas referentes a los hábitos del profesor de español. Debes usar el pronombre **nos** en las respuestas.

Modelo ¿El profesor de español los invita a ustedes a fiestas?
   Sí, nos invita a fiestas. / No, no nos invita a fiestas.

¿El profesor de español…

1. los comprende a ustedes?
2. los conoce bien?
3. los ayuda a ustedes con la tarea?
4. los escucha cuando ustedes tienen problemas?
5. los llama a casa?
6. los lleva a comer en un restaurante?
7. los saluda en los pasillos *(hallways)*?
8. los ve fuera de la clase?
9. los invita a ser sus amigos en su página de Facebook?
10. los felicita cuando hacen un buen trabajo?

La profesora siempre nos ayuda.

© Tyler Olson/Shutterstock

7.33 **¡Ayuda!** Completa la siguiente conversación con el pronombre **me, te** o **nos.**

Susana: Simón, ¡yo (1.) _____ necesito! ¡No entiendo francés!

Simón: ¿El profesor siempre habla con ustedes en francés?

Susana: Sí, solo nos habla en francés, pero no lo comprendemos a él, ni él (2.) _____ comprende a nosotros. ¿(3.) _____ ayudas con mi tarea?

Simón: Por supuesto. Yo (4.) _____ puedo ayudar esta tarde si quieres.

Susana: ¡Sí! Entonces ¿(5.) _____ vas a llamar luego?

Simón: Sí, yo (6.) _____ llamo después de trabajar.

Susana: ¡Qué bueno! ¡(7.) _____ quiero, Simón!

¿Necesitas ayuda con la tarea?

© Andresr/Shutterstock

7.34 **Una noche en el restaurante** Con un compañero, túrnense para describir lo que pasó anoche en el restaurante. Deben completar lo que dijeron las diferentes personas en cada escena, usando los pronombres de objeto directo **me, te** y **nos**.

7.35 **La telenovela** Imagínate que eres un actor de telenovelas (soap operas). Con un compañero, túrnense para leer las preguntas y las exclamaciones, y para responder de una manera original y dramática. Usen pronombres de objeto directo en las respuestas. ¡Sean creativos!

Modelo ¿Quieres a tu esposa?
　　　Estudiante 1: *¿Quieres a tu esposa?*
　　　Estudiante 2: *No, no la quiero, pero ella es muy rica.*

1. ¿Me quieres?
2. ¿Me vas a querer siempre?
3. ¿Quién te besa (kiss) cada noche?
4. ¡¿No nos vas a llevar contigo?!
5. ¡No me comprendes!

6. ¿Me estás engañando (cheating on)?
7. ¿Nos vas a abandonar?
8. ¡Nunca me escuchas!

¿Me quieres?

7.36 **Preguntas personales** Entrevista a un compañero de clase con las siguientes preguntas.

Modelo Estudiante 1: *¿Quién te cree siempre?*
　　　Estudiante 2: *Mi esposo (mi madre, mi mejor amigo, etc.) me cree siempre.*

1. ¿Quién te comprende?
2. ¿Quién te quiere mucho?
3. ¿Quién te invita a comer con frecuencia?
4. ¿Quién te llama por teléfono y habla y habla y habla… ?
5. ¿Quién te ayuda con la tarea de español?
6. ¿Quién te visita con frecuencia?
7. ¿Quién te escucha cuando tienes problemas?
8. ¿Quién te busca cuando necesita dinero?
9. ¿Quién los visita a ti y a tu familia con frecuencia?
10. ¿Quién los saluda a ti y a tus compañeros de clase todos los días?

Lectura

Antes de leer

¿Qué comidas se consideran "comida rápida" en los Estados Unidos? ¿Existe una diferencia entre comida rápida y comida chatarra *(junk food)*? ¿Cuál?

A leer

La comida rápida en Latinoamérica

has changed / century — Todos sabemos que la vida **ha cambiado** mucho en el último **siglo,** especialmente en las grandes ciudades, donde hoy en día hay poco tiempo para hacer todo lo que debemos hacer. ¿Cómo

lack of time — afecta esta **falta de tiempo** nuestros hábitos alimenticios?

Preparar comida consume mucho tiempo, así que mucha

save — gente busca soluciones para **ahorrar** ese tiempo. Las soluciones para este problema son diferentes según el país. Por ejemplo, en muchos países latinos donde pasar

make sense — tiempo con la familia es muy importante, no **tiene sentido** que una persona coma mientras maneja su automóvil. A la hora de la comida muchas amas de casa ocupadísimas se detienen en locales de comida rápida (o "comida corrida") para

homemade — comprar platillos **caseros** para su familia. De esta manera, no tienen que llegar a casa a preparar comida, solamente deben servirla. Los platillos que se compran en estos locales tienen la ventaja de ser variados y de cambiar todos los días. ¿Qué

stews — venden? ¡De todo! Diferentes variedades de sopa, carnes **guisadas,** verduras y hasta postres. Como el negocio no necesita mucho espacio y hay pocos empleados, pueden proveer comida

similar — muy **semejante** a la que se elabora en casa a un precio razonable.

Otra comida rápida popular es el pollo asado.

chains — Hay **cadenas** que lo venden
like — muy barato, **a semejanza** de las grandes compañías en los Estados Unidos que venden hamburguesas.

However — **Sin embargo,** el negocio de la comida rápida no se

> [no tiene sentido que una persona coma mientras maneja]

Las pupusas son un ejemplo de comida típica salvadoreña.

© Claudia Mejía Castillo/Shutterstock

limita a la comida para toda la familia. ¿Quién no tiene hambre a mediodía o a media tarde? Para satisfacer esos **antojos,** en cualquier pueblo o ciudad de Latinoamérica se encuentran puestos en la calle o pequeños locales donde se puede comprar comida barata de acuerdo al gusto local. Por ejemplo, en los países andinos (Perú, Ecuador y Bolivia especialmente) se compran papas en la calle, preparadas de mil maneras diferentes. En El Salvador se venden pupusas, en Puerto Rico

cravings

El chipá paraguayo

los pinchos y en el Paraguay el chipá. Aunque los ingredientes de la comida rápida no son necesariamente los mismos que los de la comida que se compra en los Estados Unidos, los resultados son igual de **apetecibles.**

appetizing

Comprensión

Decide si las siguientes afirmaciones son ciertas o falsas, según la lectura. Corrige las ideas falsas.

1. En Latinoamérica la gente tiene mucho tiempo para cocinar.
2. La gente generalmente no come mientras conduce su automóvil en los países latinos.
3. Los locales de comida rápida venden comida como hamburguesas, pizza y pollo asado.
4. El pollo asado es una comida popular.
5. Las papas pueden ser un tipo de comida rápida en algunos países como Perú y Bolivia.

Después de leer

 Con un compañero, túrnense para hacer y contestar las preguntas.

1. ¿Comes comida rápida/chatarra con frecuencia? ¿Por qué?
2. ¿Qué comidas rápidas prefieres?
3. ¿Qué más haces para ahorrar tiempo con la comida?

Redacción

Write a blog entry in which you discuss a favorite restaurant.

Paso 1 Think of a restaurant that you like. Jot down some basic information about the restaurant. Where is it located? What are its hours? What is the ambience of the restaurant like? What are the prices like? What kind of food do they serve? What do you recommend?

Paso 2 Think about a time that you visited the restaurant. When did you go and with whom? What did you and the others with you eat? How was the service? How was the food?

Paso 3 Using the information you generated in **Paso 1,** write a paragraph (in the present tense) in which you tell your readers about your favorite restaurant. Be sure to begin your paragraph with a sentence that will catch your readers' attention; a sentence such as *El Café Cielo es mi restaurante favorito.* is not going to encourage someone to continue reading.

Paso 4 Using the information you generated in **Paso 2,** write a second paragraph in which you discuss a time you visited the restaurant. You will need to use the preterite.

Paso 5 Write a brief concluding paragraph in which you sum up your thoughts about the restaurant.

Paso 6 Edit your blog entry:

1. Do all of the sentences in each paragraph support the topic sentence?
2. Are there any short sentences you can combine with **y** or **pero**?
3. Do adjectives agree with the nouns they describe?
4. Do verbs agree with the subject? Did you use the correct forms of the preterite?
5. Are there any spelling errors? Do the preterite verbs that need accents have them?

INVESTIGUEMOS EL VOCABULARIO

Here are some terms for ethnic foods commonly served in restaurants:

comida china	*Chinese food*
comida griega	*Greek food*
comida italiana	*Italian food*
comida japonesa	*Japanese food*
comida mexicana	*Mexican food*

En vivo

Entrando en materia

¿Lees los comentarios sobre los restaurantes antes de elegir un nuevo lugar para comer? ¿Por qué?

Una reseña de un restaurante

Vas a leer una bitácora que cada semana habla sobre un restaurante de la ciudad. Después de leer decide si la reseña es positiva o negativa.

GUÍA GASTRONÓMICA: COMIDA CRIOLLA

Cuando Cristóbal Colón llegó a América, la historia del mundo cambió... y las opciones para comer se multiplicaron. Aquí en la ciudad gozamos de muchas opciones de cocina internacional, pero la comida tradicional y la cocina criolla siguen siendo las favoritas. El Criollo es un nuevo restaurante que abrió el mes pasado. Antes de hablar sobre los platillos que ofrecen, **valdría la pena** recordar la diferencia entre la comida tradicional y la criolla, para que ustedes sepan qué esperar de este restaurante.

Si pensamos en la historia de Latinoamérica, recordaremos que los criollos eran hijos de europeos, pero **nacieron** en el nuevo mundo y se criaron en él. Generaciones más tarde, los hijos de los criollos siguieron llamándose criollos, hasta que la palabra llegó a significar algo **autóctono** o nacional (justamente en la época que los países latinoamericanos empezaron a independizarse de España). Algo similar ocurrió con la comida: con el intercambio de alimentos, nacieron nuevas cocinas locales que combinaban los nuevos alimentos con las prácticas culinarias locales.

Hoy en día se habla de comida tradicional y comida criolla como sinónimos, pero en realidad hay diferencias importantes. La comida tradicional es la que tradicionalmente consume un grupo cultural o etnográfico. Por ejemplo, se puede hablar de cocina tradicional **judía**. La cocina criolla se basa en una mezcla tanto de ingredientes como de técnicas para cocinar. En Latinoamérica, la cocina criolla fusiona dos (o más) gastronomías con sus técnicas, tradiciones e ingredientes. En el caso de Latinoamérica, se mezclan tradiciones culinarias prehispánicas con las europeas, las que a su vez estaban mezcladas con las de la cultura árabe y judía, entre otras.

Ahora que está aclarada la diferencia, vale la pena mencionar que en El Criollo no van a encontrar las recetas típicas peruanas, sino platillos **hechos** con ingredientes locales con un toque moderno. Las porciones son pequeñas, pero están elegantemente presentadas. El ambiente del local también es moderno, aunque un poco **ruidoso**. El servicio, para ser honesto, es un poco **lento,** pero los precios son moderados en comparación con otros restaurantes de cocina criolla. Además, El Criollo tiene un estacionamiento muy amplio, así que es un buen lugar para citarse a comer con los amigos.

¿El veredicto? Pienso regresar a El Criollo para comer con mis amigos a un buen precio.

Papas a la huancaina; papas con una salsa picante de queso

© bonchan/Shutterstock

it would be worth it

were born

made
indigenous

noisy
slow

Jewish

Comprensión

Decide si las afirmaciones son ciertas o falsas, y corrige las falsas.

1. Después de que Cristóbal Colón encontró el Nuevo Mundo, la comida se homogeneizó en todo el mundo y hubo menos variedad de platillos.
2. Los criollos eran los hijos de europeos que nacieron en América.
3. "Comida criolla" es sinónimo de "comida tradicional".
4. La cocina árabe influye en la gastronomía que trajeron los españoles a Latinoamérica.
5. El autor del blog piensa que los precios de la comida en El Criollo son buenos.
6. Al autor del blog no le gustó el restaurante.

 Más allá

Escribe una breve reseña de un restaurante en tu ciudad. ¿Lo recomiendas? ¿Por qué? Sube tu reseña y tu recomendación a Share It!

© Photos To Go

Vocabulario

Sustantivos

el berro	*watercress*
el bife de lomo	*sirloin*
la caloría	*calorie*
el (la) camarero(a)	*waiter (waitress)*
el carbón	*charcoal*
la carne (de res)	*beef*
el chimichurri	*Argentine steak sauce*
el choclo	*corn*
el chorizo	*spicy sausage*
el condimento	*spice*
la empanada	*turnover, pasty*
la especialidad	*specialty*
el matambre	*flank steak*

Adjetivos

arrollado(a)	*rolled*
hervido(a)	*boiled*
relleno(a)	*stuffed*
tierno(a)	*tender*
vegetariano(a)	*vegetarian*

Verbos

descubrir	*to discover*

Frases útiles

a fuego lento
low heat

a la parrilla
on the grill

Se corta finito.
Cut in small slices.

Se sirve caliente/frío.
Serve hot/cold.

vuelta y vuelta
cooked on both sides

DATOS IMPORTANTES

Educación: Título de chef otorgado por escuelas de cocina internacional o título universitario de licenciatura en artes culinarias y hospedaje. Para trabajar en restaurantes finos se requieren años de experiencia.

Salario: Entre $35 000 y $85 000, dependiendo de la experiencia y la categoría del restaurante

Dónde se trabaja: Restaurantes, hoteles, clubes privados, compañías de servicios para fiestas y eventos, cruceros

Vocabulario nuevo Completa con una palabra lógica.

1. No como carne porque soy _____.

2. Ponemos el chimichurri sobre _____.

3. La _____ del restaurante son las empanadas.

4. El chef va a preparar una papas _____ de carne.

5. La ensalada tiene choclo y _____.

▶ Miguel Casas, chef

Miguel Casas es el chef de un restaurante de especialidades argentinas. Trabaja en ese lugar desde hace diez años y los clientes del restaurante están muy satisfechos con la comida. En el video vas a ver al chef Casas hablar con un cliente.

Antes de ver

Un chef es el supervisor de una cocina. Debe estar al tanto de todos los platos que se preparan para que los clientes queden contentos. ¿Qué instrucciones crees que les da un chef a sus cocineros? ¿Qué tipo de conversación puede tener un chef con un cliente? ¿Qué piensas de la costumbre de algunos chefs de salir al comedor para hablar con los clientes? Explica.

Comprensión

1. ¿En qué tipo de restaurante trabaja el chef Casas?

2. ¿Quién llamó al chef Casas?

3. ¿Cómo cocinan la carne en ese restaurante?

4. ¿Qué tipo de carne comió la señorita?

5. ¿Qué ensalada comió?

6. ¿Qué tipo de vino tomó?

7. ¿Con qué rellenan las empanadas en ese restaurante?

Después de ver

En parejas, representen a un chef que sale a hablar con un cocinero muy joven y sin experiencia que hace muchas preguntas. Otra opción es representar a un chef que sale a hablar con un cliente del restaurante. ¿El cliente se queja *(complains)* o lo felicita? ¿Cómo responde el chef?

7.37 **El cumpleaños de mi esposa** Completa las siguientes oraciones con el pretérito del verbo entre paréntesis. ¡OJO! No todos los verbos son irregulares.

Ayer (1.) _____ (ser) el cumpleaños de mi esposa. Para celebrar yo

(2.) _____ (hacer) una reservación en un restaurante elegante en el centro

de la ciudad. Nosotros (3.) _____ (tener) que conducir media hora, pero

valió la pena *(it was worth it)*. Cuando llegamos, (4.) _____ (ir) directamente

a la mesa. Nosotros (5.) _____ (ver) el menú y luego (6.) _____

(pedir) nuestra comida. Cuando el mesero (7.) _____ (traer) la comida, yo

(8.) _____ (estar) muy satisfecho con mi selección. Al terminar de comer,

mi esposa (9.) _____ (querer) un postre y decidimos pedir un pastel. ¡El

pastel (10.) _____ (estar) delicioso! Después de comer (11.) yo _____

(pagar) la cuenta, (12.) _____ (dejar) una buena propina y mi esposa y yo

(13.) _____ (volver) a casa.

7.38 **Una cena en restaurante** Lee el párrafo sobre una noche que Tomás y Jimena cenaron en un restaurante. Cambia las oraciones y usa los pronombres de objeto directo para evitar *(to avoid)* las repeticiones.

Modelo Ayer fue el cumpleaños de Jimena y Tomás decidió invitar a Jimena a cenar en un restaurante.
Ayer fue el cumpleaños de Jimena y Tomás decidió invitarla a cenar en un restaurante.

(1.) El mesero llegó con los menús y Tomás y Jimena miraron los menús.
(2.) A Jimena le gusta el pollo asado y decidió pedir pollo asado. (3.) Tomás prefirió el pescado y pidió pescado. (4.) Las ensaladas parecían *(seemed)* deliciosas y los dos quisieron ensaladas. (5.) Tomás vio al mesero y llamó al mesero.
(6.) El mesero recomendó el vino blanco, pero ellos no quisieron vino blanco; prefirieron pedir vino tinto. (7.) En poco tiempo la comida llegó y ellos disfrutaron *(enjoyed)* la comida. (8.) Al final el mesero trajo la cuenta y Tomás pagó la cuenta con su tarjeta de crédito.

7.39 **¿Por o para?** Lee las siguientes oraciones y substituye las palabras en cursiva con **por** o **para**.

1. Ayer Renato decidió ir a un restaurante *a* cenar.
2. A las ocho salió de su casa *al* restaurante.
3. *A causa de* no tener una reservación, no pudo sentarse inmediatamente.
4. Esperó *durante* media hora.
5. *Al* fin, un señor lo llevó a una mesa.
6. Tenían un especial: una pizza de queso *a* 50 pesos y decidió pedirla.
7. Luego pidió un helado *de* postre.

7.40 Sondeo En grupos de tres o cuatro contesten las siguientes preguntas. Luego compartan las respuestas con la clase.

1. ¿Prefieres comer en un restaurante o en casa? ¿Por qué?
2. ¿Cuántas veces a la semana almuerzas en un restaurante?
3. ¿Cuántas veces al mes cenas en un restaurante?
4. ¿Cuál es tu restaurante favorito? ¿Qué pides allí?
5. ¿Cuándo fue la última vez *(last time)* que fuiste a un restaurante? ¿Cuál fue?

7.41 La fiesta Tu compañero y tú están planeando una cena para unos amigos, pero los invitados tienen algunas restricciones en su dieta. Uno de ustedes mira la información en esta página y el otro mira la información en el **Apéndice B.** Compartan la información sobre sus dietas y luego decidan qué van a servir del menú abajo.

aperitivo: queso, totopos con salsa

primer plato: ensalada con vinagreta, sopa de fideos *(noodles)*

segundo plato: carne asada con papas fritas, fajitas con tortillas de maíz y verduras asadas

postre: ensalada de frutas, pastel de chocolate

bebida: té helado, limonada

Invitado	Restricción
Angélica	
Lucas	Es alérgico al chocolate.
Mateo	
Regina	Está a dieta.
Javier	
Gisa	No puede consumir gluten.

7.42 La lista del supermercado Con un compañero, van a crear una lista de supermercado. Tienen un presupuesto *(budget)* limitado y solo pueden comprar diez productos.

Paso 1 Escribe una lista de diez productos que quieres comprar. Debes incluir tres verduras, tres frutas y otros cuatro productos.

Paso 2 Compara tu lista con la de tu compañero y explica por qué quieres comprar ciertos productos. Luego pónganse de acuerdo *(agree)* en los diez productos que van a comprar.

Paso 3 Compartan *(Share)* la lista con la clase y expliquen algunas de sus decisiones.

🔊 Vocabulario 1
2-5

Frutas

el durazno	*peach*
la fresa	*strawberry*
la manzana	*apple*
el melón	*melon*
la naranja	*orange*

la piña	*pineapple*
el plátano	*banana*
la sandía	*watermelon*
las uvas	*grapes*

Verduras

el brócoli	*broccoli*
la cebolla	*onion*
la lechuga	*lettuce*
el maíz	*corn*

la papa	*potato*
el pepino	*cucumber*
el tomate	*tomato*
la zanahoria	*carrot*

Lácteos y otros alimentos

la catsup	*ketchup*
el cereal	*cereal*
la crema	*cream*
el huevo	*egg*
el jamón	*ham*
la leche	*milk*
la mantequilla	*butter*

la mayonesa	*mayonnaise*
la mermelada	*jam*
la mostaza	*mustard*
el pan	*bread*
el pepinillo	*pickle*
el queso	*cheese*
el yogur	*yogurt*

Verbos

hornear	*to bake*

Palabras adicionales

la rebanada	*slice*

Los números

cien	*100*
ciento uno	*101*
doscientos	*200*
trescientos	*300*
cuatrocientos	*400*
quinientos	*500*
seiscientos	*600*

setecientos	*700*
ochocientos	*800*
novecientos	*900*
mil	*1000*
dos mil	*2000*
un millón	*1 000 000*

Diccionario personal

_____

_____

_____

_____

◀)) Vocabulario 2

Los utensilios

la copa	wine glass	la servilleta	napkin
la cuchara	spoon	la taza	cup
el cuchillo	knife	el tazón	serving bowl
el mantel	tablecloth	el tenedor	fork
el plato	plate	el vaso	glass
el plato hondo	bowl		

La comida

el arroz	rice	el jugo	juice
el azúcar	sugar	la naranja	orange
la bebida	drink	el pastel	cake
el café	coffee	el pavo	turkey
el camarón	shrimp	el pescado	fish
la carne	meat	la pimienta	pepper
el cerdo	pork	el pollo	chicken
la cerveza	beer	el postre	dessert
el coctel	cocktail	el refresco	soda
la ensalada	salad	la sal	salt
el entremés	appetizer	el sándwich	sandwich
el flan	flan	la sopa	soup
la fruta	fruit	los totopos	tortilla chips
la hamburguesa	hamburger	el vino blanco	white wine
el helado	ice cream	el vino tinto	red wine

Verbos

cenar	to eat dinner	querer	to love
dejar (una propina)	to leave (a tip)	llevar	to take along
desayunar	to eat breakfast	saludar	to greet
felicitar	to congratulate		

Palabras adicionales

al horno	baked	la cuenta	bill
el almuerzo	lunch	el desayuno	breakfast
asado(a)	grilled	frito(a)	fried
la cena	dinner	la orden	order
la comida	food, lunch	el plato principal	main dish

Diccionario personal

_____

_____

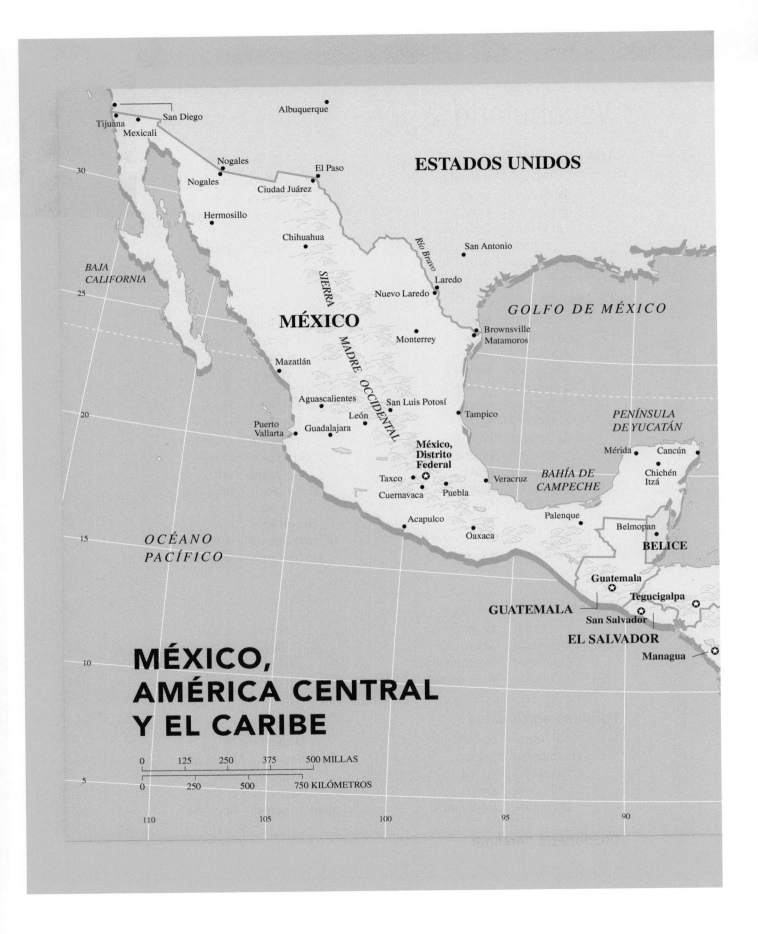

Tijuana
San Diego
Mexicali
Albuquerque
Nogales
Nogales
El Paso
Ciudad Juárez
Hermosillo
Chihuahua
San Antonio

ESTADOS UNIDOS

Río Bravo
Laredo
Nuevo Laredo

BAJA CALIFORNIA

SIERRA

MÉXICO

GOLFO DE MÉXICO

Brownsville
Matamoros
Monterrey

Mazatlán

MADRE OCCIDENTAL

Aguascalientes
León
San Luis Potosí
Tampico

PENÍNSULA DE YUCATÁN

Puerto Vallarta
Guadalajara

México, Distrito Federal

Taxco
Cuernavaca
Puebla

Veracruz

BAHÍA DE CAMPECHE

Mérida
Cancún
Chichén Itzá

Palenque

Belmopan

BELICE

Acapulco
Oaxaca

OCÉANO PACÍFICO

Guatemala

Tegucigalpa

GUATEMALA
San Salvador

EL SALVADOR

Managua

MÉXICO, AMÉRICA CENTRAL Y EL CARIBE

| 0 | 125 | 250 | 375 | 500 MILLAS |
| 0 | 250 | 500 | 750 KILÓMETROS |

110
105
100
95
90

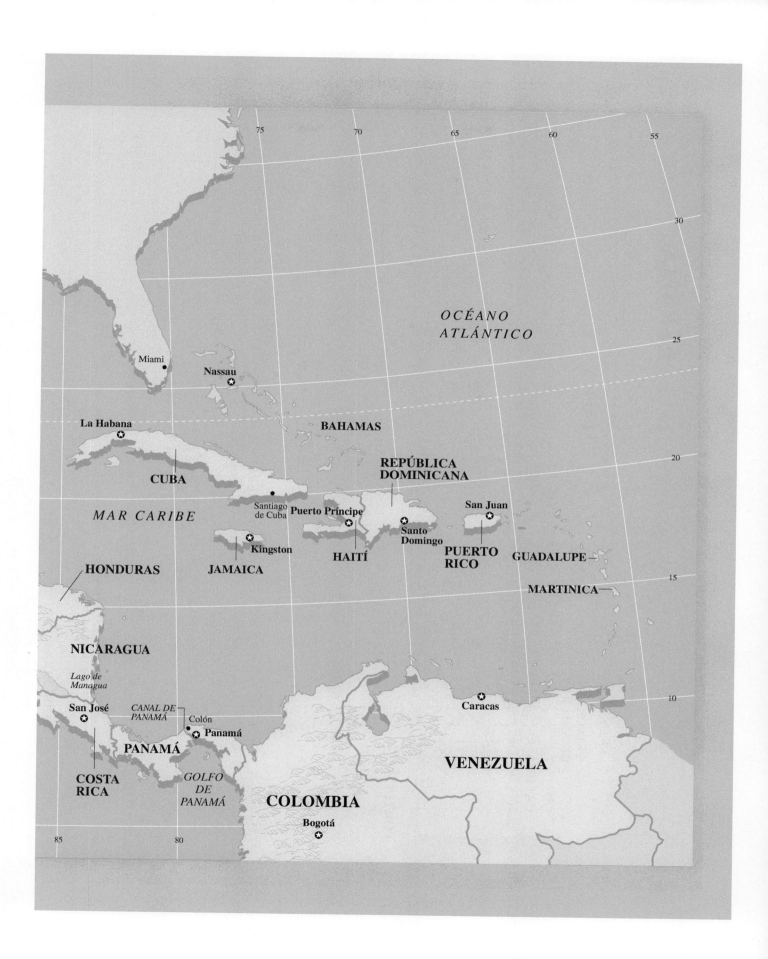

OCÉANO
ATLÁNTICO

Miami

Nassau

La Habana

BAHAMAS

REPÚBLICA
DOMINICANA

CUBA

MAR CARIBE

Santiago
de Cuba Puerto Príncipe

San Juan

Santo
Domingo

HONDURAS

Kingston

JAMAICA

HAITÍ

PUERTO
RICO

GUADALUPE

MARTINICA

NICARAGUA

Lago de
Managua

San José

CANAL DE
PANAMÁ   Colón

Panamá

Caracas

PANAMÁ

COSTA
RICA

GOLFO
DE
PANAMÁ

COLOMBIA

VENEZUELA

Bogotá

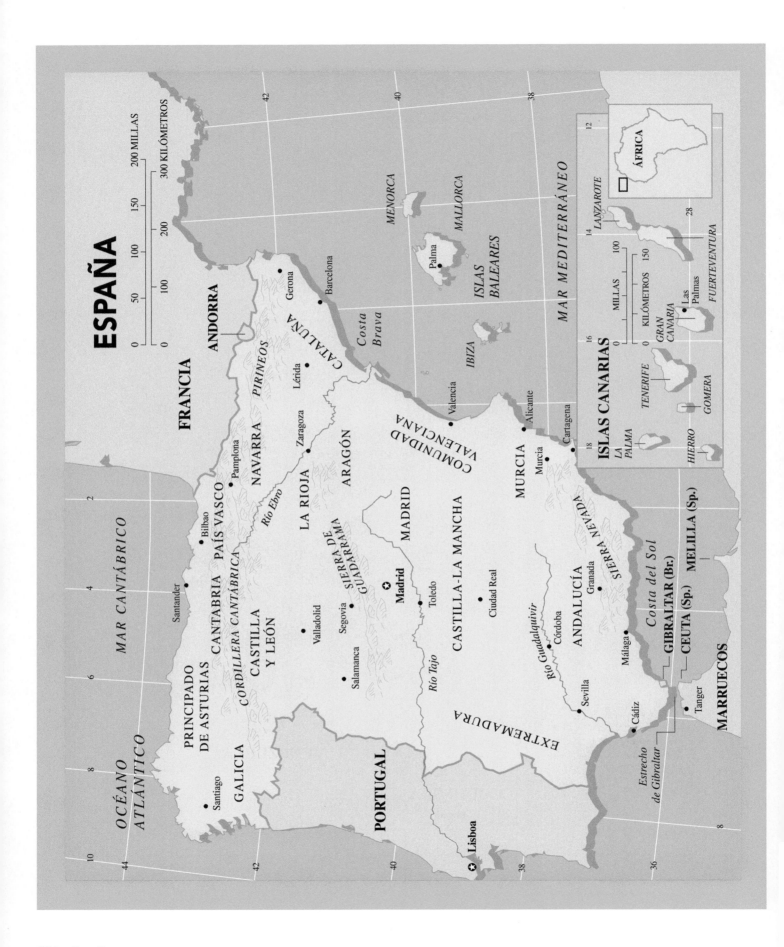

ESPAÑA

FRANCIA

ANDORRA

OCÉANO ATLÁNTICO

MAR CANTÁBRICO

PRINCIPADO DE ASTURIAS

GALICIA

• Santiago

CORDILLERA CANTÁBRICA

CANTABRIA

• Santander

• Bilbao

PAÍS VASCO

NAVARRA

• Pamplona

PIRINEOS

Río Ebro

LA RIOJA

Zaragoza •

ARAGÓN

CATALUÑA

• Lérida

Gerona •

Barcelona •

Costa Brava

CASTILLA Y LEÓN

• Valladolid

• Salamanca

Segovia •

SIERRA DE GUADARRAMA

MADRID

✪ Madrid

MADRID

Toledo •

CASTILLA-LA MANCHA

Ciudad Real •

COMUNIDAD VALENCIANA

Valencia •

Alicante •

Cartagena •

MURCIA

Murcia •

Río Tajo

EXTREMADURA

PORTUGAL

✪ Lisboa

ANDALUCÍA

Río Guadalquivir

Córdoba •

Sevilla •

Granada •

SIERRA NEVADA

Málaga •

Cádiz •

Costa del Sol

GIBRALTAR (Br.)

CEUTA (Sp.)

GIBRALTAR (Sp.)

MELILLA (Sp.)

Estrecho de Gibraltar

MARRUECOS

Tánger •

MENORCA

MALLORCA

Palma •

ISLAS BALEARES

IBIZA

MAR MEDITERRÁNEO

200 MILLAS

300 KILÓMETROS

ÁFRICA

ISLAS CANARIAS

LANZAROTE

FUERTEVENTURA

LA PALMA

TENERIFE

GRAN CANARIA

Las Palmas

GOMERA

HIERRO

MILLAS

KILÓMETROS

AMÉRICA DEL SUR

BELICE
HONDURAS
NICARAGUA
Lago de Managua
Barranquilla
Cartagena
Maracaibo
Caracas
Lago de Maracaibo
Río Orinoco
Georgetown
Paramaribo
Cayena
EL SALVADOR
GUATEMALA
PANAMÁ
COSTA RICA
San Cristóbal
VENEZUELA
GUAYANA
SURINAM
Medellín
Río Magdalena
Boa Vista
GUAYANA FRANCESA
Bogotá
Cali
COLOMBIA
ECUADOR
Río Amazonas
ISLAS GALÁPAGOS
Quito
ECUADOR
Guayaquil
Cuenca
Iquitos
A M A Z O N A S
PERÚ
BRASIL
LOS ANDES
Machu Picchu
Lima
Ayacucho
Cuzco
BOLIVIA
Brasilia
Lago Titicaca
La Paz
Santa Cruz
Sucre
Potosí
Río Paraná
Río de Janeiro
CHILE
PARAGUAY
São Paulo
Asunción
Iguazú
LOS ANDES
Río Uruguay
Córdoba
URUGUAY
OCÉANO PACÍFICO
Viña del Mar
Valparaíso
Santiago
Buenos Aires
Montevideo
Concepción
ARGENTINA
Río de la Plata
Bahía Blanca
OCÉANO ATLÁNTICO
Viedma
OCÉANO ATLÁNTICO
MAR CARIBE

ISLAS MALVINAS (Br.)
Estrecho de Magallanes
TIERRA DEL FUEGO

NIGERIA
ÁFRICA
CAMERÚN
Malabo
GUINEA ECUATORIAL
GABÓN
ÁFRICA

0   250   500   750   1,000 MILLAS
0   500   1,000   1,500 KILÓMETROS

0   MILLAS   500
0   KILÓMETROS   750

Apéndice A: Exploraciones del mundo hispano

Argentina ▶

INFORMACIÓN GENERAL

(iLrn™) Para aprender más sobre Argentina, mira el video cultural en la mediateca (*Media Library*).

Nombre oficial: República Argentina

Nacionalidad: argentino(a)

Área: 2 780 400 km² (el país de habla hispana más grande del mundo, aproximadamente 2 veces el tamaño de Alaska)

Población: 42 611 000

Capital: Buenos Aires (f. 1580) (2 891 000 hab.)

Otras ciudades importantes: Córdoba, Rosario, Mendoza, Mar del Plata, San Miguel de Tucuman

Moneda: peso (argentino)

Idiomas: español (oficial), árabe, italiano, alemán

DEMOGRAFÍA

Alfabetismo: 97,2%

Religiones: católicos (92%), protestantes (2%), judíos (2%), otros (4%)

ARGENTINOS CÉLEBRES

Jorge Luis Borges
escritor, poeta (1899–1986)

Julio Cortázar
escritor (1914–1984)

Charly García
músico (1951–)

Ernesto "Che" Guevara
revolucionario (1928–1967)

Cristina Fernández
primera mujer presidenta (1953–)

Lionel Messi
futbolista (1987–)

Adolfo Pérez Esquivel
activista, Premio Nobel de la Paz (1931–)

Eva Perón
primera dama (1919–1952)

Joaquín "Quino" Salvador Lavado
caricaturista (1932–)

© Pablo H Caridad/Shutterstock

Puerto Madero es el antiguo puerto de Buenos Aires. Fue remodelado y ahora es un barrio (*neighborhood*) moderno y popular entre los porteños (los habitantes de Buenos Aires).

Investiga en Internet

La geografía: las cataratas del Iguazú, Parque Nacional Los Glaciares, la Patagonia, las islas Malvinas, las pampas

La historia: la inmigración, los gauchos, la Guerra Sucia, la Guerra de las Islas Malvinas, Carlos Gardel, Mercedes Sosa, José de San Martín

Películas: *Valentín, La historia oficial, Golpes a mi puerta, El secreto de sus ojos, Cinco amigas*

Música: el tango, la milonga, la zamba, la chacarera, Fito Páez, Soda Stereo

Comidas y bebidas: el asado, los alfajores, las empanadas, el mate, los vinos cuyanos

Fiestas: Día de la Revolución (25 de mayo), Día de la Independencia (9 de julio)

El Obelisco, símbolo de la ciudad de Buenos Aires

El Glaciar Perito Moreno, en la Patagonia argentina, es el más visitado del país.

CURIOSIDADES

- Argentina es un país de inmigrantes europeos. A finales del siglo *(century)* XIX hubo una fuerte inmigración, especialmente de Italia, España e Inglaterra. Estas culturas se mezclaron *(mixed)* y ayudaron a crear la identidad argentina.

- Argentina se caracteriza por la calidad de su carne vacuna *(beef)* y por ser uno de los principales exportadores de carne *(meat)* en el mundo.

- El instrumento musical característico del tango, la música tradicional argentina, se llama *bandoneón* y es de origen alemán.

Bolivia ▶

INFORMACIÓN GENERAL

Nombre oficial: Estado Plurinacional de Bolivia

Nacionalidad: boliviano(a)

Área: 1 098 581 km² (aproximadamente 4 veces el área de Wyoming, o la mitad de México)

Población: 10 461 000

Capital: Sucre (poder judicial) (284 000 hab.) y La Paz (sede del gobierno) (f. 1548) (835 000 hab.)

Otras ciudades importantes: Santa Cruz de la Sierra, Cochabamba, El Alto

Moneda: peso (boliviano)

Idiomas: español, quechua, aymará (Según la Constitución de 2009 el español y las 36 lenguas indígenas son todas oficiales.)

iLrn™ Para aprender más sobre Bolivia, mira el video cultural en la mediateca (*Media Library*).

DEMOGRAFÍA

Alfabetismo: 86,7%

Religiones: católicos (95%), protestantes (5%)

BOLIVIANOS CÉLEBRES

Jaime Escalante
ingeniero, profesor de
matemáticas (1930–2010)

Evo Morales
primer indígena elegido
presidente de Bolivia (1959–)

María Luisa Pacheco
pintora (1919–1982)

Edmundo Paz Soldán
escritor (1967–)

© MP cz/Shutterstock

El Altiplano de Bolivia

Investiga en Internet

La geografía: el lago Titicaca, Tiahuanaco, el salar de Uyuni

La historia: los incas, los aymará, la hoja de coca, Simón Bolívar

Música: la música andina, las peñas, la lambada, Los Kjarkas, Ana Cristina Céspedes

Comidas y bebidas: las llauchas, la papa (más de dos mil variedades), la chicha

Fiestas: Día de la Independencia (6 de agosto), Carnaval de Oruro (febrero o marzo), Festival de la Virgen de Urkupiña (14 de agosto)

La ciudad de **Potosí** fue muy importante, pues fue el principal abastecedor *(supplier)* de plata *(silver)* para España durante la Colonia.

El Salar de Uyuni

CURIOSIDADES

- Bolivia tiene dos capitales. Una de ellas, La Paz, es la más alta del mundo a 3640 metros (11 900 pies) sobre el nivel del mar *(sea)*.

- El lago Titicaca es el lago *(lake)* navegable más alto del mundo con una altura de más de 3800 metros (12 500 pies) sobre el nivel del mar.

- El Salar de Uyuni es el desierto de sal más grande del mundo.

- En Bolivia se consumen las hojas secas *(dried leaves)* de la coca para soportar mejor los efectos de la altura extrema.

- Bolivia es uno de los dos países de Sudamérica que no tiene costa marina.

Chile ▶

INFORMACIÓN GENERAL

iLrn Para aprender más sobre Chile, mira el video cultural en la mediateca (*Media Library*).

Nombre oficial: República de Chile

Nacionalidad: chileno(a)

Área: 756 102 km² (un poco más grande que Texas)

Población: 17 217 000

Capital: Santiago (f. 1541) (5 883 000 hab.)

Otras ciudades importantes: Valparaíso, Viña del Mar, Concepción

Moneda: peso (chileno)

Idiomas: español (oficial), mapuche, mapudungun, inglés

DEMOGRAFÍA

Alfabetismo: 95,7%

Religiones: católicos (70%), evangélicos (15%), testigos de Jehová (1%), otros (14%)

CHILENOS CÉLEBRES

Isabel Allende
escritora (1942–)

Michelle Bachelet
primera mujer presidente de Chile
(1951–)

Gabriela Mistral
poetisa, Premio Nobel de Literatura
(1889–1957)

Pablo Neruda
poeta, Premio Nobel de Literatura
(1904–1973)

Violeta Parra
poetisa, cantautora (1917–1967)

Ana Tiljoux
cantante (1977–)

Santiago está situada muy cerca de los Andes.

© Tifonimages/Shutterstock

La pintoresca ciudad de Valparaíso es Patrimonio de la Humanidad.

 Investiga en Internet

La geografía: Antofagasta, el desierto de Atacama, la isla de Pascua, Parque Nacional Torres del Paine Tierra del Fuego, el estrecho de Magallanes, los pasos andinos

La historia: los indígenas mapuches, Salvador Allende, Augusto Pinochet, Bernardo O'Higgins, Pedro de Valdivia

Películas: *Obstinate Memory, La nana*

Música: el Festival de Viña del Mar, Víctor Jara, Quilapayún, La Ley, Inti Illimani, Francisca Valenzuela

Comidas y bebidas: las empanadas, los pescados y mariscos, el pastel de choclo, los vinos chilenos

Fiestas: Día de la Independencia (18 de septiembre), Carnaval Andino Con la Fuerza del Sol (enero o febrero)

Los famosos moais de la isla de Pascua

CURIOSIDADES

- Chile es uno de los países más largos del mundo, pero también es muy angosto *(narrow)*. Gracias a su longitud, en el sur de Chile hay glaciares y fiordos, mientras que en el norte está el desierto más seco *(dry)* del mundo: el desierto de Atacama. La cordillera de los Andes también contribuye a la gran variedad de zonas climáticas y geográficas de este país.

- Es un país muy rico en minerales, en particular el cobre *(copper)*, que se exporta a nivel mundial.

- En febrero del 2010, Chile sufrió uno de los terremotos *(earthquakes)* más fuertes registrados en el mundo, con una magnitud de 8,8. En 1960 Chile también sufrió el terremoto más violento en la historia del planeta, con una magnitud de 9,4.

Colombia ▶

INFORMACIÓN GENERAL

iLrn Para aprender más sobre Colombia, mira el video cultural en la mediateca (*Media Library*).

Nombre oficial: República de Colombia

Nacionalidad: colombiano(a)

Área: 1 139 914 km² (aproximadamente 4 veces el área de Arizona)

Población: 45 746 000

Capital: Bogotá D.C. (f. 1538) (7 674 000 hab.)

Otras ciudades importantes: Medellín, Cali, Barranquilla, Bucaramanga

Moneda: peso (colombiano)

Idiomas: español (oficial), chibcha, guajiro y aproximadamente 90 lenguas indígenas

DEMOGRAFÍA

Alfabetismo: 90,4%

Religiones: católicos (90%), otros (10%)

COLOMBIANOS CÉLEBRES

Fernando Botero
pintor, escultor (1932–)

Tatiana Calderón Noguera
automovilista (1994–)

Gabriel García Márquez
escritor, Premio Nobel de Literatura
(1928–2014)

Lucho Herrera
ciclista, ganador del Tour de Francia y la
Vuelta de España (1961–)

Shakira
cantante, benefactora (1977–)

Sofía Vergara
actriz (1972–)

Colombia tiene playas en el Caribe y en el océano Pacífico.

Cartagena es una de las ciudades con más historia en Colombia.

⊕ **Investiga en Internet**

La geografía: los Andes, el Amazonas, Parque Nacional el Cocuy las playas de Santa Marta y Cartagena

La historia: los araucanos, Simón Bolívar, la leyenda de El Dorado, el Museo del Oro, las FARC

Películas: *María llena de gracia, Rosario Tijeras, Mi abuelo, mi papá y yo*

Música: la cumbia, el vallenato, Juanes, Carlos Vives, Aterciopelados

Comidas y bebidas: el ajiaco, las arepas, la picada, el arequipe, las cocadas, el café, el aguardiente

Fiestas: Día de la Independencia (20 de julio), Carnaval de Blancos y Negros en Pasto (enero), Carnaval del Diablo en Riosucio (enero, cada año impar)

Bogotá, capital de Colombia

CURIOSIDADES

- El 95% de la producción mundial de esmeraldas viene del subsuelo colombiano. Sin embargo, la mayor riqueza del país es su diversidad, ya que incluye culturas del Caribe, del Pacífico, del Amazonas y de los Andes.
- Colombia, junto con Costa Rica y Brasil, es uno de los principales productores de café en Latinoamérica.
- Colombia tiene una gran diversidad de especies de flores. Es el primer productor de claveles *(carnations)* y el segundo exportador mundial de flores después de Holanda.
- Colombia es uno de los países con mayor biodiversidad del mundo.

Costa Rica ▶

INFORMACIÓN GENERAL

<img: iLrn™> Para aprender más sobre Costa Rica, mira el video cultural en la mediateca (*Media Library*).

Nombre oficial: República de Costa Rica

Nacionalidad: costarricense

Área: 51 100 km² (aproximadamente 2 veces el área de Vermont)

Población: 4 755 234

Capital: San José (f. 1521) (1 515 000 hab.)

Otras ciudades importantes: Alajuela, Cartago

Moneda: colón

Idiomas: español (oficial)

DEMOGRAFÍA

Alfabetismo: 96,3%

Religiones: católicos (76,3%), evangélicos y otros protestantes (15,7%), otros (4,8%), ninguna (3,2%)

COSTARRICENCES CÉLEBRES

Óscar Arias
político y presidente, Premio Nobel de la Paz (1949–)

Franklin Chang Díaz
astronauta (1950–)

Laura Chinchilla
primera mujer presidenta (1959–)

Carmen Naranjo
escritora (1928–2012)

Claudia Poll
atleta olímpica (1972–)

© Joe Ferrer/Shutterstock

El Teatro Nacional en San José es uno de los edificios más famosos de la capital.

Investiga en Internet

La geografía: Monteverde, Tortuguero, el Bosque de los Niños, el volcán Poás, los Parques Nacionales

La historia: las plantaciones de café, Juan Mora Fernández, Juan Santamaría

Música: El Café Chorale, Escats, Akasha

Comidas y bebidas: el gallo pinto, el café

Fiestas: Día de la Independencia (15 de septiembre), Fiesta de los Diablitos (febrero)

Costa Rica se conoce por su biodiversidad y respeto al medio ambiente.

El Volcán Poás es un volcán activo de fácil acceso para el visitante.

CURIOSIDADES

- Costa Rica es uno de los pocos países del mundo que no tiene ejército *(army)*. En noviembre de 1949, 18 meses después de la Guerra *(War)* Civil, abolieron el ejército en la nueva constitución.

- Se conoce como un país progresista gracias a su apoyo *(support)* a la democracia, el alto nivel de vida de los costarricenses y la protección de su medio ambiente *(environment)*.

- Costa Rica posee una fauna y flora sumamente ricas. Aproximadamente una cuarta parte del territorio costarricense está protegido como reserva o parque natural.

- Costa Rica produce y exporta cantidades importantes de café, por lo que este producto es muy importante para su economía. Además, el café costarricense es de calidad reconocida *(recognized)* en todo el mundo.

Cuba ▶

INFORMACIÓN GENERAL

Nombre oficial: República de Cuba

Nacionalidad: cubano(a)

Área: 110 860 km² (aproximadamente el área de Tennessee)

Población: 11 047 251

Capital: La Habana (f. 1511) (2 116 000 hab.)

Otras ciudades importantes: Santiago, Camagüey

Moneda: peso (cubano)

Idiomas: español (oficial)

DEMOGRAFÍA

Alfabetismo: 99,8%

Religiones: católicos (85%), santería y otras religiones (15%)

CUBANOS CÉLEBRES

Alicia Alonso
bailarina, fundadora del Ballet
Nacional de Cuba (1920–)

Alejo Carpentier
escritor (1904–1980)

Nicolás Guillén
poeta (1902–1989)

Wifredo Lam
pintor (1902–1982)

José Martí
político, periodista, poeta (1853–1895)

Silvio Rodríguez
poeta, cantautor (1946–)

Juan Carlos Tabío
director de cine (1942–)

iLrn™ Para aprender más sobre Cuba, mira el video cultural en la mediateca (*Media Library*).

© Kamira/Shutterstock

Catedral de la Habana

Investiga en Internet

La geografía: las cavernas de Bellamar, la Ciénaga de Zapata, la península de Guanahacabibes

La historia: los taínos, los ciboneyes, Fulgencio Batista, Bahía de Cochinos, la Revolución cubana, Fidel Castro

Películas: *Vampiros en La Habana*, *Fresa y chocolate*, *La última espera*, *Azúcar amargo*

Música: el son, Buena Vista Social Club, Celia Cruz, Pablo Milanés, Santiago Feliú, Alex Cuba

Comidas y bebidas: la ropa vieja, los moros y cristianos, el ron

Fiestas: Día de la Independencia (10 de diciembre), Día de la Revolución (1º de enero)

Los autos viejos son una vista típica en toda la isla.

El Morro, construído en 1589, para proteger la isla de invasores

CURIOSIDADES

- Cuba se distingue por tener uno de los mejores sistemas de educación del mundo, por su sistema de salud *(health)* y por su apoyo *(support)* a las artes.

- La población de la isla es una mezcla *(mix)* de los habitantes nativos (taínos), descendientes de esclavos africanos y europeos, mezcla que produce una cultura única.

- A principios *(beginning)* de la década de 1980, la nueva trova cubana (un movimiento musical) presentó al mundo entero la música testimonial.

- La santería es una religión que se originó en las islas del Caribe, especialmente en Cuba, y mezcla elementos religiosos de la religión yorubá de los esclavos de África, y elementos de la religión católica. El nombre de "santería" viene de un truco *(trick)* que los esclavos usaron para continuar adorando a los dioses *(gods)* en los que creían, burlando *(outsmarting)* la prohibición de los españoles. Así los esclavos fingían *(pretended)* que adoraban a los santos *(saints)* católicos, pero en realidad les rezaban *(prayed)* a los dioses africanos.

Ecuador ▶

INFORMACIÓN GENERAL

Nombre oficial: República del Ecuador

Nacionalidad: ecuatoriano(a)

Área: 283 561 km² (aproximadamente el área de Colorado)

Población: 15 654 411

Capital: Quito (f. 1556) (1 622 000 hab.)

Otras ciudades importantes: Guayaquil, Cuenca

Moneda: dólar (estadounidense)

Idiomas: español (oficial), quechua y otros idiomas indígenas

DEMOGRAFÍA

Alfabetismo: 91%

Religiones: católicos (95%), otros (5%)

ECUATORIANOS CÉLEBRES

Rosalía Arteaga
abogada, política, ex vicepresidenta
(1956–)

Jorge Carrera Andrade
escritor (1903–1978)

Oswaldo Guayasamín
pintor (1919–1999)

Jorge Icaza
escritor (1906–1978)

iLrn™ Para aprender más sobre Ecuador, mira el
video cultural en la mediateca (*Media Library*).

Las Peñas es un barrio muy conocido *(well-known)* de la ciudad de Guayaquil.

© Marcos Aspiazu/Shutterstock

Investiga en Internet

La geografía: La selva amazónica, las islas Galápagos, Parque Nacional Cotopaxi

La historia: José de Sucre, la Gran Colombia, los indígenas tagaeri

Música: música andina, la quena, la zampoña, Fausto Miño, Daniel Betancourt, Michelle Cordero

Comida: la papa, el plátano frito, el ceviche, la fanesca

Fiestas: Día de la Independencia (10 de agosto), Fiestas de Quito (6 de diciembre)

El parque nacional más famoso de Ecuador es el de las Islas Galápagos.

La Basílica en Quito

CURIOSIDADES

- Este país tiene una gran diversidad de zonas geográficas como costas, montañas y selva *(jungle)*. Las famosas islas Galápagos son parte de Ecuador y presentan una gran diversidad biológica. A principios *(At the beginning)* del siglo XX, estas islas fueron usadas como prisión.

- Ecuador toma su nombre de la línea ecuatorial, que divide el planeta en dos hemisferios: norte y sur.

- La música andina es tradicional en Ecuador, con instrumentos indígenas como el charango, el rondador y el bombo.

- Ecuador es famoso por sus tejidos *(weavings)* de lana *(wool)* de llama y alpaca, dos animales de la región andina.

El Salvador ▶

INFORMACIÓN GENERAL

Nombre oficial: República de El Salvador

Nacionalidad: salvadoreño(a)

Área: 21 041 km² (un poco más grande que Nueva Jersey)

Población: 6 125 512

Capital: San Salvador (f. 1524) (2 442 000 hab.)

Otras ciudades importantes: San Miguel, Santa Ana

Moneda: dólar (estadounidense)

Idiomas: español (oficial)

DEMOGRAFÍA

Alfabetismo: 84,5%

Religiones: católicos (57,1%), protestantes (21%), otros (22%)

SALVADOREÑOS CÉLEBRES

Claribel Alegría
escritora (nació en Nicaragua pero se
considera salvadoreña) (1924–)

Óscar Arnulfo Romero
arzobispo, defensor de los derechos
humanos (1917–1980)

Alfredo Espino
poeta (1900–1928)

Cristina López
atleta, medallista olímpica (1982–)

iLrn™ Para aprender más sobre El Salvador, mira el
video cultural en la mediateca (*Media Library*).

El volcán de San Vicente

© moxelotle/iStockphoto

Investiga en Internet

La geografía: el bosque lluvioso (Parque Nacional Montecristo), el puerto de Acajutla, el volcán Izalco, los planes de Renderos

La historia: Tazumal, Acuerdos de Paz de Chapultepec, José Matías Delgado, FMLN, Ana María

Películas: *Romero, Voces inocentes*

Música: Taltipac, la salsa y la cumbia (fusión), Shaka y Dres

Comidas y bebidas: las pupusas, los tamales, la semita, el atole

Fiestas: Día del Divino Salvador del Mundo (6 de agosto), Día de la Independencia (15 de septiembre)

Una de las numerosas cascadas en el área de Juayua

La catedral en San Salvador

CURIOSIDADES

- El Salvador es el país más pequeño de Centroamérica pero el más denso en población.
- Hay más de veinte volcanes y algunos están activos.
- El Salvador está en una zona sísmica, por lo que ocurren terremotos *(earthquakes)* con frecuencia. En el pasado, varios sismos le causaron muchos daños *(damage)* al país.
- Entre 1979 y 1992, El Salvador vivió una guerra *(war)* civil. Durante esos años, muchos salvadoreños emigraron a los Estados Unidos.
- La canción de U2 "Bullet the Blue Sky" fue inspirada por el viaje a El Salvador que hizo el cantante Bono en los tiempos de la Guerra Civil.

España ▶

INFORMACIÓN GENERAL

iLrn™ Para aprender más sobre España, mira el video cultural en la mediateca (*Media Library*).

Nombre oficial: Reino de España

Nacionalidad: español(a)

Área: 505 992 km² (aproximadamente 2 veces el área de Oregón)

Población: 47 738 000

Capital: Madrid (f. siglo X) (6 574 000 hab.)

Otras ciudades importantes: Barcelona, Valencia, Sevilla, Toledo, Zaragoza

Moneda: euro

Idiomas: español (oficial), catalán, vasco, gallego

DEMOGRAFÍA

Alfabetismo: 97,7%

Religiones: católicos (94%), otros (6%)

ESPAÑOLES CÉLEBRES

Pedro Almodóvar
director de cine (1949–)

Rosalía de Castro
escritora (1837–1885)

Miguel de Cervantes Saavedra
escritor (1547–1616)

Penélope Cruz
actriz (1974–)

Lola Flores
cantante, bailarina de flamenco (1923–1995)

Federico García Lorca
poeta (1898–1936)

Antonio Gaudí
arquitecto (1852–1926)

Rafael Nadal
tenista (1986–)

Pablo Picasso
pintor, escultor (1881–1973)

© Vinicius Tupinamba/Shutterstock

La Plaza Mayor es un lugar con mucha historia en el centro de Madrid.

🌐 Investiga en Internet

La geografía: las islas Canarias, las islas Baleares

La historia: la conquista de América, la Guerra Civil, el rey Fernando y la reina Isabel, la Guerra de la Independencia Española, Carlos V, Francisco Franco

Películas: *Ay, Carmela, Mala educación, Hable con ella, Mar adentro, Volver, El orfanato*

Música: las tunas, el flamenco, Paco de Lucía, Mecano, David Bisbal, Joaquín Sabina, Ana Belén, La Oreja de Van Gogh, Plácido Domingo

Comidas y bebidas: paella valenciana, tapas, tortilla española, crema catalana, vinos, sangría, horchata

Fiestas: Festival de la Tomatina (agosto), San Fermín (7 de julio), Semana Santa (marzo o abril)

Arquitectura gótica en Barcelona

El Alcázar en la ciudad de Toledo

CURIOSIDADES

- España se distingue por tener una gran cantidad de pintores y escritores. En el siglo XX se destacaron *(stood out)* los pintores Pablo Picasso, Salvador Dalí y Joan Miró. Entre los clásicos figuran Velázquez, El Greco y Goya.

- El Palacio Real de Madrid presenta una arquitectura hermosa *(beautiful)*. Contiene pinturas de algunos de los artistas mencionados arriba. Originalmente fue un fuerte *(fort)* construido por los musulmanes en el siglo IX. Más tarde, los reyes de Castilla construyeron allí el Alcázar. En 1738, el rey Felipe V ordenó la construcción del Palacio Real, que fue la residencia de la familia real hasta 1941.

- Aunque el español se habla en todo el país, cada región de España mantiene viva su propia *(own)* lengua. De todos, el más interesante quizás sea el vasco, que es la única lengua de España que no deriva del latín y cuyo origen no se conoce.

- En la ciudad de Toledo se fundó la primera escuela de traductores en el año 1126.

- En Andalucía, una región al sur de España, se ve una gran influencia árabe por los moros que la habitaron de 711 a 1492, año en el que los reyes Católicos los expulsaron durante la Reconquista.

Guatemala ▶

INFORMACIÓN GENERAL

Nombre oficial: República de Guatemala

Nacionalidad: guatemalteco(a)

Área: 108 890 km² (un poco más grande que el área de Ohio)

Población: 14 647 083

Capital: Ciudad de Guatemala (f. 1524) (2 945 000 hab.)

Otras ciudades importantes: Mixco, Villa Nueva Quetzaltenango, Puerto Barrios

Moneda: quetzal

Idiomas: español (oficial), K'iche', Mam, Q'eqchi'

DEMOGRAFÍA

Alfabetismo: 75,9%

Religiones: católicos (94%), protestantes (2%), otros (4%)

GUATEMALTECOS CÉLEBRES

Ricardo Arjona
cantautor (1964–)

Miguel Ángel Asturias
escritor (1899–1974)

Rigoberta Menchú
activista por los derechos humanos,
Premio Nobel de la Paz (1959–)

Carlos Mérida
pintor (1891–1984)

Augusto Monterroso
escritor (1921–2003)

iLrn Para aprender más sobre Guatemala, mira el video cultural en la mediateca (*Media Library*).

© SUETONE Emilio/age fotostock

Mujer tejiendo *(weaving)* en la región del departamento de Sololá

Tikal, ciudad construida por los mayas

 Investiga en Internet

La geografía: el lago Atitlán, Antigua

La historia: los mayas, Efraín Ríos Mont, la matanza de indígenas durante la dictadura, quiché, el Popul Vuh, Tecun Uman

Películas: *El norte*

Música: punta, Gaby Moreno

Comida: los tamales, la sopa de pepino, fiambre, pipián

Fiestas: Día de la Independencia (15 de septiembre), Semana Santa (marzo o abril), Día de los Muertos (1 de noviembre)

Vista del lago Atitlán

CURIOSIDADES

- Guatemala es famosa por la gran cantidad de ruinas mayas y por las tradiciones indígenas, especialmente los tejidos *(weavings)* de vivos colores.

- Guatemala es el quinto exportador de plátanos en el mundo.

- Antigua es una famosa ciudad que sirvió como la tercera capital de Guatemala. Es reconocida *(recognized)* mundialmente por su bien preservada arquitectura renacentista *(Renaissance)* y barroca. También es reconocida como un lugar excelente para ir a estudiar español.

- En Guatemala se encuentra Tikal, uno de los más importantes conjuntos *(ensembles)* arqueológicos mayas.

Guinea Ecuatorial ▶

INFORMACIÓN GENERAL

Nombre oficial: República de Guinea Ecuatorial

Nacionalidad: ecuatoguineano(a)

Área: 28 051 km² (aproximadamente el área de Maryland)

Población: 722 254

Capital: Malabo (f. 1827) (156 000 hab.)

Otras ciudades importantes: Bata, Ebebiyín

Moneda: franco CFA

Idiomas: español y francés (oficiales), fang, bubi

DEMOGRAFÍA

Alfabetismo: 94,2

Religiones: católicos y otros cristianos (95%), prácticas paganas (5%)

ECUATOGUINEANOS CÉLEBRES

Leoncio Evita
escritor del primer libro guineano y primera
novela africana en español (1929–1996)

Leandro Mbomio Nsue
escultor (1938–2012)

Eric Moussambani
nadador olímpico (1978–)

Donato Ndongo-Bidyogo
escritor (1950–)

María Nsué Angüe
escritora (1945–)

© Christine Nesbitt/AP Images

Niños jugando frente a una iglesia en Malabo

Investiga en Internet

La geografía: la isla de Bioko, el río Muni

La historia: los Bantú, los Igbo, los Fang

Música: Las Hijas del Sol, Betty Akna, Anfibio

Comidas y bebidas: la sopa banga, el pescado a la plancha, el puercoespín, el antílope, los vinos de palma, la malamba

Fiestas: Día de la Independencia (12 de octubre)

Mujeres pescando (*fishing*) en la playa

El bosque (*forest*) de la isla de Bioko

CURIOSIDADES

- Se cree que los primeros habitantes de esta región fueron pigmeos.

- Guinea Ecuatorial obtuvo su independencia de España en 1968 y es el único país en África en donde el español es un idioma oficial.

- Parte de su territorio fue colonizado por los portugueses y por los ingleses.

- Macías Nguema fue dictador de Guinea Ecuatorial hasta 1979.

- El país tiene una universidad, la Universidad Nacional de Guinea Ecuatorial, situada en la capital.

- Con el descubrimiento de reservas de petróleo y gas en la década de los años 90 se fortaleció (*strengthened*) considerablemente la economía.

- Guinea Ecuatorial tiene el más alto ingreso per cápita en África: 19,998 dólares. Sin embargo (*However*), la distribución del dinero se concentra en unas pocas familias.

Honduras ▶

INFORMACIÓN GENERAL

Nombre oficial: República de Honduras

Nacionalidad: hondureño(a)

Área: 112 090 km² (aproximadamente el área de Pennsylvania)

Población: 8 598 561

Capital: Tegucigalpa (f. 1762) (1 324 000 hab.)

Otras ciudades importantes: San Pedro Sula, El Progreso

Moneda: lempira

Idiomas: español (oficial), garífuna

DEMOGRAFÍA

Alfabetismo: 85,1%

Religiones: católicos (97%), protestantes (3%)

HONDUREÑOS CÉLEBRES

Ramón Amaya Amador
escritor (1916–1966)

Lempira
héroe indígena (1499–1537)

Carlos Mencia
comediante (1967–)

David Suazo
futbolista (1979–)

José Antonio Velásquez
pintor (1906–1983)

iLrn Para aprender más sobre Honduras, mira el video cultural en la mediateca (*Media Library*).

Copán, declarado Patrimonio de la Humanidad (*World Heritage*) por la UNESCO

© Dave Rock/Shutterstock

Investiga en Internet

La geografía: islas de la Bahía, Copán

La historia: los mayas, los garífunas, los misquitos, Ramón Villedas Morales, José Trinidad Cabañas

Música: punta, Café Guancasco, Delirium, Yerbaklan

Comidas y bebidas: el arroz con leche, los tamales, las pupusas, el atol de elote, la chicha, el ponche de leche

Fiestas: Día de la Independencia (15 de septiembre)

El esnórquel es popular en Honduras.

Vista aérea de la isla Roatán en el Caribe hondureño

CURIOSIDADES

- Los hondureños reciben el apodo *(nickname)* de "catrachos", palabra derivada del apellido Xatruch, un famoso general que combatió en Nicaragua contra el filibustero William Walker.

- El nombre original del país fue Comayagua, el mismo nombre que su capital. A mediados del siglo XIX adoptó el nombre República de Honduras, y en 1880 la capital se trasladó *(moved)* a Tegucigalpa.

- Honduras basa su economía en la agricultura, especialmente en las plantaciones de banana, cuya comercialización empezó en 1889 con la fundación de la Standard Fruit Company.

- Se dice que en la región de Yoro ocurre el fenómeno de la lluvia *(rain)* de peces, es decir que, literalmente, los peces caen del cielo *(fall from the sky)*. Por esta razón, desde 1998 se celebra en el Yoro el Festival de Lluvia de Peces.

- En 1998, el huracán Mitch golpeó *(hit)* severamente la economía nacional, destruyendo gran parte de la infraestructura del país y de los cultivos. Se calcula que el país retrocedió 25 años a causa del huracán.

México ▶

INFORMACIÓN GENERAL

iLrn Para aprender más sobre México, mira el video cultural en la mediateca (*Media Library*).

Nombre oficial: Estados Unidos Mexicanos

Nacionalidad: mexicano(a)

Área: 1 964 375 km² (aproximadamente 4 1/2 veces el área de California)

Población: 120 386 655

Capital: México D.F. (f. 1521) (21 163 000 hab.)

Otras ciudades importantes: Guadalajara, Monterrey, Puebla, Tijuana

Moneda: peso (mexicano)

Idiomas: español (oficial), aproximadamente 280 otras lenguas amerindias

DEMOGRAFÍA

Alfabetismo: 93,5%

Religiones: católicos (90,4%), protestantes (3,8%), otros (5,8%)

MEXICANOS CÉLEBRES

Carmen Aristegui
periodista (1964–)

Gael García Bernal
actor (1978–)

Alejandro González Iñarritu
director de cine (1963–)

Frida Kahlo
pintora (1907–1954)

Armando Manzanero
cantautor (1935–)

Rafa Márquez
futbolista (1979–)

Octavio Paz
escritor, Premio Nobel de Literatura (1914–1998)

Elena Poniatowska
periodista, escritora (1932–)

Diego Rivera
pintor (1886–1957)

Guillermo del Toro
cineasta (1964–)

Emiliano Zapata
revolucionario (1879–1919)

Teotihuacán, ciudad precolombina declarada Patrimonio de la Humanidad (*World Heritage*) la UNESCO.

Investiga en Internet

La geografía: el cañón del Cobre, el volcán Popocatépetl, las lagunas de Montebello, Parque Nacional Cañón del Sumidero, la sierra Tarahumara, Acapulco

La historia: mayas, aztecas, toltecas, la conquista, la colonia, Pancho Villa, Porfirio Díaz, Hernán Cortés, Miguel Hidalgo, los Zapatistas

Películas: *Amores perros, Frida, Y tu mamá también, Babel, El laberinto del fauno, La misma luna*

Música: mariachis, ranchera, Pedro Infante, Vicente Fernández, Luis Miguel, Maná, Jaguares, Juan Gabriel, Thalía, Lucero, Julieta Venegas

Comidas y bebidas: los chiles en nogada, el mole poblano, el pozole, los huevos rancheros, el tequila (alimentos originarios de México: chocolate, tomate, vainilla)

Fiestas: Día de la Independencia (16 de septiembre), Día de los Muertos (1 y 2 de noviembre)

© Colman Lerner Gerardo/Shutterstock

La Torre Latinoamericana, en la Ciudad de México, fue el primer rascacielos *(skyscraper)* del mundo construído exitosamente en una zona sísmica.

© karamysh/Shutterstock

Puerto Vallarta

CURIOSIDADES

- La Ciudad de México es una de las ciudades más pobladas del mundo. Los predecesores de los aztecas fundaron la Ciudad sobre el lago *(lake)* de Texcoco. La ciudad recibió el nombre de Tenochtitlán, y era más grande que cualquier *(any)* capital europea cuando ocurrió la Conquista.

- Millones de mariposas *(butterflies)* monarcas migran todos los años a los estados de Michoacán y México de los Estados Unidos y Canadá.

- La Pirámide de Chichén Itzá fue nombrada una de las siete maravillas del mundo moderno.

- Los olmecas (1200 a.C–400 a.C) desarrollaron *(developed)* el primer sistema de escritura en las Américas.

Nicaragua ▶

INFORMACIÓN GENERAL

iLrn Para aprender más sobre Nicaragua, mira el video cultural en la mediateca (*Media Library*).

Nombre oficial: República de Nicaragua

Nacionalidad: nicaragüense

Área: 130 370 km² (aproximadamente el área del estado de Nueva York)

Población: 5 848 641

Capital: Managua (f. 1522) (2 132 000 hab.)

Otras ciudades importantes: León, Chinandega

Moneda: córdoba

Idiomas: español (oficial), misquito

DEMOGRAFÍA

Alfabetismo: 78%

Religiones: católicos (58%), evangélicos (22%), otros (20%)

NICARAGÜENSES CÉLEBRES

Ernesto Cardenal
sacerdote, poeta (1925–)

Rubén Darío
poeta, padre del Modernismo (1867–1916)

Violeta Chamorro
periodista, presidenta (1929–)

Bianca Jagger
activista de derechos humanos (1945–)

© rchphoto/iStockphoto

Ometepe, isla formada por dos volcanes

Investiga en Internet

La geografía: el lago Nicaragua, la isla Ometepe

La historia: los misquitos, Anastasio Somoza, Augusto Sandino, Revolución sandinista, José Dolores Estrada

Películas: *Ernesto Cardenal*

Música: polca, mazurca, Camilo Zapata, Carlos Mejía Godoy, Salvador Cardenal, Luis Enrique Mejía Godoy, Perrozompopo

Comidas y bebidas: los tamales, la sopa de pepino, el triste, el tibio, la chicha

Fiestas: Día de la Independencia (15 de septiembre)

© Pablo H Caridad/Shutterstock

Catedral de Granada

© rj lerich/Shutterstock

Isla del Maíz

CURIOSIDADES

- Nicaragua se conoce como tierra *(land)* de poetas y volcanes.
- La capital, Managua, fue destruída por un terremoto *(earthquake)* en 1972. A causa de la actividad sísmica no se construyen edificios altos.
- Las ruinas de León Viejo fueron declaradas Patrimonio de la Humanidad *(World Heritage)* en el año 2000. Es la ciudad más antigua de América Central.
- Es el país más grande de Centroamérica y tiene el lago más grande de la región, el lago Nicaragua, con más de 370 islas. La isla más grande, Ometepe, tiene dos volcanes.

Panamá ▶

INFORMACIÓN GENERAL

iLrn Para aprender más sobre Panamá, mira el video cultural en la mediateca (*Media Library*).

Nombre oficial: República de Panamá

Nacionalidad: panameño(a)

Área: 75 420 km² (aproximadamente la mitad del área de Florida)

Población: 3 608 431

Capital: Panamá (f. 1519) (1 273 000 hab.)

Otras ciudades importantes: San Miguelito, David

Moneda: balboa, dólar (estadounidense)

Idiomas: español (oficial), inglés

DEMOGRAFÍA

Alfabetismo: 94,1%

Religiones: católicos (85%), protestantes (15%)

PANAMEÑOS CÉLEBRES

Joaquín Beleño
escritor y periodista (1922–1988)

Ricardo Miró
escritor (1883–1940)

Rubén Blades
cantautor, actor, abogado, político (1948–)

Omar Torrijos
militar, presidente (1929–1981)

© Marija/Shutterstock

El canal de Panamá es una de las principales fuentes *(sources)* de ingresos para el país.

Investiga en Internet

La geografía: el canal de Panamá

La historia: los Kuna Yala, la construcción del canal de Panamá, la dictadura de Manuel Noriega, Parque Nacional Soberanía, Victoriano Lorenzo

Películas: *El plomero, Los puños de una nación*

Música: salsa, Danilo Pérez, Edgardo Franco "El General", Nando Boom

Comidas y bebidas: el chocao panameño, el sancocho de gallina, las carimaolas, la ropa vieja, los jugos de fruta, el chicheme

Fiestas: Día de la Independencia (3 de noviembre)

Una isla en el archipiélago de San Blas, lugar donde habitan los Kuna Yala

La Ciudad de Panamá es famosa por sus rascacielos *(skyscrapers)*.

CURIOSIDADES

- El canal de Panamá se construyó entre 1904 y 1914. Mide *(It measures)* 84 kilómetros de longitud y funciona con un sistema de esclusas *(locks)* que elevan y bajan los barcos *(boats)* porque los océanos Atlántico y Pacífico tienen diferentes elevaciones. Cada año cruzan unos 14 000 barcos o botes por el canal, el cual estuvo bajo control de los Estados Unidos hasta el 31 de diciembre de 1999. En promedio *(On average)*, cada embarcación paga 54 000 dólares por cruzar el canal. La tarifa más baja la pagó un aventurero estadounidense, quien pagó 36 centavos por cruzar nadando en 1928.

- En la actualidad está construyéndose una ampliación al canal que permitirá que transiten por él barcos hasta tres veces más grandes que la máxima capacidad del canal actual.

- El territorio de los Kuna Yala se considera independiente. Para entrar a su territorio es necesario pagar una cuota *(fee)* y mostrar su pasaporte.

Paraguay ▶

INFORMACIÓN GENERAL

Nombre oficial: República del Paraguay

Nacionalidad: paraguayo(a)

Área: 406 750 km² (aproximadamente el área de California)

Población: 6 703 860

Capital: Asunción (f. 1537) (2 329 000 hab.)

Otras ciudades importantes: Ciudad del Este, San Lorenzo

Moneda: guaraní

Idiomas: español y guaraní (oficiales)

iLrn™ Para aprender más sobre Paraguay, mira el video cultural en la mediateca (*Media Library*).

DEMOGRAFÍA

Alfabetismo: 93,9%

Religiones: católicos (90%), protestantes (6%), otros (4%)

PARAGUAYOS CÉLEBRES

Olga Blinder
pintora (1921–2008)

Augusto Roa Bastos
escritor, Premio Cervantes de Literatura (1917–2005)

Arsenio Erico
futbolista (1915–1977)

Berta Rojas
guitarrista (1966–)

© Lukasz Kurbiel/Shutterstock

Ruinas de Misiones Jesuitas en Trinidad

Investiga en Internet

La geografía: las cataratas del Iguazú, los ríos Paraguay y Paraná, Parque Nacional Cerro Corá, la presa Itaipú, el Chaco

La historia: guaraníes, misiones jesuitas, la Guerra de la Triple Alianza, Alfredo Stroessner, Carlos Antonio López, José Félix Estigarribia

Películas: *Nosotros, Hamacas paraguayas, 7 cajas*

Música: polca, baile de la botella, arpa paraguaya, Perla, Celso Duarte

Comidas y bebidas: el chipá paraguayo, el surubí, las empanadas, la sopa paraguaya, el mate, el tereré

Fiestas: Día de la Independencia (14 de mayo), Verbena de San Juan (24 de junio)

El palacio presidencial en Asunción

Las cataratas de Iguazú, una de las siete maravillas naturales del mundo

CURIOSIDADES

- Por diversas razones históricas, Paraguay es un país bilingüe. Se calcula que el 90% de sus habitantes hablan español y guaraní, el idioma de sus habitantes antes de la llegada de los españoles. En particular, la llegada de los jesuitas tuvo importancia en la preservación del idioma guaraní. Actualmente se producen novelas y programas de radio en guaraní. Por otra parte, el guaraní ha influenciado notablemente el español de la región.

- Paraguay, igual que Bolivia, no tiene salida al mar *(sea)*.

- La presa *(dam)* de Itaipú es la mayor del mundo en cuanto a producción de energía. Está sobre el río Paraná y abastace *(provides)* el 90% del consumo de energía eléctrica de Paraguay y el 19% de Brasil.

Perú ▶

INFORMACIÓN GENERAL

Nombre oficial: República del Perú

Nacionalidad: peruano(a)

Área: 1 285 216 km² (aproximadamente 2 veces el área de Texas)

Población: 30 147 935

Capital: Lima (f. 1535) (8 769 000 hab.)

Otras ciudades importantes: Callao, Arequipa, Trujillo

Moneda: nuevo sol

Idiomas: español, quechua y aymará (oficiales), otras lenguas indígenas

iLrn™ Para aprender más sobre Perú, mira el video cultural en la mediateca (*Media Library*).

DEMOGRAFÍA

Alfabetismo: 92,9%

Religiones: católicos (81,3%), evangélicos (12,5%), otros (3,3%)

PERUANOS CÉLEBRES

Gastón Acurio
chef (1967–)

Alberto Fujimori
político y presidente (1938–)

Tania Libertad
cantante (1952–)

Claudia Llosa
directora de cine (1976–)

María Julia Mantilla
empresaria y presentadora de TV, ex Miss Universo (1984–)

Javier Pérez de Cuellar
secretario general de las Naciones Unidas (1920–)

Fernando de Szyszlo
pintor (1925–)

Mario Testino
fotógrafo (1954–)

César Vallejo
poeta (1892–1938)

Mario Vargas Llosa
escritor, político, Premio Nobel de Literatura (1936–)

© Mark Skalny/Shutterstock

Machu Picchu

Las calles de Cuzco

© Alexey Stiop/Shutterstock

La Plaza de Armas en Lima

© Neale Cousland/Shutterstock

CURIOSIDADES

- En Perú vivieron muchas civilizaciones diferentes que se desarrollaron *(developed)* entre el año 4000 a.C hasta principios *(beginning)* del siglo XVI. La más importante fue la civilización de los incas, que dominaba la región a la llegada de los españoles.

- Otra civilización importante fueron los nazcas, quienes trazaron figuras de animales que solo se pueden ver desde el aire. Hay más de 2000 km de líneas. Su origen es un misterio y no se sabe por qué las hicieron *(made)*.

- Perú es el país del mundo que tiene más platos típicos: 491.

- Probablemente la canción folclórica más famosa del Perú es "El Cóndor Pasa".

Puerto Rico ▶

INFORMACIÓN GENERAL

iLrn Para aprender más sobre Puerto Rico, mira el video cultural en la mediateca (*Media Library*).

Nombre oficial: Estado Libre Asociado de Puerto Rico (*Commonwealth of Puerto Rico*)

Nacionalidad: puertorriqueño(a)

Área: 13.790 km² (un poco menos que el área de Connecticut)

Población: 3 620 897

Capital: San Juan (f. 1521) (2 730 000 hab.)

Otras ciudades importantes: Ponce, Caguas

Moneda: dólar (estadounidense)

Idiomas: español, inglés (oficiales)

DEMOGRAFÍA

Alfabetismo: 94,1%

Religiones: católicos (85%), protestantes y otros (15%)

PUERTORRIQUEÑOS CÉLEBRES

Roberto Clemente
beisbolista (1934–1972)

Rosario Ferré
escritora (1938–)

Raúl Juliá
actor (1940–1994)

Ricky Martin
cantante, benefactor (1971–)

Rita Moreno
actriz (1931–)

Francisco Oller y Cestero
pintor (1833–1917)

Esmeralda Santiago
escritora (1948–)

Una calle en el Viejo San Juan

© Lori Froeb/Shutterstock

La cascada de La Mina en el Bosque Nacional El Yunque

 Investiga en Internet

La geografía: el Yunque, Vieques, El Morro, Parque Nacional Cavernas del Río Camuy

La historia: los taínos, Juan Ponce de León, la Guerra Hispanoamericana, Pedro Albizu Campos

Películas: *Lo que le pasó a Santiago, 12 horas, Talento de barrio*

Música: salsa, bomba y plena, Gilberto Santa Rosa, Olga Tañón, Daddy Yankee, Tito Puente, Calle 13, Carlos Ponce, Ivy Queen

Comidas y bebidas: el lechón asado, el arroz con gandules, el mofongo, los bacalaítos, la champola de guayaba, el coquito, la horchata de ajonjolí

Fiestas: Día de la Independencia de EE.UU. (4 de julio), Día de la Constitución de Puerto Rico (25 de julio)

Una playa en Fajardo

CURIOSIDADES

- A los puertorriqueños también se los conoce como (*known as*) "boricuas", ya que antes de (*before*) la llegada de los europeos la isla se llamaba Borinquen.

- A diferencia de otros países, los puertorriqueños también son ciudadanos (*citizens*) estadounidenses, con la excepción de que no pueden votar en elecciones presidenciales de los Estados Unidos si no son residentes de un estado.

- El gobierno de Puerto Rico está encabezado por un gobernador.

- El fuerte (*fort*) de El Morro fue construido en el siglo XVI para defender el puerto de los piratas. Gracias a esta construcción, San Juan fue el lugar mejor defendido del Caribe.

República Dominicana ▶

INFORMACIÓN GENERAL

Nombre oficial: República Dominicana

Nacionalidad: dominicano(a)

Área: 48 670 km² (aproximadamente 2 veces el área de Vermont)

Población: 10 349 741

Capital: Santo Domingo (f. 1492) (2 191 000 hab.)

Otras ciudades importantes: Santiago de los Caballeros, La Romana

Moneda: peso (dominicano)

Idiomas: español

iLrn Para aprender más sobre República Dominicana, mira el video cultural en la mediateca (*Media Library*).

DEMOGRAFÍA

Alfabetismo: 90,1%

Religiones: católicos (95%), otros (5%)

DOMINICANOS CÉLEBRES

Juan Bosch
escritor (1909–2001)

Charytín
cantante y conductora (1949–)

Juan Pablo Duarte
héroe de la independencia (1808–1876)

Juan Luis Guerra
músico (1957–)

Óscar de la Renta
diseñador (1932–)

David Ortiz
beisbolista (1975–)

La plaza principal en Santo Domingo

© e2dan/Shutterstock

Investiga en Internet

La geografía: Puerto Plata, Pico Duarte, Sierra de Samaná

La historia: los taínos, los arawak, la dictadura de Trujillo, las hermanas Mirabal, Juan Pablo Duarte

Películas: *Nueba Yol, Cuatro hombres y un ataúd*

Música: merengue, bachata, Wilfrido Vargas, Johnny Ventura, Milly Quezada

Comidas y bebidas: el mangú, el sancocho, el asopao, el refresco rojo, la mamajuana

Fiestas: Día de la Independencia (27 de febrero), Día de la Señora de la Altagracia (21 de enero)

Un vendedor de cocos en Boca Chica

Construido en 1976, Altos de Chavón es una recreación de un pueblo medieval de Europa.

CURIOSIDADES

- La isla que comparten *(share)* la República Dominicana y Haití, La Española, estuvo bajo control español hasta 1697, cuando la parte oeste *(western)* pasó a ser territorio francés.

- La República Dominicana tiene algunas de las construcciones más antiguas dejadas *(left)* por los españoles.

- Se cree que los restos de Cristóbal Colón están enterrados *(buried)* en Santo Domingo, pero Colón también tiene una tumba en Sevilla, España.

- En Santo Domingo se construyeron la primera catedral, el primer hospital, la primera aduana *(customs office)* y la primera universidad del Nuevo Mundo.

- Santo Domingo fue declarada Patrimonio de la Humanidad *(World Heritage)* por la UNESCO.

Uruguay ▶

INFORMACIÓN GENERAL

iLrn Para aprender más sobre Uruguay, mira el video cultural en la mediateca (*Media Library*).

Nombre oficial: República Oriental del Uruguay

Nacionalidad: uruguayo(a)

Área: 176 215 km² (casi exactamente igual al estado de Washington)

Población: 3 333 000

Capital: Montevideo (f. 1726) (1 973 000 hab.)

Otras ciudades importantes: Salto, Paysandú, Punta del Este

Moneda: peso (uruguayo)

Idiomas: español (oficial)

DEMOGRAFÍA

Alfabetismo: 98%

Religiones: católicos (47,1%), protestantes (11%), otros (42%)

URUGUAYOS CÉLEBRES

Delmira Agustini
poetisa (1886–1914)

Mario Benedetti
escritor (1920–2009)

Jorge Drexler
músico, actor, médico (1964–)

Diego Forlán
futbolista (1979–)

José "Pepe" Mujica
presidente (1935–)

Julio Sosa
cantor de tango (1926–1964)

Horacio Quiroga
escritor (1878–1937)

Alfredo Zitarrosa
compositor (1936–1989)

Plaza Independencia, Montevideo (Palacio Salvo)

© VojtechVlk/Shutterstock

Investiga en Internet

La geografía: Punta del Este, Colonia

La historia: el Carnaval de Montevideo, los tablados, José Artigas

Películas: *Whisky, 25 Watts, Una forma de bailar, Joya, El baño del Papa, El Chevrolé, El viaje hacia el mar*

Música: tango, milonga, candombe, Jorge Drexler, Rubén Rada, La vela puerca

Comidas y bebidas: el asado, el dulce de leche, la faina, el chivito, el mate

Fiestas: Día de la Independencia (25 de agosto), Carnaval (febrero)

Carnaval de Montevideo

© Kobby Dagan/Shutterstock

© Bertrandb/Dreamstime.com

Colonia del Sacramento

CURIOSIDADES

- En guaraní, "Uruguay" significa "río *(river)* de las gallinetas". La gallineta es un pájaro de esta región.

- La industria ganadera *(cattle)* es una de las más importantes del país. La bebida más popular es el mate. Es muy común ver a los uruguayos caminando con el termo bajo el brazo, listo para tomar mate en cualquier lugar.

- Los descendientes de esclavos africanos que vivieron en esa zona dieron origen a *(gave rise to)* la música típica de Uruguay: el candombe.

- Uruguay fue el anfitrión *(host)* y el primer campeón de la Copa Mundial de Fútbol en 1930.

Venezuela ▶

INFORMACIÓN GENERAL

iLrn Para aprender más sobre Venezuela, mira el video cultural en la mediateca (*Media Library*).

Nombre oficial: República Bolivariana de Venezuela

Nacionalidad: venezolano(a)

Área: 912 050 km² (2800 km de costas) (aproximadamente 6 veces el área de Florida)

Población: 28 868 486

Capital: Caracas (f. 1567) (3 051 000 hab.)

Otras ciudades importantes: Maracaibo, Valencia, Maracay Barquisimeto

Moneda: bolívar

Idiomas: español (oficial), guajiro, wayuu y otras lenguas amerindias

DEMOGRAFÍA

Alfabetismo: 95,5%

Religiones: católicos (96%), protestantes (2%), otros (2%)

VENEZOLANOS CÉLEBRES

Andrés Eloy Blanco
escritor (1897–1955)

Simón Bolívar
libertador (1783–1830)

Hugo Chávez
militar, presidente (1954–2013)

Gustavo Dudamel
músico, director de
orquesta (1981–)

Lupita Ferrer
actriz (1947–)

Rómulo Gallegos
escritor (1884–1969)

Carolina Herrera
diseñadora (1939–)

© Vadim Petrakov/Shutterstock

El Salto Ángel, la catarata (*waterfall*) más alta del mundo

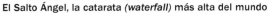

© Alexander Chaikin/Shutterstock

El Obelisco, en el centro de Plaza Francia en la ciudad de Caracas, fue en su momento la construcción más alta de la ciudad.

 Investiga en Internet

La geografía: El Salto Ángel, la isla Margarita, el Amazonas Parque Nacional Canaima

La historia: los yanomami, el petróleo, Simón Bolívar, Francisco de la Miranda

Películas: *Punto y Raya, Secuestro Express*

Música: el joropo, Ricardo Montaner, Franco de Vita, Chino y Nacho, Carlos Baute, Óscar de León

Comidas y bebidas: el ceviche, las hallacas, las arepas, el carato de guanábana, el guarapo de papelón

Fiestas: Día de la Independencia (5 de julio), Nuestra Señora de la Candelaria (2 de febrero)

© Robert Wroblewski/Shutterstock

Isla Margarita, popular destino turístico

CURIOSIDADES

- El nombre de Venezuela ("pequeña Venecia") se debe a Américo Vespucio, quien llamó así a una de las islas costeras en 1499, debido a su aspecto veneciano.

- La isla Margarita es un lugar turístico muy popular. Cuando los españoles llegaron hace más de 500 años *(more than 500 years ago)*, los indígenas de la isla, los guaiqueríes, pensaron *(thought)* que eran dioses y les dieron *(gave)* regalos y una ceremonia de bienvenida. Gracias a esto, los guaiqueríes fueron los únicos indígenas del Caribe que tuvieron el estatus de "vasallos libres".

- En la época moderna Venezuela se destaca *(stands out)* por sus concursos *(contests)* de belleza y por su producción internacional de telenovelas.

- En Venezuela hay tres sitios considerados Patrimonio de la Humanidad *(World Heritage)* por la UNESCO: Coro y su puerto, el Parque Nacional de Canaima, y la Ciudad Universitaria de Caracas.

- En Venezuela habita un roedor *(rodent)* llamado chigüire que llega a pesar hasta 60 kilos.

Los Latinos en los Estados Unidos ▶

INFORMACIÓN GENERAL

Nombre oficial: Estados Unidos de América

Nacionalidad: estadounidense

Área: 9 826 675 km² (aproximadamente el área de China o 3,5 veces el área de Argentina)

Población: 318 892 103 (2010) (aproximadamente el 15% se consideran de origen hispano)

Capital: Washington, D.C. (f. 1791) (6 000 000 hab.)

Otras ciudades importantes: Nueva York, Los Ángeles, Chicago, Miami

Moneda: dólar (estadounidense)

Idiomas: inglés (oficial), español y más de 200 otros

iLrn Para aprender más sobre Los Latinos en los Estados Unidos, mira el video cultural en la mediateca (*Media Library*).

DEMOGRAFÍA

Alfabetismo: 99%

Religiones: protestantes (51,3%), católicos (23,9%), mormones (1,7%), judíos (1,7%) y otros

HISPANOS CÉLEBRES DE ESTADOS UNIDOS

Christina Aguilera
cantante (1980–)

Julia Álvarez
escritora (1950–)

Marc Anthony
cantante (1969–)

César Chávez
activista por los derechos de los trabajadores (1927–1993)

Sandra Cisneros
escritora (1954–)

Junot Díaz
escritor (1968–)

Eva Longoria
actriz (1975–)

Soledad O'Brien
periodista, presentadora (1966–)

Ellen Ochoa
astronauta (1958–)

Edward James Olmos
actor (1947–)

Sonia Sotomayor
Juez Asociada de la Corte Suprema de Justicia de EE.UU. (1954–)

La Pequeña Habana en Miami, Florida

© Jeff Greenberg/The Image Works

© FRILET Patrick/age fotostock

Un mural de Benito Juárez en Chicago, Illinois

 Investiga en Internet

La geografía: regiones que pertenecieron a México, lugares con arquitectura de estilo español, Plaza Olvera, Calle 8, La Pequeña Habana

La historia: el Álamo, la Guerra Mexicoamericana, la Guerra Hispanoamericana, Antonio López de Santa Anna

Películas: *A Day without Mexicans, My Family, Stand and Deliver, Tortilla Soup*

Música: salsa, tejano (Tex-Mex), merengue, hip hop en español, Jennifer López, Selena

Comidas y bebidas: los tacos, las enchiladas, los burritos, los plátanos fritos, los frijoles, el arroz con gandules, la cerveza con limón

Fiestas: Día de la Batalla de Puebla (5 de mayo)

© Brandon Seidel/Shutterstock

El Álamo, donde Santa Anna derrotó *(defeated)* a los tejanos en una batalla de la Revolución de Texas.

CURIOSIDADES

- Los latinos son la primera minoría de Estados Unidos (más de 46 millones). Este grupo incluye personas que provienen de los veintiún países de habla hispana y a los hijos y nietos de estas que nacieron *(were born)* en los Estados Unidos. Muchos hablan español perfectamente y otros no lo hablan para nada. El grupo más grande de latinos es el de mexicanoamericanos, ya que territorios como Texas, Nuevo México, Utah, Nevada, California, Colorado y Oregón eran parte de México.

- Actualmente todas las culturas latinoamericanas están representadas en los Estados Unidos.

Partner Activities

Capítulo 1

1.5 **Correo electrónico** You and your partner are in charge of your school's Club Internacional. You have information for half of the new members on this page and your partner has the other half on page 5. Ask each other questions to complete the tables. You will need the following words: **arroba** (@) and **punto** (dot).

Modelo Estudiante 1: *¿Cuál es el correo electrónico de Pilar?*
Estudiante 2: *pilybonita@uden.es → p-i-l-y-b-o-n-i-t-a, arroba, u-d-e-n, punto, e-s*

Nombre	Correo electrónico
1. Marina	marichiqui@ubbi.ar
2. Gabriel	
3. Alejandro	elmeroale@claro.mex
4. Valeria	

1.22 **La fila** Work with a partner to figure out the names of the people in the stands. One of you will look at this page, and the other will look at the picture on page 19. Take turns giving the name of a person and a description, so your partner will know who it is.

© Cengage Learning

1.37 **Diferencias** Working with a partner, one of you will look at the picture on this page, and the other will look at the picture on page 35. Take turns describing the pictures using the expression **hay**, numbers, and the classroom vocabulary. Find the eight differences.

> Modelo Estudiante 1: *Hay una computadora.*
> Estudiante 2: *Sí, y hay una silla.*
> Estudiante 1: *No, no hay una silla.*

© Cengage Learning

Capítulo 2

2.5 **Una familia** You and your partner each have half of the information about the Navarro family. One of you will look at the drawing on this page, the other one will look at the drawing on page 41. Take turns asking the names of the different people.

> Modelo Estudiante 1: *¿Cómo se llama el hermano de Sofía?*
> Estudiante 2: *Se llama Miguel.*

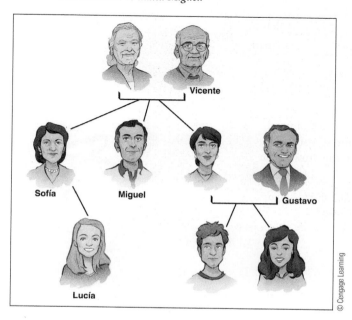

Vicente

Sofía   Miguel   Gustavo

Lucía

© Cengage Learning

2.23 **La graduación** In order to graduate, each student must take one class in each of the following categories: natural science, social science, math, humanities (**las humanidades**), and language. You and your partner must check the schedules of four students to determine which courses they have taken, and which ones they need. One of you will look at the information on this page and the other will look at page 55.

Modelo   Estudiante 1: *¿Tiene (has) Raúl Ruiz Costa una clase de ciencias naturales?*
          Estudiante 2: *Sí, Raúl tiene biología.*
          Estudiante 1: *¿Tiene Raúl una clase de humanidades?*
          Estudiante 2: *No, él necesita una clase de humanidades.*

Ramón Ayala Pérez	Andrea Gómez Ramos	Diana Salazar Casas	Hugo Vargas Díaz
arte		**ingeniería**	
química		**física**	
informática		**alemán**	
geografía		**cálculo**	
educación física			

2.41 **Datos personales** Working with a partner, look at the chart below while your partner looks at the chart on page 71. Take turns asking questions to fill in the missing information.

Modelo   *¿Cuántos años tiene Diego?*   *Diego tiene veinte años.*
          ¿Qué parientes hay en la familia de Diego?   *Diego tiene dos hermanos.*
          ¿Qué clase tiene Diego?   *Diego tiene informática.*

Nombre	Edad	Familia	Clase
Diego	20	dos hermanos	informática
Alonso		una sobrina	
Magdalena			esquia
Cristina	30	cinco primos	
Pablo	62		
Gabriel	25		cálculo
Rufina		un esposo	alemán

Capítulo 3

3.5 **Los regalos** A friend sent a care package for the rest of your friends but forgot to label who everything was for, so you and a classmate need to clarify. One of you will look at the drawing on this page, and the other at the drawing on page 79.

Modelo   Estudiante 1: *¿Para quién (For whom) son los calcetines rojos?*
          Estudiante 2: *Los calcetines rojos son para Emilia.*

3.25 **La tele** En parejas túrnense para preguntar a qué hora son los programas y en qué canal son. Uno mira la programación y las preguntas aquí y el otro mira la página 93. *(With a partner, take turns asking what times the shows are on and on what channel. One will look at the guide and questions here, and the other will look at page 93).*

Modelo Estudiante 1: *¿A qué hora es* Vacaciones en familia?
Estudiante 2: *Veredicto final es a las dos de la tarde.*
Estudiante 1: *¿En qué canal es?*
Estudiante 2: *Es en Cine Canal.*

PROGRAMACIÓN ○ Películas ○ Especiales ○ Deportes ○ Nuevos

		14:00	14:30	15:00	15:30	16:00	16:30	17:00	17:30	18:00	18:30	19:00
Canal 5		Veredicto final			Será anunciada				Difícil de creer		Quiero amarte	
Discovery Channel	Cable 35	MythBusters: Cazadores		Cazadores de Monstruos		Adictos	Adictos	Rides 3		Los Archivos del FBI		
TNT	Cable 37	(:15)★★ "Aprendiendo a Vivir" (1995) Peter Falk, D.B. Sweeney.					★ "Las Aventuras de Rocky y Bullwinkle" (2000)				Harry Potter	
Cine Canal	Digital 482	"Vacaciones en Familia"		(:10)★★★ "Las Ballenas de Agosto" (1987, Drama)				(16:55) "Durmiendo con el Enemigo"			Seducción	

Jueves 10 de agosto

© Cengage Learning

¿A qué hora es… ?

1. El Chapulín Colorado
2. Dos Ilusiones
3. A los 30 Años
4. Gritos del Más Allá

3.41 **Ocho diferencias** Trabaja con un compañero. Uno mira la ilustración aquí y el otro mira la ilustración en la página 109. Túrnense para describir su ilustración y buscar las ocho diferencias. *(Work with a partner. One of you will look at the illustration on this page and the other will look at the illustration on page 109. Take turns describing the illustrations to find the eight differences.)*

© Cengage Learning

Capítulo 4

4.5 **Planes para el fin de semana** Trabaja con un compañero para descubrir cuáles son las actividades de Jazmín, Lila y Arturo durante el fin de semana y dónde las hacen. Uno de ustedes va a ver la información en esta página, y el otro va a ver la información en la página 115.

Modelo Estudiante 1: *¿Qué hace Lila el sábado por la mañana?*
Estudiante 2: *Lila corre.*
Estudiante 1: *¿Dónde corre?*
Estudiante 2: *En el gimnasio.*

	Jazmín	Lila	Arturo
sábado por la mañana		correr (el gimnasio)	
sábado por la tarde	caminar (el parque)		tomar fotos (el zoológico)
sábado por la noche	bailar (un club)	comer (un café)	
domingo por la mañana			buscar libros (la librería)

4.23 **Comparemos** Trabaja con un compañero. Uno de ustedes mira la casa en esta página mientras el otro mira la casa en la página 129. Túrnense para describir las casas y busquen las seis diferencias.

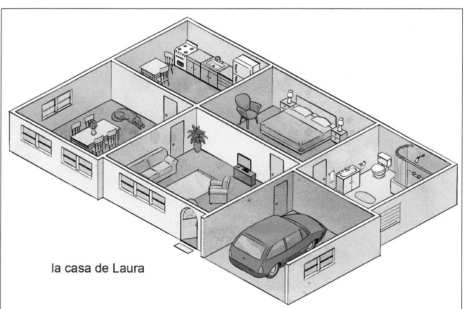

la casa de Laura

© Cengage Learning

4.37 **Seis diferencias** Trabaja con un compañero. Uno mira el dibujo aquí y el otro mira el dibujo en la página 145. Túrnense para describirlos y buscar seis diferencias.

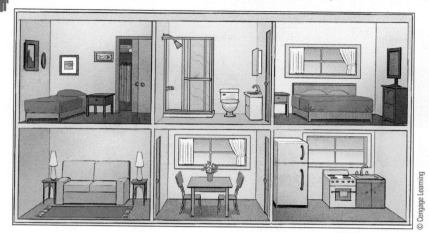

© Cengage Learning

Capítulo 5

5.6 **Los chismes** *(gossip)* Imagina que tu compañero y tú están intercambiando información sobre cómo están todos sus amigos. Uno de ustedes va a ver la tabla en esta página, y el otro va a ver la página 153. **¡OJO!** ¡Presta atención a la concordancia *(agreement)*!

Modelo Estudiante 1: *¿Cómo está Ramira?*
Estudiante 2: *Está contenta.*
Estudiante 1: *¿Por qué?*
Estudiante 2: *Porque va a ir de vacaciones a Venezuela.*

Nombre	¿Cómo está(n)?	¿Por qué?
Ramira	contento	Va a ir de vacaciones a Venezuela.
Emanuel y Arturo		Tienen mucha tarea.
Gisela		
Alex	avergonzado	
Karina e Iliana	enamorado	Sus novios son perfectos.
Gerardo		Va a tener varios exámenes difíciles.
Javier y Manuel	aburrido	

5.23 **Personas famosas** Trabaja con un compañero para completar la información. Uno de ustedes debe ver la tabla en esta página y el otro debe ver la tabla en la página 167. Túrnense para preguntar y responder.

Nombre	Profesión	País de origen
Alicia Alonso		Cuba
Óscar de la Renta	diseñador	
Andrea Serna		
Baruj Benacerraf	médico	Venezuela
Gabriela Mistral		Chile
Luis Federico Leloir	científico	

5.40 Información, por favor Trabaja con un compañero para completar la información. Uno debe mirar el gráfico en esta página y el otro debe mirar el gráfico en la página 183. Atención al uso de **ser** y **estar**.

Nombre	Profesión	Origen	Localización	Emoción
Carlota	pintora			alegre
Éric	arquitecto	Bogotá		
César			el café	
Paloma		Santiago		nerviosa
Samuel	escritor			ocupado
Camila		Montevideo	el teatro	

Capítulo 6

6.6 Unos monstruos Trabaja con un compañero. Uno debe mirar el dibujo aquí y el otro va a mirar el dibujo en la página 189. Túrnense para describir los monstruos y encontrar las cinco diferencias.

© Cengage Learning

6.25 Actividades de verano Los organizadores de los eventos de verano para una pequeña ciudad están intercambiando información sobre el equipo que necesitan y las actividades que tienen planeadas. Trabaja con un compañero para completar la información. Uno de ustedes debe ver la información en esta página y el otro debe ver la información en la página 203.

Evento	Lugar del evento	Equipo que tienen	Equipo/recursos que necesitan
1. Torneo de fútbol	la universidad		
2.		sacos de dormir	tiendas de campaña
3. Clases de natación		la piscina	
4.	el gimnasio de la preparatoria		raquetas
5. Torneo de voleibol			pelotas

6.41 **¿Qué hizo?** Dante es estudiante de secundaria pero no es muy aplicado *(dedicated)*. Con un compañero, túrnense para completar la información sobre lo que hizo *(what he did)* esta mañana. Uno de ustedes va a mirar la información en esta página y el otro va a mirar la página 219.

Modelo Estudiante 1: *¿Qué hizo a medianoche?*
        Estudiante 2: *Se acostó.*

12:00	acostarse
7:00	levantarse
7:30	
7:40	
8:00	cepillarse los dientes
8:55	
9:35	dormirse en clase
9:58	despertarse y correr a otra clase
10:10	
10:30	volver a clase
11:00	

Capítulo 7

7.6 **¿Cuánto cuesta?** Trabaja con un compañero. Uno de ustedes va a ver la información en esta página y el otro debe ver la página 227. Imagínense que están en dos supermercados diferentes en Chile. Llámense por teléfono para preguntar cuánto cuestan los productos de cada ilustración. Los precios que tu compañero necesita están abajo. Tomen notas y al final sumen *(add)* los totales. ¿Quién va a gastar más?

Tu compañero quiere comprar...

Tú quieres comprar...

1 kilo • 500 gramos • 500 gramos • 250 gramos • 3 kilos

Un ananás (piña) $1650
choclo (maíz), un kilo $1432
mantequilla ($522)
queso, un kilo $1725

plátanos, un kilo $439
uvas, un kilo, $811
crema, 200 gramos, $715
pan, $1150

7.24 **Comparemos** Trabaja con un compañero. Uno va a mirar el dibujo en esta página y el otro va a mirar el dibujo en la página 241. Túrnense para describir los dibujos y encontrar cinco diferencias.

© Cengage Learning

7.41 **La fiesta** Tu compañero y tú están planeando una cena para unos amigos, pero los invitados tienen algunas restricciones en su dieta. Uno de ustedes mira la información en esta página y el otro mira la información en la página 257. Compartan la información sobre sus dietas y luego decidan qué van a servir del menú abajo.

> **aperitivo:** queso, totopos con salsa
>
> **primer plato:** ensalada con vinagreta, sopa de fideos *(noodles)*
>
> **segundo plato:** carne asada con papas fritas, fajitas con tortillas de maíz y verduras asadas
>
> **postre:** ensalada de frutas, pastel de chocolate
>
> **bebida:** té helado, limonada

Invitado	Restricción
Angélica	Es vegetariana.
Lucas	
Mateo	No puede consumir cafeína.
Regina	
Javier	Es intolerante a la lactosa.
Gisa	

Capítulo 8

8.6 **Compañeros de casa** Javier, Marcos y Emanuel decidieron vivir juntos y quieren organizarse para hacer los quehaceres de la casa que les gustan. Trabaja con un compañero para completar la tabla. Uno de ustedes va a ver la información en esta página, y el otro debe ver la información en la página 263. Primero completen el gráfico y después decidan quién va a hacer cada quehacer. Cada persona debe tener dos obligaciones.

Quehacer	Javier	Marcos	Emanuel	¿Quién va a hacerlo?
Lavar los platos	Le gusta.		No le gusta.	
Limpiar los baños		No le gusta.		
Trapear la cocina			No le gusta.	
Pasar la aspiradora	Le gusta.	No le gusta.	No le gusta.	
Cortar el césped	No le gusta.			
Regar las plantas		Le gusta.		

8.25 **Las actividades favoritas** Irma y Mario tienen que cuidar a varios niños todo el sábado. Irma quiere ir de excursión con la mitad de los niños, pero Mario quiere cuidarlos desde su casa porque tiene que trabajar. Trabaja con un compañero para saber qué actividades le gustan a los niños y después decidir cuáles son los niños que van a ir con Irma y quiénes se van a quedar con Mario. Un compañero debe mirar la tabla en la página 277.

Modelo *¿Cuál es la actividad favorita de Manuela?*
¿A quién le gusta volar cometas?

Niño	Actividad favorita	¿Con quién debe pasar el sábado?
Manuela	volar cometas	
	ir de paseo	
Nadia	nadar	
Alejandro	navegar por Internet	
	dibujar	
	trepar árboles	
Humberto	jugar juegos de mesa	

8.41 **Regalos** Tu compañero necesita comprar regalos para el cumpleaños de los hijos gemelos *(twins)* de un amigo (un niño y una niña). Encontró buenos regalos en un sitio web, pero no dan los precios. Tu compañero llama y pregunta cuánto cuestan los juguetes para decidir qué les va a comprar. Mira la lista de precios y contesta sus preguntas.

Modelo *¿Cuánto cuesta el muñeco azul?*
Cuesta $32.

Capítulo 9

9.5 **Las tradiciones** Hay muchas tradiciones interesantes con las que las personas reciben el año nuevo. Trabaja con un compañero. Uno de ustedes va a ver la ilustración en esta página y el otro va a describir la ilustración en página 301. Describan sus ilustraciones (sin ver la otra) para encontrar las seis diferencias.

9.22 Contradicciones Tu compañero y tú son testigos de un accidente, pero hay diferencias entre sus dos versiones. Uno de ustedes va a observar la ilustración en esta página y el otro va a observar la ilustración en la página 315. Encuentren las cinco diferencias.

9.39 El periodista Un periodista habla con un testigo sobre el accidente que vio. Trabaja con un compañero. Uno de ustedes es el periodista y hace las preguntas en la página 331, prestando atención al uso del pretérito o el imperfecto. El otro es el testigo y mira los dibujos en esta página para responder las preguntas.

Capítulo 10

10.6 ¿Vamos por tren o por avión? Tu compañero y tú están estudiando en Quito, Ecuador y quieren viajar este fin de semana. Deben decidir si van a viajar por avión a Cuenca, o por tren a Latacunga. Uno de ustedes puede ver la información para viajar por tren en esta página y el otro va a ver la información para viajar por avión en la página 337. Intercambien la información y tomen notas. Después van a ponerse de acuerdo *(agree)* en cómo van a viajar y a qué hora. Compartan toda la información antes de decidir.

TREN ECUADOR.COM

Ruta "Avenida de los volcanes", Quito–Machachi–El Boliche–Latacunga–Quito

Salida	Llegada	Regreso*	Precio por pasajero
4:20 AM	12:00 PM	3:30 PM	$38,00
8:00 AM	1:00 PM	3:30 PM	$40,00
10:00 AM	2:45 PM	5:45 PM	$44,95

*Regreso el mismo día

10.24 **¿Qué hotel elegir?** Tu compañero y tú están planeando unas vacaciones en Costa Rica y hablan por teléfono para decidir qué hotel elegir. Hay solamente dos hoteles que tienen habitaciones disponibles. Uno de ustedes va a mirar la información en esta página y el otro debe mirar la página 351. Pregúntense sobre los servicios y decidan al final en qué hotel van a quedarse.

Hotel Bellavista Monteverde

Descripción: 40 habitaciones, localizado en el centro de Monteverde, cerca de bancos y restaurantes.

Servicios: baño privado, televisor, Internet inalámbrico, cafetería abierta de 6:00 AM a 10:00 PM.

Precio: 115.000 colones (habitación doble/triple).

10.42 **En la agencia de viajes** Trabaja con un compañero. Uno de ustedes es el agente de viajes y mira la información en la página 367. El otro es el cliente y mira la información en esta página. El cliente llama al agente de viajes para comprar un boleto. El agente de viajes debe intentar encontrar el mejor boleto para el cliente y conseguir su información (nombre, teléfono, etcétera) y su tarjeta de crédito.

El cliente

Necesitas viajar a Santiago, Chile para una reunión el viernes por la mañana.

- Quieres viajar el jueves.
- Prefieres viajar por la tarde.
- No quieres tener escalas.
- Te gusta sentarte al lado de la ventanilla.
- No quieres pagar más de $750.

Capítulo 11

11.5 **Diferencias** Trabaja con un compañero para encontrar las ocho diferencias. Uno de ustedes va a mirar la ilustración en esta página y el otro va a mirar el dibujo en la página 375. Túrnense para describir la escena y encontrar las diferencias.

11.23 Una exhibición de arte Un museo local quiere montar una exhibición con obras de diferentes artistas hispanos, pero solo tiene el presupuesto *(budget)* para tres artistas diferentes. Tu compañero y tú deben compartir la información sobre los artistas y después decidir qué artistas presentar. Estén preparados para explicar por qué.

Artista	Medio	País	Año	Nombre del cuadro y estilo
1. Oswaldo Guayasamín		Ecuador		*El Presidente,* cubista
2. Mario Carreño			1981	*Mascarón de Proa,* surrealista
3. Joan Miró	pintura, escultura			
4. Marisol Escobar	escultura		2006	*El Padre Damian,* ecléctico
5. Diego Rivera		México	1928	
6. Roberto Matta	pintura	Chile		

11.39 Un pedido Trabaja con un compañero. Uno de ustedes es el vendedor y el otro es el cliente. El cliente necesita ropa para un viaje a la playa. Debe ver la información del catálogo en la página 405 y llamar para hacer un pedido. Necesita comprar tres prendas. El vendedor necesita ver esta página para contestar las preguntas del cliente y conseguir su información (nombre, teléfono, etcétera) y su tarjeta de crédito.

Modelo   Estudiante 1: *Buenas tardes.*
Estudiante 2: *Buenas tardes. Necesito una camiseta de algodón azul en talla extra grande.*
Estudiante 1: *Lo siento. No la tenemos en talla extra grande.*
Estudiante 2: *¿Qué colores tienen en talla extra grande?*

INFORMACIÓN DEL INVENTARIO:

C1050 Camiseta de algodón
Colores: azul (P, M, G), amarillo (P, M, G),
negro (agotado *sold out*), beige (M, G, XG)
Precio: 25 € (Rebajado a 20 €)

C4325 Camisa con estampado hawaiano
Colores: azul (agotado), verde
(M, G, XG), rojo (P, XG)
Precio: 35 €

B2219 Blusa de lunares
Colores: blanco/negro (P, G, XG); negro/rosado
(P, M, XG), rojo/blanco (P, M, G, XG)
Precio: 42 €

P6750 Pantalones cortos a rayas
Colores: blanco/azul (P, M, G), blanco/verde
(P, M, G, XG), gris/negro (agotado), café/beige
(M, G)
Precio: 55 €

P7382 Pantalones cortos a cuadros
Colores: azul/verde (P, M, G, XG), negro/rojo
(P, G, XG), rosado/gris (P, M)
Precio: 48 €

F9124 Falda con estampado de flores
Colores: blanco/rosado (P, G, XG), azul
marino/rojo (P, M, XG), anaranjado/amarillo
(P, M, G, XG)
Tallas: P, M, G, XG
Precio: 57 €

S5320 Sandalias de cuero
Colores: café (35, 37, 39, 41, 43), negro
(36, 38, 40, 42)
Precio: 70 €

Capítulo 12

12.5 **Las descripciones** Trabaja con un compañero.
Uno de ustedes (Estudiante 1) va a describirle el dibujo en la página 411 a su compañero (Estudiante 2) quien debe dibujar lo que escucha sin ver la ilustración. Al terminar comparen el original y el nuevo dibujo. Después el Estudiante 2 debe describir el dibujo en esta página, y el Estudiante 1 va a dibujarlo.

12.25 **Donaciones** Imagina que un compañero y tú trabajan para el *World Wildlife Fund*.
Uno de ustedes va a trabajar con la tabla en esta página, y el otro va a completar la tabla en la página 425. Compartan la información para completarla, y después decidan para qué animal deben hacer la siguiente campaña para recibir más donaciones.

ESPECIE	DONACIONES	PAÍS/ REGIÓN
1. Pingüino imperial		
2. El orangután		Indonesia
3. El jaguar		Latinoamérica
4. El oso frontino	$129.467,00	
5. El cóndor andino	$871.034,00	
6. El oso polar	$1.209.654,00	El ártico

12.41 **La granja** Mira uno de los dibujos y tu compañero va a mirar el otro en la página 441.
Túrnense para describir las granjas y encontrar las cinco diferencias.

13.6 Una relación La siguiente es una historia ilustrada de cómo evolucionó la relación entre Mercedes y Juan Sebastián. Trabaja con un compañero y túrnense para describir sus dibujos (numerados del 1 al 8) y completar la historia. Uno de ustedes va a describir las imágenes en esta página, y el otro las de la página 449.

13.24 En familia Trabaja con un compañero para descubrir las cinco diferencias. Uno de ustedes mira este dibujo y el otro mira el dibujo en la página 463. Túrnense para describirlos y encontrar las cinco diferencias.

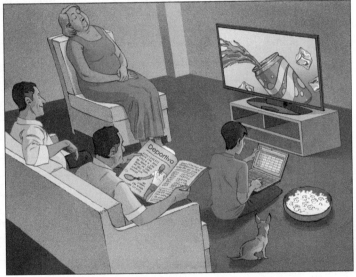

13.41 ¿Cuál es la pregunta? Trabaja con un compañero. Uno de ustedes debe ver las preguntas en esta página, y el otro debe verlas en la página 479. Es una competencia y el ganador *(winner)* es quien tenga más puntos. Obtienes puntos cuando adivinas la pregunta <u>exacta</u> que tiene tu compañero. Para ayudarte, tu compañero te va a decir la respuesta a la pregunta. Tienes tres oportunidades para adivinar cada pregunta.

Modelo ¿Qué es extrañar?
      Estudiante 1: *Es cuando no estás con una persona y estás triste. Piensas mucho en la*
            persona.
      Estudiante 2: *¿Qué es extrañar?*

Puntos	Preguntas
10	¿Qué es el noviazgo?
20	¿Qué hay en una recepción?
30	¿Qué es la unión libre?
40	¿Qué hacemos en la vejez?
50	¿Quién es la prometida?
100	¿Qué es comprometerse?

Capítulo 14

14.5 **Diferencias** Trabaja con un compañero. Uno mira el dibujo en esta página y el otro mira el dibujo en la página 485. Túrnense para describir sus dibujos y encontrar las cinco diferencias.

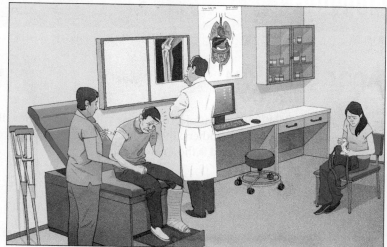

14.23 **El Mundial** Un amigo y tú quieren sorprender a todos sus amigos con fiestas para ver los juegos del Mundial de Fútbol. Tu compañero debe mirar la información en la página 499. Túrnense para completar las nacionalidades de sus amigos y el horario de los partidos. Al final encontrarán las cinco fechas cuando deberán tener las fiestas.

Preguntas posibles: *¿Cuál es la nacionalidad de Juan José?*
¿Cuándo es el juego número uno? / ¿Quiénes juegan el juego número uno?

Amigos:

NOMBRE	Mundo	Jazmín	Marco	Pío	Marcelo	Yolanda
PAÍS		colombiana			ecuatoriano	paraguaya

Horario de juegos:

Juego 1		10 de junio	Juego 5	España vs. EEUU	
Juego 2	Colombia vs. México		Juego 6		19 de junio
Juego 3	Argentina vs. Chile		Juego 7	Bélgica vs. Paraguay	
Juego 4		16 de junio	Juego 8		24 de junio

¿Cuáles son los cinco partidos que deben ver y cuándo?

14.39 **Un diagnóstico** Imagínate que eres médico y que vas a consultar con otro médico sobre algunos pacientes. Trabaja con un compañero para completar la información. Uno va a mirar la información en esta página y el otro va a mirar la información en la página 515.

Modelo Olivia Aragón   estornudos, ojos irritados
   Estudiante 1: *Olivia Aragón estornuda mucho y tiene ojos irritados.*
   Estudiante 2: *Debe tomar pastillas para las alergias y no salir al jardín en la primavera.*

Nombre	Síntomas	Remedio
Bruno Medina		tomar pastillas, reducir el sodio
Lourdes Montes	falta de energía, insomnio	
Saúl Reyes		tomar jarabe para el resfriado
Aranza Rivera	náusea, mareos	
Ileana Castro		tomar antibióticos, quedarse en cama
Esteban Peña	dolor de cabeza, mareos	

Acentuación

In Spanish, as in English, all words of two or more syllables have one syllable that is stressed more forcibly than the others. In Spanish, written accents are frequently used to show which syllable in a word is the stressed one.

Words without written accents

Words without written accents are pronounced according to the following rules:

A. Words that end in a vowel (**a, e, i, o, u**) or the consonants **n** or **s** are stressed on the next to last syllable.

tardes   capi**tal**es   **gran**de   es**tu**dia   **no**ches   **co**men

B. Words that end in a consonant other than **n** or **s** are stressed on the last syllable.

bus**car**   ac**triz**   espa**ñol**   liber**tad**   ani**mal**   come**dor**

Words with written accents

C. Words that do not follow the two preceding rules require a written accent to indicate where the stress is placed.

ca**fé**   sim**pá**tico   fran**cés**   na**ción**   José **Pé**rez

Words with a strong vowel (a, o, u) next to a weak vowel (e, i)

D. Diphthongs, the combination of a weak vowel (**i, u**) and a strong vowel (**e, o, a**), or two weak vowels, next to each other, form a single syllable. A written accent is required to separate diphthongs into two syllables. Note that the written accent is placed on the weak vowel.

seis	estu**dia**	inter**ior**	**ai**re	**au**to	**ciu**dad
re**ír**	**dí**a	**rí**o	ma**íz**	ba**úl**	veinti**ún**

Monosyllable words

E. Words with only one syllable never have a written accent unless there is a need to differentiate it from another word spelled exactly the same. The following are some of the most common words in this category.

Unaccented	Accented	Unaccented	Accented
como (like, as)	cómo (how)	que (that)	qué (what)
de (of)	dé (give)	si (if)	sí (yes)
el (the)	él (he)	te (you D.O., to you)	té (tea)
mas (but)	más (more)	tu (your)	tú (you informal)
mi (my)	mí (me)		

F. Keep in mind that in Spanish, the written accents are an extremely important part of spelling since they not only change the pronunciation of a word, but may change its meaning and/or its tense.

publico (I publish)   **público** (public)   **publicó** (he/she/you published)

Los verbos regulares

Simple tenses

	Present Indicative	Imperfect	Preterite	Future	Conditional	Present Subjunctive	Past Subjunctive	Commands
hablar (to speak)	hablo	hablaba	hablé	hablaré	hablaría	hable	hablara	
	hablas	hablabas	hablaste	hablarás	hablarías	hables	hablaras	habla (no hables)
	habla	hablaba	habló	hablará	hablaría	hable	hablara	hable
	hablamos	hablábamos	hablamos	hablaremos	hablaríamos	hablemos	habláramos	hablemos
	habláis	hablabais	hablasteis	hablaréis	hablaríais	habléis	hablarais	hablad (no habléis)
	hablan	hablaban	hablaron	hablarán	hablarían	hablen	hablaran	hablen
aprender (to learn)	aprendo	aprendía	aprendí	aprenderé	aprendería	aprenda	aprendiera	
	aprendes	aprendías	aprendiste	aprenderás	aprenderías	aprendas	aprendieras	aprende (no aprendas)
	aprende	aprendía	aprendió	aprenderá	aprendería	aprenda	aprendiera	aprenda
	aprendemos	aprendíamos	aprendimos	aprenderemos	aprenderíamos	aprendamos	aprendiéramos	aprendamos
	aprendéis	aprendíais	aprendisteis	aprenderéis	aprenderíais	aprendáis	aprendierais	aprended (no aprendáis)
	aprenden	aprendían	aprendieron	aprenderán	aprenderían	aprendan	aprendieran	aprendan
vivir (to live)	vivo	vivía	viví	viviré	viviría	viva	viviera	
	vives	vivías	viviste	vivirás	vivirías	vivas	vivieras	vive (no vivas)
	vive	vivía	vivió	vivirá	viviría	viva	viviera	viva
	vivimos	vivíamos	vivimos	viviremos	viviríamos	vivamos	viviéramos	vivamos
	vivís	vivíais	vivisteis	viviréis	viviríais	viváis	vivierais	vivid (no viváis)
	viven	vivían	vivieron	vivirán	vivirían	vivan	vivieran	vivan

Compound tenses

Present progressive

estoy	estamos		
estás	estáis	hablando	aprendiendo	viviendo
está	están		

Present perfect indicative

he	hemos		
has	habéis	hablado	aprendido	vivido
ha	han		

Past perfect indicative

había	habíamos		
habías	habíais	hablado	aprendido	vivido
había	habían		

Los verbos con cambios en la raíz

Infinitive / Present Participle / Past Participle	Present Indicative	Imperfect	Preterite	Future	Conditional	Present Subjunctive	Past Subjunctive	Commands
pensar *to think* **e → ie** pensando pensado	**pienso** **piensas** **piensa** pensamos pensáis **piensan**	pensaba pensabas pensaba pensábamos pensabais pensaban	pensé pensaste pensó pensamos pensasteis pensaron	pensaré pensarás pensará pensaremos pensaréis pensarán	pensaría pensarías pensaría pensaríamos pensaríais pensarían	**piense** **pienses** **piense** pensemos penséis **piensen**	pensara pensaras pensara pensáramos pensarais pensaran	**piensa (no pienses)** **piense** pensemos pensad (no penséis) **piensen**
acostarse *to go to bed* **o → ue** acostándose acostado	me **acuesto** te **acuestas** se **acuesta** nos acostamos os acostáis se **acuestan**	me acostaba te acostabas se acostaba nos acostábamos os acostabais se acostaban	me acosté te acostaste se acostó nos acostamos os acostasteis se acostaron	me acostaré te acostarás se acostará nos acostaremos os acostaréis se acostarán	me acostaría te acostarías se acostaría nos acostaríamos os acostaríais se acostarían	me **acueste** te **acuestes** se **acueste** nos acostemos os acostéis se **acuesten**	me acostara te acostaras se acostara nos acostáramos os acostarais se acostaran	acuéstate (no te acuestes) acuéstese acostémonos acostaos (no os acostéis) acuéstense
sentir *to feel* **e → ie, i** sintiendo sentido	**siento** **sientes** **siente** sentimos sentís **sienten**	sentía sentías sentía sentíamos sentíais sentían	sentí sentiste **sintió** sentimos sentisteis **sintieron**	sentiré sentirás sentirá sentiremos sentiréis sentirán	sentiría sentirías sentiría sentiríamos sentiríais sentirían	**sienta** **sientas** **sienta** sintamos sintáis **sientan**	sintiera sintieras sintiera sintiéramos sintierais sintieran	siente (no sientas) sienta sintamos (no sintáis) sentid sientan
pedir *to ask for* **e → i, i** pidiendo pedido	**pido** **pides** **pide** pedimos pedís **piden**	pedía pedías pedía pedíamos pedíais pedían	pedí pediste **pidió** pedimos pedisteis **pidieron**	pediré pedirás pedirá pediremos pediréis pedirán	pediría pedirías pediría pediríamos pediríais pedirían	**pida** **pidas** **pida** pidamos pidáis **pidan**	pidiera pidieras pidiera pidiéramos pidierais pidieran	pide (no pidas) pida pidamos pedid (no pidáis) pidan
dormir *to sleep* **o → ue, u** durmiendo dormido	**duermo** **duermes** **duerme** dormimos dormís **duermen**	dormía dormías dormía dormíamos dormíais dormían	dormí dormiste **durmió** dormimos dormisteis **durmieron**	dormiré dormirás dormirá dormiremos dormiréis dormirán	dormiría dormirías dormiría dormiríamos dormiríais dormirían	**duerma** **duermas** **duerma** durmamos durmáis **duerman**	durmiera durmieras durmiera durmiéramos durmierais durmieran	duerme (no duermas) duerma durmamos dormid (no durmáis) duerman

Los verbos con cambios de ortografía

Infinitive / Present Participle / Past Participle	Present Indicative	Imperfect	Preterite	Future	Conditional	Present Subjunctive	Past Subjunctive	Commands
comenzar (e → ie) to begin; **z → c before e** comenzando comenzado	comienzo comienzas comienza comenzamos comenzáis comienzan	comenzaba comenzabas comenzaba comenzábamos comenzabais comenzaban	**comencé** comenzaste comenzó comenzamos comenzasteis comenzaron	comenzaré comenzarás comenzará comenzaremos comenzaréis comenzarán	comenzaría comenzarías comenzaría comenzaríamos comenzaríais comenzarían	**comience** **comiences** **comience** **comencemos** **comencéis** **comiencen**	comenzara comenzaras comenzara comenzáramos comenzarais comenzaran	comienza (**no comiences**) **comience** **comencemos** comenzad (**no comencéis**) **comiencen**
conocer to know; **c → zc before a, o** conociendo conocido	**conozco** conoces conoce conocemos conocéis conocen	conocía conocías conocía conocíamos conocíais conocían	conocí conociste conoció conocimos conocisteis conocieron	conoceré conocerás conocerá conoceremos conoceréis conocerán	conocería conocerías conocería conoceríamos conoceríais conocerían	**conozca** **conozcas** **conozca** **conozcamos** **conozcáis** **conozcan**	conociera conocieras conociera conociéramos conocierais conocieran	conoce (**no conozcas**) **conozca** **conozcamos** conoced (**no conozcáis**) **conozcan**
pagar to pay; **g → gu before e** pagando pagado	pago pagas paga pagamos pagáis pagan	pagaba pagabas pagaba pagábamos pagabais pagaban	**pagué** pagaste pagó pagamos pagasteis pagaron	pagaré pagarás pagará pagaremos pagaréis pagarán	pagaría pagarías pagaría pagaríamos pagaríais pagarían	**pague** **pagues** **pague** **paguemos** **paguéis** **paguen**	pagara pagaras pagara pagáramos pagarais pagaran	paga (**no pagues**) **pague** **paguemos** pagad (**no paguéis**) **paguen**
seguir (e → i, i) to follow; **gu → g before a, o** siguiendo seguido	**sigo** sigues sigue seguimos seguís siguen	seguía seguías seguía seguíamos seguíais seguían	seguí seguiste siguió seguimos seguisteis siguieron	seguiré seguirás seguirá seguiremos seguiréis seguirán	seguiría seguirías seguiría seguiríamos seguiríais seguirían	**siga** **sigas** **siga** **sigamos** **sigáis** **sigan**	siguiera siguieras siguiera siguiéramos siguierais siguieran	sigue (**no sigas**) **siga** **sigamos** seguid (**no sigáis**) **sigan**
tocar to play, to touch; **c → qu before e** tocando tocado	toco tocas toca tocamos tocáis tocan	tocaba tocabas tocaba tocábamos tocabais tocaban	**toqué** tocaste tocó tocamos tocasteis tocaron	tocaré tocarás tocará tocaremos tocaréis tocarán	tocaría tocarías tocaría tocaríamos tocaríais tocarían	**toque** **toques** **toque** **toquemos** **toquéis** **toquen**	tocara tocaras tocara tocáramos tocarais tocaran	toca (**no toques**) **toque** **toquemos** tocad (**no toquéis**) **toquen**

Appendix G

Los verbos irregulares

Infinitive / Present Participle / Past Participle	Present Indicative	Imperfect	Preterite	Future	Conditional	Present Subjunctive	Past Subjunctive	Commands
andar (to walk) andando andado	ando / andas / anda / andamos / andáis / andan	andaba / andabas / andaba / andábamos / andabais / andaban	anduve / anduviste / anduvo / anduvimos / anduvisteis / anduvieron	andaré / andarás / andará / andaremos / andaréis / andarán	andaría / andarías / andaría / andaríamos / andaríais / andarían	ande / andes / ande / andemos / andéis / anden	anduviera / anduvieras / anduviera / anduviéramos / anduvierais / anduvieran	anda (no andes) / ande / andemos / andad (no andéis) / anden
*dar (to give) dando dado	doy / das / da / damos / dais / dan	daba / dabas / daba / dábamos / dabais / daban	di / diste / dio / dimos / disteis / dieron	daré / darás / dará / daremos / daréis / darán	daría / darías / daría / daríamos / daríais / darían	dé / des / dé / demos / deis / den	diera / dieras / diera / diéramos / dierais / dieran	da (no des) / dé / demos / dad (no deis) / den
*decir (to say, tell) diciendo dicho	digo / dices / dice / decimos / decís / dicen	decía / decías / decía / decíamos / decíais / decían	dije / dijiste / dijo / dijimos / dijisteis / dijeron	diré / dirás / dirá / diremos / diréis / dirán	diría / dirías / diría / diríamos / diríais / dirían	diga / digas / diga / digamos / digáis / digan	dijera / dijeras / dijera / dijéramos / dijerais / dijeran	di (no digas) / diga / digamos / decid (no digáis) / digan
*estar (to be) estando estado	estoy / estás / está / estamos / estáis / están	estaba / estabas / estaba / estábamos / estabais / estaban	estuve / estuviste / estuvo / estuvimos / estuvisteis / estuvieron	estaré / estarás / estará / estaremos / estaréis / estarán	estaría / estarías / estaría / estaríamos / estaríais / estarían	esté / estés / esté / estemos / estéis / estén	estuviera / estuvieras / estuviera / estuviéramos / estuvierais / estuvieran	está (no estés) / esté / estemos / estad (no estéis) / estén
haber (to have) habiendo habido	he / has / ha [hay] / hemos / habéis / han	había / habías / había / habíamos / habíais / habían	hube / hubiste / hubo / hubimos / hubisteis / hubieron	habré / habrás / habrá / habremos / habréis / habrán	habría / habrías / habría / habríamos / habríais / habrían	haya / hayas / haya / hayamos / hayáis / hayan	hubiera / hubieras / hubiera / hubiéramos / hubierais / hubieran	he (no hayas) / haya / hayamos / habed (no hayáis) / hayan
*hacer (to make, to do) haciendo hecho	hago / haces / hace / hacemos / hacéis / hacen	hacía / hacías / hacía / hacíamos / hacíais / hacían	hice / hiciste / hizo / hicimos / hicisteis / hicieron	haré / harás / hará / haremos / haréis / harán	haría / harías / haría / haríamos / haríais / harían	haga / hagas / haga / hagamos / hagáis / hagan	hiciera / hicieras / hiciera / hiciéramos / hicierais / hicieran	haz (no hagas) / haga / hagamos / haced (no hagáis) / hagan

*Verbs with irregular yo forms in the present indicative

(continued)

Infinitive / Present Participle / Past Participle	Present Indicative	Imperfect	Preterite	Future	Conditional	Present Subjunctive	Past Subjunctive	Commands
ir / to go / yendo / ido	voy	iba	fui	iré	iría	vaya	fuera	
	vas	ibas	fuiste	irás	irías	vayas	fueras	ve (no vayas)
	va	iba	fue	irá	iría	vaya	fuera	vaya
	vamos	íbamos	fuimos	iremos	iríamos	vayamos	fuéramos	vamos (no vayamos)
	vais	ibais	fuisteis	iréis	iríais	vayáis	fuerais	id (no vayáis)
	van	iban	fueron	irán	irían	vayan	fueran	vayan
*oír / to hear / oyendo / oído	oigo	oía	oí	oiré	oiría	oiga	oyera	
	oyes	oías	oíste	oirás	oirías	oigas	oyeras	oye (no oigas)
	oye	oía	oyó	oirá	oiría	oiga	oyera	oiga
	oímos	oíamos	oímos	oiremos	oiríamos	oigamos	oyéramos	oigamos
	oís	oíais	oísteis	oiréis	oiríais	oigáis	oyerais	oíd (no oigáis)
	oyen	oían	oyeron	oirán	oirían	oigan	oyeran	oigan
poder (o → ue) / can, to be able / pudiendo / podido	puedo	podía	pude	podré	podría	pueda	pudiera	
	puedes	podías	pudiste	podrás	podrías	puedas	pudieras	puede (no puedas)
	puede	podía	pudo	podrá	podría	pueda	pudiera	pueda
	podemos	podíamos	pudimos	podremos	podríamos	podamos	pudiéramos	podamos
	podéis	podíais	pudisteis	podréis	podríais	podáis	pudierais	poded (no podáis)
	pueden	podían	pudieron	podrán	podrían	puedan	pudieran	puedan
*poner / to place, to put / poniendo / puesto	pongo	ponía	puse	pondré	pondría	ponga	pusiera	
	pones	ponías	pusiste	pondrás	pondrías	pongas	pusieras	pon (no pongas)
	pone	ponía	puso	pondrá	pondría	ponga	pusiera	ponga
	ponemos	poníamos	pusimos	pondremos	pondríamos	pongamos	pusiéramos	pongamos
	ponéis	poníais	pusisteis	pondréis	pondríais	pongáis	pusierais	poned (no pongáis)
	ponen	ponían	pusieron	pondrán	pondrían	pongan	pusieran	pongan
querer (e → ie) / to like / queriendo / querido	quiero	quería	quise	querré	querría	quiera	quisiera	
	quieres	querías	quisiste	querrás	querrías	quieras	quisieras	quiere (no quieras)
	quiere	quería	quiso	querrá	querría	quiera	quisiera	quiera
	queremos	queríamos	quisimos	querremos	querríamos	queramos	quisiéramos	queramos
	queréis	queríais	quisisteis	querréis	querríais	queráis	quisierais	quered (no queráis)
	quieren	querían	quisieron	querrán	querrían	quieran	quisieran	quieran
*saber / to know / sabiendo / sabido	sé	sabía	supe	sabré	sabría	sepa	supiera	
	sabes	sabías	supiste	sabrás	sabrías	sepas	supieras	sabe (no sepas)
	sabe	sabía	supo	sabrá	sabría	sepa	supiera	sepa
	sabemos	sabíamos	supimos	sabremos	sabríamos	sepamos	supiéramos	sepamos
	sabéis	sabíais	supisteis	sabréis	sabríais	sepáis	supierais	sabed (no sepáis)
	saben	sabían	supieron	sabrán	sabrían	sepan	supieran	sepan

*Verbs with irregular yo forms in the present indicative

Infinitive Present Participle Past Participle	Present Indicative	Imperfect	Preterite	Future	Conditional	Present Subjunctive	Past Subjunctive	Commands
*salir	salgo	salía	salí	saldré	saldría	salga	saliera	
to go out	sales	salías	saliste	saldrás	saldrías	salgas	salieras	sal (no salgas)
saliendo	sale	salía	salió	saldrá	saldría	salga	saliera	salga
salido	salimos	salíamos	salimos	saldremos	saldríamos	salgamos	saliéramos	salgamos
	salís	salíais	salisteis	saldréis	saldríais	salgáis	salierais	salid (no salgáis)
	salen	salían	salieron	saldrán	saldrían	salgan	salieran	salgan
ser	soy	era	fui	seré	sería	sea	fuera	
to be	eres	eras	fuiste	serás	serías	seas	fueras	sé (no seas)
siendo	es	era	fue	será	sería	sea	fuera	sea
sido	somos	éramos	fuimos	seremos	seríamos	seamos	fuéramos	seamos
	sois	erais	fuisteis	seréis	seríais	seáis	fuerais	sed (no seáis)
	son	eran	fueron	serán	serían	sean	fueran	sean
*tener	tengo	tenía	tuve	tendré	tendría	tenga	tuviera	
(e → ie)	tienes	tenías	tuviste	tendrás	tendrías	tengas	tuvieras	ten (no tengas)
to have	tiene	tenía	tuvo	tendrá	tendría	tenga	tuviera	tenga
teniendo	tenemos	teníamos	tuvimos	tendremos	tendríamos	tengamos	tuviéramos	tengamos
tenido	tenéis	teníais	tuvisteis	tendréis	tendríais	tengáis	tuvierais	tened (no tengáis)
	tienen	tenían	tuvieron	tendrán	tendrían	tengan	tuvieran	tengan
*traer	traigo	traía	traje	traeré	traería	traiga	trajera	
to bring	traes	traías	trajiste	traerás	traerías	traigas	trajeras	trae (no traigas)
trayendo	trae	traía	trajo	traerá	traería	traiga	trajera	traiga
traído	traemos	traíamos	trajimos	traeremos	traeríamos	traigamos	trajéramos	traigamos
	traéis	traíais	trajisteis	traeréis	traeríais	traigáis	trajerais	traed (no traigáis)
	traen	traían	trajeron	traerán	traerían	traigan	trajeran	traigan
*venir	vengo	venía	vine	vendré	vendría	venga	viniera	
(e → ie, i)	vienes	venías	viniste	vendrás	vendrías	vengas	vinieras	ven (no vengas)
to come	viene	venía	vino	vendrá	vendría	venga	viniera	venga
viniendo	venimos	veníamos	vinimos	vendremos	vendríamos	vengamos	viniéramos	vengamos
venido	venís	veníais	vinisteis	vendréis	vendríais	vengáis	vinierais	venid (no vengáis)
	vienen	venían	vinieron	vendrán	vendrían	vengan	vinieran	vengan
ver	veo	veía	vi	veré	vería	vea	viera	
to see	ves	veías	viste	verás	verías	veas	vieras	ve (no veas)
viendo	ve	veía	vio	verá	vería	vea	viera	vea
visto	vemos	veíamos	vimos	veremos	veríamos	veamos	viéramos	veamos
	veis	veíais	visteis	veréis	veríais	veáis	vierais	ved (no veáis)
	ven	veían	vieron	verán	verían	vean	vieran	vean

*Verbs with irregular yo forms in the present indicative

Supplemental Structures

1. Perfect tenses

In **Capítulo 12** you learned that the perfect tense is formed by combining the present indicative of the verb **haber** with the past participle. Similarly, you learned in **Capítulo 14** that the past perfect is formed by combining the imperfect of the verb **haber** with the past participle. The future perfect and conditional perfect tenses are formed by combining the imperfect, future, and conditional of **haber** with the past participle.

Future perfect		Conditional perfect	
habré		habría	
habrás		habrías	
habrá	+ past	habría	+ past
habremos	participle	habríamos	participle
habréis		habríais	
habrán		habrían	

In general, the use of these perfect tenses parallels their use in English.

Para el año 2015, **habremos terminado** nuestros estudios aquí.
Yo lo **habría hecho** por ti.

By the year 2015, we will have finished our studies here.
I would have done it for you.

The present perfect subjunctive and past perfect subjunctive are likewise formed by combining the present subjunctive and past subjunctive of **haber** with the past participle.

Present perfect subjunctive		Past perfect subjunctive	
haya		hubiera	
hayas		hubieras	
haya	+ past	hubiera	+ past
hayamos	participle	hubiéramos	participle
hayáis		hubierais	
hayan		hubieran	

These tenses are used whenever the independent clause in a sentence requires the subjunctive and the verb in the dependent clause represents an action completed prior to the time indicated by the verb in the independent clause. If the time of the verb in the independent clause is present or future, the present perfect subjunctive is used; if the time is past or conditional, the past perfect subjunctive is used.

Dudo que lo **hayan leído.**
Si **hubieras llamado,** no tendríamos este problema ahora.

I doubt that they have read it.
If you had called, we would not have this problem now.

2. Past progressive tense

In **Capítulo 5** you learned that the present progressive tense is formed with the present indicative of **estar** and a present participle. The past progressive tense is formed with the imperfect of **estar** and a present participle.

The past progressive tense is used to express or describe an action that was in progress at a particular moment in the past.

Past progressive tense	
estaba	
estabas	
estaba	+ present
estábamos	participle
estabais	
estaban	

Estábamos comiendo cuando llamaste.	*We were eating when you called.*
¿Quién **estaba hablando** por teléfono?	*Who was talking on the phone?*

Another past progressive tense can also be formed with the preterite of **estar** and the present participle. However, its use is of much lower frequency in Spanish.

3. Stressed possessive adjectives and pronouns

In **Capítulo 2** you learned to express possession using **de** or the possessive adjectives **mi(s), tu(s), su(s), nuestro(a, os, as), vuestro(a, os, as).** Possession may also be expressed using the stressed possessive adjectives equivalent to the English *of mine, of yours, of ours, of theirs.*

Stressed possessive adjectives and pronouns					
mío **míos**	**mía** **mías**	*my, (of) mine*	**nuestro** **nuestros**	**nuestra** **nuestras**	*our, (of) ours*
tuyo **tuyos**	**tuya** **tuyas**	*your, (of) yours*	**vuestro** **vuestros**	**vuestra** **vuestras**	*your, (of) yours*
suyo **suyos**	**suya** **suyas**	*its, his, (of) his hers, (of) hers your, (of) yours*	**suyo** **suyos**	**suya** **suyas**	*their, (of) theirs your, (of) yours*

A. As adjectives, the stressed possessives must agree in number and gender with the thing possessed.

Una amiga **mía** viene a visitarme hoy.	*A friend of mine is coming to visit me today.*
¿Qué hay en las maletas **suyas**, señor?	*What do you have in those suitcases of yours, sir?*
El coche **nuestro** nunca funciona.	*Our car never works.*

Note that stressed possessive adjectives *always* follow the noun they modify. Also note that the noun must be preceded by an article.

B. Stressed possessive adjectives can be used as possessive pronouns by eliminating the noun.

¿Dónde está **la suya,** señor?   *Where is yours, sir?*
El nuestro nunca funciona.   *Ours never works.*

Note that both the article and possessive adjective must agree in number and gender with the noun that has been eliminated.

C. A stressed possessive pronoun may be used without the article after the verb **ser.**

Esta maleta no es **mía,** señor.   *This suitcase is not mine, sir.*
¿Es **suya,** señora?   *Is it yours, ma'am?*

4. Present subjunctive of stem-changing verbs

A. Stem-changing -**ar** and -**er** verbs follow the same stem changes in the present subjunctive as in the present indicative. Note that the stems of the **nosotros** and **vosotros** forms do not change.

contar (ue)	
c**ue**nte	contemos
c**ue**ntes	contéis
c**ue**nte	c**ue**nten

perder (ie)	
p**ie**rda	perdamos
p**ie**rdas	perdáis
p**ie**rda	p**ie**rdan

B. Stem-changing -**ir** verbs follow the same pattern in the present subjunctive, except for the **nosotros** and **vosotros** forms. These change **e → i** or **o → u.**

morir (ue)	
m**ue**ra	m**u**ramos
m**ue**ras	m**u**ráis
m**ue**ra	m**ue**ran

preferir (ie)	
pref**ie**ra	pref**i**ramos
pref**ie**ras	pref**i**ráis
pref**ie**ra	pref**ie**ran

pedir (i)	
p**i**da	p**i**damos
p**i**das	p**i**dáis
p**i**da	p**i**dan

5. Present subjunctive of verbs with spelling changes

As in the preterite, verbs that end in -**car, -gar,** and -**zar** undergo a spelling change in the present subjunctive in order to maintain the consonant sound of the infinitive.

A. -**car:**   **c** changes to **qu** in front of **e**

  buscar: bus**que,** bus**ques,** bus**que**...

B. -**zar:**   **z** changes to **c** in front of **e**

  almorzar: almuer**ce,** almuer**ces,** almuer**ce**...

C. -**gar:**   **g** changes to **gu** in front of **e**

  jugar: jue**gue,** jue**gues,** jue**gue**...

D. -**ger:**   **g** changes to **j** in front of **a**

  proteger: prote**ja,** prote**jas,** prote**ja**...

6. Irregular verbs in the present subjunctive

The following verbs are irregular in the present subjunctive:

dar	dé, des, dé, demos, deis, den
haber	haya, hayas, haya, hayamos, hayáis, hayan
ir	vaya, vayas, vaya, vayamos, vayáis, vayan
saber	sepa, sepas, sepa, sepamos, sepáis, sepan
ser	sea, seas, sea, seamos, seáis, sean

7. Past subjunctive and Conditional *Si* clauses

The past subjunctive of *all* verbs is formed by removing the **-ron** ending from the **ustedes** form of the preterite and adding the past subjunctive verb endings: **-ra, -ras, -ra, -ramos, -rais, -ran.** Thus, any irregularities in the **ustedes** form of the preterite will be reflected in all forms of the past subjunctive. Note that the **nosotros** form requires a written accent.

comprar		tener		ser	
compra~~ron~~		tuvie~~ron~~		fue~~ron~~	
comprara	compráramos	tuviera	tuviéramos	fuera	fuéramos
compraras	comprarais	tuvieras	tuvierais	fueras	fuerais
comprara	compraran	tuviera	tuvieran	fuera	fueran

An alternate form of the past subjunctive uses the verb endings **-se, -ses, -se, -semos, -seis, -sen.** This form is used primarily in Spain and in literary writing.

A. The past subjunctive has the same uses as the present subjunctive, except that it generally applies to past events or actions.

Insistieron en que **fuéramos.**	*They insisted that we go.*
Era imposible que lo **terminaran** a tiempo.	*It was impossible for them to finish it on time.*

B. In Spanish, as in English, conditional sentences express hypothetical conditions usually with an *if*-clause: *I would go if I had the money.* Since the actions are hypothetical and one does not know if they will actually occur, the past subjunctive is used in the *if*-clause.

Iría a Perú si **tuviera** el dinero.	*I would go to Peru if I had the money.*
Si **fuera** necesario, pediría un préstamo.	*If it were necessary, I would ask for a loan.*

C. Conditional sentences in the present use either the present indicative or the future tense. The present subjunctive is never used in *if*-clauses.

Si me **invitas,** iré contigo.	*If you invite me, I'll go with you.*

Grammar Guide

For more detailed explanations of these grammar points, consult the Index on pages 619–622 to find the places where these concepts are presented.

ACTIVE VOICE (La voz activa) A sentence written in the active voice identifies a subject that performs the action of the verb.

Juan	cantó	la canción.
Juan	***sang***	***the song.***
subject	verb	direct object

In the sentence above Juan is the performer of the verb **cantar**.

(*See also* **Passive Voice.**)

ADJECTIVES (Los adjetivos) are words that modify or describe **nouns** or **pronouns** and agree in **number** and generally in **gender** with the nouns they modify.

Las casas **azules** son **bonitas**.
*The **blue** houses are **pretty.***

Esas mujeres **mexicanas** son mis **nuevas** amigas.
*Those **Mexican** women are my **new** friends.*

- **Demonstrative adjectives** (Los adjetivos demostrativos) point out persons, places, or things relative to the position of the speaker. They always agree in **number** and **gender** with the **noun** they modify. The forms are: **este, esta, estos, estas / ese, esa, esos, esas / aquel, aquella, aquellos, aquellas.** There are also neuter forms that refer to generic ideas or things, and hence have no gender: **esto, eso, aquello.**

Este libro es fácil.	***This** book is easy.*
Esos libros son difíciles.	***Those** books are hard.*
Aquellos libros son pesados.	***Those** books **(over there)** are boring.*
Eso es impotante.	***That** is important.*

Demonstratives may also function as **pronouns**, replacing the **noun** but still agreeing with it in **number** and **gender:**

Me gustan esas blusas verdes.	*I like those green blouses.*
¿Cuáles, **estas**?	*Which ones, **these?***
No. Me gustan **esas**.	*No. I like **those.***

- **Stressed possessive adjectives** (Los adjetivos posesivos tónicos) are used for emphasis and follow the noun that they modifiy. These adjectives may also function as pronouns and always agree in **number** and in **gender**. The forms are: **mío, tuyo, suyo, nuestro, vuestro, suyo.** Unless they are directly preceded by the verb **ser,** stressed possessives must be preceded by the **definite article.**

Ese perro pequeño es **mío**.	*That little dog is **mine.***
Dame el **tuyo**; el **nuestro** no funciona.	*Give me **yours; ours** doesn't work.*

- **Possessive adjectives** (Los adjetivos posesivos) demonstrate ownership and always precede the **noun** that they modify.

La señora Elman es **mi** profesora.	*Mrs. Elman is **my** professor.*
Debemos llevar **nuestros** libros a clase.	*We should take **our** books to class.*

ADVERBS (Los adverbios) are words that modify **verbs, adjectives,** or other adverbs and, unlike **adjectives,** do not have **gender** or **number.** Here are examples of different classes of adverbs:

Practicamos **diariamente**.	*We practice **daily.** (adverb of frequency)*
Ellos van a salir **pronto**.	*They will leave **soon.** (adverb of time)*
Jennifer está **afuera**.	*Jennifer is **outside.** (adverb of place)*
No quiero ir **tampoco**.	*I don't want to go **either.** (adverb of negation)*
Paco habla **demasiado**.	*Paco talks **too much.** (adverb of quantity)*
Esta clase es **extremadamente** difícil.	*This class is **extremely** difficult. (modifies adjective)*
Ella habla **muy** poco.	*She speaks **very** little. (modifies adverb)*

AGREEMENT (La concordancia) refers to the correspondence between parts of speech in terms of **number, gender,** and **person.** Subjects agree with their verbs; articles and adjectives agree with the nouns they modify, etc.

Toda**s** la**s** lengua**s** son interesante**s.**	*All languages are interesting.* (number)
Ella es bonit**a.**	*She is pretty.* (gender)
Nosotros somos de España.	*We are from Spain.* (person)

ARTICLES (Los artículos) precede nouns and indicate whether they are definite or indefinite persons, places, or things.

- **Definite articles (Los artículos definidos)** refer to particular members of a group and are the equivalent of *the* in English. The definite articles are: **el, la, los, las.**

El hombre guapo es mi padre.	*The handsome man is my father.*
Las mujeres de esta clase son inteligentes.	*The women in this class are intelligent.*

- **Indefinite articles (Los artículos indefinidos)** refer to any unspecified member(s) of a group and are the equivalent of *a(n)* and *some.* The indefinite articles are: **un, una, unos, unas.**

Un hombre vino a nuestra casa anoche.	*A man came to our house last night.*
Unas niñas jugaban en el parque.	*Some girls were playing in the park.*

CLAUSES (Las cláusulas) are subject and verb combinations; for a sentence to be complete it must have at least one main clause.

- **Main clauses** (Independent clauses) **(Las cláusulas principales)** communicate a complete idea or thought.

Mi hermana va al hospital.	*My sister goes to the hospital.*

- **Subordinate clauses** (Dependent clauses) **(Las cláusulas subordinadas)** depend upon a main clause for their meaning to be complete.

Mi hermana va al hospital	cuando está enferma.
My sister goes to the hospital	*when she is ill.*
main clause	**subordinate clause**

In the sentence above, *when she is ill* is not a complete idea without the information supplied by the main clause.

COMMANDS (Los mandatos) (*See* **Imperatives.**)

COMPARISONS (Las comparaciones) are statements that describe one person, place, or thing relative to another in terms of quantity, quality, or manner.

- **Comparisons of equality (Las formas comparativas de igualdad)** demonstrate an equal share of a quantity or degree of a particular characteristic. These statements use a form of **tan** or **tanto(a)(s)** and **como.**

Ella tiene **tanto** dinero **como** Elena.	*She has **as much** money **as** Elena.*
Fernando trabaja **tanto como** Felipe.	*Fernando works **as much as** Felipe.*
Jim baila **tan** bien **como** Anne.	*Jim dances **as** well **as** Anne.*

- **Comparisons of inequality (Las formas comparativas de desigualdad)** indicate a difference in quantity, quality, or manner between the compared subjects. These statements use **más/menos... que** or comparative **adjectives** such as **mejor/peor, mayor/menor.**

México tiene **más** playas **que** España.	*Mexico has **more** beaches **than** Spain.*
Tú hablas español **mejor que** yo.	*You speak Spanish **better than** I.*

(*See also* **Superlative statements.**)

CONJUGATIONS (Las conjugaciones) are the forms of the verb as they agree with a particular subject or person.

Yo bailo los sábados.	*I dance on Saturdays.* (1st-person singular)
Tú bailas los sábados.	*You dance on Saturdays.* (2nd-person singular)
Ella baila los sábados.	*She dances on Saturdays.* (3rd-person singular)
Nosotros bailamos los sábados.	*We dance on Saturdays.* (1st-person plural)
Vosotros bailáis los sábados.	*You dance on Saturdays.* (2nd-person plural)
Ellos bailan los sábados.	*They dance on Saturdays.* (3rd-person plural)

CONJUNCTIONS (Las conjunciones) are linking words that join two independent clauses together.

Fuimos al centro **y** mis amigos compraron muchas cosas.
*We went downtown, **and** my friends bought a lot of things.*

Yo quiero ir a la fiesta, **pero** tengo que estudiar.
*I want to go to the party, **but** I have to study.*

CONTRACTIONS (Las contracciones) in Spanish are limited to preposition/article combinations, such as **de + el = del** and **a + el = al,** or preposition/pronoun combinations such as **con + mí = conmigo** and **con + ti = contigo.**

DIRECT OBJECTS (Los objetos directos) in sentences are the direct recipients of the action of the verb. Direct objects answer the questions *What?* or *Whom?*

¿Qué hizo?
Ella hizo **la tarea.**
Y luego llamó **a su amiga.**

What did she do?
*She did her **homework.***
*And then called **her friend.***

(*See also* **Pronoun, Indirect Object, Personal *a*.**)

EXCLAMATORY WORDS (Las palabras exclamativas) communicate surprise or strong emotion. Like interrogative words, exclamatory words also carry accents.

¡Qué sorpresa!
¡Cómo canta Miguel!

***What** a surprise!*
***How well** Miguel sings!*

(*See also* **Interrogatives.**)

GERUNDS (Los gerundios) in Spanish refer to the present participle. In English gerunds are verbals (based on a verb and expressing an action or a state of being) that function as nouns. In most instances where the gerund is used in English, the infinitive is used in Spanish.

(El) **Ser** cortés no cuesta nada.
Mi pasatiempo favorito es **viajar.**
Después de **desayunar,** salió de la casa.

***Being** polite is not hard.*
*My favorite pasttime is **traveling.***
*After **eating** breakfast, he left the house.*

(*See also* **Present Participle.**)

IDIOMATIC EXPRESSIONS (Las frases idiomáticas) are phrases in Spanish that do not have a literal English equivalent.

Hace mucho frío.

It is very cold. (Literally, It makes a lot of cold.)

IMPERATIVES (Los imperativos) represent the mood used to express requests or commands. It is more direct than the **subjunctive** mood. Imperatives are commonly called commands and fall into two categories: affirmative and negative. Spanish speakers must also choose between using formal commands and informal commands based upon whether one is addressed as **usted** (formal) or **tú** (informal).

Habla conmigo.
No me hables.
Hable con la policía.
No hable con la policía.
Hablen con la policía.
No hablen con la policía
Hablad con la policía.
No habléis con la policía.

Talk to me. (informal, singular, affirmative)
Don't talk to me. (informal, singular, negative)
Talk to the police. (formal, singular, affirmative)
Don't talk to the police. (formal, singular, negative)
Talk to the police. (formal, plural, affirmative)
Don't talk to the police. (formal, plural, negative)
Talk to the police. (informal [Spain], plural, affirmative)
Don't talk to the police. (informal [Spain], plural, negative)

(*See also* **Mood.**)

IMPERFECT (El imperfecto) The imperfect tense is used to make statements about the past when the speaker wants to convey the idea of 1) habitual or repeated action, 2) two actions in progress simultaneously, or 3) an event that was in progress when another action interrupted. The imperfect tense is also used to emphasize the ongoing nature of the middle of the event, as opposed to its beginning or end. Age and clock time are always expressed using the imperfect.

Cuando María **era** joven, ella **cantaba** en el coro.
*When María **was** young, she **used to sing** in the choir.*

Aquel día **llovía** mucho y el cielo **estaba** oscuro.
*That day **it was raining** a lot and the sky **was dark**.*

Juan **dormía** cuando sonó el teléfono.
*Juan **was sleeping** when the phone rang.*

(*See also* **Preterite.**)

IMPERSONAL EXPRESSIONS (Las expresiones impersonales) are statements that contain the impersonal subjects of *it* or *one*.

Es necesario estudiar.   *It is necessary to study.*
Se necesita estudiar.   *One needs to study.*

(*See also* **Passive Voice.**)

INDEFINITE WORDS (Las palabras indefinidas) are **articles**, **adjectives**, **nouns** or **pronouns** that refer to unspecified members of a group.

Un hombre vino.   *A man came.* (indefinite article)
Alguien vino.   *Someone came.* (indefinite noun)
Algunas personas vinieron.   *Some people came.* (indefinite adjective)
Algunas vinieron.   *Some came.* (indefinite pronoun)

(*See also* **Articles.**)

INDICATIVE (El indicativo) The indicative is a mood, rather than a tense. The indicative is used to express ideas that are considered factual or certain and, therefore, not subject to speculation, doubt, or negation.

Josefina **es** española.   *Josefina **is** Spanish.*
(present indicative)
Ella **vivió** en Argentina.   *She lived in Argentina.*
(preterite indicative)

(*See also* **Mood.**)

INDIRECT OBJECTS (Los objetos indirectos) are the indirect recipients of an action in a sentence and answer the questions *To whom?* or *For whom?* In Spanish it is common to include an indirect object **pronoun** along with the indirect object.

Yo **le** di el libro **a Sofía**.   *I gave the book **to Sofía**.*
Sofía **les** guardó el libro **a sus padres**.   *Sofía kept the book **for her parents**.*

(*See also* **Direct Objects** *and* **Pronouns.**)

INFINITIVES (Los infinitivos) are verb forms that are uninflected or **not conjugated** according to a specific **person**. In English, infinitives are preceded by *to: to talk, to eat, to live.* Infinitives in Spanish end in **-ar (hablar)**, **-er (comer)**, and **-ir (vivir)**.

INTERROGATIVES (Las formas interrogativas) are used to pose questions and carry accent marks to distinguish them from other uses. Basic interrogative words include: **quién(es)**, **qué**, **cómo**, **cuánto(a)(s)**, **cuándo**, **por qué**, **dónde**, **cuál(es)**.

¿Qué quieres?   ***What** do you want?*
¿Cuándo llegó ella?   ***When** did she arrive?*
¿De **dónde** eres?   ***Where** are you from?*

(*See also* **Exclamatory Words.**)

MOOD (El modo) is like the word *mode*, meaning *manner* or *way*. It indicates the way in which the speaker views an action, or his/her attitude toward the action. Besides the **imperative** mood, which is simply giving commands, there are two moods in Spanish: the **subjunctive** and the **indicative**. Basically, the subjunctive mood communicates an attitude of uncertainty toward the action, while the indicative indicates that the action is certain or factual. Within each of these moods there are many **tenses**. Hence you have the present indicative and the present subjunctive, the present perfect indicative and the present perfect subjunctive, etc.

- **Indicative mood** (El indicativo) is used to talk about actions that are regarded as certain or as facts: things that happen all the time, have happened, or will happen. It is used in contrast to situations where the speaker is voicing an opinion, doubts, or desires.

Yo **quiero** ir a la fiesta.   *I **want** to go to the party.*
¿Quieres ir conmigo?   *Do **you want** to go with me?*

- **Subjunctive mood (El subjuntivo)** indicates a recommendation, a statement of uncertainty, or an expression of opinion or emotion.

Yo recomiendo que tú **vayas** a la fiesta.	*I recommend that **you go** to the party.*
Dudo que **vayas** a la fiesta.	*I doubt that **you'll go** to the party.*
No creo que **vayas** a la fiesta.	*I don't believe that **you'll go** to the party.*
Si **fueras** a la fiesta, te divertirías.	*If **you were to go** to the party, you would have a good time.*

- **Imperative mood (El imperativo)** is used to make a command or request.

¡**Ven** conmigo a la fiesta!	***Come** with me to the party!*

(*See also* **Mood, Indicative, Imperative,** *and* **Subjunctive.**)

NEGATION (La negación) takes place when a negative word, such as **no,** is placed before an affirmative sentence. In Spanish, double negatives are common.

Yolanda va a cantar esta noche.	*Yolanda will sing tonight.* (affirmative)
Yolanda **no** va a cantar esta noche.	*Yolanda will **not** sing tonight.* (negative)
Ramón quiere algo.	*Ramón wants something.* (affirmative)
Ramón **no** quiere **nada.**	*Ramón **doesn't** want **anything.*** (negative)

NOUNS (Los sustantivos) are persons, places, things, or ideas. Names of people, countries, and cities are proper nouns and are capitalized.

Alberto	*Albert* (person)
el pueblo	*town* (place)
el diccionario	*dictionary* (thing)

ORTHOGRAPHY (La ortografía) refers to the spelling of a word or anything related to spelling, such as accentuation.

PASSIVE VOICE (La voz pasiva), as compared to **active voice (la voz activa),** places emphasis on the action itself rather than the subject (the person or thing that is responsible for doing the action). The passive **se** is used when there is no apparent subject.

Luis vende los coches.	*Luis sells the cars.* (active voice)
Los coches **son vendidos por** Luis.	*The cars **are sold by** Luis.* (passive voice)
Se venden los coches.	*The cars **are sold.*** (passive voice)

(*See also* **Active Voice.**)

PAST PARTICIPLES (Los participios pasados) are verb forms used in compound tenses such as the **present perfect.** Regular past participles are formed by dropping the **-ar** or **-er/-ir** from the **infinitive** and adding **-ado** or **-ido.** Past participles are generally the equivalent of verb forms ending in *-ed* in English. They may also be used as **adjectives,** in which case they agree in **number** and **gender** with their nouns. Irregular past participles include: **escrito, roto, dicho, hecho, puesto, vuelto, muerto, cubierto.**

Marta ha **subido** la montaña.	*Marta has **climbed** the mountain.*
Hemos **hablado** mucho por teléfono.	*We have **talked** a lot on the phone.*
La novela **publicada** en 1995 es su mejor novela.	*The novel **published** in 1995 is her best novel.*

PERFECT TENSES (Los tiempos perfectos) communicate the idea that an action has taken place before now (present perfect) or before a moment in the past (past perfect). The perfect tenses are compound tenses consisting of the auxiliary verb **haber** plus the **past participle** of a second verb.

Yo **he comido.**	*I have eaten.* (present perfect indicative)
Antes de la fiesta, yo ya **había comido.**	*Before the party **I had already eaten.*** (past perfect indicative)
Yo espero que **hayas comido.**	*I hope that **you have eaten.*** (present perfect subjunctive)
Yo esperaba que **hubieras comido.**	*I hoped that **you had eaten.*** (past perfect subjunctive)

PERSON (La persona) refers to changes in the subject pronouns that indicate if one is speaking (first person), if one is spoken to (second person), or if one is spoken about (third person).

Yo hablo.	*I speak.* (1st-person singular)
Tú hablas.	*You speak.* (2nd-person singular)
Ud./Él/Ella habla.	*You/He/She speak(s).* (3rd-person singular)
Nosotros(as) hablamos.	*We speak.* (1st-person plural)
Vosotros(as) habláis.	*You speak.* (2nd-person plural)
Uds./Ellos/Ellas hablan.	*They speak.* (3rd-person plural)

PERSONAL A (La *a* personal) The personal **a** refers to the placement of the preposition **a** before a person or a pet when it is the **direct object** of the sentence.

Voy a llamar **a** María.	*I'm going to call María.*
El veterinario curó **al** perro.	*The veterinarian treated the dog.*

PREPOSITIONS (Las preposiciones) are linking words indicating spatial or temporal relations between two words.

Ella nadaba **en** la piscina.	*She was swimming **in** the pool.*
Yo llamé **antes de** las nueve.	*I called **before** nine o'clock.*
El libro es **para** ti.	*The book is **for** you.*
Voy **a** la oficina.	*I'm going **to** the office.*
Jorge es **de** Paraguay.	*Jorge is **from** Paraguay.*

PRESENT PARTICIPLE (El participio del presente) is the Spanish equivalent of the *-ing* verb form in English. Regular participles are created by replacing the infinitive endings (**-ar, -er/-ir**) with **-ando** or **-iendo**. They are often used with the verb **estar** to form the present progressive tense. The present progressive tense places emphasis on the continuing or progressive nature of an action. In Spanish, the participle form is referred to as a gerund.

Miguel está **cantando** en la ducha.	*Miguel is **singing** in the shower.*
Los niños están **durmiendo** ahora.	*The children are **sleeping** now.*

(*See also* **Gerunds**)

PRETERITE (El pretérito) The preterite tense, as compared to the **imperfect tense,** is used to talk about past events with specific emphasis on the beginning or the end of the action, or emphasis on the completed nature of the action as a whole.

Anoche yo **empecé** a estudiar a las once y **terminé** a la una.
*Last night I **began** to study at eleven o'clock and **finished** at one o'clock.*

Esta mañana **me desperté** a las siete, **desayuné, me duché** y **vine** al campus para las ocho.
*This morning **I woke up** at seven, **I ate breakfast, I showered,** and **I came** to campus by eight.*

PRONOUNS (Los pronombres) are words that substitute for **nouns** in a sentence.

Yo quiero **este.**	*I want **this one.*** (demonstrative—points out a specific person, place, or thing)
¿Quién es tu amigo?	***Who** is your friend?* (interrogative—used to ask questions)
Yo voy a llamar**la.**	*I'm going to call **her.*** (direct object—replaces the direct object of the sentence)
Ella va a dar**le** el reloj.	*She is going to give **him** the watch.* (indirect object—replaces the indirect object of the sentence)
Juan **se** baña por la mañana.	*Juan bathes **himself** in the morning.* (reflexive—used with reflexive verbs to show that the agent of the action is also the recipient)
Es la mujer **que** conozco.	*She is the woman **that** I know.* (relative—used to introduce a clause that describes a noun)
Nosotros somos listos.	***We** are clever.* (subject—replaces the noun that performs the action or state of a verb)

SUBJECTS (Los sujetos) are the persons, places, or things which perform the action of a verb, or which are connected to a description by a verb. The **conjugated** verb always agrees with its subject.

Carlos siempre baila solo.	***Carlos** always dances alone.*
Colorado y **California** son mis estados preferidos.	***Colorado** and **California** are my favorite states.*
La cafetera produce el café.	*The **coffee pot** makes the coffee.*

(*See also* **Active Voice.**)

SUBJUNCTIVE (El subjuntivo) The subjunctive mood is used to express speculative, doubtful, or hypothetical situations. It also communicates a degree of subjectivity or influence of the main clause over the subordinate clause.

No creo que **tengas** razón.	*I don't think that **you're** right.*
Si yo **fuera** el jefe, les pagaría más a mis empleados.	*If I **were** the boss, I would pay my employees more.*
Quiero que **estudies** más.	*I want **you to study** more.*

(*See also* **Mood, Indicative.**)

SUPERLATIVE STATEMENTS (Las frases superlativas) are formed by adjectives or adverbs to make comparisons among three or more members of a group. To form superlatives, add a definite article **(el, la, los, las)** before the comparative form.

Juan es **el más alto** de los tres.	*Juan is **the tallest** of the three.*
Este coche es **el más rápido** de todos.	*This car is **the fastest** of them all.*
En mi opinión, ella es **la mejor** cantante.	*In my opinion, she is **the best** singer.*

(*See also* **Comparisons.**)

TENSES (Los tiempos) refer to the manner in which time is expressed through the verb of a sentence.

Yo estudio.	*I study.* (present tense)
Yo estoy estudiando.	*I am studying.* (present progressive)
Yo he estudiado.	*I have studied.* (present perfect)
Yo había estudiado.	*I had studied.* (past perfect)
Yo estudié.	*I studied.* (preterite tense)
Yo estudiaba.	*I was studying.* (imperfect tense)
Yo estudiaré.	*I will study.* (future tense)

VERBS (Los verbos) are the words in a sentence that communicate an action or state of being.

Helen **es** mi amiga y ella **lee** muchas novelas.	*Helen **is** my friend and she **reads** a lot of novels.*

- **Auxiliary verbs (Los verbos auxiliares)** or helping verbs **haber, ser,** and **estar** are used to form the passive voice, compound tenses, and verbal periphrases.

Estamos estudiando mucho para el examen mañana.	***We are** studying a lot for the exam tomorrow. (verbal periphrases)*
Helen **ha** trabajado mucho en este proyecto.	*Helen **has** worked a lot on this project. (compound tense)*
La ropa **fue** hecha en Guatemala.	*The clothing **was** made in Guatemala. (passive voice)*

- **Reflexive verbs (Los verbos reflexivos)** use reflexive **pronouns** to indicate that the person initiating the action is also the recipient of the action.

Yo **me afeito** por la mañana.	***I shave (myself)** in the morning.*

- **Stem-changing verbs (Los verbos con cambios de raíz)** undergo a change in the main part of the verb when conjugated. To find the stem, drop the -**ar**, -**er**, or -**ir** from the **infinitive: dorm-, empez-, ped-.** There are three types of stem-changing verbs: **o** to **ue**, **e** to **ie** and **e** to **i**.

dormir: Yo d**ue**rmo en el parque.	*I sleep in the park.* (**o** to **ue**)
empezar: Ella siempre emp**ie**za su trabajo temprano.	*She always starts her work early.* (**e** to **ie**)
pedir: ¿Por qué no p**i**des ayuda?	*Why don't you ask for help?* (**e** to **i**)

Functional Glossary

Asking questions
Question words

¿Adónde? To where?
¿Cómo? How?
¿Cuál(es)? Which? What?
¿Cuándo? When?
¿Cuánto/¿Cuánta? How much?
¿Cuántos/¿Cuántas? How many?
¿Dónde? Where?
¿Para qué? For what reason?
¿Por qué? Why?
¿Qué? What?
¿Quién(es)? Who? Whom?

Requesting information

¿Cómo es su (tu) profesor(a) favorito(a)? What's your favorite professor like?
¿Cómo se (te) llama(s)? What's your name?
¿Cómo se llama? What's his/her name?
¿Cuál es su (tu) facultad? What's your school/department?
¿Cuál es su (tu) número de teléfono? What's your telephone number?
¿De dónde es (eres)? Where are you from?
¿Dónde hay...? Where is/are there . . .?
¿Qué estudia(s)? What are you studying?

Asking for descriptions

¿Cómo es...? What is . . . like?
¿Cómo son...? What are . . . like?

Asking for clarification

¿Cómo? What?
Dígame (Dime) una cosa. Tell me something.
Más despacio. More slowly.
No comprendo./No entiendo. I don't understand.
¿Perdón? Pardon me?
¿Qué? Otra vez, por favor. What? One more time, please.
Repita (Repite), por favor. Please repeat.
¿Qué significa...? What does . . . mean?

Asking about and expressing likes and dislikes

¿Te (le) gusta(n)? Do you like it (them)?
No me gusta(n). I don't like it (them).
Sí, me gusta(n). Yes, I like it (them).

Asking for confirmation

... ¿de acuerdo? . . . agreed? (*Used when some type of action is proposed.*)
... ¿no? . . . isn't that so? (*Not used with negative sentences.*)

... ¿no es así? . . . isn't that right?
... ¿vale? . . . okay?
... ¿verdad? ¿cierto? . . . right?
... ¿está bien? . . . OK?

Complaining

Es demasiado caro/cara (costoso/costosa). It's too expensive.
No es justo. It isn't fair.
¡No, hombre/mujer! No way!
No puedo esperar más. I can't wait anymore.
No puedo más. I can't take this anymore.

Expressing belief

Es cierto/verdad. That's right./That's true.
Estoy seguro/segura. I'm sure.
Lo creo. I believe it.
No cabe duda de que... There can be no doubt that . . .
No lo dudo. I don't doubt it.
No tengo la menor duda. I haven't the slightest doubt.
Tiene(s) razón. You're right.

Expressing disbelief

Hay dudas. There are doubts.
Es poco probable. It's doubtful/unlikely.
Lo dudo. I doubt it.
No lo creo. I don't believe it.
Estás equivocado(a). You're wrong.
Tengo mis dudas. I have my doubts.

Expressing frequency of actions and length of activities

¿Con qué frecuencia...? How often . . .?
de vez en cuando from time to time
durante la semana during the week
frecuentemente frequently
los fines de semana on the weekends
nunca never
por la mañana/por la tarde/por la noche in the morning/afternoon/evening
siempre always
todas las tardes/todas las noches every afternoon/evening
todos los días every day
Hace un año/dos meses/tres semanas que... for a year/two months/three weeks

Listening for instructions in the classroom

Abran los libros en la página... Open your books to page . . .
Cierren los libros. Close your books.

Complete (Completa) (Completen) la oración. Complete the sentence.
Conteste (Contesta) (Contesten) en español. Answer in Spanish.
Escriban en la pizarra. Write on the board.
Formen grupos de... estudiantes. Form groups of . . . students.
Practiquen en parejas. Practice in pairs.
¿Hay preguntas? Are there any questions?
Lea (Lee) en voz alta. Read aloud.
Por ejemplo... For example . . .
Preparen... para mañana. Prepare . . . for tomorrow.
Repita (Repite), (Repitan) por favor. Please repeat.
Saquen el libro (el cuaderno, una hoja de papel). Take out the book (the notebook, a piece of paper).

Greeting and conversing
Greetings

Bien, gracias. Fine, thanks.
Buenas noches. Good evening.
Buenas tardes. Good afternoon.
Buenos días. Good morning.
¿Cómo está(s)? How are you?
¿Cómo le (te) va? How is it going?
Hola. Hi.
Mal. Bad./Badly.
Más o menos. So so.
Nada. Nothing.
No muy bien. Not too well.
¿Qué hay de nuevo? What's new?
¿Qué tal? How are things?
Regular. Okay.
¿Y usted (tú)? And you?

Introducing people

¿Cómo se (te) llama(s)? What is your name?
¿Cómo se llama(n) él/ella/usted(es)/ellos/ellas? What is (are) his/her, your, their name(s)?
¿Cuál es su (tu) nombre? What is your name?
El gusto es mío. The pleasure is mine.
Encantado(a). Delighted.
Igualmente. Likewise.
Me llamo... My name is . . .
Mi nombre es... My name is . . .
Mucho gusto. Pleased to meet you.
Quiero presentarle(te) a... I want to introduce you to . . .
Se llama(n)... His/Her/Their name(s) is/are . . .

Entering into a conversation

Escuche (Escucha). Listen.
(No) Creo que... I (don't) believe that . . .
(No) Estoy de acuerdo porque... I (don't) agree because . . .

Pues, lo que quiero decir es que... Well, what I want to say is . . .
Quiero decir algo sobre... I want to say something about . . .

Saying goodbye

Adiós. Goodbye.
Chao. Goodbye.
Hasta la vista. Until we meet again.
Hasta luego. See you later.
Hasta mañana. Until tomorrow.
Hasta pronto. See you soon.

Chatting

(Bastante) bien. (Pretty) well, fine.
¿Cómo está la familia? How's the family?
¿Cómo le (te) va? How's it going?
¿Cómo van las clases? How are classes going?
Fenomenal. Phenomenal.
Horrible. Horrible.
Mal. Bad(ly).
No hay nada de nuevo. There's nothing new.
¿Qué hay de nuevo? What's new?
¿Qué tal? How's it going?

Reacting to comments

¡A mí me lo dice(s)! You're telling me!
¡Caray! Oh! Oh no!
¿De veras?/¿De verdad? Really? Is that so?
¡Dios mío! Oh, my goodness!
¿En serio? Seriously? Are you serious?
¡Estupendo! Stupendous!
¡Fabuloso! Fabulous!
¡No me diga(s)! You don't say!
¡Qué barbaridad! How unusual! Wow! That's terrible!
¡Qué bien! That's great!
¡Qué desastre! That's a disaster!
¿Qué dijo (dijiste)? What did you say?
¡Qué gente más loca! What crazy people!
¿Qué hizo (hiciste)? What did you do?
¡Qué horrible! That's horrible!
¡Qué increíble! That's amazing!
¡Qué lástima! That's a pity! That's too bad!
¡Qué mal! That's really bad!
¡Qué maravilla! That's marvelous!
¡Qué pena! That's a pain! That's too bad!
¡Ya lo creo! I (can) believe it!

Extending a conversation using fillers and hesitations

A ver... Let's see . . .
Buena pregunta... That's a good question . . .
Bueno... Well . . .
Es que... It's that . . .
Pues... no sé. Well . . . I don't know.
Sí, pero... Yes, but . . .
No creo. I don't think so.

Expressing worry

¡Ay, Dios mío! Good grief!
¡Es una pesadilla! It's a nightmare!
¡Eso debe ser horrible! That must be horrible!
¡Pobre! Poor thing!
¡Qué espanto! What a scare!
¡Qué horror! How horrible!
¡Qué lástima! What a pity!
¡Qué mala suerte/pata! What bad luck!
¡Qué terrible! How terrible!
¡Qué triste! How sad!
¡Qué pena! What a shame!

Expressing agreement

Así es. That's so.
Cierto./Claro (que sí)./Seguro. Certainly. Sure(ly).
Cómo no./Por supuesto. Of course.
Correcto. That's right.
Es cierto/verdad. It's true.
Eso es. That's it.
(Estoy) de acuerdo. I agree.
Exacto. Exactly.
Muy bien. Very good. Fine.
Perfecto. Perfect.
Probablemente. Probably.

Expressing disagreement

Al contrario. On the contrary.
En absoluto. Absolutely not. No way.
Es poco probable. It's doubtful/not likely.
Incorrecto. Incorrect.
No es así. That's not so.
No es cierto. It's not so.
No es verdad. It's not true.
No es eso. That's not it.
No está bien. It's no good/not right.
No estoy de acuerdo. I don't agree.
Todo lo contrario. Just the opposite./ Quite the contrary.

Expressing sympathy

Es una pena. It's a pity.
Lo siento mucho. I'm very sorry.
Mis condolencias. My condolences.
¡Qué lástima! What a pity!

Expressing obligation

Necesitar + *infinitive* To need to . . .
(No) es necesario + *infinitive* It's (not) necessary to . . .
(No) hay que + *infinitive* One must(n't) . . ., One does(n't) have to . . .
(Se) debe + *infinitive* (One) should (ought to) . . .
Tener que + *infinitive* To have to . . .

In the hospital
Communicating instructions

Aplicar una pomada. Apply cream/ ointment.
Bañarse con agua fría/caliente. Take a bath in cold/hot water.

Lavar la herida. Wash the wound.
Llamar al médico. Call the doctor.
Pedir información. Ask for information.
Poner hielo. Put on ice.
Poner una tirita/una venda. Put on a Band-Aid®/a bandage.
Quedarse en la cama. Stay in bed.
Sacar la lengua. Stick out your tongue.
Tomar la medicina/las pastillas después de cada comida (dos veces al día/antes de acostarse). Take the medicine/the pills after each meal (two times a day/ before going to bed).

Describing symptoms

Me duele la cabeza/la espalda, etc. I have a headache/backache, etc.
Me tiemblan las manos. My hands are shaking.
Necesito pastillas (contra fiebre, mareos, etc.). I need pills (for fever, dizziness, etc.).
Necesito una receta (unas aspirinas, un antibiótico, unas gotas, un jarabe). I need a prescription (aspirin, antibiotics, drops, cough syrup).

Invitations
Extending invitations

¿Le (Te) gustaría ir a... conmigo? Would you like to go to . . . with me?
¿Me quiere(s) acompañar a...? Do you want to accompany me to . . .?
¿Quiere(s) ir a...? Do you want to go to . . .?
Si tiene(s) tiempo, podemos ir a... If you have time, we could go to . . .

Accepting invitations

Sí, con mucho gusto. Yes, with pleasure.
Sí, me encantaría. Yes, I'd love to.
Sí, me gustaría mucho. Yes, I'd like to very much.

Declining invitations

Lo siento mucho, pero no puedo. I'm very sorry, but I can't.
Me gustaría, pero no puedo porque... I'd like to, but I can't because . . .

Making reservations and asking for information

¿Dónde hay...? Where is/are there . . .?
¿El precio incluye...? Does the price include . . .?
Quisiera reservar una habitación... I would like to reserve a room . . .

Opinons
Asking for opinions

¿Cuál prefiere(s)? Which do you prefer?
¿Le (Te) gusta(n)...? Do you like . . .?

¿Le (Te) interesa(n)...? Are you interested in . . .?

¿Qué opina(s) de...? What's your opinion about . . .?

¿Qué piensa(s)? What do you think?

¿Qué le (te) parece(n)? How does/do . . . seem to you?

Giving opinions

Creo que... I believe that . . .

Es bueno. It's good.

Es conveniente. It's convenient.

Es importante. It's important.

Es imprescindible. It's indispensable.

Es mejor. It's better.

Es necesario./Es preciso. It's necessary.

Es preferible. It's preferable.

Me gusta(n)... I like . . .

Me interesa(n)... I am interested in . . .

Me parece(n)... It seems . . . to me. (They seem . . . to me.)

Opino que... It's my opinion that . . .

Pienso que... I think that . . .

Prefiero... I prefer . . .

Adding information

A propósito/De paso... By the way . . .

Además... In addition . . .

También... Also . . .

Negating and contradicting

¡Imposible! Impossible!

¡Jamás!/¡Nunca! Never!

Ni hablar. Don't even mention it.

No es así. It's not like that.

No está bien. It's not right.

Making requests

¿Me da(s)...? Will you give me . . .?

¿Me hace(s) el favor de...? Will you do me the favor of . . .?

¿Me pasa(s)...? Will you pass me . . .?

¿Me puede(s) dar...? Can you give me . . .?

¿Me puede(s) traer...? Can you bring me . . .?

¿Quiere(s) darme...? Do you want to give me . . .?

Sí, cómo no. Yes, of course.

In a restaurant
Ordering a meal

¿Está incluida la propina? Is the tip included?

Me falta(n)... I need . . .

¿Me puede traer..., por favor? Can you please bring me . . .?

¿Puedo ver la carta/el menú/la lista de vinos? May I see the menu/the wine list?

¿Qué recomienda usted? What do you recommend?

¿Qué tarjetas de crédito aceptan? What credit cards do you accept?

Quisiera hacer una reservación para... I would like to make a reservation for . . .

¿Se necesitan reservaciones? Are reservations needed?

¿Tiene usted una mesa para...? Do you have a table for . . .?

Tráigame la cuenta, por favor. Please bring me the check/bill.

Shopping
Asking how much something costs and bargaining

¿Cuánto cuesta...? How much is . . .?

El precio es... The price is . . .

Cuesta alrededor de... It costs around . . .

¿Cuánto cuesta(n)? How much does it (do they) cost?

De acuerdo. Agreed. All right.

Es demasiado. It's too much.

Es una ganga. It's a bargain.

No más. No more.

No pago más de... I won't pay more than . . .

solo only

última oferta final offer

Describing how clothing fits

Me queda(n) bien/mal. It fits (They fit) me well/badly.

Te queda(n) bien/mal. It fits (They fit) you well/badly.

Le queda(n) bien/mal. It fits (They fit) him/her/you well/badly.

Getting someone's attention

Con permiso. Excuse me.

Discúlpeme. Excuse me.

Oiga (Oye). Listen.

Perdón. Pardon.

Expressing satisfaction and dissatisfaction

El color es horrible. The color is horrible.

El modelo es aceptable. The style is acceptable.

Es muy barato(a). It's very inexpensive.

Es muy caro(a). It's very expensive.

Me gusta el modelo. I like the style.

Thanking

De nada./Por nada./No hay de qué. It's nothing. You're welcome.

¿De verdad le (te) gusta? Do you really like it?

Estoy muy agradecido(a). I'm very grateful.

Gracias. Thanks./Thank you.

Me alegro que le (te) guste. I'm glad you like it.

Mil gracias. Thanks a lot.

Muchas gracias. Thank you very much.

Muy amable de su (tu) parte. You're very kind.

Spanish-English Vocabulary

This vocabulary includes all the words and expressions listed as active vocabulary in **Exploraciones**. The number following the definition refers to the chapter in which the word or phrase was first used actively. For example, an entry followed by **13** is first used actively in **Capítulo 13**. Nouns that end in **-o** are maculine and in **-a** are feminine unless unless otherwise indicated.

All words are alphabetized according to the 1994 changes made by the Real Academia: **ch** and **ll** are no longer considered separate letters of the alphabet.

Stem-changing verbs appear with the vowel change in parentheses after the infinitive: **(ie), (ue), (i), (ie, i), (e, i), (ue, u),** or **(i, i).** Most cognates, conjugated verb forms, and proper nouns used as passive vocabulary in the text are not included in this glossary.

The following abbreviations are used:

adj. adjective	*n.* noun	*dem.* demonstrative	*prep.* preposition
adv. adverb	*pl.* plural	*dir. obj.* direct object	*pron.* pronoun
art. article	*pp.* past participle	*f.* feminine	*refl.* reflexive
conj. conjunction	*poss.* possessive	*f.* feminine	

form. formal	*s.* singular
indir. obj. indirect object	*subj.* subject
interj. interjection	*v.* verb
m. masculine	

A

a to, at; **a causa de** on account of; **a cuadros** checkered; plaid (11); **a fin de que** so that (14); in order that (14); **a la derecha de** to the right of (4); **a la izquierda de** to the left of (4); **a lo largo (de)** along; **a lunares** polka-dotted; **a menos que** unless (14); **a menudo** frequently, often; **a pesar de** in spite of; **a propósito** by the way; **a rayas** striped (11); **a tiempo completo** full-time; **a tiempo** on time (10); **al horno** baked (7); **al igual que** like; **al lado (de)** alongside (of); beside, next to (4); **al mes** per month
abajo *adv.* below; **abajo de** under
abogado(a) lawyer (5); attorney
abordar to board (10); **pase** *m.* **de abordar** boarding pass (10)
abrazar (c) to hug (13)
abrigo coat (3)
abril *m.* April (3)
abrir to open (3)
abstracto(a) abstract (11); **arte** *m.* **abstracto** abstract art (11)
abuelo(a) grandfather/grandmother (2)
aburrido(a) bored (5); boring (1)
aburrir to bore (8); **aburrirse** to become bored (9)
acabar to finish (11); **acabar de** (+ *inf.*) to have just (*done something*)
acampar to go camping
acaso perhaps
acción *f.* action
aceite *m.* oil
aceituna olive
aceptar to accept
acera sidewalk (9)
acercarse (qu) to approach
acompañar to accompany
acondicionado(a): aire acondicionado *m.* air-conditioning
acontecimiento event
acostarse (ue) to lie down (6); to go to bed (6)
actividad activity
actor *m.* actor (5)
actriz *f.* actress (5)
actual current
acuerdo agreement; **de acuerdo** agreed, all right; **estar de acuerdo** to agree
adelgazar (c) to lose weight
además besides; furthermore; in addition
adiós goodbye (1)
adolescencia adolescence (13)
adolescente *m. f.* adolescent (13)
¿adónde? to where? (4)
aduana customs (10)
adulto adult (13)

aéreo(a) *adj.* air; **línea aérea** airline
aeropuerto (internacional) airport (4); (international) airport (10)
afeitarse to shave (6)
aficionado(a) fan (6)
afuera *adv.* outside
agente *m. f.* agent; **agente de aduana** customs official; **agente de seguridad** security agent (10); **agente de viajes** travel agent (5)
agosto August (3)
agradecido(a) grateful
agresivo(a) aggressive (1)
agua *f.* (*but* **el agua**) water
aguacate *m.* avocado
águila *f.* (*but* **el águila**) eagle
ahí there
ahora now (3) (6); **hasta ahora** up to now, so far
ajedrez *m.* chess (8)
ajo garlic
alberca swimming pool
albergue estudiantil *m.* youth hostel
alegrarse to become happy (9)
alegre happy (5)
alemán *m.* German (*language*) (2)
alergia allergy (14)
alfombra carpet (4); rug
algo something
algodón *m.* cotton (11)
alguien someone, somebody
aliviar to relieve, alleviate
allá over there
allí there
almacén *m.* department store
almohada pillow
almorzar (ue) (c) to have lunch (4)
almuerzo lunch (7)
aló hello (*telephone response in some countries*)
alojamiento lodging (10)
alojarse to lodge, to stay (*in a hotel*) (10)
alpinismo mountain climbing; **hacer alpinismo** to climb mountains (6)
alquilar to rent (4)
alto(a) high; tall (1); **presión** *f.* **alta** high blood pressure (14)
amable kind (1)
amar to love (13)
amarillo(a) yellow (3)
ambiente *m.* atmosphere, environment
ambulancia ambulance (9)
amigo(a) friend (2)
amo(a) de casa homemaker (5)
anaranjado(a) orange (3)
ándale there you go
andar to walk; **andar en** to ride (8); **andar en bicicleta** to ride a bike (6)

andén *m.* platform (10)
anfibio amphibian (12)
anfitrión(-ona) host
anillo ring (13)
animado(a) excited; **dibujos animados** cartoons (13)
aniversario (wedding) anniversary (9)
anoche last night (6)
ante todo first of all, first and foremost
anteayer the day before yesterday
anterior before, prior
antes previously; **antes de** (+ *inf.*) before (*doing something*) (6); **antes (de) que** before (14)
antipático(a) unfriendly (1)
anuncio comercial commercial (13)
añadir to add
año year; **Año Nuevo** New Year (3); **el año pasado** last year; **los quince años** girl's fifteenth birthday celebration (9); **tener... años** to be . . . years old (2)
apagar (gu) to turn off (11)
aparcamiento parking lot
apartamento apartment (4)
aplicarse (qu) to apply
apreciar to appreciate; to enjoy (11)
aprender (a +*inf.*) to learn (*to do something*) (3)
apretado(a) tight (11)
aprobar (ue) to approve
aquel(la) *adj.* that (over there); *pron.* that (one) (over there)
aquello *pron.* that (one)
aquellos(as) *adj.* those (over there); *pron.* those (over there)
aquí here; **hasta aquí** up to now, so far
árbol *m.* tree (12); **trepar un árbol** to climb a tree (8)
ardilla squirrel (12)
arena sand (12)
argentino(a) Argentine (14)
armario closet, armoire (4)
arquitecto(a) architect (5)
arreglar to arrange; **arreglarse** to fix oneself up (6); to get ready (6)
arriba up (with)
arroz *m.* rice (7)
arte *m.* art (2); **arte abstracto** abstract art (11); **arte dramático** theater; **artes marciales** *f. pl.* martial arts; **bellas artes** *f. pl.* fine arts
arterial: presión *f.* **arterial** blood pressure
artesanías handicrafts
artículo article; **artículos de limpieza** cleaning materials
asado(a) grilled (7)
ascensor *m.* elevator (10)

así like this, thus, in this manner; **así es** that's so; **así que** thus, therefore; **¿no es así?** isn't that so?

asiento seat (10)

asistente *m. f.* **de vuelo** flight attendant (5)

asistir (a) to attend (3)

aspiradora vacuum cleaner; **pasar la aspiradora** to vacuum (8)

aspirante *m. f.* job candidate

aspirina aspirin (14)

asustado(a) scared (5)

asustarse to become frightened (9)

atender (ie) a to wait on; to attend to; to pay attention to (*other people*)

aterrizar (c) to land (10)

ático small attic apartment

atlético(a) athletic (1)

atletismo track and field (6)

atracción *f.* attraction; **parque** *m.* **de atracciones** amusement park

atrasado(a) late; **estar atrasado(a)** to be late

atravesar (ie) to cross (9)

atropellar to run over (9)

atún *m.* tuna

audiencia audience (13)

audífonos headphones (13)

auditorio auditorium (2)

aumento increase

aunque although, though

auto car

autorretrato self-portrait (11)

auxilio help; **primeros auxilios** first aid (14)

ave *f.* (*but* **el ave**) poultry; bird (12)

avergonzado(a) embarrassed (5)

avión *m.* plane

ayer yesterday (6)

ayudar to help (2)

ayuntamiento city hall

azafata *f.* flight attendant

azúcar *m.* sugar (7)

azul blue (3)

B

bádminton *m.* badminton (6)

bahía bay (12)

bailar to dance (2)

bailarín/bailarina dancer

bajar de to get out of (*a vehicle*) (9)

bajo(a) short (1); **presión** *f.* **baja** low blood pressure (14)

ballena whale (12)

balneario spa

balón *m.* (volley)ball

baloncesto basketball

banco bank (4)

bandera flag (1)

banderines streamers (9)

bañarse to bathe, to take a bath; to shower (*Mex.*) (6)

bañera bathtub (4)

baño bath; bathtub; bathroom (4); **traje de baño** bathing suit

bar *m.* bar (4)

barato(a) inexpensive, cheap (11)

barbilla chin

barco ship, boat

barrer to sweep (8)

básquetbol *m.* basketball (6)

bastante rather

basura trash, garbage, litter (8); **bote** *m.* **de basura** trashcan (8); **sacar (qu) la basura** to take the trash out (8)

batido(a) whipped

bautizo baptism (9)

beber to drink (3)

bebida drink (7)

beca scholarship (14)

béisbol *m.* baseball (6)

bellas artes *f. pl.* fine arts

beneficios benefits

besar to kiss (13)

biblioteca library (2)

bibliotecario(a) librarian

bicicleta bicycle; **andar en bicicleta** to ride a bike (6)

bien fine (1); well; **llevarse bien** to get along well (13); **pasarlo bien** to have a good time; **¡qué bien te queda esa falda!** that skirt really fits you well! (11); **sentirse (e, i) bien** to feel well

billete *m.* ticket

biología biology (2)

birth nacimiento (13)

bisabuela great grandmother

bisabuelo great grandfather

blanco(a) white (3); **vino blanco** white wine (7)

blusa blouse (3)

bluyíns *m., pl.* blue jeans (3)

boca mouth (6)

bocadillo snack (9)

boda wedding (9)

boleto ticket (10)

bolígrafo pen (1)

boliviano(a) Bolivian (14)

bolsa bag; purse (3); handbag

bolso bag; beach bag; purse; handbag

bombero(a) firefighter; **estación** *f.* **de bomberos** fire station

bonito(a) pretty (1); **¡qué color tan bonito!** what a pretty color! (11)

borracho(a) drunk (5)

borrador *m.* (chalk) eraser

bosque *m.* forest (12); wood(s)

bota boot (3)

bote *m.* **de basura** trashcan (8)

botella bottle

botones *m. f., sing. pl.* bellhop (10)

brazo arm (6)

brindar to toast (9)

brindis *m.* toast (*with a drink*) (9)

brócoli *m.* broccoli (7)

bucear con tubo de respiración to snorkel

bucear to scuba dive (6)

buen/bueno(a) good (1); **buen provecho** enjoy your meal; **buenas noches** good night (1); **buenas tardes** good afternoon (1); **buenos días** good morning (1); **hace buen tiempo** it's nice weather (3); **¡que tengas un buen día!** have a nice day! (1)

bufanda scarf (3)

buscador *m.* search engine (13)

buscar (qu) to look for (2)

butaca seat (*theater*) (13)

C

caballero gentleman

caballo horse (2); **montar a caballo** to ride horseback

cabello hair

caber to fit; **no cabe duda** there can be no doubt

cabeza head (6); **me duele la cabeza** I have a headache

cabo: al fin y al cabo after all; when all is said and done

cada each, every

cadera hip

caer(se) to fall (9); **caer bien (mal)** to like (dislike) a person (8)

café *m.* coffee (7); café (4); brown (3); **tomar café** to drink coffee

cafetera coffee maker (4)

cafetería cafeteria (2)

caja cash register (11)

calabacita zucchini

calabaza squash; pumpkin

calcetines *m. pl.* socks (3)

calefacción *f.* heat

caliente warm, hot

calle *f.* street (4)

calor *m.* warmth; heat; **hace calor** it's hot; **tener (mucho) calor** to be (very) hot (2)

calvo(a) bald (1)

cama bed (4); **cama matrimonial** double bed; **coche** *m.* **cama** sleeping car (10); **hacer la cama** to make the bed (8)

camarero(a) (hotel) maid (10)

camarón *m.* shrimp (7)

cambiar to change

cambio change; **en cambio** on the other hand

camilla stretcher (9)

caminar to walk (2)

camisa shirt (3)

camiseta T-shirt (3)

campo field (6)

cáncer *m.* cancer (14)

cancha court (*sports*) (6)

cansado(a) tired (5)

cantante *m. f.* singer (5)

cantar to sing (2)

cara face (6)

¡caray! oh!; oh no!

cariñoso(a) loving (1)

carne *f.* meat (7); **carne de res** beef; **carne de vacuno** beef

carnicería butcher shop

caro(a) expensive (11); **¡qué caro(a)!** how expensive! (11)

carretera highway (9)

carrito toy car (8)

carta letter (4); menu; *pl.* playing cards (8)

cartel *m.* poster (1)

cartera billfold, wallet

casa house

casarse (con) to get married to (9)

cascada waterfall (*small*) (12)

caso: en caso (de) (que) in case (that) (14)

catarata waterfall (12)

catorce fourteen (1)

catsup *f.* ketchup (7)

causa cause; **a causa de** on account of

causar to cause

caza hunting (12)

cazar (c) to hunt (12)

CD *m.* CD; **reproductor de CDs** CD player (13)

cebolla onion (7)

cebra zebra (12)

ceja eyebrow

celebrar to celebrate (9)

celos *m. pl.* jealousy; **tener celos** to be jealous

celoso(a) jealous (5)

cena dinner (7)

cenar to eat dinner (7)

censurar to censor (13)

centro center; **centro comercial** shopping center; **centro estudiantil** student center (2); **centro de negocios** business center (10)

cepillarse to brush (6)

cerca (de) close (to) (4)

cerdo pork (7); pig (12)

ceremonia ceremony (13)

cereza cherry

cero zero (1)

cerrar (ie) to close (4); to shut

cerro hill
certeza certainty
cerveza beer (7)
césped *m.* lawn; **cortar el césped** to mow the lawn (8)
ceviche (cebiche) *m. raw fish marinated in lime juice*
chalet *m.* villa
champán *m.* champagne (9)
champú *m.* shampoo (6)
chao Bye (1)
chaqueta jacket (3)
charlar to chat
charlatán(-ana) gossipy
chatear to chat (*online*) (8)
cheque *m.* check; **cheque de viaje** traveler's check; **cheque de viajero** traveler's check
chico(a) child; *adj.* small (11)
chileno(a) Chilean (14)
chimenea fireplace
chismear to gossip
chiste *m.* joke (8)
chocar (qu) (con) to crash (*into something*) (9)
ciclista *m. f.* cyclist (9)
cielo sky (12)
cien/ciento one hundred (1) (7); **cien mil** (one) hundred thousand; **cien millones** (one) hundred million; **ciento uno** one hundred one (1) (7); **por ciento** percent (11)
ciencias *f. pl.* science; **ciencias naturales** natural science (2); **ciencias políticas** political science (2); **ciencias sociales** social science (2)
científico(a) scientist (5)
cierto(a) *adj.* sure, certain, true; *adv.* certainly, surely; **¿cierto?** right?
cinco five (1)
cincuenta fifty (1)
cine *m.* movie theater (4); cinema
cintura waist
cinturón *m.* belt; **cinturón de seguridad** safety (seat) belt (10)
cirugía surgery (14)
cita date (13)
ciudadano(a) citizen (14)
claro(a) *adj.* sure; clear; light, pale (11); *adv.* certainly, surely; **claro que no** of course not; **claro que sí** certainly, surely, of course
clase *f.* class; **compañero(a) de clase** classmate (2); **primera clase** first class (10); **salón** *m.* **de clases** classroom (1); **segunda clase** second class (10)
clasificación *f.* rating (13)
clic: hacer clic (en) to click on (13)
cliente *m. f.* client
clínica clinic
club *m.* club (4)
coche *m.* car; **coche cama** sleeping car (10)
cochera garage (4)
cocina kitchen (4); **papel de cocina** paper towel
cocinar to cook (2)
cocinero(a) cook
cocodrilo crocodile (12)
coctel *m.* cocktail (7)
codo elbow (6)
cognado cognate
cola line, queue; **hacer cola** to stand in line
coleccionar to collect
colegio school (*secondary*)
colgar (ue) to hang (8)

colina hill (12)
collar *m.* necklace
colmo height; **¡esto es el colmo!** this is the last straw!
colombiano(a) Colombian (14)
color *m.* color; **¡qué color tan bonito!** what a pretty color! (11)
columna vertebral spinal column
comedor *m.* dining room (4)
comenzar (ie) (c) to begin (4); to start
comer to eat (3)
comercial: anuncio comercial commercial (13); **centro comercial** shopping center (4)
comerciante *m. f.* merchant
comercio: tratado de comercio trade agreement (14)
comestibles *m. pl.* groceries
cometa kite (8)
cómico(a) funny (1); **tira cómica** comic strip (8)
comida meal; food (7); lunch (7)
como like, as; **como consecuencia** as a consequence; **como resultado** as a result
¿cómo? how? (4); what?; **¿cómo está usted?** how are you? (*form.*) (1); **¿cómo estás?** how are you? (*fam.*) (1); **cómo no** of course
cómoda chest of drawers; bureau
cómodo(a) comfortable (3)
compañero(a) companion, significant other, partner; **compañero(a) de clase** classmate (2); **compañero(a) de cuarto** roommate
comparado(a) con compared with
compartir to share
competencia competition
competir (i, i) to compete (4)
completar to complete; to fill out
completo(a) complete; **a tiempo completo** full-time; **pensión** *f.* **completa** full board
complicado(a) complex (11)
comprar to buy (2)
comprender to understand (3)
comprobante *m.* voucher, credit slip
comprometerse (con) to get engaged (to) (13)
compromiso engagement (13)
computación: ciencias de la computación computer science
computadora computer (1)
con with; **con mucho gusto** with pleasure; **con tal (de) que** provided (that) (14)
concluir (y) to conclude
concurso contest; game show (13)
conducir (zc) to drive (5)
conductor(a) driver (9); TV host (13)
conejo rabbit (12)
conexión *f.* connection (10)
conferencia lecture; **sala de conferencias** conference center (10)
confundido(a) confused (5)
conjunto outfit
conmigo with me
conocer (zc) to know; to be acquainted with (5)
conocimiento knowledge
consecuencia consequence; **como consecuencia** as a consequence
conseguir (i, i) to get, obtain
consejero(a) adviser
conserje *m. f.* concierge
conservador(a) conservative (1)
construir (y) to build, construct
consultar to look up (a webpage,

a text, etc.); to consult
consultorio doctor's office
contabilidad *f.* accounting
contable *m. f.* accountant
contador(a) accountant (5)
contaminación pollution; contamination (12)
contar (ue) to count; to tell (a story) (8)
contener (*like* tener) to contain
contento(a) happy (5)
contestar to answer
contra against
contradecir to contradict
contrario(a) opposite, contrary; **al contrario** on the contrary; **al contrario de** unlike
control *m.* control; **control de pasaporte** passport control; **control de seguridad** security check; **control remoto** remote control (13)
copa wine glass (7)
corazón *m.* heart (14)
corbata tie (3)
cordero lamb
cordillera mountain range
correcto(a) that's right
correo mail; post office (4); **oficina de correos** post office
correr to run (3); **pista de correr** track
cortacésped *m.* lawnmower (8)
cortar to cut (8); **cortarse** to cut (oneself) (6) (14); **cortar el césped** to cut, to mow the lawn (10)
cortina curtain (4)
corto(a) short (1); **pantalones** *m. pl.* **cortos** shorts
cosa thing
costa coast (12)
costar (ue) to cost (4)
costarricense *m. f.* Costa Rican (14)
costoso(a) expensive
crédito credit; **tarjeta de crédito** credit card (11)
creer to believe (3); to think
crema cream (7); **crema batida** whipped cream
cremoso(a) creamy
criminología criminology (2)
cruce *m.* crosswalk (9)
crucigrama *m.* crossword puzzle
cruel cruel (1)
cruzar (c) to cross (9)
cuaderno notebook (1)
cuadro square; painting (4); picture (4); **a cuadros** checkered; plaid (11)
¿cuál(es)? which? (4)
cuando when
¿cuándo? when? (1)
cuanto: en cuanto as soon as (14)
¿cuánto(a)? how much? (4)
¿cuántos(as)? how many? (4)
cuarenta forty (1)
cuarto quarter (*of an hour*); room; **cuarto de baño** bathroom; **cuarto oscuro** darkroom
cuarto(a) *adj.* fourth (4)
cuatro four (1)
cuatrocientos(as) four hundred (7)
cubano(a) Cuban (14)
cubierto(a) covered
cubiertos *m. pl.* table setting; cutlery
cubista *m. f.* cubist (11)
cuchara soupspoon (7)
cucharita teaspoon
cuchillo knife (7)
cuello neck (6)

cuenta bill (*restaurant*) (7); check
cuento story (8)
cuerda jumping rope (8)
cuero leather
cuerpo body
cuidado care; **tener (mucho) cuidado** to be (very) careful (2)
cuidar (de) to take care (of)
culpa fault
cultivar el jardín to garden (*flowers*)
cumpleañero(a) birthday boy (girl)
cumpleaños *m. sing., pl.* birthday (3) (9); **fiesta de cumpleaños** birthday party
curita small adhesive bandage (14)
cuyo(a), cuyos(as) whose

D

dama lady; *pl.* checkers (8)
dañado(a) damaged; **estar dañado(a)** to be damaged (9)
dañar to damage (9)
dar to give (5); **dar a luz** to give birth (13); **darse cuenta de** to realize; **dar la vuelta** to take a walk or a ride (8)
de of, from; **de acuerdo** agreed, all right; **¿de dónde eres tú?** where are you (*fam.*) from? (1); **¿de dónde?** from where? (4); **de lunares** with polka dots (11); **de moda** fashionable (11); **de nuevo** new; again; **de paso** by the way; **de repente** suddenly (9); **¿de veras?** really, is that so?; **de verdad** really; **del mismo modo** similarly
debajo (de) below; under (4)
deber (+ *inf.*) should/ought to (*do something*) (3)
décimo(a) tenth (4)
decir to say, to tell (5); **querer decir** to mean
declarar to declare; **algo que declarar** something to declare
decorar to decorate (9)
dedo finger (6); **dedo del pie** toe (6)
definido(a) definite
deforestación *f.* deforestation (12)
dejar to leave; **dejar una propina** to leave a tip (7)
delante (de) in front (of)
delantero(a) front
delgado(a) thin (1)
demasiado(a) too, too much
dentro (de) inside (of) (4)
dependiente(a) clerk (5)
deportes *m. pl.* sports; **practicar (qu) deportes** to play sports (2)
deportivo(a) related to sports, sporting
deprimido(a) depressed (5)
derecha right; **a la derecha (de)** to the right (of) (4)
derecho law; right; **derechos humanos** human rights (14); **seguir (i) derecho** to go straight (10)
desacuerdo disagreement
desayunar to eat breakfast (7)
desayuno breakfast (7)
descansar to rest (14)
descomponer to break down (*a machine*) (11)
descuento discount (11)
desear to wish (2) (13); to desire (13); to want
desechos industriales industrial waste (12)
desembarcar (qu) to deplane
desempleado(a) unemployed
desempleo unemployment (14)
desfile *m.* parade (9)
deshacer la maleta to unpack one's suitcase
desierto desert (12)

desmayarse to faint (14)
desmayo faint (14)
despacio slowly
despedida farewell; **despedida de soltera** bridal shower; **despedida de soltero** bachelor party
despedir (i, i) to fire; **despedirse** to say goodbye
despegar (gu) to take off (10)
despejado(a) clear (*weather*) (3)
despertador *m.* alarm clock (6)
despertarse (ie) to wake up (6)
después then, next; **después de (que)** after (14); **después de (+ *inf.*)** after (*doing something*) (6)
destino destination
destruir (y) to destroy (12)
desván *m.* attic
detergente *m.* **para platos** dish detergent
detrás (de) in back (of); behind (4)
devolver (ue) to return (*something*) (4)
día *m.* day (3); **al día** per day; **día de santo** saint's day; **día feriado** holiday (3); **¡que tengas un buen día!** have a nice day! (1); **todos los días** every day (3)
diabetes *f.* diabetes (14)
diario(a) daily
diarrea diarrhea (14)
dibujar to draw (8)
dibujos animados cartoons (13)
diccionario dictionary (1)
diciembre *m.* December (3)
dictadura dictatorship (14)
diecinueve nineteen (1)
dieciocho eighteen (1)
dieciséis sixteen (1)
diecisiete seventeen (1)
diente *m.* tooth (6)
diez ten (1)
diferencia difference; **a diferencia de** unlike; in contrast to
diferente different; **diferente de** unlike
dinero money (4); **el dinero en efectivo** cash (11)
Dios *m.* God; **Dios mío** oh, my goodness
dirección *f.* direction; address (4)
discoteca nightclub (4)
disculparse to excuse oneself
diseñador(a) designer (5)
diseñar to design (11)
disfrutar to enjoy (9)
disponible available (10)
distraerse to get distracted (9)
diversión *f.* entertainment; hobby, pastime
divertido(a) funny (5); fun
divertirse (ie, i) to have fun (6)
divorciarse (de) to divorce (13)
doblar to bend; to turn (10)
doble double (10); **habitación doble** double room
doce twelve (1)
docena dozen
documental *m.* documentary (13)
doler (ue) to hurt (14); **me duele la cabeza** I have a headache
dolor *m.* pain (14); ache
doméstico(a) domestic, household
domingo *m.* Sunday (3)
dominicano(a) Dominican (14)
dominó *sing.* dominos (8)
donde where
¿dónde? where? (1) (4); **¿de dónde?** from where? (4); **¿de dónde eres tú?** where are you (*fam.*) from? (1)
dormir (ue, u) to sleep (4); **dormirse (ue, u)** to fall asleep (6); **saco de dormir** sleeping bag (6)

dormitorio bedroom (4)
dos two (1)
doscientos(as) two hundred (7)
dramático(a) dramatic; **arte** *m.* **dramático** theater
ducha shower (4)
ducharse to shower (6)
duda doubt; **no cabe duda** there can be no doubt
dudar to doubt (12)
dudoso(a) doubtful
dulce sweet; **salsa de tomate dulce** tomato sauce; ketchup; *n. pl.* candies (9)
durazno peach (7)
duro(a) tough, hard

E

ecología ecology (12)
economía economics; economy (2)
económico(a) *adj.* economical; inexpensive; **ciencias económicas** economics; **hotel** *m.* **económico** inexpensive hotel
ecuatoguineano Equatorial Guinean (14)
ecuatoriano(a) Ecuadorian (14)
edificio building (4)
efectivo cash (11); **el dinero en efectivo** cash (11)
eficiente efficient
egoísta selfish (1)
ejemplo example; **por ejemplo** for example
ejercicio exercise; **ejercicios aeróbicos** aerobics
el *def. art. m.* the; **el cual(es)** which, whom; **el que** that, which, whom, the one
él *sub. pron.* he
elefante *m.* elephant (12)
elegante elegant; **¡qué pantalones tan elegantes!** what elegant pants! (11)
elegir (i, i) (j) to elect; to choose (11)
ella she
embarazada pregnant; **estar embarazada** to be pregnant (13)
embargo: sin embargo nevertheless; however
emergencia: sala de emergencias emergency room (14)
emigración *f.* emigration (14)
emigrar to emigrate (14)
emisora de radio radio station
empatar to tie (*score*)
empezar (ie) (c) to begin (4); **empezar a** to begin to do something (4); to start; **para empezar** to begin with
empresa firm, business; **administración** *f.* **de empresas** business and management
en in; on; at; **en cambio** on the other hand; **en caso (de) (que)** in case (that) (14); **en conclusión** in conclusion; **en particular** in particular; **en principio** in principle; **en resumen** in summary; **en suma** in conclusion; **en venta** on sale; **en voz alta** aloud
enamorado(a) (de) in love (*with*) (5)
encantado(a) delighted; nice to meet you (1)
encantador(a) enchanting
encantar to love, to be delighted (8)
encender (ie) to turn on (4)
encerrar (ie) to lock up (4)
encima (de) on top (of) (4)
encontrar (ue) to find (4)
enero January (3)
enfermero(a) nurse (5)
enfermo(a) sick (5)
enfrente (de) in front (of) (4)
engordar to gain weight
enojado(a) angry (5)
enojarse to become angry (9)

ensalada salad (7)

enseñar to teach (2)

entender (ie) to understand (4)

entonces then, next

entrada entrance; cover charge; ticket (6)

entrar to enter

entre among; between (4)

entregar (gu) to hand in, hand over

entremés *m.* appetizer (7)

entrenador(a) coach

entrenar to train, to coach

entreplanta loft

entrevista interview (5)

entusiasta enthusiastic

envolver (ue) to wrap

equipaje *m.* luggage (10); **facturar equipaje** to check luggage (10); **reclamo de equipaje** baggage claim (10); **revisión** *f.* **de equipaje** luggage screening (10)

equipo team (6); equipment (6); **equipo escolar** school supplies

equivocado(a) wrong (5)

equivocarse (qu) to make a mistake

escala layover (10); **hacer escala** to make a stop, layover

escalera stairs (7)

escoba broom (8)

escolar *adj.* school; **equipo escolar** school supplies

escondidas *f.* hide and seek (8)

escribir (un mensaje) to write (a message) (3)

escritor(a) writer (5)

escritorio desk; teacher's desk (1)

escuchar to listen (2)

escuela school (4)

esculpir to sculpt (11)

escultura sculpture (11)

ese(a) *adj.* that; *pron.* that (one)

esmog *m.* smog (12)

eso *pron.* that (one); **por eso** therefore

esos(as) *adj.* those; *pron.* those

espalda back (6)

espanto fright

España Spain

español *m.* Spanish (*language*)

español(a) *m.* (*f.*) native of Spain; *adj.* Spanish (14)

espejo mirror

espera: sala de espera waiting room (10)

esperar to hope (for) (13); to expect; to wait (9)

espinaca spinach

esponja sponge

esposo(a) husband/wife; spouse (2)

esqueleto skeleton (14)

esquí acuático *m.* water-skiing

esquiar to ski (2); **esquiar en el agua** to water ski (6); **esquiar en tabla** to snowboard (6)

esquina corner (9)

estación *f.* station; season; **estación de autobuses** bus station; **estación de bomberos** fire station; **estación de ferrocarril** train station; **estación de policía** police station

estacionarse to park (9)

estadio stadium (2)

Estados Unidos United States

estadounidense *m. f.* citizen of the United States

estampado(a) patterned (11)

estante *m.* shelf

estar to be (4); **¿cómo está usted?** how are you (*form.*)? (1); **¿cómo estás?** how are you (*fam.*)? (1); **estar embarazada** to be pregnant (13); **estar atrasado(a)** to

be late; **estar dañado(a)** to be damaged (9); **estar de acuerdo** to agree; **estar de moda** to be in style; **estar herido(a)** to be injured (9); **estar mareado(a)** to be dizzy (14); **está lloviendo** it's raining; **está nevando** it's snowing; **está nublado** it is cloudy (3); **está despejado** it is clear (3); **fuera de** outside of (4)

estatura height

este(a) *adj.* this; *pron.* this (one)

estilográfico(a): pluma estilográfica fountain pen

estirarse to stretch (6)

esto *pron.* this (one); **¡esto es el colmo!** this is the last straw!

estómago stomach (6)

estornudar to sneeze (14)

estornudo sneeze (14)

estos(as) adj. these

éstos(as) *pron.* these

estrecho strait

estreñimiento constipation

estudiante *m. f.* student (1)

estudiantil *adj.* student; **albergue estudiantil** *m.* youth hostel; **centro estudiantil** student center (2)

estudiar to study (2)

estudio efficiency apartment, studio

estufa stove (4)

exacto(a) exactly

examen *m.* exam (2); **examen médico** medical examination

examinar to examine (14)

excursión: ir de excursión to hike (6)

excusarse to make an excuse

exhibición *f.* exhibition (11)

exhibir to exhibit (11)

éxito success; **éxito de taquilla** box office hit (13); **tener (mucho) éxito** to be (very) successful (2)

expresión *f.* expression; **expresión oral** speech (2)

extinción: peligro de extinción danger of extinction (12)

extranjero: al extranjero abroad

extranjero(a) foreigner

extrañar to miss (13)

extraño strange, odd (11)

extremidad *f.* extremity

extrovertido(a) extrovert

F

fábrica factory

fácil easy (1)

facturar equipaje to check luggage (10)

facultad *f.* school, college

falda skirt (3); **¡qué bien te queda esa falda!** that skirt really fits you well! (11)

falta lack

famoso(a) famous (1)

farmacéutico(a) pharmacist

farmacia pharmacy (4)

fascinante fascinating

fascinar to fascinate, be fascinated by (8)

favor *m.* favor; **por favor** please

febrero February (3)

fecha date (*calendar*) (3)

felicitar to congratulate (7)

feliz happy (5); **ponerse feliz** to become happy

feo(a) ugly (1)

ferrocarril *m.* railroad; **estación** *f.* **de ferrocarril** train station

festejado(a) guest of honor

festejar to entertain, to celebrate

festejo party, celebration (9)

festival *m.* festival

festivo: día *m.* **festivo** holiday

fiambre *m.* luncheon meat, cold cut

fiebre *f.* fever

fiesta party; **fiesta de canastilla** baby shower; **fiesta de cumpleaños** birthday party; **fiesta sorpresa** surprise party

filosofía philosophy (2); **filosofía y letras** liberal arts

fin *m.* end; **fin de semana** weekend (3); **a fin de que** so (that), in order that (14); **al fin y al cabo** after all; when all is said and done; **por fin** finally

final *m.* end; **al final** in the end

finalmente finally

física physics (2)

físico(a) physical

flan *m.* flan (7)

flojo(a) loose

flor *f.* flower (4); **de flores** floral, flowered

forma shape; **mantenerse** (*like* **tener**) **en forma** to stay fit, keep in shape

foto *f.* photo(graph); **revelar fotos** to develop photos; **sacar (qu) fotos** to take photos

fotógrafo(a) photographer (5)

fracturarse to fracture (14)

francés *m.* French (*language*) (2)

frase *f.* phrase

fregadero kitchen sink (4)

fregar (ie) (gu) to mop; to scrub

frente a facing

frente *f.* forehead

fresa strawberry (7)

fresco(a) fresh, cool; **hace fresco** it's cool (*weather*)

frijol *m.* bean

frío(a) cold; **hace frío** it's cold (*weather*); **tener (mucho) frío** to be (very) cold (2)

frito(a) fried (7)

frustrado(a) frustrated (5)

frustrarse to become frustrated (9)

fruta fruit (7)

frutería fruit store

fuego fire; **fuegos artificiales** fireworks (9)

fuera (de) outside (of) (4)

fútbol *m.* soccer (6); **fútbol americano** football

futbolista *m. f.* football (soccer) player

G

gafas *pl.* glasses; **gafas de sol** sunglasses

galería gallery (11)

gallina hen (12)

gallo rooster (12)

gamba shrimp

gana desire, wish; **tener ganas de** (+ *inf.*) to feel like (*doing something*) (2)

ganar to earn (5); to win

ganga bargain

garganta throat; **dolor** *m.* **de garganta** sore throat; **inflamación** *f.* **de la garganta** strep throat

gastar to spend

gato(a) cat (2)

gemelo(a) twin

general: por lo general generally

generalmente generally

generoso(a) generous (1)

gente *f.* people

geografía geography (2)

gerente *m. f.* manager

gimnasio gym(nasium) (2)

gis *m.* chalk

globalización *f.* globalization (14)
globo balloon (9)
gobierno government (14)
golf *m.* golf (6)
golfo gulf
golosina candy (13)
goma (pencil) eraser
gordo(a) fat (1); plump
gorila gorilla (12)
gorra cap
gorro cap (3)
gota drop (14)
grabado engraving (11); print (11)
grabadora tape recorder
gracias thanks, thank you
gracioso(a) funny; charming
graduación *f.* graduation (9)
gran/grande great; big (1); large (11)
granja farm (12)
gripe *f.* flu (14)
grupo group; **grupo de música** music group (9); band (9)
guante *m.* glove (3)
guapo(a) handsome (1)
guardar to keep; to put away (8)
guatemalteco(a) Guatemalan (14)
guerra war (14)
guisante *m.* pea
gustar to like; to please; to be pleasing; **me gusta** I like (3); **le gusta** he/she likes (3); **te gusta** you (*fam. sing.*) like (3)
gusto pleasure; taste; **con mucho gusto** with pleasure; **mucho gusto** nice to meet you (1)

H

habitación *f.* room (4) (10); **habitación doble** double room; **habitación sencilla** single room; **servicio a la habitación** room service (10)
hablar to talk (2); to speak; **hablar por teléfono** to talk on the phone (2)
hacer to do (5); to make (5); **hace buen tiempo** the weather is nice (3); **hace calor** it's hot (3); **hace fresco** it's cool (*weather*) (3); **hace frío** it's cold (*weather*) (3); **hace mal tiempo** the weather is bad (3); **hace sol** it's sunny (3); **hace viento** it's windy (3); **hacer alpinismo** to climb mountains (6); **hacer clic (en)** to click on (13); **hacer juego** to match (11); **hacer la cama** to make the bed (8); **hacer la maleta** to pack one's suitcase; **hecho(a) a mano** handmade (11); **¿qué tiempo hace?** what's the weather like?
hambre *f.* hunger; **tener (mucha) hambre** to be (very) hungry (2)
hamburguesa hamburger (7)
hasta until; **hasta ahora** up to now, so far; **hasta aquí** up to now, so far; **hasta hace poco** until a little while ago; **hasta luego** see you later (1); **hasta mañana** see you tomorrow (1); **hasta pronto** see you soon (1); **hasta que** until
hay there is/are (1); **hay que** (+ *inf.*) one should (+ *verb*); it's necessary to (+ *verb*); **¿qué hay de nuevo?** what's new? (1)
helada frost
helado ice cream (7)
hembra female (12)
herida wound
herido(a): estar herido(a) to be injured (9)
hermanastro(a) stepbrother/stepsister
hermano(a) brother/sister (2); **medio(a) hermano(a)** half brother/half sister (2)
hermoso(a) beautiful

hielo ice; **patinar sobre hielo** to ice skate
hierba grass
hígado liver (14)
hijastro(a) stepson/stepdaughter
hijo(a) son/daughter (2)
hipertensión *f.* hypertension; high blood pressure (14)
historia history (2); **historia médica** medical history
hogar *m.* home
hoja de papel piece of paper
hola hello (1)
holandés(esa) Dutch
hombre *m.* man (1)
hombro shoulder (6)
hondureño(a) Honduran (14)
honesto(a) honest (1)
hora time (*of day*)
hornear to bake (7)
horno oven (4); **al horno** baked (7)
hospital *m.* hospital (4)
hostal *m.* hostel
hotel *m.* hotel (4); **hotel económico** inexpensive hotel; **hotel de lujo** luxury hotel; **hotel de primera clase** first-class hotel
hoy today (3) (6)
huelga strike
hueso bone (14)
huésped *m. f.* guest (10)
huevo egg (7)

I

ida: de ida one-way; **de ida y vuelta** round-trip
idealista idealist (1)
identificación *f.* identification
idioma *m.* language (14)
iglesia church (4)
igual equal; **al igual que** like
igualmente likewise
impaciente impatient (1)
impermeable *m.* raincoat (3)
importancia importance
importante important
importar to be important (8)
imposible impossible
imprescindible indispensable
impresionante impressive
impresionista impressionist (11)
impresora printer
impuesto tax
incluido(a) included
incluir (y) to include
incorrecto(a) not right, incorrect
infantil childish, for children (13)
inferior lower
infinitivo infinitive
inflamación *f.* **de la garganta** strep throat
informática computer science (2)
ingeniería engineering (2)
ingeniero(a) engineer
inglés *m.* English (*language*)
inicialmente initially
inmigración *f.* immigration (14)
inmigrar to immigrate (14)
inodoro toilet (4)
insistir (en + *inf.*) to insist (*on*) (13)
insomnio insomnia (14)
inteligente intelligent (1)
interesado(a) interested (5)
interesante interesting (1)
interesar to interest, be interested in (8)
internacional international; **aeropuerto internacional** international airport

(10); **organismo internacional** international organization (14)
Internet inalámbrico *m.* wireless Internet (10)
interno(a) internal
intestino intestine (14)
introvertido(a) introvert
invierno winter (3)
invitación *f.* invitation (9)
invitado(a) guest (9)
inyección *f.* injection (14); shot; **poner(le) una inyección** to give (him/her) an injection
ir to go (3); **irse** to leave, go away (6); **ir de excursión** to hike (6); **ir de pesca** to go fishing (6)
isla island (12)
italiano Italian (2)
izquierda left; **a la izquierda (de)** to the left (of) (4)

J

jabón *m.* soap (6); **jabón para platos** dish soap (8)
jade *m.* jade; **objeto de jade** jade object
jaguar *m.* jaguar (12)
jamás never (6)
jamón *m.* ham (7)
jarabe *m.* cough syrup (14)
jardín *m.* yard; garden (4); **jardín botánico** botanical garden; **cultivar el jardín** to garden (*flowers*)
jardinería gardening; **hacer jardinería** to do yardwork (8)
jaula cage (12)
jirafa giraffe (12)
joven (*pl.* **jóvenes**) young (1)
jubilado(a) retired
judía verde green bean
juego game; **juego de mesa** board game (8); **hacer** *irreg.* **juego** to match (11)
jueves *m.* Thursday (3)
jugar (ue, u) (gu) to play (4); **jugar a los bolos** to go bowling (8)
jugo juice (7)
juguete *m.* toy (8)
juicio judgment
julio July (3)
junio June (3)
junto a beside, next to
jurar to swear, give one's word
justo(a) fair
juventud *f.* youth (13)

K

kiosco kiosk, stand

L

la *f.* the; *d.o.* her/it/you (*form. sing.*)
labio lip
laboratorio laboratory (2)
lado side; **al lado (de)** alongside (of); beside, next to (4)
lago lake (6)
lámpara lamp (4)
lana wool (11)
langosta lobster
lápiz *m.* (*pl.* **lápices**) pencil(s) (1)
largo(a) long (1); **a lo largo (de)** along
las *f. pl.* the; *d.o. pron.* you (*form. pl.*) them
lástima pity
lavabo bathroom sink (4)
lavadora washing machine (4)

lavandería laundry, laundry room
lavaplatos *m. sing., pl.* dishwasher (4)
lavar(se) to wash (6); **lavar platos** to do dishes (8); **lavar ropa** to do laundry (8)
le *i.o.* you (*form. sing.*); to/for him, her, it; **le presento a...** I'd like to introduce you (*form.*) to . . . (1)
leal loyal
lección *f.* lesson
leche *f.* milk (7)
lechería dairy store
lechuga lettuce (7)
leer to read (3)
lejos (de) far (from) (4)
lengua language (2); tongue; **lenguas modernas** modern languages; **sacar (qu) la lengua** to stick out one's tongue
lentes *m. pl.* glasses (3)
león *m.* lion
les *i.o. pron.* to, for you (*form. pl.*), them
letras: filosofía y letras liberal arts
levantar to lift; **levantarse** to get up (6); **levantar pesas** to lift weights (6)
ley *f.* law (14)
liberal liberal (1)
libra pound
libre free; **unión** *f.* **libre** common-law union (13)
librería bookstore (2)
libro book (1)
licuado smoothie made with fruits, juices, and ice
limitar to limit (13)
límite *m.* **de velocidad** speed limit (9)
limón *m.* lemon; lime
limpiador *m.* liquid cleaner; **limpiador para el hogar** all-purpose cleaner
limpiar to clean (2)
limpieza: artículos de limpieza cleaning materials
limpio(a) clean
lindo(a) pretty; **¡qué lindos zapatos!** what pretty shoes! (11)
línea aérea airline
lino linen (11)
liquidación *f.* sale
liso(a) solid (*color*) (11)
lista list
litera bunk (bed)
literatura literature (2)
litro liter
llama llama (12)
llamar to call (2); **llamarse** to be called/named; **me llamo...** my name is . . . (1)
llano plains (12)
llave *f.* key (10)
llegada arrival (10)
llegar (gu) to arrive (2)
lleno(a) full
llevar to take (3); to carry (3); to wear (3); to take along (7); **llevar puesto** to be wearing (3)
llevarse bien/mal to (not) get along (13)
llover (ue) to rain (4); **está lloviendo** it's raining; **llueve** it is raining, it rains (3)
lluvia rain
lo *m. d.o.* you (*form. sing.*); him,/it; **lo cual** which; **lo que** what, which; **lo siento (mucho)** I'm (very) sorry
lobo wolf (12)
loco(a) crazy (5); **volverse loco(a)** to go crazy
locutor(a) announcer (13)
los *def. art. m. pl.* the; *d.o.* them/you (*form. pl.*)
lucha fight, struggle

luchar to fight, struggle
lucir (zc) to wear; to show off, sport (*wear*)
luego then, next (6); **hasta luego** see you later (1)
lugar *m.* place; **tener lugar** to take place
lujo luxury; **de lujo** luxurious (10); **hotel** *m.* **de lujo** luxury hotel
luna de miel honeymoon (13)
lunar: de lunares polka-dotted (11)
lunes *m.* Monday (3)
luz *f.* (*pl.* **luces**) light (11); **dar a luz** to give birth (13)

M

macho male (12)
madrastra stepmother
madre *f.* mother (2)
madrina godmother (13)
maestro(a) teacher; **maestro(a) de ceremonias** master of ceremony
maíz *m.* corn (7); **palomitas de maíz** popcorn (13)
mal *adv.* badly; bad (1), not well; **hace mal tiempo** the weather is bad (3); **llevarse mal** to not get along (13); **sentirse (e, i) mal** to feel bad, ill
mal, malo(a) bad (1)
maleta suitcase (10); **deshacer la maleta** to unpack one's suitcase; **hacer la maleta** to pack one's suitcase
maletero porter
mamá mother (2)
mamífero mammal (12)
manantial *m.* spring (of water)
mandar to order (13); **mandar (un mensaje)** to send (a message) (2)
mandato command
manejar to drive (2)
manera way
manguera hose (8)
mano *f.* hand (6); **equipaje** *m.* **de mano** hand luggage (10); **hecho(a) a mano** handmade (11)
mantel *m.* tablecloth
mantenerse (*like* **tener) en forma** to stay fit, keep in shape
mantequilla butter (7)
manzana apple (7)
mañana tomorrow (3) (6); morning; **de la mañana** A.M.; **hasta mañana** see you tomorrow (1); **por la mañana** in the morning (3)
mapa *m.* map (1)
maquillarse to put on make-up (6)
mar *m.* sea (12)
maravilla marvel, wonder
marca: de marca name brand (11)
marcador *m.* marker
marcharse to leave, to go away
marcial: artes marciales *f. pl.* martial arts
mareado dizzy; **estar mareado(a)** to be dizzy (14)
marearse to feel dizzy
mareo dizziness; **tener mareos** to be dizzy
mariscal *m. raw shellfish marinated in lime juice*
mariscos shellfish
marrón brown
martes *m.* Tuesday (3)
marzo March (3)
más more; plus (*in mathematical functions*); **más que** more than; **más tarde** later (6)
máscara mask (11)
masticar (qu) to chew
matemáticas *pl.* mathematics (2)

materia course, subject
matrimonial: cama matrimonial double bed
matrimonio: marriage **proponer matrimonio** to propose marriage (13)
mayo May (3)
mayonesa mayonnaise (7)
mayor older (11); **el/la mayor** the oldest
me *d.o., i.o. pron.* me
mecánico(a) mechanic (5)
media stocking
mediano(a) medium (11)
medianoche *f.* midnight (3)
medias *pl.* panty hose
medicamento medication
médico(a) *adj.* medical; **examen** *m.* **médico** medical examination; **historia médica** medical history; **receta médica** prescription (14)
médico(a) *n.* doctor (5)
medio(a) half; **medio(a) hermano(a)** half brother/half sister (2); **media pensión** half board (*breakfast and one other meal*)
mediodía *m.* noon (3)
mejilla cheek
mejillón *m.* mussel
mejor better (11); **el/la mejor** the best
melón *m.* melon (7)
menor younger (11); **el/la menor** the youngest
menos less; minus (*in mathematical functions*); **menos que** less than; **a menos que** unless (14)
mentir (ie, i) to lie (4)
menudo: a menudo frequently, often (6)
mercado market
merecer (zc) to deserve
merendar (ie) to eat a snack
merienda snack
mermelada jam
mes *m.* month
mesa table; **poner la mesa** to set the table (8); **recoger (j) la mesa** to pick up the table (8); to clear the table (8)
mesero(a) (*Mex.*) (*restaurant*) waitperson; waiter (5)
meseta plateau
mesita coffee table (4); end table; **mesita de noche** night table
metro subway
mexicano(a) Mexican (14)
mezclilla denim (11)
mezquita mosque (4)
mi my
microondas *m.* microwave (4)
miedo fear; **tenerle miedo a** to be afraid of (*person*); **tener (mucho) miedo** to be (very) afraid (2)
miel *f.* honey; **luna de miel** honeymoon (13)
miembro member
mientras while (6)
miércoles *m.* Wednesday (3)
mil one thousand (7); **cien mil** (one) hundred thousand; **dos mil** two thousand (7)
millón *m.* million (7); **cien millones** (one) hundred million
mío(a) mine
mirar (la tele) to watch (TV) (2); to look (at)
misa mass
mismo(a) same; **del mismo modo** similarly
mochila backpack (1)
moda fashion, style; **de moda** fashionable (11); **estar de moda** to be in style (11); **pasado(a) de moda** out of style

modelo *m. f.* model (5)
moderno(a) modern; **lenguas modernas** modern languages
modista dressmaker
modo way; **del mismo modo** similarly
molestar to bother (8), be bothered by
mono monkey (12)
montaña mountain (12)
montañoso(a) mountainous
montar to climb; get on; **montar a** to ride (an animal) (6)
morado(a) purple (3)
moreno(a) dark-skinned/dark-haired (1), brunette
morir (ue, u) to die (4)
mostaza mustard (7)
mostrador *m.* counter (10)
mostrar (ue) to show (8)
moto(cicleta) motorcycle (8)
mover (ue) to move (*something*)
MP3 *m.* MP3 (13)
mucho(a) much; many; a lot (2); **lo siento (mucho)** I'm (very) sorry; **mucho gusto** nice to meet you (1)
mudarse to move (14)
muebles *m. pl.* furniture
muerte *f.* death (13)
muerto(a) dead; **naturaleza muerta** still life (11)
mujer *f.* woman (1); **mujer policía** police officer (5)
multa fine (9); ticket (9)
municipalidad *f.* city hall
muñeca wrist
muñeco(a) doll (8)
mural *m.* mural (11)
muscular muscular; **dolor** *m.* **muscular** muscle ache
museo museum (4)
música music (2)
músico(a) musician (5)
muslo thigh (6)
muy very (1)

N

nacer (zc) to be born (13)
nacionalidad *f.* nationality
nada nothing (1)
nadar to swim (2)
nadie no one, nobody
naipes *m. pl.* (playing) cards
naranja orange (7) (8)
nariz *f.* nose (6)
natación swimming (6)
natural natural; **recursos naturales** natural resources (12)
naturaleza nature (12); **naturaleza muerta** still life (11)
navegar (gu) a la vela to sail; **navegar el Internet** to surf the web (8)
Navidad Christmas (3)
necesario(a) necessary
necesitar to need (2)
negar (ie) (gu) to deny, to negate
negocio business (4); **negocios** *pl.* business (2); **centro de negocios** business center (10)
negro(a) black (3)
nevar (ie) to snow (4); **está nevando** it's snowing; **nieva** it is snowing, it snows (3)
ni... ni neither . . . nor
nicaragüense *m. f.* Nicaraguan (14)
niebla fog
nieto(a) grandson/granddaughter (2)
nieve *f.* snow

nilón *m.* nylon
ningún/ninguno(a) none, not any
niñera babysitter (8)
niñez *f.* childhood (13)
no no; **¿no?** isn't that so?; **¿no es así?** isn't that right?; **no obstante** however
noche *f.* night; **de la noche** P.M.; **mesita de noche** night table; **por la noche** in the evening (3)
nombre *m.* name
noreste *m.* northeast
normalmente normally (6)
noroeste *m.* northwest
norte *m.* north
norteamericano(a) North American
nos *d.o.* us; *i.o.* to/for us; *refl. pron.* ourselves; **nos vemos** see you later (1)
nosotros(as) *subj. pron.* we
nota grade (2); **nota adhesiva** sticky note; **sacar (qu) una buena/mala nota** to get a good/bad grade
noticiario news (13)
novecientos(as) nine hundred (7)
novelista *m. f.* novelist
noventa ninety (1)
noviazgo engagement (13); relationship (13)
noviembre *m.* November (3)
novio(a) groom/bride; fiancé(e); boyfriend/girlfriend (2); *pl.* bride and groom (9)
nube *f.* cloud (12)
nublado(a) cloudy; **está nublado** it is cloudy (3)
nuboso(a) cloudy
nuera daughter-in-law
nuestro(a) *poss.* our
nueve nine (1)
nuevo(a) new; **Año Nuevo** New Year (3); **de nuevo** new; again; **¿Qué hay de nuevo?** What's new? (1)
número number; size (*shoe*) (11)
nunca never (6)

O

o or; **o...o** either . . . or
obesidad *f.* obesity (14)
objeto object; **objeto directo** direct object; **objeto indirecto** indirect object
obligación *f.* obligation
obra work (*of art, literature, theater, etc.*) (11)
obscuro(a) dark (11)
obstante: no obstante however
obstinado(a) obstinate, stubborn
obtener to get
obvio(a) obvious
océano ocean
ochenta eighty (1)
ocho eight (1)
ochocientos(as) eight hundred (7)
octubre *m.* October (3)
ocupado(a) busy (5)
ocurrir to occur
odiar to hate (13)
oferta offer; sale (event, reduction of prices) (11)
oficina office (4); **oficina de correos** post office
oficio occupation
oído inner ear
oír to hear (5)
ojalá (que) I hope (that)
ojo eye

ola wave (12)
óleo oil painting (11)
oler (ue) to smell
olfato sense of smell
olla de cerámica ceramic pot
olvidar to forget (11)
once eleven (1)
onomástico saint's day
opinar to give one's opinion
opinión *f.* opinion
optimista *m., f.* optimist (1)
oración *f.* sentence
orden *f.* order (7)
ordenador *m.* computer
ordenar to tidy up (8); to straighten up (8)
oreja (*outer*) ear (6)
organismo internacional international organization (14)
organizar (c) to organize, to tidy up
órgano organ; **órgano vital** vital organ (14)
orgulloso(a) (de) proud (of)
origen *m.* origin
oro gold
os *d.o.* (*Sp.*) you (*fam. pl.*); *i.o.* (*Sp.*) to/for you (*fam. pl.*); *refl. pron.* (*Sp.*) yourselves (*fam. pl.*)
oscuro(a) dark; **cuarto oscuro** darkroom (8)
osito teddy bear (8)
oso bear (12)
otoño autumn (3)
otro(a) other; **otra vez** again; **por otra parte** moreover; on the other hand
oveja sheep (12)

P

pachanga (rowdy) party
paciente patient (1) (14)
padrastro stepfather (2)
padre *m.* father (2); *pl.* parents
padrino best man, godfather (13)
pagar (gu) to pay; **pagar y marcharse** to check out (10)
página page
país *m.* country (14)
paisaje *m.* landscape (11)
pájaro bird
palabra word
palacio palace
paleta pallet (11)
palmera palm tree (12)
palomitas de maíz popcorn (13)
pampa grasslands (12)
pan *m.* bread (7)
panadería bakery
panameño(a) Panamanian (14)
pantalla screen (13)
pantalones *m. pl.* pants (3); **pantalones cortos** shorts (3)
papá *m.* father (2)
papa potato (7)
papel *m.* paper (1); **hoja de papel** piece of paper; **papel de cocina** paper towel
paperas mumps
paquete package (4)
para for; in order to; to (*in the direction of*); **para empezar** to begin with; **para que** so (that) (14); **¿para qué?** for what reason?
parada stop (10)
paraguas *m. sing., pl.* umbrella (3)
paraguayo(a) Paraguayan (14)
paramédico paramedic (9)
parcial partial; **a tiempo parcial** part-time
PARE: pasarse una señal de PARE to run a STOP sign (9)
parecer (zc) to seem

parecerse a to look like; to be similar/like
pared *f.* wall
pareja pair; couple (2) (13); partner (2)
pariente relative (2)
párpado eyelid
parque *m.* park (4); **parque de atracciones** amusement park
parquímetro parking meter (9)
parte *f.* part; **por otra parte** moreover; on the other hand
particular: en particular in particular
partido match; game (*sports*) (6)
pasa raisin
pasado(a) past; last; **el año pasado** last year; **la semana pasada** last week (6); **pasado(a) de moda** out of style
pasaje *m.* ticket (*transportation*)
pasajero(a) passenger (10)
pasaporte *m.* passport (10); **control de pasaporte** passport control
pasar to pass; to happen; **pasar la aspiradora** to vacuum (8); **pasarlo bien** to have a good time; **pasar por seguridad** to go through security (10); **pasar tiempo** to spend time (8); **pasarse un semáforo en rojo** to run a red light (9); **pasarse una señal de PARE** to run a STOP sign (9); **¿qué pasa?** what's going on? (1)
pase: pase *m.* **de abordar** boarding pass (10)
pasear to walk
paseo: ir de paseo to go for a walk (8)
pasillo hallway; aisle (10)
paso: de paso by the way
pasta de dientes toothpaste (6)
pastel *m.* pastry; cake (7) (9)
pastelería pastry shop
pastilla pill (14)
pasto grass, pasture (12)
patín *m.* skate
patinar to skate (6); **patinar en hielo** to ice skate (6); **patinar sobre ruedas** to roller-skate, roller-blade
patineta skateboard (8)
patio patio (4); courtyard; yard; flower garden
pato duck (12)
patrulla police car (9)
pavo turkey (7) (12)
paz *f.* peace (14)
pecho chest (6)
pedagogía pedagogy; **ciencias de la pedagogía** education
pedir (i, i) to ask for (4); to request
peinarse to comb/style one's hair (6)
pelear to fight (8); to argue (8)
película movie (4); film
peligro (de extinción) danger (of extinction) (12)
pelirrojo(a) red-haired (1)
pelo hair (6)
pelota ball (6)
península peninsula (12)
pensar (ie) to think (4); to intend
peor worse (11); **el/la peor** the worst
pepinillo pickle (8)
pepino cucumber (7)
pequeño(a) small (1)
pera pear
perder (ie) to lose (4); to miss (a flight, a train) (10)
perdón *m.* pardon
perdonarse to excuse oneself
perezoso(a) lazy (1)

periodismo journalism (2)
periodista *m. f.* journalist (5)
permiso permission (8)
pero *conj.* but
perro dog (2)
persona person
peruano(a) Peruvian (14)
pesa weight; **levantar pesas** to lift weights (6)
pesadilla nightmare
pésame *m. sing.* condolences
pesar to weigh
pesar: a pesar de in spite of
pesca: ir de pesca to go fishing (6)
pescadería fish store, fish market
pescado fish (*food*) (7)
pescar (qu) to fish (6)
pesimista *adj. m. f.* pessimist (1)
pestaña eyelash
petróleo oil (12)
pez *m.* (*pl.* **peces**) fish (2)
piano piano; **tocar (qu) el piano** to play the piano
picar (qu) to snack
pico mountain peak
pie *m.* foot (6)
piel *f.* skin; leather (11)
pierna leg (6)
pijama *m. sing.* pajamas (3)
piloto *m. f.* pilot (5)
pimienta pepper (7)
pincel *m.* paintbrush (11)
ping-pong *m.* ping-pong; **jugar al ping-pong** to play ping-pong (6)
pingüino penguin (12)
pintor(a) painter (5)
pintura paint
piña pineapple (7)
piñata piñata (9)
Pirineos Pyrenees
piscina swimming pool (4)
piso apartment; floor (*of a building*) (4)
pista (de correr) track
pizarra chalkboard (1)
plancha iron (8)
planchar to iron (8); **tabla de planchar** ironing board (8)
planta plant (4); floor (*building*)
plata silver
plátano banana (7)
platillo saucer
plato plate; dish; **detergente** *m.* **para platos** dish detergent; **jabón** *m.* **para platos** dish soap (8); **lavar platos** to wash the dishes (8); **plato principal** main dish (7)
playa beach (4)
plaza city square (4)
pluma (estilográfica) (fountain) pen
pobre poor (1)
pobreza poverty (14)
poco(a) little, few (2); **hasta hace poco** until a little while ago
poder to be able to (4)
policía *f.* police (*force*); **estación** *f.* **de policía** police station
policía *m.* police officer (5); **mujer** *f.* **policía** police officer (5)
poliéster *m.* polyester
político(a) *n.* politician (5); *adj.* political; **ciencias políticas** political science (2)
pollo chicken (7); chick (12)
pomada cream; ointment
poner to put, place; to put on; to put up; **poner la mesa** to set the table (8); **poner(le) una inyección** to give (him/

her) an injection; **ponerse** to get (+ *adj.*); to become (+ *adj.*); **ponerse feliz** to become happy; **ponerse la ropa** to put on clothing (6); **ponerse triste** to become sad
por by; through; because of; due to; on account of; times (*in mathematical functions*); **por adelantado** in advance; **por ciento** percent (11); **por ejemplo** for example; **por eso** therefore; **por favor** please; **por fin** finally; **por lo general** generally; **por otra parte** moreover; on the other hand; **por otro lado** on the other hand; **¿por qué?** why? (1); **por supuesto** of course; **por último** lastly, finally
porque because
portero door attendant
posada inn; *pl.* nine-day celebration before Christmas
posar to pose (11)
posesivo(a) possessive
postre *m.* dessert (7)
postura posture
práctica activity; practice
practicar (qu) to practice; **practicar deportes** to play sports (2)
prado meadow
precio price
precioso(a) precious; lovely; beautiful
preferible preferable
preferir (ie, i) to prefer (4)
pregunta question
preguntar to ask (2)
preguntón(-ona) inquisitive
prenda garment (11); article of clothing
preocupación *f.* worry
preocupado(a) worried (5)
preocuparse to worry
preposición *f.* preposition
presentar to introduce; **le presento a...** I'd like to introduce you (*form.*) to . . . (1); **te presento a...** I'd like to introduce you (*fam.*) to . . . (1)
preservar to preserve (12)
presidente *m. f.* president
presión *f.* **arterial** blood pressure; **presión alta/baja** high/low blood pressure (14); **tomar la presión** to take someone's blood pressure (14)
prestar to lend (8)
pretérito preterite
previamente previously
primavera spring (3)
primer, primero(a) first; **hotel** *m.* **de primera clase** first-class hotel; **primera clase** first class (10); **Primera Comunión** *f.* First Communion; **primeros auxilios** first aid (14)
primo(a) cousin (2)
principal main; **plato principal** main dish (7)
principio beginning; principle; **al principio** at the beginning; **en principio** in principle
prisa hurry, haste; **tener (mucha) prisa** to be in a (big) hurry (2)
privado(a) private
probablemente probably
probador *m.* dressing room (11); fitting room
probar(se) (ue) to try (on) (11); to test
problema *m.* problem
problemático(a) problematic
profesión *f.* profession
profesor(a) professor (1)
profundo(a) deep
programación *f.* programming (13)

programador(a) programmer
prohibir to prohibit
prometer to promise
prometido(a) fiancé(e) (13)
pronombre *m.* pronoun
pronto soon (6); **hasta pronto** see you soon (1); **tan pronto como** as soon as (14)
propina tip; **dejar una propina** to leave a tip (7)
proponer (matrimonio) to propose (marriage) (13)
propósito: a propósito by the way
propuesta proposal
proteger (j) to protect (12)
protesta protest
provecho: buen provecho enjoy your meal
prueba test
psicología psychology (2)
psicólogo(a) psychologist (5)
público(a) public; **funcionario(a) público(a)** public official
puerta door (1); **puerta de salida** gate (10)
puerto port, harbor
puertorriqueño(a) Puerto Rican (14)
puesto de trabajo position, job
pulgar *m.* thumb
pulmón *m.* lung (14)
pulpo octopus
pulsera bracelet
punto point
pupitre *m.* student desk (1)

Q

que that, which; than; **¡que tengas un buen día!** have a nice day (1)
¡qué! what!; **¡qué bien te queda esa falda!** that skirt really fits you well! (11); **¡qué caro(a)!** how expensive! (11); **¡qué color tan bonito!** what a pretty color! (11); **¡qué lindos zapatos!** what pretty shoes! (11); **¡qué pantalones tan elegantes!** what elegant pants! (11)
¿qué? what? (1); **¿qué hay de nuevo?** what's new? (1); **¿qué pasa?** what's going on? (1); **¿qué tal?** how's it going? (1); **¿qué tiempo hace?** what's the weather like?
quedar to remain (11); to fit (11); **quedarse** to stay (10); **¡qué bien te queda esa falda!** that skirt really fits you well! (11)
quedarle to fit
quehacer *m.* chore (8)
quejarse to complain
quemadura de sol sunburn
querer to want (4); to love (7) (13); **querer decir** to mean; **quisiera** I would like
queso cheese (7)
quien(es) who, whom
¿quién(es)? who? (1) (4)
química chemistry (2)
quince fifteen (1); **los quince años** girl's fifteenth birthday celebration (9)
quinceañera girl celebrating her fifteenth birthday (9)
quinientos(as) five hundred (7)
quitarse to take off (*clothing*)
quizá(s) perhaps

R

racional rational
radio: emisora de radio radio station
radiografía X-ray (14)
raíz *f.* (*pl.* **raíces**) root
rana frog (12)
rápido fast

raqueta racket (6)
ráquetbol *m.* racquetball
raro(a) strange
ratón *m.* mouse (2)
raya stripe; **a rayas** striped (11)
rayos X X-rays; **sacar (qu) rayos X** to take X-rays
razón *f.* reason; **no tener razón** to be wrong; **tener razón** to be right (2)
realista realist (1)
rebajado(a) on sale (11); **estar rebajado(a)** to be on sale (11)
recepción *f.* reception (desk) (10); wedding reception (13)
recepcionista *m. f.* desk clerk; receptionist (10)
receta médica prescription (14)
rechazar (c) to decline, reject
recibir to receive (3); **recibir un regalo** to receive a gift (3)
recibo receipt
reciclaje *m.* recycling (12)
recién casado(a) newlywed (13)
recinto campus
reclamo de equipaje baggage claim (10)
recoger (j) la mesa to clear the table (8); to pick up the table (8)
recomendación *f.* recommendation
recomendar (ie) to recommend
recordar (ue) to remember (4)
recreación *f.* recreation; **sala de recreación** rec room
recuperarse to recover (14)
recursos naturales natural resources (12)
red *f.* net
redacción *f.* writing (2)
redes *f. pl.* **sociales** social networks (13)
refresco soda (7)
refrigerador *m.* refrigerator (4)
refugiado(a) refugee (14)
regalo gift (3); **recibir un regalo** to receive a gift (3)
regar (ie) (gu) to water (8)
regatear to bargain
registrarse to register (10)
regla ruler
regresar (a casa) to return (home) (2)
regular so-so (1); okay
reír (í, i) to laugh (4)
relación *f.* relationship
relacionado(a) related
relámpago lightning
rellenar to fill out
reloj *m.* clock (1); watch
remediar to remedy
remedio remedy
remoto: control *m.* **remoto** remote control (13)
renunciar to resign
reparar to repair
repente: de repente suddenly (9)
repetir (i, i) to repeat (4)
representante *m. f.* representative
reproductor: reproductor de CDs CD player (13); **reproductor de DVDs** DVD player (13)
reptil *m.* reptile (12)
res: carne de res beef
resaca hangover
reservación *f.* reservation
resfriado cold (*illness*) (14)
resguardo voucher; credit slip
residencia residence hall (2)
resistir to resist
resolución *f.* resolution
resolver (ue) to solve

respiración *f.* breathing; **bucear con tubo de respiración** to snorkel
respirar to breathe (14)
responder to respond
responsabilizar (c) to make (someone) responsible
responsable responsible
respuesta reply, answer
restaurante *m.* restaurant (4)
resultado result; **como resultado** as a result
resultar (de/en) to result (in)
resumen *m.* summary
retrasado(a) delayed (10)
retrato portrait (11)
revelar fotos to develop photographs
revisar to inspect
revisión *f.* **de equipaje** luggage screening (10)
revisor *m.* controller
revista magazine (13)
rezar (c) to pray (4)
rico(a) rich (1); delicious
riñón *m .* kidney
río river (12)
riqueza wealth (14)
rocoso(a) rocky
rodilla knee (6)
rojo(a) red (3); **pasarse un semáforo en rojo** to run a red light (9)
romántico(a) romantic
romper(se) to break (9) (11); **romper con** to break up with (relationship) (13)
ropa clothes; clothing; **lavar ropa** to do laundry (8)
ropero closet
rosado(a) pink (3); **vino rosado** rosé wine
rotulador *m.* marker
rubio(a) blond(e) (1)
rueda wheel; **patinar sobre ruedas** to roller-skate, roller-blade
rutina routine

S

sábado *m.* Saturday (3)
saber to know (*facts, how to do something*) (5)
sabroso(a) delicious
sacar (qu) to take (out); **sacar fotos** to take photographs; **sacar la basura** to take the trash out (8); **sacar la lengua** to stick out one's tongue; **sacar una buena/mala nota** to get a good/bad grade; **sacar rayos X** to take X-rays
saco suit coat; sport coat; **saco de dormir** sleeping bag
sacudidor *m.* duster (8)
sacudir to dust (8)
sal *f.* salt (7)
sala living room (4); **sala de conferencias** conference center (10); **sala de emergencias** emergency room (14); **sala de espera** waiting room (10); **sala de recreación** rec room; **sala de recreo** rec room
salado(a) salty
salchicha sausage
salida departure (10); **puerta de salida** gate (10)
salir to leave, to go out; **salir (a + *inf.*)** to go out (to do something) (8)
salmón *m.* salmon
salón *m.* living room; sitting room; hall; **salón de clases** classroom (1)
salsa de tomate (dulce) tomato sauce; ketchup
saltar to jump (8)
salud *f.* health (5) (14)
saludar to greet (7)

saludo greeting
salvadoreño(a) Salvadorian (14)
salvaje wild
sandalia sandal (3)
sandía watermelon
sándwich *m.* sandwich (7)
sangrar to bleed (14)
sangre *f.* blood
sano(a) healthy
santo saint; saint's day (9); **día** *m.* **de santo** saint's day
sastre *m.* tailor
satisfacción *f.* satisfaction
satisfecho(a) full (*stomach*); satisfied
sauna *m.* sauna (10)
secadora dryer (4)
secar(se) (qu) to dry (oneself) (6); to dry (8)
secretario(a) secretary (5)
sed *f.* thirst; **tener (mucha) sed** to be (very) thirsty (2)
seda silk (11)
seguir (i, i) to follow (5); **seguir (i) derecho** to go straight (10)
segundo(a) second; **segunda clase** second class (10)
seguridad *f.* security; **agente de seguridad** security agent (10); **cinturón** *m.* **de seguridad** safety (seat) belt (10); **control de seguridad** security check; **pasar por seguridad** to go through security (10)
seguro(a) *adj.* sure (5); *adv.* certainly; surely
seis six (1)
seiscientos(as) six hundred (7)
selva jungle (12); **selva tropical** tropical rain forest
semáforo stoplight; **pasarse un semáforo en rojo** to run a red light (9)
semana week (3); **fin de semana** weekend (3); **semana pasada** last week (6)
semestre semester (2)
sencillo(a) single (*room*) (10); simple (11); **habitación** *f.* **sencilla** single room
sensacional sensational
sensible sensitive
sentarse (ie) to sit (down)
sentido sense
sentir (ie, i) to feel; **lo siento (mucho)** I'm (very) sorry; **sentirse bien** to feel well; **sentirse mal** to feel bad, ill
señal *f.* sign; **pasarse una señal de PARE** to run a STOP sign (9)
separarse (de) to separate (from) (13)
septiembre *m.* September (3)
ser *m.* **humano** human being
ser to be (1); **¿de dónde eres tú?** where are you (*fam.*) from? (1); **yo soy de...** I'm from . . . (1)
serenata serenade (9)
serio(a) serious (1)
serpiente *f.* snake (12)
servicio a la habitación room service (10)
servicios utilities
servilleta napkin (7)
servir (i, i) to serve (4)
sesenta sixty (1)
setecientos(as) seven hundred (7)
setenta seventy (1)
si if, whether
sí yes
sicología psychology
sicólogo(a) psychologist
SIDA *m. sing.* AIDS (14)
siempre always (6); **casi siempre** almost always (6); **siempre y cuando** as long as (14)

sierra mountain range
siete seven (1)
silla chair (1)
sillón *m.* armchair (4)
sin without; **sin embargo** nevertheless; however; **sin que** without (14)
sino but (rather), instead; **sino (que)** *conj.* but
sobre on; on top of; over; about
sobremesa after-dinner conversation
sobrino(a) nephew/niece (2)
social social; **redes** *f. pl.* **sociales** social networks (13)
sociología sociology
sofá *m.* couch (4)
sol *m.* sun; **gafas de sol** sunglasses; **hace sol** it's sunny; **quemadura de sol** sunburn
solicitar to apply
solicitud *f.* application (5); want ad (5)
solidaridad *f.* solidarity
solo only
soltero(a) single person; unmarried person (13); **despedida de soltera** bridal shower; **despedida de soltero** bachelor party
solución *f.* solution
solucionar to solve
sombrero hat (3)
sombrilla beach umbrella
sonreír (i, i) to smile (4)
soñar (ue) to dream (*about*) (4)
sopa soup (7)
sorprenderse to be surprised (9)
sorprendido(a) surprised (5)
sorpresa surprise; **fiesta sorpresa** surprise party
sostener to support
sótano basement
su *poss.* your (*form. sing., pl.*); his; her; its; their
subir to go up, to take something up (10); **subir a** to get into (*a vehicle*) (9)
sucio(a) dirty (8)
suegro(a) father-in-law/mother-in-law (2)
sueldo salary (5)
suelo floor
sueño dream; sleep; **tener (mucho) sueño** to be (very) sleepy (2)
suerte *f.* luck; **tener (mucha) suerte** to be (very) lucky (2)
suéter *m.* sweater (3)
sugerencia suggestion
sugerir (ie, i) to suggest (13)
suma sum; summary; **en suma** in conclusion
súper super (*used as prefix*)
superar to overcome
superior superior; upper
supermercado supermarket (4)
supersticioso(a) superstitious
supuesto: por supuesto of course
sur *m.* south
sureste *m.* southeast
suroeste *m.* southwest
surrealista *m. f.* surrealist (11)
suspender to fail

T

tabla: esquiar en tabla to snowboard (6); **tabla de planchar** ironing board (8)
tablero keyboard (13)
tacto touch
tal vez perhaps
tal: ¿qué tal? how's it going? (1); **con tal (de) que** provided that (14)
taller *m.* workshop; garage
también also (1); in addition
tan so; **tan... como** as . . . as; **tan pronto como** as soon as (14); **¡qué color tan bonito!** what a pretty color! (11); **¡qué**

pantalones tan elegantes! what elegant pants! (11)
tanto(a) *adj.* so much; *pl.* so many; **tanto(s)/ tanta(s)... como** as many . . . as
tapete *m.* throw rug
taquilla ticket window (10); box office; **éxito de taquilla** box office hit (13)
tarde *adv.* late (6)
tarde *f.* afternoon; **de la tarde** P.M.; **más tarde** later (6); **por la tarde** in the afternoon (3)
tarea homework
tarjeta de crédito credit card (11)
tarta pie
taza cup
tazón *m.* soup bowl
te *d.o.* you (*fam. sing.*); *i.o.* to/for you (*fam. sing.*); *refl.* yourself; **te presento a...** I'd like to introduce you (*fam.*) to . . . (1)
té *m.* tea, afternoon tea
teatro theater (2) (4)
techo ceiling
técnico(a) technician
tejer to knit (8)
tela fabric
teléfono telephone; **teléfono celular** cell phone (8)
telenovela soap opera (13)
televidente *m. f.* television viewer (13)
televisión *f.* television (*medium*); **televisión por satélite** satellite television (13)
televisor *m.* television set (1)
temblar (ie) to shake; **me tiemblan las manos** my hands are shaking
temer to fear
temperatura temperature
templo temple (4)
temprano early (6)
tenedor *m.* fork (7)
tener to have; **tener que** (+ *inf.*) to have to (+ *verb*) (2); **no tener razón** to be wrong; **¡que tengas un buen día!** have a nice day (1); **tener (mucha) hambre** to be (very) hungry (2); **tener (mucha) prisa** to be in a (big) hurry (2); **tener (mucha) sed** to be (very) thirsty (2); **tener (mucha) suerte** to be (very) lucky (2); **tener (mucho) calor** to be (very) hot (2); **tener (mucho) cuidado** to be (very) careful (2); **tener (mucho) éxito** to be (very) successful (2); **tener (mucho) frío** to be (very) cold (2); **tener (mucho) miedo** to be afraid of (2); **tener (mucho) sueño** to be (very) sleepy (2); **tener celos** to be jealous; **tener ganas de** (+ *inf.*) to feel like (*doing something*) (2); **tener lugar** to take place; **tener mareos** to be dizzy; **tener razón** to be right (2); **tener... años** to be . . . years old (2); **tenerle miedo a** to be afraid of (*person*)
tenis *m.* tennis (6); tennis shoes (3)
terminar to finish (3) (9)
ternera veal
terraza terrace
testigo *m. f.* witness
textura texture
tiburón *m.* shark (12)
tiempo time; weather; **a tiempo** on time (10); **a tiempo completo** full-time; **a tiempo parcial** part-time; **hace buen tiempo** the weather is nice (3); **hace mal tiempo** the weather is bad (3); **pasar tiempo** to spend time (8); **¿Qué tiempo hace?** What's the weather like?

tienda shop; store (4); **tienda de campaña** camping tent (6)
tierno(a) tender
Tierra Earth (*planet*) (12)
tierra land, earth
tigre *m.* tiger (12)
tinta ink (11)
tinto: vino tinto red wine (7)
tintorería dry cleaners
tío(a) uncle/aunt (2)
tiza chalk
toalla towel (6); **toalla de papel** paper towel
tobillo ankle (6)
tocador *m.* dressing table
tocar (qu) to touch; **tocar (el piano)** to play (*the piano*) (8); to touch
tocino bacon
todavía still (6)
todo(a) all, every; **todos los días** every day (6)
tomar to take (2); **tomar (café)** to drink (coffee) (2); **tomar la presión** to take someone's blood pressure (14)
tomate *m.* tomato (7); **salsa de tomate (dulce)** tomato sauce; ketchup
tonto(a) dumb (1)
topografía topography
torcerse (ue) (z) to twist (14)
tormenta storm
toro bull (12)
toronja grapefruit
torre *f.* tower
tortuga turtle (12)
toser to cough (14)
totopos *pl.* tortilla chips (7)
trabajador(a) *adj.* hardworking (1)
trabajador(a) social social worker (5)
trabajar to work (2)
trabajo work; job (5); **solicitud** *f.* **de trabajo** job application
tradicional traditional (11)
traductor(a) translator
traer to bring (5)
traidor(a) traitorous
traje *m.* suit (3); **traje de baño** swimming suit (3)
tranquilo(a) tranquil; calm
transicional transitional
transmitir to broadcast (13)
transporte *m.* transportation (10)
trapeador *m.* mop (8)
trapear to mop (8)
trapo dust cloth; rag (8); cloth (8)
tratado de comercio trade treaty (14)
tratamiento treatment (14)
trece thirteen (1)
treinta thirty (1)
tren *m.* train
trepar (un árbol) to climb (a tree) (8)
tres three (1)
trescientos(as) three hundred (7)
trimestre quarter (2)
triple triple (10)
triste sad (5); **ponerse triste** to become sad
tronco trunk
tropezar (ie) (c) to trip (9)
tropical tropical; **selva tropical** tropical rain forest
trucha trout

trueno thunder
tú *subj. pron.* you (*fam. sing.*); **¿de dónde eres tú?** where are you (*fam.*) from? (1); **¿y tú?** and you (*fam.*)? (1)
tu(s) *poss.* your (*fam. sing.*)
tubo: bucear con tubo de respiración to snorkel
tuna cactus fruit
turista *m. f.* tourist (10)

U

ubicación *f.* location
último(a) final; last; **por último** lastly; finally
un/uno(a) a, an, one (1)
único(a) unique; only
unión *f.* **libre** common-law union (13)
universidad *f.* university
unos(as) some
urgente urgent
uruguayo(a) Uruguayan (14)
usado(a) used
usar to use (2)
usted *subj. pron.* you (*form. sing.*); **¿cómo está usted?** how are you (*form.*)? (1); **¿y usted?** and you (*form.*)? (1)
usualmente usually
uva grape (7)

V

vaca cow (12)
vacaciones *f. pl.* vacation
vacuna vaccine (14)
vacunar to vaccinate
vacuno: carne de vacuno beef
vagón *m.* car, wagon (10)
valer to be worth; to cost; **¿vale?** okay?
valiente valiant, courageous
valle *m.* valley (12)
valor *m.* value
vanguardista *m. f.* revolutionary (11); avant-garde (11)
varicela chicken pox
varios(as) several (2)
vaso glass
veinte twenty (1)
veinticinco twenty-five (1)
veinticuatro twenty-four (1)
veintidós twenty-two (1)
veintinueve twenty-nine (1)
veintiocho twenty-eight (1)
veintiséis twenty-six (1)
veintisiete twenty-seven (1)
veintitrés twenty-three (1)
veintiuno twenty-one(1)
vejez *f.* old-age (13)
vela candle (9)
velocidad: límite *m.* **de velocidad** speed limit (9)
vena vein
venado deer (12)
venda bandage
vendaje *m.* bandage (14)
vendedor(a) salesperson (5)
vender to sell (3)
venezolano(a) Venezuelan (14)
venir to come (5)
venta sale (transaction) (11); **en venta** on sale

ventana window (1); **limpiador para ventanas** window cleaner
ventanilla window (10)
ver to see (5); **verse** to see oneself (6); **a ver** let's see; **nos vemos** see you later (1)
verano summer (3)
verbo verb
verdad *f.* truth; **¿verdad?** right?; **de verdad** really
verde green (3)
verduras *f. pl.* vegetables
vestido dress (3)
vestirse (i, i) to get dressed (6)
veterinaria veterinary medicine
veterinario(a) veterinarian (5)
vez *f.* time; **a veces** sometimes (6); **de vez en cuando** from time to time; **dos veces** two times, twice
viajar to travel (2)
viaje *m.* trip; **agente de viajes** travel agent (5); **cheque** *m.* **de viaje** traveler's check; **viaje todo pagado** all-inclusive trip
viajero(a) traveler; **cheque** *m.* **de viajero** traveler's check
videojuego videogame (8)
viejo(a) old (1)
viento wind; **hace viento** it's windy
viernes *m.* Friday (3)
VIH *m.* HIV
vinagre *m.* vinegar
vino wine; **vino blanco** white wine (7); **vino rosado** rosé wine; **vino tinto** red wine (7)
visa visa (10)
visitar to visit
vista view; sight
viudo(a) widower/widow (13)
vivienda housing
vivir to live (3)
volar (ue) to fly (8)
volcán *m.* volcano (12)
voleibol *m.* volleyball (6)
voleibolista *m. f.* volleyball player
volver (ue) to return; to come back (4); **volverse loco(a)** to go crazy
vomitar to vomit (14)
vosotros(as) *subj. pron.* you (*fam. pl.*) (*Sp.*)
votar to vote (14)
voz *f.* voice; **en voz alta** aloud
vuelo flight (10); **asistente** *m. f.* **de vuelo** flight attendant
vuestro(a) *poss.* your (*fam. sing.*) (*Sp.*)

Y

y and; **¿y tú?** and you (*fam.*)? (1); **¿y usted?** and you (*form.*)? (1)
ya already (6); **ya no** no longer (6)
yerno son-in-law
yeso cast (14)
yo I; **yo soy de...** I'm from . . . (1)
yogur yogurt (7)

Z

zanahoria carrot (7)
zapatilla slipper
zapato shoe (3); **¡qué lindos zapatos!** what pretty shoes! (11)
zona area
zoológico zoo (4)
zorro fox (12)

Vocabulario 1

🔊 1–8

Saludos

bien	*fine*
Buenas noches.	*Good night.*
Buenas tardes.	*Good afternoon.*
Buenos días.	*Good morning.*
¿Cómo estás (tú)?	*How are you? (informal)*
¿Cómo está (usted)?	*How are you? (formal)*
gracias	*thank you*
hola	*hello*
mal	*bad*
nada	*nothing*
¿Qué hay de nuevo?	*What's new?*
¿Qué pasa?	*What's going on?*
¿Qué tal?	*How's it going?*
regular	*so-so*
¿Y tú?	*And you? (informal)*
¿Y usted?	*And you? (formal)*

Presentaciones

Encantado(a).	*Nice to meet you.*
Me llamo...	*My name is . . .*
Mucho gusto.	*Nice to meet you.*
Le presento a...	*I'd like to introduce you to . . . (formal)*
Te presento a...	*I'd like to introduce you to . . . (informal)*

Despedidas

Adiós.	*Goodbye.*
Chao.	*Bye.*
Hasta luego.	*See you later.*
Hasta mañana.	*See you tomorrow.*
Hasta pronto.	*See you soon.*
Nos vemos.	*See you later.*
¡Que tengas un buen día!	*Have a nice day!*

El salón de clases

la bandera	*flag*
el bolígrafo	*pen*
el cartel	*poster*
la computadora	*computer*
el cuaderno	*notebook*
el diccionario	*dictionary*
el escritorio	*teacher's desk*
el (la) estudiante	*student*
el lápiz	*pencil*
el libro	*book*
el mapa	*map*
la mesa	*table*
la mochila	*backpack*
el papel	*paper*
la pizarra	*chalkboard*
el (la) profesor(a)	*professor*
la puerta	*door*
el pupitre	*student desk*
el reloj	*clock*
el salón de clases	*classroom*
la silla	*chair*
el televisor	*television set*
la ventana	*window*

Gramática

Gender and number of nouns

1. A noun is a person, place, or thing. In order to make a noun plural, add an **-s** to words ending in a vowel. Add **-es** to words ending in a consonant, unless that consonant is **-z** in which case the **-z** changes to **-c** before adding **-es**. (lápiz → lápices)

2. Some nouns lose an accent mark or gain an accent mark when they become plural. (examen → exámenes) You will learn more about accents in **Capítulo 2.**

3. Nouns have gender (masculine / feminine) whether or not they refer to people. In general, if they are not referring to people, nouns that end in **-o** are masculine, and nouns that end in **-a** are feminine. Exceptions include **el** día (m.), **el** mapa (m.), **el** problema (m.), **la** mano (f.), **la** foto (f.), and **la** moto (f.).

Definite and indefinite articles

1. Definite articles mean *the*, and are used to refer to specific nouns or nouns already mentioned. They agree in gender and number with the noun they modify.

	masculino	femenino
singular	**el**	**la**
plural	**los**	**las**

2. Indefinite articles mean *a, an* or *some*, and are used to refer to non-specific nouns or nouns not yet mentioned. They also agree in gender and number with the noun they modify.

	masculino	femenino
singular	**un**	**una**
plural	**unos**	**unas**

Hay

1. **Hay** means *there* is when followed by a singular noun and *there are* when followed by a plural noun.

> Hay un libro en el pupitre.
> *There is a book on the desk.*

> Hay veinte estudiantes en la clase.
> *There are twenty students in the class.*

Palabras adicionales

¿De dónde eres tú?	*Where are you from?*
hay	*there is/there are*
Yo soy de...	*I am from . . .*

Palabras interrogativas

¿Dónde?	*Where?*
¿Cuándo?	*When?*
¿Cuántos(as)?	*How many?*
¿Qué?	*What?*
¿Quién?	*Who?*
¿Por qué?	*Why?*

Los números

uno	*one*
dos	*two*
tres	*three*
cuatro	*four*
cinco	*five*
seis	*six*
siete	*seven*
ocho	*eight*
nueve	*nine*
diez	*ten*
once	*eleven*
doce	*twelve*
trece	*thirteen*
catorce	*fourteen*
quince	*fifteen*
dieciséis	*sixteen*
diecisiete	*seventeen*
dieciocho	*eighteen*
diecinueve	*nineteen*
veinte	*twenty*
veintiuno	*twenty-one*
veintidós	*twenty-two*
veintitrés	*twenty-three*
veinticuatro	*twenty-four*
veinticinco	*twenty-five*
veintiséis	*twenty-six*
veintisiete	*twenty-seven*
veintiocho	*twenty-eight*
veintinueve	*twenty-nine*
treinta	*thirty*

Vocabulario 2

🔊 1-9

Adjetivos para describir la personalidad

aburrido(a)	boring
agresivo(a)	aggressive
amable	kind
antipático(a)	unfriendly
atlético(a)	athletic
bueno(a)	good
cariñoso(a)	loving
cómico(a)	funny
conservador(a)	conservative
cruel	cruel
egoísta	selfish
famoso(a)	famous
generoso(a)	generous
honesto(a)	honest
idealista	idealist
impaciente	impatient
inteligente	intelligent
interesante	interesting
liberal	liberal
malo(a)	bad
optimista	optimist
paciente	patient
perezoso(a)	lazy
pesimista	pessimist
pobre	poor
realista	realist
rico(a)	rich
serio(a)	serious
simpático(a)	nice
sociable	sociable
tímido(a)	timid, shy
tonto(a)	dumb
trabajador(a)	hardworking

Adjetivos para describir el aspecto físico

alto(a)	tall
bajo(a)	short
bonito(a)	pretty
calvo(a)	bald
delgado(a)	thin
feo(a)	ugly
gordo(a)	fat
grande	big
guapo(a)	good-looking
joven	young
moreno(a)	dark-skinned/ dark-haired
pelirrojo(a)	red-haired
pequeño(a)	small
rubio(a)	blond(e)
viejo(a)	old

Otros adjetivos

corto(a)	short (length)
difícil	difficult
fácil	easy
largo(a)	long

Gramática

Subject pronouns

1. The subject pronouns in Spanish are **yo, tú, él, ella, usted, nosotros/nosotras, vosotros/ vosotras, ellos, ellas,** and **ustedes.**

2. **Tú** and **usted (Ud.)** both mean *you*. **Tú** is informal, **usted** is formal.

3. The subject pronouns **nosotros, vosotros,** and **ellos** must be made feminine when referring to a group of only females (**nosotras, vosotras, ellas**). If there is a mixed-gender group, the subject pronouns remain in the masculine form.

4. **Vosotros** and **ustedes** both mean *you* (plural). **Vosotros** is used in Spain with a familiar group of people, and **ustedes** is always used to address a group formally. In Latin America, it is also used to address a familiar group.

Ser

1. The verb **ser** means *to be,* and its forms are as follows:

yo *(I)*	**soy**	nosotros / nosotras *(we)*	**somos**
tú *(you)*	**eres**	vosotros / vosotras *(you, plural)*	**sois**
usted *(you)*	**es**	ustedes *(you, plural)*	**son**
él *(he)* / ella *(she)*	**es**	ellos / ellas *(they)*	**son**

2. **Ser** is used when describing someone's traits (tall, intelligent, etc.) and to say where someone is from.

Adjective agreement

1. Adjectives describe a person, place, or thing. In Spanish, adjectives must agree in gender and number with the nouns that they modify.

2. If a singular masculine adjective ends in **-o**, the ending must be changed to **-a** when modifying a feminine noun (**alto → alta**).

3. If a singular masculine adjective ends in **-a** or **-e**, it does not need to be changed when modifying a feminine noun (**idealista, paciente**).

4. If a singular masculine adjective ends in a consonant, it does not need to be made feminine, unless the ending is **-or,** in which case you would add an **-a** (**trabajador → trabajadora**).

5. Once you have made the adjective agree in gender, you must make it also agree in number. To modify plural nouns, you add **-s** to adjectives that end in vowels or **-es** to adjectives that end in consonants (**bajos, liberales**).

Verbos

ser	to be

Palabras adicionales

el hombre	man
la mujer	woman
muy	very
el (la) niño(a)	child
pero	but
un poco	a little
también	also
y	and

Vocabulario 1

🔊 1–14

La familia

el (la) abuelo(a)	grandfather / grandmother
el (la) amigo(a)	friend
el (la) esposo(a)	spouse
el (la) hermanastro(a)	stepbrother / stepsister
el (la) hermano(a)	brother / sister
el (la) hijo(a)	son / daughter
la madrastra	stepmother
la madre (mamá)	mother
el (la) medio(a) hermano(a)	half brother / half sister
el (la) nieto(a)	grandson / granddaughter
el (la) novio(a)	boyfriend / girlfriend
el padrastro	stepfather
el padre (papá)	father
la pareja	couple; partner
el pariente	relative
el (la) primo(a)	cousin
el (la) sobrino(a)	nephew / niece
el (la) suegro(a)	father-in-law / mother-in-law
el (la) tío(a)	uncle / aunt

Las mascotas

el caballo	horse
el (la) gato(a)	cat
el pájaro	bird
el (la) perro(a)	dog
el pez	fish
el ratón	mouse

Los verbos

ayudar	to help
bailar	to dance
buscar	to look for
caminar	to walk
cantar	to sing
cocinar	to cook
comprar	to buy
desear	to wish
enseñar	to teach
escuchar	to listen
esquiar	to ski
estudiar	to study
hablar (por teléfono)	to talk (on the phone)
limpiar	to clean
llamar	to call
llegar	to arrive
mandar (un mensaje)	to send (a message)
manejar	to drive
mirar (la tele)	to look, to watch (TV)
nadar	to swim
necesitar	to need
practicar (deportes)	to practice; to play (sports)
preguntar	to ask
regresar (a casa)	to return (home)
tomar (café)	to take; to drink (coffee)
trabajar	to work
usar	to use
viajar	to travel

Gramática

Possessive adjectives

1. The possessive adjectives in Spanish are as follows:

mi(s)	my	nuestro(a)(s)	our
tu(s)	your	vuestro(a)(s)	your (plural, informal)
su(s)	his, her, its, your (formal)	su(s)	their, your (plural, informal or formal)

2. Possessive adjectives, like other adjectives, must agree in gender and number with the nouns that they modify. **Nuestro** and **vuestro** are the only possessive adjectives that need to change for gender.

Nuestra familia es muy grande.   *Our family is very big.*
Mis primos son jóvenes.   *My cousins are young.*

3. In Spanish, the 's does not exist. Instead, if you want to be more specific about who something belongs to, it is necessary to use **de.**

Elena es la hija **de** Juan.
Elena is Juan's daughter.

4. When **de** is followed by **el** in Spanish, you form the contraction **del.**

Anita es una amiga **del** profesor.
Anita is the professor's friend.

Regular -ar verbs

1. The verbs presented on the left are in the *infinitive* form. This form identifies the action, and is translated as *to (do something)* in English. (**Bailar** means *to dance*.)

2. Verbs in the infinitive form need to be conjugated when you are identifying the person who is doing the action. Regular **-ar** verbs are all conjugated in the same way. To form a present tense verb, the **-ar** is dropped from the infinitive and an ending is added that reflects the subject (the person doing the action).

nadar

yo	**-o**	nad**o**	nosotros(as)	**-amos**	nad**amos**
tú	**-as**	nad**as**	vosotros(as)	**-áis**	nad**áis**
él / ella / usted	**-a**	nad**a**	ellos / ellas / ustedes	**-an**	nad**an**

3. When using two verbs together that are dependent upon each other, the second verb remains in the infinitive.

Los estudiantes **necesitan estudiar.**
The students need to study.

However, both verbs are conjugated if they are not dependent on each other.

Mi primo **trabaja, practica** deportes y **estudia** en la universidad.
My cousin works, plays sports, and studies at the university.

4. Place the word **no** before the conjugated verb to make a statement negative.

Mis padres **no** toman café.
*My parents **don't** drink coffee.*

5. To form a yes/no question, you simply use intonation to raise your voice and place the subject after the conjugated verb. There is no need for a helping word in Spanish.

¿Cocinas tú bien?
Do you cook well?

Vocabulario 2

🔊 1–15

Las materias académicas

el alemán	German
el álgebra	algebra
el arte	art
la biología	biology
el cálculo	calculus
las ciencias naturales	natural science
las ciencias políticas	political science
las ciencias sociales	social science
la criminología	criminology
la economía	economy
la educación física	physical education
la expresión oral	speech
la filosofía	philosophy
la física	physics
el francés	French
la geografía	geography
la geometría	geometry
la historia	history
la informática	computer science
la ingeniería	engineering
el inglés	English
el italiano	Italian
las lenguas	languages
la literatura	literature
las matemáticas	mathematics
la música	music
los negocios	business
el periodismo	journalism
la psicología	psychology
la química	chemistry
la redacción	writing
el teatro	theater
la veterinaria	veterinary medicine

Los lugares en la universidad

el auditorio	auditorium
la biblioteca	library
la cafetería	cafeteria
el centro estudiantil	student center
el estadio	stadium
el gimnasio	gymnasium
el laboratorio	laboratory
la librería	bookstore
las residencias	residence halls

Expresiones con *tener*

tener... años	to be . . . years old
tener (mucho) calor	to be (very) hot
tener (mucho) cuidado	to be (very) careful
tener (mucho) éxito	to be (very) successful
tener (mucho) frío	to be (very) cold
tener ganas de + infinitive	to feel like doing something

tener (mucha) hambre	to be (very) hungry
tener (mucho) miedo	to be (very) afraid
tener (mucha) prisa	to be in a (big) hurry
tener que + infinitive	to have to do something
tener (mucha) razón	to be right
tener (mucha) sed	to be (very) thirsty
tener (mucho) sueño	to be (very) sleepy
tener (mucha) suerte	to be (very) lucky

Gramática

The verb *tener*

1. The verb **tener** means *to have*, and its forms are as follows:

yo	**tengo**	nosotros(as)	**tenemos**
tú	**tienes**	vosotros(as)	**tenéis**
él / ella / usted	**tiene**	ellos / ellas / ustedes	**tienen**

2. The verb **tener** can also mean *to be* when used in certain expressions. See **expresiones con *tener*** in the left-hand column of this page.

> Mi mejor amiga **tiene** diecinueve años.
> *My best friend **is** nineteen years old.*

> Yo siempre **tengo** hambre antes del almuerzo.
> *I **am** always hungry before lunch.*

3. As you remember from **Capítulo 2**, other than adjectives of quantity, adjectives are generally placed behind the noun they modify. However, there are some other exceptions. **Bueno** and **malo** are often used in front of the noun they modify, and they drop the **o** when used in front of a masculine singular noun.

> La señora es una **buena** profesora.
> *The woman is a **good** teacher.*

> Es un **mal** día.
> *It is a **bad** day.*

Adjective Placement

1. In Spanish, adjectives are generally placed after the noun they describe.

> La química no es una clase **fácil**.
> *Chemistry is not an **easy** class.*

2. Adjectives such as **mucho, poco,** and **varios** that indicate quantity or amount are placed in front of the object.

> Tengo **varias** clases los jueves, pero no tengo clase los viernes.
> *I have **several** classes on Thursdays, but I don't have class on Fridays.*

3. When using more than one adjective to describe a noun, use commas between adjectives and **y** (*and*) before the last adjective.

> Mis clases son largas, difíciles **y** aburridas.
> *My classes are long, difficult, **and** boring.*

Palabras adicionales

el (la) compañero(a) de clase	classmate
el examen	exam
mucho	a lot
la nota	grade
poco	few
el semestre	semester
la tarea	homework
el trimestre	quarter
varios	several

Vocabulario 1

🔊 1–20

La ropa y los accesorios

el abrigo	coat
la blusa	blouse
los bluyines	blue jeans
la bolsa	purse
las botas	boots
la bufanda	scarf
los calcetines	socks
la camisa	shirt
la camiseta	T-shirt
la chaqueta	jacket
la corbata	tie
la falda	skirt
el gorro	cap
los guantes	gloves
el impermeable	raincoat
los lentes	glasses
los pantalones	pants
los pantalones cortos	shorts
el paraguas	umbrella
la pijama	pajamas
las sandalias	sandals
el sombrero	hat
el suéter	sweater
los tenis	tennis shoes
el traje	suit
el traje de baño	swimming suit
el vestido	dress
los zapatos	shoes

El tiempo

Está despejado.	It is clear.
Está nublado.	It is cloudy.
Hace buen tiempo.	The weather is nice.
Hace calor.	It's hot.
Hace fresco.	It is cool.
Hace frío.	It's cold.
Hace mal tiempo.	The weather is bad.
Hace sol.	It's sunny.
Hace viento.	It is windy.
Llueve.	It rains. / It is raining.
Nieva.	It snows. / It is snowing.

Las estaciones

el invierno	winter
el otoño	fall
la primavera	spring
el verano	summer

Los verbos

abrir	to open
aprender (a + infinitive)	to learn (to do something)
asistir (a)	to attend
beber	to drink
comer	to eat
comprender	to understand
correr	to run
creer	to believe
deber	should, ought to
decidir	to decide
escribir	to write
leer	to read

recibir (un regalo)	to receive (a gift)
vender	to sell
vivir	to live

Palabras adicionales

cómodo(a)	comfortable
llevar	to wear, to carry; to take
llevar puesto(a)	to be wearing

Gramática

The verb *gustar*

1. The Spanish equivalent of *I like* is **me gusta**, which literally means *it pleases me*. The expression **me gusta** (*I like*) is followed by singular nouns.

   Me gusta la clase.
   I like the class. (The class pleases me.)

   No me gusta la pizza.
   I don't like pizza. (Pizza doesn't please me.)

2. When followed by a plural noun, the verb becomes **gustan**.

   No me gustan los exámenes.
   I don't like exams.

   Me gustan el francés y el italiano.
   I like French and Italian.

3. When followed by a verb or a series of verbs, the singular form **gusta** is used.

   A Julio **le gusta** practicar deportes y leer.
   Julio likes to play sports and read.

4. **Gustar** can also be used to ask about or indicate what other people like.

me gusta(n)	I like
nos gusta(n)	we like
te gusta(n)	you like
os gusta(n)	you like (plural, Spain)
le gusta(n)	he/she likes
les gusta(n)	they, you (plural) like

5. When using **gustar** with a noun, you must use the definite article as well.

   No me gusta **el** invierno.
   I don't like winter.

6. To clarify who he or she is, it is necessary to use an **a** in front of the name.

   A Marta le gusta correr.
   Marta likes to run.

7. To express different degrees, use the terms **mucho** (*a lot*), **poco** (*a little*), and **para nada** (*not at all*).

   No me gusta trabajar **para nada**.
   *I don't like working **at all**.*

Regular *-er* and *-ir* verbs

1. Regular **-er** and **-ir** verbs follow a pattern very similar to that of regular **-ar** verbs.

2. The endings for regular **-er** verbs are as follows:

comer

yo	-o	como	nosotros(as)	-emos	comemos
tú	-es	comes	vosotros(as)	-éis	coméis
él / ella / usted	-e	come	ellos / ellas / ustedes	-en	comen

3. The endings for regular **-ir** verbs are as follows:

vivir

yo	-o	vivo	nosotros(as)	-imos	vivimos
tú	-es	vives	vosotros(as)	-ís	vivís
él / ella / usted	-e	vive	ellos / ellas / ustedes	-en	viven

Expresiones importantes

me gusta	I like
te gusta	you like
le gusta	he/she likes
nos gusta	we like
os gusta	you (plural) like (Spain)
les gusta	they, you (plural) like

Vocabulario 2

🔊 1-21

Los días de la semana

el lunes	*Monday*
el martes	*Tuesday*
el miércoles	*Wednesday*
el jueves	*Thursday*
el viernes	*Friday*
el sábado	*Saturday*
el domingo	*Sunday*

Los meses

enero	*January*
febrero	*February*
marzo	*March*
abril	*April*
mayo	*May*
junio	*June*
julio	*July*
agosto	*August*
septiembre	*September*
octubre	*October*
noviembre	*November*
diciembre	*December*

Los verbos

ir	*to go*
terminar	*to finish*

Palabras adicionales

ahora	*now*
el Año Nuevo	*New Year*
el cumpleaños	*birthday*
el día	*day*
el día feriado	*holiday*
la fecha	*date*
el fin de semana	*weekend*
hoy	*today*
mañana	*tomorrow*
la medianoche	*midnight*
el mediodía	*noon*
Navidad	*Christmas*
la semana	*week*
por la mañana /	*in the morning /*
tarde / noche	*afternoon / evening*
todos los días	*every day*

Gramática

The verb *ir*

1. The verb **ir** means *to go*:

voy	vamos
vas	vais
va	van

2. To tell where someone is going, it is necessary to use the preposition **a** *(to)*. When asking where someone is going, the preposition **a** is added to the word **dónde (adónde).** When **a** is followed by the definite article **el,** you must use the contraction **al.**

> ¿**Adónde** van?
> *(To) **Where** are they going?*

> Mis amigos van **al** museo.
> *My friends are going **to the** museum.*

Ir + a + infinitive

1. Similar to English, the verb **ir** can be used to talk about the future. To tell what someone is going to do use the structure ir + a + infinitive.

> El viernes **vamos a bailar.**
> *On Friday we're going to dance.*

> Miguel **va a estudiar** este fin de semana.
> *Miguel is going to study this weekend.*

3. It is common to use the verb **ir** in the present tense to tell where someone is going at that moment.

> Mi amiga **va** a la universidad ahora.
> *My friend **is going** to the university now.*

4. The verb **ir** is used in a variety of expressions.

> **ir de compras** *to go shopping*
> **ir de excursión** *to go hiking*
> **ir de paseo** *to go for a walk*
> **ir de viaje** *to take a trip*

2. To ask what someone is going to do, use the verb **hacer** in the question. When responding, the verb **hacer** is not necessary.

> ¿Qué vas a hacer (tú)?
> *What are you going to do?*

> (Yo) Voy a estudiar (trabajar, comer, etcetera).
> *I am going to study (work, eat, etc.).*

Vocabulario 1

🔊 1–26

Los lugares

el aeropuerto	airport
el banco	bank
el bar	bar
el café	cafe
la calle	street
el centro comercial	mall
el cine	movie theater
el club	club
el correo	post office
la discoteca	nightclub
el edificio	building
la escuela	school
la farmacia	pharmacy
el hospital	hospital
el hotel	hotel
la iglesia	church
el mercado	market
la mezquita	mosque
el museo	museum
el negocio	business
la oficina	office
el parque	park
la piscina	swimming pool
la playa	beach
la plaza	city square
el restaurante	restaurant
la sinagoga	synagogue
el supermercado	supermarket
el teatro	theater
el templo	temple
la tienda	store
el zoológico	zoo

Los verbos

almorzar	to have lunch
alquilar	to rent
costar	to cost
depositar	to deposit
devolver	to return (something)
dormir	to sleep
encontrar	to find
estar	to be
jugar	to play
llover	to rain
morir	to die
poder	to be able to
recordar	to remember
rezar	to pray
soñar (con)	to dream (about)
volver	to come back

Palabras adicionales

la carta	letter
el dinero	money
el paquete	package
la película	movie

Gramática

Stem changing verbs (o → ue)

1. Most of the verbs that appear in the **verbos** section of vocabulary to the left are stem-changing verbs. That means there is a change in the stem or the root of the verb. All of the endings are the same as other **-ar**, **-er**, and **-ir** verbs.

2. **Poder** is an **o → ue** stem-changing verb. Notice that **o** changes to **ue** in all forms except **nosotros** and **vosotros.**

p**ue**do	podemos
p**ue**des	podéis
p**ue**de	p**ue**den

3. The verb **jugar** follows the same pattern, but its stem changes from **u → ue:**

j**ue**go	jugamos
j**ue**gas	jugáis
j**ue**ga	j**ue**gan

Estar with prepositions

1. **Estar** means *to be* and is used to talk about position or location. Its forms are as follows:

estoy	estamos
estás	estáis
está	están

2. You will always use **estar** when using any of the prepositions listed on the left of this page.

> El café **está entre** la farmacia y la biblioteca.
> *The coffee shop is (located) between the pharmacy and the library.*

3. Note that most of the prepositional phrases listed in this chapter include the word **de.** Remember to form the contraction **del** when **de** is followed by the definite article **el.**

> Vivo lejos **del** supermercado.
> *I live far from the supermarket.*

Las preposiciones

a la derecha de	to the right of
al lado de	beside, next to
a la izquierda de	to the left of
cerca de	near
debajo de	under
dentro de	inside
detrás de	behind
en	in, on, at
encima de	on top of
enfrente de	in front of
entre	between
fuera de	outside
lejos de	far from

Vocabulario 2

🔊 1-27

Habitaciones de la casa

el baño	bathroom
la cochera	garage
la cocina	kitchen
el comedor	dining room
el dormitorio	bedroom
el jardín	garden
el patio	patio
la sala	living room

Muebles, utensilios y aparatos electrodomésticos

la alfombra	carpet
el armario	closet, armoire
la bañera	bathtub
la cafetera	coffee maker
la cama	bed
las cortinas	curtains
el cuadro	painting, picture
la ducha	shower
el espejo	mirror
la estufa	stove
la flor	flower
el fregadero	kitchen sink
el horno	oven
el (horno de) microondas	microwave (oven)
el inodoro	toilet
la lámpara	lamp
el lavabo	bathroom sink
la lavadora	washer
el lavaplatos	dishwasher
la mesita	coffee table
las plantas	plants
el refrigerador	refrigerator
la secadora	dryer
el sillón	armchair
el sofá	couch

Los verbos

cerrar	to close
comenzar (a)	to begin (to do something)
competir	to compete
empezar (a)	to begin (to do something)
encender	to turn on
entender	to understand
mentir	to lie
nevar	to snow
pedir	to ask for
pensar	to think
perder	to lose
preferir	to prefer
reír	to laugh
repetir	to repeat
querer	to want
servir	to serve
sonreír	to smile

Gramática

Interrogatives

1. In most questions:
   - the subject is placed after the verb.
   - the question word is often the first word of the question.
   - it is not necessary to have a helping word such as *do* or *does*.
   - it is necessary to have an inverted question mark at the beginning of the questions and another question mark at the end.

2. Prepositions (**a, con, de, en, por, para**, etc.) cannot be placed at the end of the question. They must be in front of the question word.

   > ¿**Con** quién estudias?
   > ***With** whom do you study?*

Stem-changing verbs e → ie and e → i

1. Most of the verbs that appear in the **verbos** section of vocabulary to the left are stem-changing verbs. That means there is a change in the stem or the root of the verb. All of the endings are the same as other **-ar**, **-er**, and **-ir** verbs.

2. **Querer** is an e → **ie** stem-changing verb. Notice that **i** changes to **ie** in all forms except **nosotros** and **vosotros**.

quiero	queremos
quieres	queréis
quiere	quieren

3. The e → **ie** stem-changing verbs **comenzar** and **empezar** are followed by the preposition **a** when used with an infinitive.

3. **Quién** and **cuál** must agree in number with the noun that follows, and **cuánto** and **cuántos** must agree in gender with the preceding noun.

4. There are two ways to express *What?* or *Which?*: When asking *which*, use **qué** in front of a noun and **cuál** in front of a verb or with the preposition **de**. When asking *what*, use **cuál** with the verb **ser** with the exception of the question ¿**Qué es?** *(What is it?)*. Use **qué** with all other verbs.

   > ¿**Qué** electrodomésticos necesitas?
   > ***What (Which)** appliances do you need?*

   > ¿**Cuáles** de los libros te gustan más?
   > *Which of the books do you like the most?*

   > **Empieza a** llover.
   > *It's starting to rain.*

4. **Pedir** is an e → **i** stem-changing verb. Note that **pedir** means to ask *for* something or to order, where as **preguntar** means to ask a question. Here are the forms of **pedir**:

pido	pedimos
pides	pedís
pide	piden

5. The verbs **reír** and **sonreír** require accents on the **í** in the conjugated forms.

   > Los niños **sonríen** en la foto.
   > *The children smile in the photo.*

Palabras adicionales

el apartamento	apartment
la dirección	address
la habitación	room
el mueble	furniture
la planta baja	ground floor
el (primer) piso	(first) floor

Palabras interrogativas

¿adónde?	to where?
¿cómo?	how?
¿cuál(es)?	which?
¿cuándo?	when?
¿cuánto(a)?	how much?
¿cuántos(as)?	how many?
¿de dónde?	from where?
¿dónde?	where?
¿por qué?	why?
¿qué?	what?
¿quién(es)?	who?

Vocabulario 1

🔊 1–32

Los estados de ánimo y otras expresiones con el verbo *estar*

aburrido(a)	*bored*
alegre	*happy*
asustado(a)	*scared*
avergonzado(a)	*embarrassed*
borracho(a)	*drunk*
cansado(a)	*tired*
celoso(a)	*jealous*
confundido(a)	*confused*
contento(a)	*happy*
deprimido(a)	*depressed*
divertido(a)	*entertained; in a good mood*
enamorado(a) (de)	*in love (with)*
enfermo(a)	*sick*
enojado(a)	*angry*
equivocado(a)	*wrong*
feliz	*happy*
frustrado(a)	*frustrated*
interesado(a)	*interested*
loco(a)	*crazy*
nervioso(a)	*nervous*
ocupado(a)	*busy*
preocupado(a)	*worried*
sano(a)	*healthy*
seguro(a)	*sure*
sorprendido(a)	*surprised*
triste	*sad*

Palabras adicionales

la salud	*health*

Gramática

Estar with adjectives and present progressive

1. Remember that **estar** is an irregular verb:

estar	
estoy	estamos
estás	estáis
está	están

2. Apart from indicating location, the verb **estar** is also used to express an emotional, mental, or physical condition.

> Mis padres **están** felices.
> *My parents are happy.*

3. The verb **estar** is also used with present participles to form the present progressive. The present progressive is used to describe actions in progress. To form the present participle, add **-ando** (**-ar** verbs) or **–iendo** (**-er** and **-ir** verbs) to the stem of the verb.

> El profesor **está hablando** con Tito ahora.
> *The professor is talking to Tito now.*

4. The present participle of the verb **ir** is **yendo**. However, it is much more common to use the present tense of the verb when the action is in progress.

5. When the stem of an **-er** or an **-ir** verb ends in a vowel, **-yendo** is used instead of **-iendo**.

> leer – le**yendo**   oír – o**yendo**

6. Stem-changing **-ir** verbs have an irregular present participle. An **e** in the stem becomes an **i**, and an **o** in the stem becomes a **u**.

> mentir – m**i**ntiendo   dormir – d**u**rmiendo

7. In the present progressive, the verb **estar** must agree with the subject; however, you will notice that the present participle does NOT agree in gender (masculine/feminine) or number (singular/plural) with the subject.

> Mis hijos están estudiando inglés.
> *My children are studying English.*

Ser and *estar*

1. The verb **ser** is used in the following ways:
  a. to describe characteristics of people, places, or things

> La profesora **es** inteligente.
> *The professor is intelligent.*

  b. to identify a relationship, occupation, or nationality

> Mi novia **es** peruana.
> *My girlfriend is Peruvian.*

  c. to express origin

> Yo **soy** de Bolivia.
> *I am from Bolivia.*

  d. to express possession

> El libro **es** de Álvaro.
> *The book belongs to Álvaro.*

  e. to tell time and give dates

> **Son** las dos.
> It **is** two o'clock.

2. The verb **estar** is used in the following ways:
  a. to indicate location

> Ella **está** en la casa.   She **is** in the house.

  b. to express an emotional, mental, or physical condition

> Mi madre **está** enferma hoy.
> *My mother is sick today.*

  c. in the present progressive

> **Estoy** estudiando.   *I am studying.*

3. It is important to realize that the use of **ser** and **estar** with some adjectives can change the meaning of the adjectives. The use of **ser** indicates a characteristic or a trait, while the use of **estar** indicates a condition. Some common adjectives that change meaning are: **aburrido(a), alegre, feliz, bueno(a), malo(a), guapo(a), listo(a),** and **rico(a).**

> Carlos **es** aburrido.
> *Carlos is boring. (personality)*

> Graciela **está** aburrida.
> *Graciela is bored. (present condition)*

Vocabulario 2

🔊 1–33

Las profesiones

el (la) abogado(a)	lawyer
el actor	actor
la actriz	actress
el (la) agente de viajes	travel agent
el amo(a) de casa	homemaker
el (la) arquitecto(a)	architect
el (la) asistente de vuelo	flight attendant
el bailarín/ la bailarina	dancer
el (la) cantante	singer
el (la) científico(a)	scientist
el (la) cocinero(a)	cook
el (la) consejero(a)	adviser
el (la) contador(a)	accountant
el (la) dependiente	clerk
el (la) deportista	athlete
el (la) diseñador(a)	designer
el (la) enfermero(a)	nurse
el (la) escritor(a)	writer
el (la) fotógrafo(a)	photographer
el (la) ingeniero(a)	engineer
el jefe/la jefa	boss
el (la) maestro(a)	elementary/high school teacher
el (la) mecánico(a)	mechanic
el (la) médico(a)	doctor
el (la) mesero(a)	waiter
el (la) modelo	model
el (la) músico(a)	musician
el (la) periodista	journalist
el (la) piloto	pilot
el (la) pintor(a)	painter
el policía/la mujer policía	police officer
el (la) psicólogo(a)	psychologist
el (la) político(a)	politician
el (la) secretario(a)	secretary
el (la) trabajador(a) social	social worker
el (la) vendedor(a)	salesperson
el (la) veterinario(a)	veterinary

Palabras adicionales

el (la) cliente	client
la entrevista	interview
la solicitud	application; want ad
el sueldo	salary
el trabajo	job

Los verbos

conducir	to drive
conocer	to know, to be acquainted with
dar	to give
decir	to say, to tell
ganar	to earn
hacer	to do, to make
oír	to hear
poner	to put; to set
saber	to know (facts; how to do something)
salir	to go out, to leave
seguir	to follow
traer	to bring
venir	to come
ver	to see

Gramática

Verbs with changes in the first person

1. The following verbs have irregular first person forms:

poner → pongo   conducir → conduzco
salir → salgo   dar → doy
traer → traigo   ver → veo

2. The following verbs are not only irregular in the first person form, but also have other changes:

decir

digo	decimos
dices	decís
dice	dicen

venir

vengo	venimos
vienes	venís
viene	vienen

seguir

sigo	seguimos
sigues	seguís
sigue	siguen

oír

oigo	oímos
oyes	oís
oye	oyen

Saber and conocer

1. *Saber* and *conocer* are irregular in the first person form.

saber

sé	sabemos
sabes	sabéis
sabe	saben

conocer

conozco	conocemos
conoces	conocéis
conoce	conocen

2. While the verbs *saber* and *conocer* both mean *to know*, they are used in different contexts. *Saber* is used to express knowledge of facts or information as well as skills. *Conocer* is used to express acquaintance or familiarity with a person, place or thing.

Ana **conoce** Chile.   (*familiarity*)
Ana **sabe** dónde está Chile.   (*fact*)

3. When using *saber* to mean to *know how to do something*, it is followed by the infinitive.

El profesor **sabe** enseñar.
*The professor **knows how to** teach.*

4. When expressing knowledge or familiarity with general concepts or subjects, the verb *conocer* is used.

El artista conoce el arte prehispánico.
*The artist **knows** (is familiar with) pre-Hispanic art.*

La enfermera conoce la medicina.
*The nurse **knows** (is familiar with) medicine.*

5. Remember to use the *personal a* with *conocer* when referring to a person or a pet.

Conozco al piloto.   *I **know** the pilot.*

Vocabulario 1

🔊 1–37

Los verbos reflexivos

acostarse (ue)	to lie down; to go to bed
afeitarse	to shave
arreglarse	to fix oneself up; get ready
bañarse	to bathe; to shower (Mex.)
cepillarse	to brush
cortarse	to cut
despertarse	to wake up
divertirse	to have fun
dormirse	to fall asleep
ducharse	to shower
estirarse	to stretch
irse	to leave, to go away
lavarse	to wash
levantarse	to get up
maquillarse	to put on make-up
peinarse	to comb or style one's hair
ponerse (la ropa)	to put on (clothing)
quitarse (la ropa)	to take off (clothing)
secarse	to dry oneself
sentarse	to sit down
verse	to look at oneself
vestirse	to get dressed

Las partes del cuerpo

la boca	mouth
el brazo	arm
la cabeza	head
la cara	face
el codo	elbow
el cuello	neck
el dedo	finger
el dedo (del pie)	toe
el diente	tooth
la espalda	back
el estómago	stomach
el hombro	shoulder
la mano	hand
el muslo	thigh
la nariz	nose
el ojo	eye
la oreja	ear
el pecho	chest
el pelo	hair
el pie	foot
la pierna	leg
la rodilla	knee
el tobillo	ankle

Adverbios

a menudo	often
a veces	sometimes
ahora	now
antes de + infinitive	before (doing something)
después de + infinitive	after (doing something)
hoy	today
luego	later
mañana	tomorrow
más tarde	later
mientras	while
normalmente	normally, usually
(casi) nunca	(almost) never
pronto	soon
(casi) siempre	(almost) always

Gramática

Reflexive verbs

1. Reflexive verbs are verbs whose subject also receives the action performed. Simply put, they describe what one does to oneself. In Spanish, these verbs are characterized by the reflexive pronoun **se** that follows the infinitive form of the verb. Many of the verbs used to talk about daily routine are reflexive verbs.

2. Reflexive verbs are conjugated like regular verbs, except that the reflexive pronoun **se** must also be changed to reflect the subject.

levantarse	
me levanto	**nos** levantamos
te levantas	**os** levantáis
se levanta	**se** levantan

3. The reflexive pronoun can always go in front of the conjugated verb. If you are using two verbs, it will precede the first verb.

> **Nos lavamos** las manos antes de comer.
> *We wash our hands before eating.*

> Paula **se está estirando.**
> *Paula is stretching.*

4. When using a reflexive verb with the infinitive, you can attach the pronoun to the infinitive.

Adverbs of time and frequency

1. One of the functions of an adverb is to tell when an action occurs. The following common adverbs of time may be used either before or after the action:

ahora	luego	pronto
a menudo	mañana	todos los días
hoy	más tarde	

2. The following adverbs of time usually come before the verb:

a veces*	(casi) siempre
mientras*	todavía
normalmente	ya
(casi) nunca	ya no

*If using a subject in the sentence, these adverbs are placed in front of the subject.

When using a reflexive verb with the present participle, you can attach the pronoun to the present participle, but you must then add an accent to maintain the original stress. The pronoun will still always agree with the subject.

> ¿**Vas a ducharte** antes de salir?
> Gilberto **está poniéndose** la ropa en su habitación.

5. Verbs may be reflexive or nonreflexive depending on who receives the action.

> Roberto **se lava.**
> Roberto **lava** a su perro.

6. Use the definite article rather than the possessive adjective after a reflexive verb.

> Mariana **se cepilla** los dientes.

7. Using a reflexive pronoun changes the meaning of some verbs.

> Vivián **se va** porque está enojada con su novio.
> *Vivian left because she was angry at her boyfriend.*

> Mi prima **va** a la iglesia a las diez.
> *My cousin goes to church at ten.*

3. To say what someone does before or after another activity, use the expressions **antes de** + *infinitive* and **después de** + *infinitive*.

> **Antes de acostarse, mi hijo lee un libro.**
> *Before going to bed, my son reads a book.*

When using a verb after a preposition, such as **de,** it is necessary to use the infinitive. **Antes** and **después** can be used without the preposition **de** and followed by a conjugated verb; however, the meaning changes slightly, and they are translated as *beforehand* and *afterwards*, respectively.

> **Me ducho y después me acuesto.**
> *I shower and afterwards I go to bed.*

4. When saying how often you do something, use the word **vez.**

> Me cepillo los dientes **dos veces al día.**
> *I brush my teeth **twice a day.***

Notice that the adverbial expression comes after the activity.

todavía	still
todos los días	every day
ya	already
ya no	no longer

Palabras adicionales

el champú	shampoo
la pasta de dientes	toothpaste
el despertador	alarm clock
el jabón	soap
tarde	late
temprano	early
la toalla	towel

Vocabulario 2

🔊 1–38

Los deportes

el atletismo	track and field
el bádminton	badminton
el básquetbol	basketball
el béisbol	baseball
el fútbol	soccer
el fútbol americano	American football
el golf	golf
la natación	swimming
el tenis	tennis
el voleibol	volleyball

El equipo

el equipo	equipment, team
el patín	skate
la pelota	ball
la raqueta	racquet
la red	net
el saco de dormir	sleeping bag
la tienda de campaña	camping tent

Verbos

acampar	to go camping
andar en bicicleta	to ride a bicycle
bucear	to scuba dive
esquiar en el agua	to water-ski
esquiar en tabla	to snowboard
hacer alpinismo	to climb mountains
ir de excursión	to hike
ir de pesca	to go fishing
jugar al ping-pong	to play ping-pong
levantar pesas	to lift weights
montar a	to ride (an animal)
patinar	to skate
patinar en hielo	to ice skate
pescar	to fish

Palabras adicionales

el (la) aficionado(a)	fan (of a sport)
anoche	last night
ayer	yesterday
el campo	field
la cancha	court
la entrada	ticket
el lago	lake
el partido	game
la semana pasada	last week

Gramática

The preterite

1. The preterite is used to discuss actions completed in the past. To form the preterite of regular **-ar** verbs, add these endings to the stem of the verb.

ballar			
yo	bail**é**	nosotros(as)	bail**amos**
tú	bail**aste**	vosotros(as)	bail**asteis**
él / ella / usted	bail**ó**	ellos / ellas / ustedes	bail**aron**

José **viajó** a México.　　José **traveled (did travel)** to Mexico.

2. The preterite endings for regular **-er** and **-ir** verbs are identical. They are as follows:

beber / vivir			
yo	beb**í** / viv**í**	nosotros(as)	beb**imos** / viv**imos**
tú	beb**iste** / viv**iste**	vosotros(as)	beb**isteis** / viv**isteis**
él / ella / usted	beb**ió** / viv**ió**	ellos / ellas / ustedes	beb**ieron** / viv**ieron**

¿**Escribiste** tú una carta?　　**Did you write** a letter?

3. **-Ar** and **-er** verbs that have stem changes in the present tense do not change in the preterite tense. You will learn about stem-changing **-ir** verbs below.

4. Verbs ending in **-car, -gar,** and **-zar** have spelling changes in the **yo** form in the preterite. Notice that the spelling changes preserve the original sound of the infinitive for **-car** and **-gar** verbs.

car → **qué**　　**Busqué** el libro. *I looked for the book.*

gar → **gué**　　**Llegué** tarde a la fiesta. *I arrived late to the party.*

zar → **cé**　　**Empecé** a estudiar español el año pasado. *I started studying Spanish last year.*

5. The third person singular and plural of **oír** and **leer** also have spelling changes when conjugated in the preterite tense. These verbs carry accents in all forms of the preterite except for the third person plural.

oír → **oyó, oyeron**　　leer → **leyó, leyeron**

Stem-changing verbs in the preterite

1. **-Ir** verbs that have stem changes in the present tense also have stem changes in the preterite. The third person singular and plural change **e → i** and **o → u**.

pedir		dormir	
pedí	pedimos	dormí	dormimos
pediste	pedisteis	dormiste	dormisteis
p**i**dió	p**i**dieron	d**u**rmió	d**u**rmieron

Mi hermano **pidió** pollo, pero yo **pedí** la sopa.
*My brother **ordered** chicken, but I ordered soup.*

2. Other common stem-changing verbs:

conseguir (i)	morir (u)	repetir (i)	servir (i)
divertirse (i)	preferir (i)	seguir (i)	vestirse (i)

Vocabulario 1

🔊 2–5

Frutas

el durazno	peach
la fresa	strawberry
la manzana	apple
el melón	melon
la naranja	orange
la piña	pineapple
el plátano	banana
la sandía	watermelon
las uvas	grapes

Verduras

el brócoli	broccoli
la cebolla	onion
la lechuga	lettuce
el maíz	corn
la papa	potato
el pepino	cucumber
el tomate	tomato
la zanahoria	carrot

Lácteos y otros alimentos

la catsup	ketchup
el cereal	cereal
la crema	cream
el huevo	egg
el jamón	ham
la leche	milk
la mantequilla	butter
la mayonesa	mayonnaise
la mermelada	jam
la mostaza	mustard
el pan	bread
el pepinillo	pickle
el queso	cheese
el yogur	yogurt

Verbos

hornear	to bake

Palabras adicionales

la rebanada	slice

Los números

cien	100
ciento uno	101
doscientos	200
trescientos	300
cuatrocientos	400
quinientos	500
seiscientos	600
setecientos	700
ochocientos	800
novecientos	900
mil	1000
dos mil	2000
un millón	1 000 000

Gramática

Irregular verbs in the preterite

1. There are a number of verbs that are irregular in the preterite. **Ser** and **ir** have the same forms in the preterite.

ser/ir	
fui	fuimos
fuiste	fuisteis
fue	fueron

2. The verbs **dar** and **ver** have similar conjugations in the preterite.

dar		ver	
di	dimos	vi	vimos
diste	disteis	viste	visteis
dio	dieron	vio	vieron

3. Other irregular verbs can be divided into three groups. Notice that there are no accents on these verbs and that they all take the same endings (with the exception of the 3rd person plural of the verbs with **j** in the stem).

Verbs with *u* in the stem: tener	
tuve	tu**vimos**
tu**viste**	tu**visteis**
tu**vo**	tu**vieron**

Verbs with *i* in the stem: venir	
vine	vin**imos**
vin**iste**	vin**isteis**
vin**o**	vin**ieron**

Verbs with *j* in the stem: traer	
traje	traj**imos**
traj**iste**	traj**isteis**
traj**o**	traj**eron**

Other verbs with **u** in the stem: **andar** (**anduv-**), **estar** (**estuv-**), **poder** (**pud-**), **poner** (**pus-**), **saber** (**sup-**) and **tener** (**tuv-**).

Other verbs with **i** in the stem: **hacer** (**hic-**) and **querer** (**quis-**)

Other verb with **j** in the stem: **conducir** (**conduj-**), **decir** (**dij-**), **producir** (**produj-**) and **traducir** (**traduj-**)

4. The preterite tense of **hay** is **hubo**.

> **Hubo** mucha información para estudiar.

Por and *para* and prepositional pronouns

1. **Por** and **para** can both be translated as *for* in English, but they have different uses in Spanish. **Por** is used to indicate:

a. cause, reason, or motive *(because of, on behalf of)*

> Nos tuvimos que poner los abrigos **por** el frío.

b. duration, period of time *(during, for)*

> El presidente habló **por** una hora y media.

c. exchange *(for)*

> Mi padre pagó diez mil dólares **por** el coche.

d. general movement through space *(through, around, along, by)*

> Pasamos **por** el parque porque es más bonito.

e. expressions:

por ejemplo	*for example*
por eso	*that's why*
por favor	*please*
por fin	*finally*
por supuesto	*of course*

2. **Para** is used to indicate:

a. goal or purpose *(in order to, used for)*

> Fueron al cine **para** ver una película.
> *They went to the movie theater **to** see a film.*

b. recipient *(for)*

> La abuela preparó la comida **para** sus nietos.
> *The grandmother prepared the food **for** her grandchildren.*

c. destination *(to)*

> Vamos **para** la playa este verano.
> *We're going **to** the beach this summer.*

d. deadline *(for, due)*

> Tenemos que leer el texto **para** el lunes.
> *We have to read the text **for** Monday.*

e. contrast to what is expected.

> **Para** estar a dieta, come mucho.
> *For being on a diet, he eats a lot.*

f. expressions:

para colmo	*to top it all off*
para nada	*not at all*
para siempre	*forever*
para variar	*for a change*

3. After a preposition, use the same pronoun that you use as a subject pronoun, except for **yo** and **tú**. **Yo** becomes **mí** after a preposition, and **tú** becomes **ti**.

> La habitación grande es **para ti**.
> *The large room is **for you**.*

4. Instead of **mí** or **ti** with **con**, **conmigo** and **contigo** are used.

> ¿Puedo ir **contigo**?
> *Can I go with you?*

> ¡Claro que sí! Puedes venir **conmigo**.
> *Of course! You can come with me.*

Vocabulario 2

 2–6

Los utensilios

la copa	wine glass
la cuchara	spoon
el cuchillo	knife
el mantel	tablecloth
el plato	plate
el plato hondo	bowl
la servilleta	napkin
la taza	cup
el tazón	serving bowl
el tenedor	fork
el vaso	glass

La comida

el arroz	rice
el azúcar	sugar
la bebida	drink
el café	coffee
el camarón	shrimp
la carne	meat
el cerdo	pork
la cerveza	beer
el coctel	cocktail
la ensalada	salad
el entremés	appetizer
el flan	flan
la fruta	fruit
la hamburguesa	hamburger
el helado	ice cream
el jugo	juice
la naranja	orange
el pastel	cake
el pavo	turkey
el pescado	fish
la pimienta	pepper
el pollo	chicken
el postre	dessert
el refresco	soda
la sal	salt
el sándwich	sandwich
la sopa	soup
los totopos	tortilla chips
el vino blanco	white wine
el vino tinto	red wine

Verbos

cenar	to eat dinner
dejar (una propina)	to leave (a tip)
desayunar	to eat breakfast
felicitar	to congratulate
llevar	to take along
querer	to love
saludar	to greet

Palabras adicionales

al horno	baked
el almuerzo	lunch
asado(a)	grilled
la cena	dinner
la comida	food, lunch
la cuenta	bill
el desayuno	breakfast
frito(a)	fried
la orden	order
el plato principal	main dish

Gramática

Direct object pronouns I

1. Direct object pronouns are used to replace the direct object, or the noun that receives the action of the verb. In Spanish, the direct object pronoun must agree in gender and number with the noun that it replaces.

> Esteban dejó **la propina.**
> *Esteban left the tip. (Tip is the direct object.)*

> Esteban **la** dejó.
> *Esteban left it. (**La**, to reflect the feminine gender of **la propina**.)*

2. Here are the direct object pronouns for the third person:

	singular	plural
masculino	**lo** *it, him, you*	**los** *them, you*
femenino	**la** *it, her, you*	**las** *them, you*

3. Note that the direct object pronoun is placed before the conjugated verb.

> ¿Comiste el pescado?
> *Did you eat the fish?*

> Sí, **lo** comí.
> *Yes, I ate it.*

> ¿Hiciste la tarea?
> *Did you do the homework?*

> **La** estoy haciendo ahora.
> *I am doing it now.*

4. The direct object pronoun can also be attached to the infinitive or the present participle. An accent is necessary when adding the pronoun to the end of the present participle.

> ¿Quieres ver**los** mañana?
> *Do you want to see them tomorrow?*

> **Lo** está preparando. / Está preparándo**lo**.
> *She is preparing it.*

Direct object pronouns II

1. The direct object pronouns outlined above are only for the third person. Here are all of the direct object pronouns:

	singular	plural
first person	**me** *me*	**nos** *us*
second person	**te** *you*	**os** *you (plural)*
third person	**lo / la** *it, him, her, you*	**los / las** *them, you (plural)*

2. The following verbs are frequently used with direct object pronouns:

ayudar	escuchar	querer
buscar	felicitar	saludar
conocer	invitar	ver
creer	llamar	visitar
encontrar	llevar	